BLOOD of the MARTYRS

How the Slaves in Rome
Found Victory in Christ

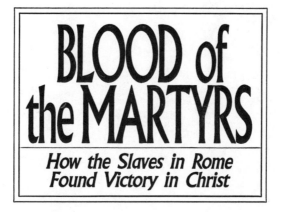

CHRISTIAN EPICS

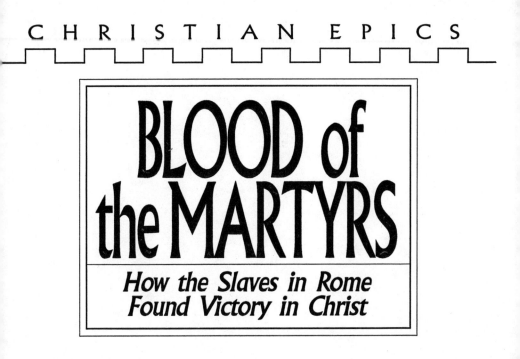

BLOOD of the MARTYRS

How the Slaves in Rome
Found Victory in Christ

NAOMI MITCHISON

EDITED AND INTRODUCED BY JAMES S. BELL, JR.

MOODY PRESS
CHICAGO

ISBN: 0-8024-7107-2

1 3 5 7 9 10 8 6 4 2

Printed in the United States of America

*To my aunt and uncle
Priscilla and John Powers—
faithful adherents to the Christian Epic Series.
They understand well that unless a grain of wheat
falls into the earth and dies, it remains alone,
but if it dies, it bears much fruit (John 12:24).*

Naomi Mitchison was born in Edinburgh in 1897 and educated at the Dragon School and St. Anne's College Oxford. She is one of the foremost historical novelists of her generation. She wrote more than 70 publications, including several books: *The Conquered, The Corn King and the Spring Queen,* and *The Bull Calves.* Some of her entertaining memoirs have been published as *You May Well Ask.*

James S. Bell, Jr. (B.A., College of the Holy Cross; M.A., University College, Dublin) has recast *Blood of the Martyrs* in today's language while remaining true to the author's purpose and style. An experienced editor, he has revised and updated many books, including *Ben Hur, Simon of Cyrene, Soul on Fire, Bold Galilean, Silver Chalice,* and *Devotional Prayers.* He has worked as director of religious publishing at Doubleday and as executive director at Bridge Publishing. Several years ago he came to Moody Press as editorial director. He lives in West Chicago with his wife and four children.

Contents

Introduction

Jesus Christ gave us some hint of the composition of heaven when He said things would be upside down: The last in this world (the prostitutes and tax collectors) would hold high position, while the first (the powerful rich and those building their religious empires) would fall. Certainly the woman who sinned much was forgiven much and had a strong motive to enter the Kingdom, but are the "last" merely the worst sinners or rather those who had little on this earth to live for?

Indeed, these who responded in numbers to the message of a future glorious hope were the lower class poor. In the very hub of Rome, the church was filled with a certain kind of dispossessed, abused, and completely exploited form of chattel— slaves. Mere pieces of property collected from throughout the Empire, slaves had no rights whatever. Their very existence was dependent upon the whim of their masters. Some received equitable treatment, but many were underfed, overworked, and beaten.

Blood of the Martyrs inexorably draws us into both the pulsating inner world and tumultuous surroundings of an entire array of the slave class. Exotic dancers, bakers, litter-bearers, metalworkers, secretaries, and a host of others coalesce in their common bond of servitude.

What are the choices when the group is as powerless as the individual—dumb submission, internal rebellion, external revolt? None bring true freedom, nor do the upper-class philosophies of the refined Stoics and Epicureans. Suddenly a humble carpenter dies and rises again to bequeath a glorious kingdom to the disenfranchised, the oppressed, and the poor, who have no hope in this present world. Finally they had a viable choice of another way, a way to authentically resist despotic power—through acceptance, faith, but most of all through love, especially love of their oppressors.

9

Mitchison's story revolves around the households of two Roman senators, Flavius Crispus and Aelius Balbus, at the time of Emperor Nero. Many of the slaves in these houses have become Christians, unbeknownst to their masters. The two worlds collide in the person of Beric, adopted by Crispus, and the son of Caradoc, king of East Britain.

Beric is not a Roman citizen but enjoys its status and privilege through Crispus. Beric is enticed with the beauty and allure of Flavia, daughter of Crispus, representing the beauty, wealth, and power of all that is Rome. Yet he is magnetically drawn to the coterie of slaves who enjoy a holy ecstasy of peace, joy, and love in their master Jesus.

They speak constantly of "the Kingdom," where there will be no exploitation but only love based on mutual service. As they break bread at their love feasts and speak "the Words," hope is born for an earthly Christian society as well as the promise of eternal bliss regardless of their present circumstances. They invite Beric and others in his class, including Claudia Acte, Nero's mistress, to join them in this dream, and much of the action in this novel focuses on slaves, freedmen, and noblemen living out equality and fraternity in Christ.

Receiving the Kingdom means internal security but not necessarily "happiness ever after" in this life. The upper class misunderstand the Way as being a crowd of cannibals and atheists overthrowing the State. Nero conveniently deflects his responsibility for Roman discontent onto the Christians by means of the great fire, and they will pay the price of death.

That ultimate price is willing to be paid by most of the slaves, though realistically there is some cowardice and betrayal. How can death be tolerated? It is a deliverance from a less than happy life, though most will not depart willingly.

"But to be burned alive! When you begin to think what that is going to be like—could any of us bear it?"

"Not by ourselves. But just because we aren't alone any longer, we can bear it. We're all with one another in this pain and this death, and Jesus is with us all, showing us how . . . if the Kingdom could come without our dying for it, yes . . . it's made out of people's lives and deaths."

One of the early church Fathers said that the blood of the martyrs was the seed of the church. Through their heroism, humility, community, and succor for enemies, a corrupt and decadent empire crumbled. Whether dead or alive, they stand together: Lalage, Sophrosyne, Eunice, Manasses, Argas, Persis, Niger, Euphemia, and other slaves and freed people. Jew, Greek, and barbarian stand defenseless against the pagan state. Will Beric join them?

Others stand in awe of the spectacle, wavering and reconsidering, transfixed by their holy countenances. Echoing across the decades can be heard "Surely, this man was the Son of God!" Immediately, there are willing volunteers to replace the dead.

Martyr means witness, and you the reader will witness the poignant struggles of flesh and spirit in their sufferings and joys, their naïveté and aspirations.

Though ignorant of sophisticated doctrine and even unsure of some morality (the church was young), they excelled in long-suffering and childlike trust in each other and the inevitability of the Kingdom of their God.

In some ways we will be transported by the inner world of these characters—at a time when both they and their religion were truly outsiders. Indeed the novel is dominated by the multitude of characters, demonstrating in various facets the One whom they serve.

Paul himself appears in the novel, and we learn from him in his epistles not to seek release from physical bondage to our circumstances but rather from spiritual bondage. These martyrs and their cohorts sought this very thing. If *Blood of the Martyrs* teaches anything, it is the need to become slaves of Christ. We can find freedom for ourselves and others only in Him, regardless of the adverse circumstances in this life.

JAMES S. BELL, JR.

Cast of Characters

Roman Citizens and Their Families

The emperor Nero
His wife, the empress Poppaea
Ofonius Tigellinus, prefect of the Praetorian Guards
L. Junius Gallio, ex-proconsul of Achaea
T. Flavius Crispus, a senator
His daughter, Flavia
His mother, Domina Aelia
Flavius Scaevinus, his cousin, a senator
Aelius Balbus, a senator
His son, M. Aelius Candidus, an officer in the
  Praetorian Guards
Annaeus Lucan, a poet, Gallio's nephew
T. Satellius, a tanner
His wife, Megallis
Casperius, a prison official
Eprius, a city guard
Marulla, a poor citizen's wife
Sex. Papinius Calvinus, an Italian citizen
M. Antonius Paulus (Paul), a provincial citizen

Non-citizens and Freedmen or Freedwomen

Beric, son of Caradoc, or Caratacus, king of East
  Britain
Clinog, his brother
Erasixenos, an Alexandrian
Luke, a provincial doctor
Claudia Acte, Nero's freedwoman
Asterope, daughter of one of Nero's nurses
Lalage, a professional dancer, Claudia Acte's
  freedwoman
Her accompanist, Sophrosyne
Phineas-bar-Gedaliah, owner of a fish shop
His wife, Sapphira
His father, Gedaliah-bar-Jorim, a carpet weaver
His brothers, Amariah and Jorim, and his sister-in-
  law, Joanna

His mother, Tabitha, and his sister, Noumi, all
  carpet weavers
Hadassa, a widow
Blephano, Toxulus, Cario, and Harpax, prison
  officials
Montanus, the overseer at Aelius Balbus's house
Nausiphanes, a tutor, freedman of Flavius Crispus
Eunice, a baker, freedwoman of Flavius Crispus
Euphemia, a shopkeeper
Rhodon, a metalworker
Sotion, a rent collector
Carpus, a potter

Slaves

BELONGING TO FLAVIUS CRISPUS

Argas, dining-room slave
Hermeias, secretary and dining-room slave
Manasses, dining-room slave
Phaon, son of Eunice, dining-room slave
Lamprion, dining-room slave
Sannio, dining-room slave
Mikkos, dining-room slave
Pistos, dining-room slave
Persis, a ladies' maid
Josias, kitchen slave
Dapyx, kitchen slave

BELONGING TO AELIUS BALBUS

Felicio, secretary
Niger, litter slave
Zyrax, litter slave
Abgar, a runaway

1

Beric

In the hot afternoon, Beric, who was no longer a child, had been with Flavia, who was no longer a child either. She had amused herself, but it was beginning to be dangerous. Supposing Beric came out of the dream in which he stroked and kissed her, in which he did what she wanted and no more? Well, there would soon be something better to think about than Beric—by no means a dream this time, but real.

But Beric did not know. It was no business of the Briton's to whom she was betrothed. She was more than certain that her father had not mentioned it in his presence so far. It would be amusing when he knew.

And suddenly she was bored with his light wavy hair and the red sunburn on his neck and shoulders, and his fingers merely repeating an old story. She sat up sharply, saying that she must dress.

His hands tried to hold her, but she pushed him off, and he, as his dreams subsided, remembered that he had to see to his arrangements for the dinner party that evening. He would have liked to kiss her gently good-bye, but she, suddenly brisk, would have none of it and shoved him impatiently, so that he knocked over a basket of grapes from the little table.

He would have picked them up, but now she couldn't bear him in the room one moment longer. "Let the slaves!" she said, stomping. "What are they there for! And go quietly, you big ox!"

When he went out, she pushed her toes into one of the fallen grape bunches. The juice was warm and sticky and a lovely color on her feet. She pushed it around a little on the tiled floor, then clapped her hands.

Little Persis came running in, with anxious eyes on her mistress, who was now slipping off her short sweaty cotton gown, dropping it, one hem in the grape juice, as Persis saw with some concern, and called for powder.

As Persis powdered her all over, Flavia stretched again and again, and thrust her fingers into her brown hair, pulling it back in crisp, hot masses from her cheeks and neck. Her face was the right kind of face for a sixteen-year-old Roman aristocrat. She had enjoyed herself so far; she was going to enjoy herself much more when she left home. She had not yet made anyone do what she wanted except the slaves and Beric, but that was going to happen too.

The other slaves came in to dress her and admire her and brush her hair—the old woman who was supposed to be so good but whom Flavia didn't trust an inch, and the round-faced Italian maid who giggled.

Persis was the youngest and newest and easiest to hurt. She began to clear up the squashed grapes. Her sleek black head bent to the floor; there was a tempting patch of brown shoulder. Flavia tiptoed and gave it a quick pinch.

Persis jumped and squealed. The other two slaves laughed, applauding their mistress and wondering what she was going to try on them.

She looked round idly and viciously for something to do or throw or hurt.

The Italian girl ran and brought in her pet monkey, hoping she would tease it instead of teasing them.

In the meantime the dinner party had to be arranged. The food, of course, had been ordered days before. Both the head cook and Beric had been to the market, though actually most of the meat, poultry, vegetables, fruit, and cheese had come in from Flavius Crispus's country estate, a pleasant little place to which old Domina Alia, the grandmother, had retired. The flowers for the garlands had come from there too, but in this heat it was difficult to keep the roses from drooping.

As for entertainment, Beric had put the two dancing boys through a rehearsal of their new mime—Ulysses and the Cyclops —with the gouging out of the eye done as realistically as possible. Phaon was a tiresome, temperamental little brat, but the dancing boys were bound to be rather spoiled. He had been born in the house. His mother, Eunice, had been freed five years back and now ran a little bakery. Sometimes she brought in some extra fancy rolls—there would be some today, shaped like swans and butterflies.

Phaon was fifteen, and his legs were pretty enough to eat. He knew that all right, and half the time he was showing off like a regular Greek, which was what the guests liked, and then suddenly he'd go queer and sullen, as if he hated the kind of life he was leading, which was stupid and ungrateful of him. Not many slaves were as well treated and as well trained as Flavius Crispus's dancing boys.

The other was a young Jew, Manasses, older than Phaon and with much more experience. In fact, it was he who had taught Phaon. He was easier to deal with, and his dark curls and dark sidelong eyes made him a good contrast with the little Greek.

But Beric didn't like him much. Jews were a nuisance in a household anyhow, with all the different kinds of food they refused to eat, and their praying, and trying to sneak off from work one day a week. In the Jewish Quarter in Rome, you could go there that day and there wouldn't be a soul about, not so much as chopping wood or drawing water.

Of course, there were certain things which he, Beric, did not eat—goose, for instance. Naturally—no Britons ate goose! It always made him feel uncomfortable to see the Romans actually enjoy eating it, especially Flavia. It made him feel squeamish, as though he didn't want to touch her for an hour or two afterwards.

But everybody knew that pork was one of the best foods there is! He remembered helping in a great game one day when the rest of the household made the Jew slaves eat it—held them down and jammed it into their mouths. Most of them were sick afterwards. It was all in fun, of course, and the rest of them had laughed like mad. Some of the others had manhandled Manasses a bit that time.

The rest of the slaves were always jealous of the dancing boys, and, on the whole, Beric saw the point of that. Of course, all the dining-room slaves had a better time. They had the pick of what was left over—they were not supposed to, but neither Beric nor Crispus was going to be hard on them. When there were no guests, they often talked to the slaves who were waiting on them. Naturally they were more intelligent and trustworthy—and better-looking than the rest too! They were mostly Greeks—Lamprion, Sannio, Argas, Mikkos, and the rest.

By now Beric did most of the running of the household, thus (as he sometimes said to himself) saving the price and keep of an overseer. Today, for instance, he had hired a professional dancing girl entirely on his own. Well, as a matter of fact, Flavius Crispus had seen her somewhere when he was dining out, but it was Beric who had found out her name and where she lived.

Sometimes he wondered what was going to happen to him later on, when he was a grown man with a great brown mustache like his father. Not that he wasn't big and strong enough now—they all said so at the gymnasium. He could throw most of his friends. But—later on? Some day soon he must ask Flavius Crispus.

Thirteen years ago, the British king Caradoc, son of Cymbeline, had been chased out of Essex by the legions, west along the Thames valley and into Wales. There had been fighting there, the usual betrayal of barbarians by one another, and in the end Caradoc and his wife and children had been taken to Rome, where old Emperor Claudius had, on one of his good days, seen and pardoned them—not, of course, to go back to Britain, but to live on as clients in Rome. And the youngest boy was given to Flavius Crispus to be brought up with his own motherless little girl.

Beric had howled and kicked at first, but it was all a long time ago. Caradoc and his wife were dead years back, and Beric had not grieved much. He had never tried to get in touch with his brothers, who were probably somewhere in Italy, nor did he think of himself as the son of a king except sometimes when with Flavia. When they were quite little, she had made him crowns out of anything that came to hand and pretended to do him homage.

And again this last year, who he was seemed to heighten everything for her. She had whispered it at him, "King's son, king's son," making him do this or that, touch her or not touch her, thinking of new games to play with him as the afternoons burned and blazed from winter into July. And inside the shutters, the square, dusky, rose-scented room was her practice ground where she would make him follow and beg or cry with rage or laugh low with delight.

The slave girls whispered to one another sometimes that he was a king's son, but he didn't know or care about that. He wasn't interested in slave girls, though last year at Saturnalia he had given special presents to Flavia's maids—but not for what they said; only for what they left unsaid.

Now he went along to see if there were any more directions for the dinner party. He found Crispus quite worried, and indeed it was a rather awkward party. Beric had never bothered much about Roman politics, but even he couldn't help knowing that no senator could enjoy having the present prefect of the Praetorians to dinner.

He was sorry and worried that Crispus should have to do it, sorry from affection and worried because—well, Crispus had never held any important office of state, had never been involved in any kind of scandal or conspiracy, but still . . . Even Beric felt uneasy when he thought about what had been happening in Rome lately.

Beric knew most of the other guests already, old friends of the family: a second cousin, Flavius Scaevinus; Aelius Balbus, a cousin on the other side of the family; Junius Gallio, the ex-proconsul of Achaea; and Gallio's nephew, young Annaeus Lucan, the poet; also Aelius Candidus, Balbus's son, who had just left one of the Praetorians. Hence Ofonius Tigellinus, the prefect. There was one other guest, whom Beric did not know, Erasixenos, an Alexandrian, exceedingly rich. He was to sit next to Tigellinus. They were said to have tastes in common—Crispus coughed a little over this—and Beric was to see, above all, that they were to have everything they wanted in the way of entertainment.

Beric did not always come to the dinner parties—only when he was wanted to make up numbers—and he usually sat at the lowest end of the third couch, where he could supervise the service. Often he didn't get much conversation, and he knew he wouldn't tonight, as his neighbor would be Lucan, who was sure to be bored anyhow and would probably leave early.

He said soothingly to Crispus that he was quite sure the dinner would be a success. The partridges especially were sure to be delicious. He had got hold of the recipe for that new stuffing and had just been down to the kitchen to taste it himself.

Crispus began to say something to him about Aelius Candidus and then stopped. He patted Beric on the shoulder. "You're a good boy," he said.

Beric found the dinner party as dull as he had expected. There were awkward moments too. None of the aristocrats liked sitting at the same table as Tigellinus. Flavius Scaevinus was positively rude and left early. That was stupid of him. Times had changed, and it was no use supposing one was living under Augustus. Even Beric knew that.

The partridges, however, were a great success, though Tigellinus had rather a coarse way of biting out the breast and throwing the rest to the floor. Lucan, who affected plain living and high thinking, and had come in a plain green tunic with mended stitches in several places, talked to Beric for a few minutes. Apparently he had an idea that because Britain was damp, foggy, full of unpleasant wild animals and without heating, it was also the home of freedom and nobility.

Beric agreed enthusiastically, trying to look the part, but when Lucan began talking across the table to Erasixenos about some new Alexandrian religion, he couldn't help remembering the way his father, King Caradoc, and his big brothers, Prince Rudri and Prince Clinog, had spoken and thought about the peasants and servants and men at arms—not the tall, fair Britons Lucan was thinking of, the conquerors, the seagoers, the ones that fetched the big prices on the slave market—but the ordinary, middle-height, middle-colored countrymen who were there all the time, however much their huts were burned and their beasts stolen, and they themselves kicked and prodded and made to fight behind the palisades, half armed, while the long-haired warriors marched around and sang war songs.

Freedom? That was how King Caradoc had been able to speak up in front of the Divine Claudius. He wasn't afraid. He was free and noble and all that, just right for the Stoics to make up stories about. And he, Beric—he could look handsome and strong and free. But it wasn't the whole story about Britain. Well, who cared? Suddenly he began to feel sad and wished it were true, wished Britain had been a kind of Stoic paradise. He wanted something, he didn't know what, but something real.

Erasixenos was talking about Egyptian religions. Lucan apparently had been, or was going to, write one of his poems about Egypt. Beric had an idea that Lucan's notions about Egypt were as cockeyed as his ideas about Britain. Probably Egypt was full of ordinary stupid men and women, and the ghosts and devils were a different shape, but you had to get rid of them the same sort of way. For that matter he had seen a crocodile with his own eyes in the arena.

Why were the Romans always so interested in new kinds of gods? They had plenty of gods of their own, only they weren't— what was it?—they weren't active, not in people's lives. Not any longer. So the Romans had to go somewhere else to get rid of the devils and spirits and bits of bad luck that were always floating round. They had to go somewhere else to get that feeling you get out of the gods when you know they are there, the way they had been when he was a child. But the Romans had killed the Druids, and if he saw a Druid now he wouldn't look twice.

Beric watched the slaves clear away the empty sea urchins, the fish bones, the half-eaten hams, and the roast boar and ducks and sucking pig, the pie crust and broken rolls and blobs of honey—it would all get finished up in the kitchen—the walnut shells and fruit rinds. Everyone had eaten much too much, of course, but what was the use of being rich if you weren't going to have as much as possible of everything?

It was sweaty weather though, even between the water-cooled marble walls. A slave went around to each diner with wet towels, fans, a nice little earthenware pot amusingly and appropriately painted, and fresh cushions to lie on.

Then the two boys began dancing their mime, all dressed up with the new masks and stiff short tunics. The little round bottom of Phaon as a rather frivolous Ulysses flipped up now and then, and once Tigellinus reached over and pinched him. Tigellinus also watched with interest the mimed gouging out of the Cyclops's eye. It seemed to be the kind of thing he knew about. The Stoics, naturally, found it boring, but Aelius Candidus liked it. At the end, the boys pulled their masks off and bowed.

Tigellinus clapped and beckoned Phaon to come over. Phaon didn't want to, but Beric caught his eye and glared at him to do what he was told. Tigellinus wasn't going to eat him, after all. Spoiled little brat!

Garlands were brought around by some of the girls. Tigellinus had a little fun with his. At any rate, he went to a party to enjoy himself, which was more than the Stoics did! Lucan insisted on a garland of plain leaves, though he didn't go quite so far as to ask for poetic bay leaves.

Aelius Balbus was appointed toastmaster, and everybody shifted a bit and settled down to the drinking, beginning with the emperor of course. Unfortunately this started Tigellinus and Erasixenos off on several new stories about the doings of the Divine Nero, and, as one of them was about a girl who happened to be the niece of Gallio's sister-in-law, it was all rather a pity.

In any case, Gallio was in a bad temper. However, he would probably get better when the wine had warmed him up a little. Poor old Crispus really disliked hearing that kind of story about the emperor; he tried hard to disbelieve them. Aelius Candidus obviously thought them grand but was a little shy, with his father there, of telling any himself.

After that there were drinks and compliments all around the table, not to Beric, of course, except from his neighbor Lucan, who was really drinking to Freedom, even if she had fled to the barbarians.

Beric wasn't sure if he liked being called a barbarian. He always rather hated it when he was explained away to guests, as that tin soldier Aelius Candidus was doing now at the far side of the table to Tigellinus, who got it a bit wrong and said loudly that it must be awkward having one of these Germans around the place, especially if there was a pretty daughter.

At that Beric shut himself away, closing himself against everything but his own dream. As the toasts went around he drank more deeply than usual. The slaves refilled his cup, but he did not notice their hands on the heavy jugs. It was as though he were back in the room with Flavia.

Circles of color swelled and burst across his mind, golden and rose, golden and hot black. Out of childhood a great blue pond swam up, almost level to the marshes, the high reeds, the very green, slimy marsh plants. Fish rose, turning, bursting bubbles; enormous dragonflies planed, touched the surface of the pond to shivers, almost, almost submerging in one long ripple the willing marshes. The Horse-Goddess lifting circles of color for the delight of warriors, golden and rose, golden and hot-black, stepped with one hot, hard hoof sizzling into the great pond of childhood, that he knew now as the great, reed-blocked Thames, few-forded, flooding suddenly, king-river of Britain. He was the king's son, master of rushes and water and the golden Goddess.

But now Crispus was proposing the health of Aelius Candidus in a long and involved speech, since he had by now got outside a good deal of his own excellent wine, as indeed they all had. "Here's a young fellow," he said, beaming around the table, "excellent young fellow. Going to have a most distinguished career. Going to start it by marrying my daughter!"

Everyone clapped. And the dream, found out, shriveled into contemptible childishness. It would never visit Beric again. That had been said. That.

Crispus went on. "So now I ask you all to drink to the health and prosperity of my future son-in-law, Marcus Aelius Candidus!"

It was only then that Beric noticed the red splash on his tunic where the wine had spilled when he jerked his cup. He didn't care, but Argas came round and wiped it up. Argas laid a hand on his shoulder for a moment, but Beric didn't seem to feel it.

Now Candidus was drinking Flavia's health, and there was plenty of applause, and Balbus asked if the little lady herself might not be induced to honor them with her company for a short time.

Crispus, pleased, hesitated and asked Beric what sort of show the dancer was going to give them.

Beric answered low that it was classical dancing—this seemed to disappoint Tigellinus—and that he was sure there was nothing Flavia could mind, at which Candidus shouted over at him to ask the little beauty to give them the pleasure of her company.

Beric turned furiously to Crispus—he wasn't even going to say yes or no to Candidus! But Crispus sent one of the slaves.

Lucan took his leave now. Women bored him, and ladies bored him even more than women.

Two of the slaves held back the curtains for Flavia to make an entrance. Beric, alone at his end of the couch, would not even look at her, but the others did, and a pretty picture she made, eyes downcast, cheeks flushed, lightly veiled over girlish curls, a white flower in place, silver sandals. At once the atmosphere of the dining-room responded.

"If I were perfectly certain I could stand on my feet," said Candidus, "I'd take my garland and lay it at yours!"

Daintily she stepped around and sat on the edge of the middle couch between her father and future father-in-law. Offered wine, she duly refused it. In any case, she didn't like it much. Tigellinus gave her a good stare and whispered to Erasixenos.

Now it was time for the dancer.

"Ah—what is the young person's name, again?" asked Crispus.

Beric answered that it was Lalage, and someone inevitably quoted Horace.

Lalage appeared with her accompanist, a little old woman who crouched down in a corner with her harp and double flutes. The dancer was a striking young woman, black-haired, rather angular, fairly tall, expressionless. She was wearing a long heavy cloak which she threw off, abruptly, holding it for a moment at the end of one muscular arm. Under it she was wearing the traditional maenad dress, the wide, finely pleated skirt, flaring out from the hips, the vine leaves low on the waist and the fawn skin over one shoulder, leaving the other breast professionally bared.

Her accompanist played a single chord on the harp, and Lalage took up her position. She looked at the supper party, then over her shoulder to the harpist. "If they talk, stop playing!"

The dancing was definitely good. After a few formal movements, the maenad awoke, turning a succession of rapid cartwheels all in the same square yard of floor. She spun this way and that, and the skirt twirled into queer shapes. For a moment she sank into a slower rhythm; they could hear her panting.

The dance came to an end, was applauded, and Candidus threw a couple of gold coins. Lalage kicked them with one bare heel over to the harpist, who picked them up, and Flavia observed that she was glad she was going to have such a generous husband.

Candidus glared at her, then at the dancer. But it wasn't either of them—it was that Briton. At the table—speaking like one of themselves! *So you've got to do something about it; got to put him in his place once and for all. Wouldn't do to let these fellows behave as if they were citizens.* His future father-in-law had been soft, obviously. So it was up to him.

Even Tigellinus was feeling all the more amiable for his wine, but a wave of cruel and efficient sobriety had come over Candidus. He walked over to the Briton. The slaves dodged quickly out of his way. Flavia caught her breath.

"Do you know what you are?" he said heavily, leaning toward Beric. "An impudent foreigner taking advantage of the privileges Rome gives you. But that isn't allowed, Mister Briton."

For a moment Beric could think of nothing to say.

"No. Not allowed," said Candidus and smacked Beric's face.

Flavia, peeping around her father, laughed out loud. So did Tigellinus.

Beric jumped to his feet, but Crispus reached over and caught his hand. "No, Beric!"

"If I weren't under *this* roof—" said Beric, low and heavily.

And Flavia, peeping around again, rubbed it in. "No, you'd never abuse your father's hospitality, would you, Beric?"

Candidus walked back to his own place almost steadily, and Beric dropped his head in his hands. Nobody paid any attention to him. He heard Balbus scolding Candidus, saying he must always avoid getting involved in quarrels with persons not of his own race and class. He heard Tigellinus tickling Lalage and getting his ears boxed and laughing enormously. He heard Crispus telling Flavia that it was time for her to say good night.

On the way out she pinched him, but still he didn't look up. Then he began to hear a discussion about foreigners in Rome. Balbus and Crispus were talking rather low about the way each of these foreign immigrants now had streets of their own: Syrians here, Phrygians there, Egyptians over by the Tiber, the Jews in their own quarter protected by the Empress Poppaea. Greeks everywhere. Every kind of poisonous foreigner, prostitutes and abortionists and murders, men and women who would hire themselves out to anyone for anything! And probably the worst of the lot were a sect of Jews called Christians, who hadn't even any respectable people among them but worshiped all kind of obscene animals, fishes, and donkeys.

Beric took a breath and sat up straight. On the couch in front of him Tigellinus and Erasixenos were teasing Lalage, but she was a sufficiently muscular and sharp-tongued young woman to be able to deal with them. Her old accompanist watched from a corner as she must have watched the same thing evening after evening at other houses.

Candidus was by now in a rather disconnected stage of drink. He seemed to be asleep for a few minutes, then he woke up and bit Lalage's toe. Gallio clapped his hands, and Phaon came running with the damp cloths and little pot. Crispus and Balbus were still talking about foreigners.

Then—was it after all possible that Crispus thought of him, Beric, as a foreigner? As an impudent foreigner taking advantage of what wasn't his? And she—Flavia had laughed at him. There was no getting over that.

A black slave with a horribly long knife at his belt came in, rattled the knife hilt to make Tigellinus attend, and handed him a set of tablets.

He looked at them and swore, then heaved himself rapidly up, shedding Lalage like a blanket. She was on her feet at once and shook herself.

Tigellinus explained to his host that he must go; it was an imperial summons. "I'm sorry, Crispus," he said, "very sorry. This was just developing into a most agreeable evening." He added that it might mean a turn-out of the Praetorians and prodded Candidus, who got up, remarking that when duty called, beauty must wait.

Beric got up too. It was *his* duty to see the guests off, to light their torches and hunt out their slaves. Tigellinus tipped him— inadvertently perhaps, not as a deliberate insult. Candidus merely hiccuped when Beric, holding himself in, wished them good night.

A minute or two later Erasixenos left too, though very politely; he was one of the foreigners. But if one had plenty of money it wouldn't matter. Anyhow, the Greeks were different. Beric walked back through the main courtyard of the house, under the midsummer stars. He didn't want to go into the dining room again. The slaves would look at him—he knew they had seen—and he'd take it out of them next morning if they said a word—looked at him as if . . . as if . . . But perhaps they knew.

For a few minutes he stood with his back to a pillar, looking up at that soft, thick star-glow. The Stoics found comfort in contemplation of the movement of the stars. He didn't. He went through the small courtyard with the little fountain and flowerpots.

There was Flavia. He wanted to hit her, but he couldn't. He couldn't even say anything angry and splendid. He only said, "You might have told me."

"Yes," she said, "I might, but I didn't. You're not very good at concealing your feelings, are you?"

"I didn't have to. This afternoon, Flavia—you knew about this then!"

"Of course I did. It was no business of yours. It's no business of yours now! You've got a lot to learn, Beric."

"I see. And *you've* been learning on me, just because I happened to be there."

"Well, if you hadn't happened to be there, it wouldn't have been you I learned on!" She giggled.

And suddenly, instead of being hurt and ashamed, he was wildly angry. He said, "I think I am going to tell your father—everything."

Flavia answered lightly but with anger answering his. "But, you see, he wouldn't believe you, because naturally I wouldn't dream of admitting it, and he'd have the skin taken off your back for saying such a thing!"

Could she really have said that? Flavia? He tried to struggle back. "I am the son of a king, Flavia!"

"Very possibly," she said and tucked in a curl that was beginning to slip, "but no one remembers that any longer except you. Actually you wouldn't be here at all if the Divine Claudius hadn't

27

happened to be rather sloppy. All the emperors get like that. Gaius wanted to make his horse a consul."

He gasped at that, and she went on, still lightly, "And the thing about horses is that there's always a groom to keep them in their places—with a whip. Natives have to be kept in order in much the same way. You heard what Gallio said. *And* felt it!"

"Flavia!" he said. "Flavia! You don't mean it!"

"Oh yes, I do," she said. "I waited here to tell you, because I've made up my mind to have nothing more to do with creatures like you. No, don't try to touch me. I mean what I say."

He half shouted, "I won't stand this! I won't have you treating me like dirt!"

"You *are* dirt," said Flavia, "and you'd better get used to it," and she turned her back and left him.

The three old men in the dining room were still talking. For a time they discussed these Christians, a little nervously. It was odd to find oneself at a party, even after absorbing the drink and sobering down, talking about such an unpleasant subject, but they had been upset by Tigellinus. They were wondering now about the whole structure of the state, which these Christians, alone among the foreigners and atheists, definitely wished to destroy or at any rate did not support.

"They believe in nothing, I understand," said Balbus. "They have no temples, no priests, and they say they are going to destroy the world!"

"They always talk in terms of destruction—flames and judgment and violence," Crispus said. "They seem unable to understand what the State is."

"That's because they are stateless, slaves and worse. When the police hear of a Christian meeting, depend on it, it's in one of the tenements in the Aventine. They swarm in there. It ought to be cleared."

"Nothing but a fire's going to clear that. You know, Balbus, those tenements are a disgrace, and I don't care who the landlords are! Full of thieves and poisoners and Christians and cheap astrologers and the gods alone know what else!"

"The common Jews aren't so bad. They're fine fighters, and they make good citizens so long as they don't quarrel with their

neighbors. And at any rate they don't push their superstitions. I've met some very decent Jews."

"Of course. You must have had plenty to do with Jews in your time, Gallio."

"Eh?" said Gallio, starting awake. "Jews. Yes, yes. Much more honest than the Greeks. Often won't take a bribe. But excitable. Dear me, yes."

"You never came across any Christians, did you?"

"Oh, sometimes. The strict Jews can't stand them. Seems they're slack about religious observances. Don't insist on all this nonsense about special food."

"I told you so," said Balbus. "Atheists! Even the Jews think so. Sometimes I wonder, Gallio, whether it isn't the worst of a career like yours—and a fine career too—that in provincial administration you're having to deal all the time with inferior races, Jews and Greeks and that class of person. It must have been intolerably tedious."

Gallio looked at him and scratched in his beard a moment. "Sure they are inferior?"

"Well—" Balbus was almost shocked "—naturally!"

"I don't know," Gallio said. "Seems different when you're not in Rome. There was one Jew at Corinth. A little dark man. Queer way of looking at you—that's why I remember him. Paul or some such name. Yes, Marcus Antonius Paulus. Curious how they remember Anthony still in the East. Kind of immortality, that."

"What had this Paul done?"

"Nothing. Made some rather good tents. As a matter of fact, I bought some from him. But the other Jews wanted his blood. He'd put their backs up somehow."

"But was he one of these Christians?"

"Don't know. He seemed perfectly respectable. I let him go, of course. He didn't strike me as inferior."

"All the same, these Levantines . . ."

"There seem to be so many of them," Crispus said. "Now this fellow Erasixenos, I wouldn't have asked him two or three years ago. But now . . ." He shrugged his shoulders.

"Yes," said Balbus, "our Divine Nero admires their taste so much! And the rest of us have to ask them to dinner."

Crispus looked around. Two or three of the slaves were still there. "Boys, you may go," he said quickly, "all of you."

"Ah, thanks," said Balbus, "though I wasn't going to say anything treasonable! Only that Tigellinus makes me sick. To see the way he looked at your daughter!"

"We're old-fashioned, I'm afraid. Perhaps he isn't as bad as he seems. I can't believe everything I hear about the emperor."

"You'd better start practicing, then," said Gallio and laughed shortly.

But Crispus went rambling on with his regrets. The wine made him reminiscent and long-winded. But there was no hurry. No hurry for any of them. Nothing left for three old men, all more or less retired from public life, to do or change. So they could go on talking.

"It was so different those first five years, Gallio," he said, "when your brother Seneca was Nero's tutor. We all thought he might be going to be the philosopher-king at last—the old dream. Yes, yes. But it was only because things had got so bad just before, with all the informers and murders and confiscations and scandals, and women and slaves in high places. But, you know, Balbus, it seemed like a fresh start with every emperor, and then. . . ." He shook his head and emptied his wine cup.

"I was only a child when the Divine Augustus died," said Balbus, reminiscent too, "but I can remember the grief there was in all classes. And I remember, too, my father saying that we'd got a scholar and philosopher in Tiberius, a true Roman, hardworking, modest. Well, there, we all know what came of it, and my poor father knew too, to his cost, before the end."

"I was out of Rome those last five years of Tiberius," said Crispus. "A young man on my first job in the provinces. It wasn't till I came back that I realized how things were at home."

"It was the gloom, the blackness on everything, wasn't it, Gallio?" Balbus said. "You couldn't enjoy yourself nor feel secure. There was that unhappy madman, betrayed by his wife and his friends and at last by his own scholarship, pouncing between here and Capri. And then when he died and young Gaius took over—Caligula they called him, remember, Crispus?—it seemed like the good old days. Yes, the exiles came back, there were free

elections and free speech again. We thought Rome could be Rome. But it was hardly a year before the prosecutions and the tyranny came back. Gaius was as mad as Tiberius. The things we had to put through in the Senate! Enough to make one ashamed to bear one's grandfather's name.

"And then Gaius was murdered, and the Divine Claudius came shambling and stammering on. But still, he was no tyrant. No, Gallio, he kept the provinces together, and he might have done well for Rome but for trusting his wives and his freedmen. It didn't send him mad, being Caesar, but whether Nero is going the same way as Tiberius and Gaius—what do you think, Gallio?"

"He's not mad; he's bad," Gallio answered. "It would take more than my poor brother and Burrus to hold a boy like that. He took after his mother. And she was a devil. But he only murdered her for a worse woman yet. Women and slaves!"

"But, oh dear, why must the gods treat us like this?" said Crispus.

"Why? I'll tell you. We're to blame ourselves. Power's a nasty, dangerous stuff, bad enough for a grown man. Poison to a boy. Even if Nero hadn't had that mother. And we've been so afraid of civil war again—and the gods know we had reason to be afraid—that we let these Julio-Claudians have power. Tons of it. Enough to burst them, to send them mad. We gave it to them with both hands—anything to keep us out of a civil war. We couldn't see that it was more than they could stand, any of them."

"Augustus stood it."

"He didn't have it from childhood. And it wasn't all in his hands, either. There was still a Senate and People of Rome with a will of its own that it could make known. And certain powers not given up. But now, think! We've given everything. Civil and military power. Judicial and executive. Haven't we, Balbus?"

"It's not possible to run an empire efficiently unless there's power at the center. What we complain about is its misuse. It keeps on getting into the wrong hands. Creatures like Pallas and Narcissus in the last reign—not even Italians! And now men like Tigellinus and all those clever little snakes of freedmen, who can't even get the whip-marks off their backs, and women like Poppaea

—the Divine Empress creeping from one bed to another—oh, it makes my blood boil!"

Gallio laughed. "Drink and cool down. It's our doing. Not that we could have helped it, being what we are. And the world as it is. The people who want power are the ones who get it, and it's not a thing that decent people want. You wouldn't like to be emperor, would you, Crispus?"

"The gods forbid!"

"Nor I. We've some regard for our souls. It's the ones without souls—women and half-men like these imperial Ganymedes, and brutes without education like our dear Tigellinus. They're the kind that want power. And take it."

"But the emperors?"

"Can an emperor have a soul? Ask my brother: Seneca'll tell you fast enough! Poor little silly imperial soul, smothered to death with flattery and luxury and pride and anger uncontrolled. No, you can't have it both ways. Not power and a soul."

"At any rate," said Crispus, "it isn't so bad in the provinces. They say that in Gaul, for instance, there is something nearer the old Roman life."

"Comes of being a week's journey from the capital. Gaul can't be gathered up into the same bundle of power as Rome. But suppose now—well, I'm no poet; this is more my nephew's line! —but say one could get letters and legions to and from the provinces in a matter of hours. Flying horses! Well, then, they'd be under the same power too, and no different."

"In the same fear and shame as we are."

"Yes, but mark you, Crispus, the Empire'd be that much more efficient. The imperial administration that much more unified. No rebellions possible. Can't have it both ways. See, Crispus?"

Balbus, who had been calming down, swirling the wine around in his cup, broke in. "I'm not so sure, Gallio. Is it all so efficient? What about the finances? Rome could live on what she made and took—well, in the usual way!—under the Republic. If you were a citizen, that meant a decent security. But an Imperial Court with all the trimmings is a different matter. It's upset the balance of things. It has to be fed and paid for, with imports all the time, and I'm not sure if that's going so nicely. Here in Rome, half the citizens are on the dole. And I'd like to know just how the Treasury is paying for these pageants and parades and cardboard imitations of the Olympic Games that are got up to keep their minds off reality!"

Crispus laughed. "We all need to have our minds taken off reality these days. It's nice to think of those two young people starting life together. Though I could have wished your Candidus hadn't chosen to go into the Praetorians."

"He's set his heart on it," said Balbus, "and it's certainly a career. When the old ways of looking at things are breaking down—the continuity of the family and all that—well, young people want to make their own lives. We shall have to see the astrologers, Crispus, and get them to fix a day."

Gallio grunted. "Astrologers! Mean to say you believe in that sort of nonsense, Balbus?"

"Well, my dear fellow, there's a lot in it, you know."

"Lots of moonshine. Well, good night, Crispus, and thanks. Coming, Balbus? Yes, of course I'm walking. Think I'm going to be carried about in a litter like one of Nero's nancies? You don't know old Gallio!"

When he had seen his two old friends off, Crispus went along to bed, still sighing and shaking his head and wondering if it could be true that the emperor was no better than the rest, that something was really wrong, so badly wrong that it could not be put right by going back—back to the manners and decencies and truthfulness and civilization of Augustus. Or farther.

The slaves, however, waited to clear up, and Lalage was waiting to be paid. Hearing Crispus call for his personal servant to give him the usual ten minutes' bedtime massage, Argas came back to the dining room.

But by then Beric was there again, sitting on the end of the couch where Candidus had been. He shouted at Argas to get out and keep out. Argas, who had seen what happened, the spilled wine and the blow!

Argas shrugged his shoulders and went out. "No good," he said to Sannio. "The Briton's there. And a nasty temper he's in."

"Well," said Sannio, "the little cat's done the dirty on him. Sitting there as if butter wouldn't melt in her claws. Oh my, oh my!"

Phaon was crying, clutching and rubbing himself where Tigellinus had pinched him. "I hate him!" he said. "I hate him. I'd like to kill him!"

Argas caught hold of him. "No, you don't," he said. "You don't, Phaon." And he whispered some words to Phaon that seemed to calm him down.

The slaves yawned. They would have liked to go to bed, but they knew they'd catch it if they left the clearing up till morning. Lalage was talking in a corner to Manasses, quite low, about something that seemed to interest them both. Sannio made a dirty joke, but Argas didn't laugh.

At last Lalage said, "Well, I shall go in, temper or no temper, and make that precious Briton of yours pay up. And extra for Tigellinus!" She patted Phaon, and he smiled a little. The accompanist had nodded to sleep on a bench.

Lalage went into the room quietly, for she could be very quiet, and found herself behind Beric. She stood and watched him, for something seemed to be happening to him that was the kind of thing she understood. He was standing beside the couch where Candidus had been, and he was talking to empty air, but, as Lalage listened, it became quite plain what he was doing.

"Now, you swine," he snarled, "you Aelius Candidus, you've struck me. Struck me before witnesses. Me, a king's son." He clutched about with his hands, felt at his belt, drew out a knife and pulled its edge across his thumb. Then he lifted it and held it point down and spoke again to emptiness, again from snarling misery. "No, go down on your knees, Roman, and beg for your miserable life. Say it. Say it after me. I, Aelius Candidus, in fear and trembling, beg of you, Beric, son of Caradoc the king . . ."

But already the harsh aching voice was quivering and dropping. He let the knife go, and, as it dropped with a little clatter, he turned and saw Lalage.

In the moment before his anger, she spoke, gently. "But it wouldn't have been any good, you know, even if you had done it then."

"It would have been!" said Beric. "Now—now, oh, she said I was dirt and I'd got to get used to it!"

"Who said that?"

34

"Flavia."

"Was she—your Flavia?"

"I thought she was. I don't know. Oh, I don't know anything now! It's all gone!" He made a wild gesture. "All my life, Romans are going to be able to treat me like that—like dirt! She said—"

"I know," said Lalage soothingly, "and now you can remember all the things you didn't say to her. Poor king's son!"

"King's son!" he said. "Yes, and then—dirt. Impudent native. She'd have me whipped. And now I'm blubbering about it to a dancing girl!"

"Why not?" said Lalage. "I'm dirt too." And she smiled at him.

Suddenly he grabbed at her, pulled her down beside him. "Listen!" he said. "I've never thought about it before—hardly ever—but it's all true. I *am* dirt. I'm nothing. I'm only here by the accident of Claudius Caesar being soft! My father's dead. It's all just a mistake that I'm not a chained slave. And it's a mistake they might take back. Then I'd be a slave really."

"And couldn't you bear it?"

"No. *No!* I thought I was happy, and now I know it's all lost."

"All lost. But that's the best time in life. No, look at me, Beric, son of Caradoc, listen. When everything is lost, you can be born again."

"I wish I could! As a Roman. The equal of anyone. Instead of dirt!"

"Dirt? You?" She shook him.

He felt in her hands and arms that she was strong, a dancer at the top of her physical powers, and he listened, feeling an increasing strangeness and excitement.

"Look at you. You're wearing a clean tunic. I expect you've got a dozen more put away. You've got gold pins at your shoulders. You're not hungry. You're not in pain. You've only been hit once. If it comes to dirt, I'm more like the real thing. I used to belong to an old woman who hired me out. To anyone. That makes you feel properly dirty. Coming back dirty in the mornings and knowing it was all going to happen again. Well, I made enough to pay her off and start on my own. And even now—you saw for yourself what I have to put up with and look as if I liked it.

But I don't feel as if I was dirt. All that had to happen to me just so as to give me a chance to become myself—to be reborn as my real self." She stopped.

Beric wanted her to go on. "How?" he said. "Tell me some more!"

But Lalage made a funny movement with her right hand, touching her forehead and chest in a queer way. She was silent for a moment, looking away from him.

And all at once he became wildly impatient. "Go on!" he half shouted at her.

Lalage turned to him again, speaking very firmly. "This is only the beginning. You're going to have His help. Even I can see that."

Now Beric was completely bewildered. *"Whose* help?"

"The help of One who lives for us who've lost hope and found it again and been reborn. Who promised that He would feed the hungry and give their turn to the humble and meek. Who will see there is equal justice at last, not one scale weighted. Not Romans and natives, Beric. Not masters and servants. Not ladies and whores."

He thought he was beginning to understand. "Is it—a leader? Against Rome?" Rome had killed King Cymbeline, his grandfather. And King Caradoc, his father. And Togodumnus, his uncle. And the queen of the Iceni—and oh, everywhere, the king of the Parthians, the queen of Egypt, the king of the Jews . . . But Lalage was speaking again, and he wanted to listen.

"He's not the kind of leader you're thinking of still. He's not an earthly king. But yet He's stronger than all the rich and all the power they've got. He's the strength of the poor. My strength. I would like to tell you about Him," she went on, slowly and softly.

Beric found he was wanting to put himself into her hands. "I promise . . ." he began and then wondered what he had meant to promise.

She seemed to accept it, though. She took a deep breath and began to explain. "You see, the whole thing has to come from us. The dirt. People can't be reborn if they're all mixed with ruling others. Thinking about the things they own. The lucky ones are allowed to start from the very bottom, without possessions, without power, without love."

"I don't understand," said Beric. "How can a man be lucky when he's penniless and helpless and alone?"

"Not alone anymore," said Lalage. "He's with us. He lived among us, among poor people and women like me. And in the end He got the whip on His back and the nails in His hands and feet. He had to be crucified, because that's the worst, filthiest kind of death. Nothing worse than that happens to the lowest of the dirt. He couldn't have helped us if He hadn't taken on our life and died our death."

"But then he's dead. Crucified. Like a slave. Do you mean your leader is dead, Lalage?"

"He had to suffer everything before He became our leader. Life and death."

Beric considered all this. There obviously was a leader, alive or dead. Lalage wasn't making it up. He thought he had heard about leaders who came back . . . but it was too puzzling to talk about anymore. Instead he asked, "Lalage, what was that you did with your hands just now?"

"That? Oh, that's His sign, the sign of the poor and the hurt and the ones who are kind to one another. The brothers. See if you can make it." She guided his hands into the sign of the cross.

It was a kind of magic, he thought. He felt dazed and rather happy. He sat quite quiet, and she sat quiet too.

The slaves came in. "Will it be all right if we clean up, sir?" asked Argas, and Beric nodded.

They began to clear away, talking to one another in whispers. Sannio and Mikkos took out the cups and dishes to wash up. Manasses and Phaon were tidying the couches. Suddenly Phaon began shaking the cushions violently and sobbing again. They were the cushions Tigellinus had been lying on.

"Steady on, child," said Manasses, "you'll have the stuffing out."

"Wish I had *his* stuffing out!" said Phaon.

Manasses said low, "Don't be a fool. You'll be lucky if you don't get worse done to you than that before you're much older. There's some houses—"

"You've told me that already!" said Phaon, and his voice rose to a squeak. "But I won't stand it! Not always."

Argas looked up, frowning, from his bucket and rags, and Manasses caught the boy by the wrist and said very quietly, "It won't go on always. We know that."

Phaon choked and swallowed. "Yes," he whispered. "Yes. We are not to be oppressed. He shall fill the hungry with good things."

Manasses whispered back, "And the rich He shall send empty away."

But Argas was watching Beric and Lalage, scrubbing towards them. Half aloud, he said to Lalage, "Got your pay yet?"

Lalage answered rather oddly, "I think I am being paid now."

Beric was disturbed by her speaking. He looked up and saw Argas, but he did not seem to mind now that Argas had seen the spilled wine and the blow. Perhaps Argas also had once been free and proud and then lost everything—what was it?—lost power, lost possessions, lost love.

He had never thought of Argas that way before. He had been one of the slaves, just one of the slaves. Now their glances met, fumbling, and he heard Lalage saying into his ear, "Make the sign, Beric, son of Caradoc the king, the way I showed you."

Uncertainly he made the sign, and Argas, sitting back on his heels in the dirty water, answered him quick with the same sign, and Manasses and Phaon came slipping around from the other couch and made it too.

Manasses whispered urgently to Lalage, "Does he know the Words too?"

"The words?" said Beric, bewildered. "I don't know what you're all talking about! I don't even know the name of the one you follow."

Manasses, behind, whispered, "Take care!"

But Argas, watching him steadily, said, "We follow Jesus, the Christ, who died for us and arose."

Something in Beric gave a sickening jump. He said in horror, "Then you're—Christians?" And he looked from one to the other. He was in a trap. Somehow the slaves had got him down, tangled him, as Flavia had. Only it was Lalage this time!

38

She answered him, "Yes, friend," and the others nodded.

He blurted out, increasingly upset, "You, Manasses. You poured me out my wine this evening. And you were a Christian all the time!"

He clenched his fists. He wanted to hurt Manasses. If only Manasses hadn't stayed so quiet. If only Manasses hadn't smiled and said, "Do I look as if I wanted to poison you?"

"But," said Beric, "Christians are—"

"Dirt," said Lalage. "So we are. I told you."

"But you dance in all the best houses, Lalage!" said Beric desperately. "And Manasses . . . Argas . . . little Phaon . . . I can't understand it. In this house! And you look just the same as you always did!"

"Do we?" said Argas.

Beric stood up, looked from him to Manasses, went over to Phaon and tilted up his face and stared at it. "No," he said, "you don't. No. You don't look like slaves. You look like men. So that's what it does."

Manasses said, "We've been reborn. We've been like this ever since, but you've only just seen it. Friend."

"Why are you calling me friend?" Beric asked. He only wanted to know, but Manasses and the other slaves took it as a rebuke and stood silent and uncomfortable.

It was Lalage who answered. "Because you made our sign. After that none of us could help calling you friend. Don't you like him to say it? Isn't it a good word?"

"I—I think I like it," said Beric.

Suddenly Phaon said, "She laughed at you—I saw her. They do laugh. When one of us is hurt. They don't think of us as people. We're only people when—when He's with us."

Beric flushed, for a moment hating that anyone should speak of her laughing. And of him and the slaves in the same breath, the same thought!

Young Argas was watching him. A slave has to know what the masters are thinking. He said, "I'm a man, am I not? As it might be—your brother."

Beric did not answer.

Argas said humbly, "You don't like to think that?" What was going to happen? What was their master going to make happen?

Argas was still kneeling in the dirty water. He had been doing the dirty work all evening while Beric lay on a couch among the noblemen. While Tigellinus had been pulling Phaon and Lalage about, treating them like animals, like things.

And he, Beric, he hadn't noticed that they were people. He had been thinking about himself, had been sorry for himself, wrapped up in himself like a snail in its stupid shell. Now he had looked out and seen the others. "I don't mind—brother," he said.

2

Manasses and Josias

Eleazar the son of Esrom and Nathan the son of Berechiah took their instructions and set out together, northward through Galilee, barefoot, without money or even a change of clothes. That was nothing. They were both brave and simple men who had been convinced that a certain course of action was right. If others could be convinced of it, well and good. But if they were not open to conviction, then the two would go on.

According to the country, much of which was very hilly and difficult, and according to how long they stopped in any village or group of houses, they would cover anything from three to twenty miles in a day. But sometimes they would stop for several days in a village, talking about the new way of life and healing the sick and casting out evil spirits.

These two men were convinced that there was a kind of relationship between people that was attainable, as they knew from their own experience, and that was worth everything else in life. When people were in this relationship, they loved and trusted and understood each other without too many words. They were no longer separated by fear and suspicion and competition and class. In this relationship, men and women could at last meet without each thinking the other was hoping to do some evil.

When the relationship happened, those who experienced it were very happy. They did not any longer want power and glory and possessions. If everybody in the world could have it, then nobody would want these things, and there would be no more tyranny and hatred and privilege and oppression of the poor by the rich. In the meantime, it seemed not possible for the rich to enter into this relationship, because their possessions put up a barrier of envy and greed between them and their neighbors. They could not have this happiness, which was blessing, unless they separated themselves from their possessions, and indeed some of them did so, because they wanted to come into the Kingdom of Heaven so much more than they had ever in their lives wanted anything else.

Eleazar and Nathan were so confident about all this, as indeed they had every reason to be, that people were constantly asking them for help. So few men walked about the world with that look of certainty about them, that look of being removed from ordinary human insecurity and fear, that it seemed as though they could deal with all difficulties. When men and women came to them with pains and terrors, they could usually take them away, and they themselves were not in the least afraid of darkness and wild beasts and all those things that ordinarily send village folk flying to shelter. But when they spoke about the Kingdom of Heaven, some people were always frightened, because this was an idea that contradicted everything that they had been brought up to believe in. It meant that people would no longer care about making money or having a grand position. It meant that women would be the equals of their fathers and husbands, and that parents could have no right to the labor of their sons.

So, although the doctrine of the Kingdom of Heaven was plain and obvious sense, yet there were many who hated it and who tried to hurt the two who were carrying it about. Still, they always escaped, for there were always some to help them, and they did not think evil of those who persecuted them. They were only sorry for them and sometimes puzzled.

They thought it was very probable that some of those who were carrying the doctrine might be caught and killed, and above all they thought that Jesus-bar-Joseph, from whom they had taken their instructions, might Himself be killed, for He was a man who always spoke His mind, and, although He was very clever and could make those who argued against Him look fools and worse, yet sooner or later He would fall into the hands of His enemies. And indeed He had said Himself that this might happen.

But all the same, the Kingdom was to grow and flourish until it spread over all Judea. Then, they believed, there would be no more kings in one palace and governors in another, no more high priests and rich merchants who ate up the lives and happiness of the Am Harez, the common people. And a nation that had become one in trust and amity and comradeship would be able to stand even against Rome.

So after a time they heard that Jesus-bar-Joseph had gone to Jerusalem for Passover, to teach the new way of life to the Passover pilgrims, and the rich had caught Him at last and crucified Him. And they were very sad, but they knew that the Kingdom must go on and that the things that had convinced them the year before were still true.

And a few months later, they heard that this same Jesus, whose disciples they were, had been seen again, alive, after His death and burial. This did not surprise them, because they had always supposed that He was of such a kind that this sort of thing might happen, and they hoped that they too might one day see Him again.

Usually they were given food at the village where they came in the evening. Sometimes they worked for it. Nathan had been a shepherd, and he would go out and watch the flocks on the hills with the other shepherds and talk to them. Eleazar had been a fisherman, and whenever they came to a village by a river where they did netting, he could at least mend nets in the evening.

Both of them tried to stay over the Sabbath in whatever village or town they happened to be, but, if they had either to walk or to work on that day, they did not worry about it very much. But they kept the Law as far as they could, and, though they wandered away north into Phoenicia, they only preached in the Jewish villages or streets. They never thought of preaching to the Gentiles.

By and by Nathan died suddenly, in the sun by the roadside, smiling, and Eleazar went on alone. But he was beginning to get more easily tired, and his beard was streaked with white. Often he saw angels and other strange beings both by day and night. Sometimes he came back to villages where they had taught earlier, and people remembered them and welcomed him, but so strong is the force of habit that few had changed their way of life much. If they had done so, they would usually form a little community rather apart from the rest of the village where they lived.

So it was that Eleazar came back to a village in the hills near Beth Zanita and found just such a community. He was tired, and when they asked him to stay, he said he would for a time, and then it seemed as though one of the angels gave him leave to stay always. So he stayed.

There were about twelve families in the community, and most of the land belonged to two or three of them, but now they held it all in common and all worked on it, digging, sowing, leading the water in little channels to the roots of the crops and then shutting it off, gathering fruit or grain. The boys herded the goats and sheep of the community, and the women spun and wove and made pots, and once a week they all met and said the prayer and talked about what had to be done, and Eleazar or another spoke about the Kingdom. But mostly they asked him to tell them stories about Jesus-bar-Joseph, how He had looked and what He had said, and, above all, what He had done in love or anger or doubt or eagerness. There was little money used, except what they needed for paying the yearly taxes.

They were only ten miles or so from the sea, but it was out of sight behind the hills, and even when you got there the fishermen of Achzib were not friendly. So they got little news of the outside world. But one year all the villages heard something terrible. The emperor of the Romans had decreed that his statue was to be set up and worshiped in Jerusalem, perhaps in the temple, and two legions had been landed to force this thing on the people.

It was the time of the autumn sowing, but no one could work. Those who had swords brought them out and sharpened them. Others had axes or metal-pointed hoes that would make spears. The streets were full of crying women. In the community they talked this way and that. It was the first time there had been very hard words and even blows, for some said that even this must be forgiven, and others said that the forgiving of enemies meant the enemies of one's own village or at least nation and that it never could have been said of the Gentiles. In the end nothing came of it, and the emperor was killed in Rome and went to the everlasting fire, and the temple was safe, and in the community they went on saying the prayer, but it meant different things to different people.

Things were unsettled after that in Judea and all about the coasts. Now and again some man would get followers and arm them and call himself king, and those who hated the Romans would follow him, and it would be weeks or even months before the legions could put down the rebellion. The flocks and the crops would suffer, and it was bad for everyone.

It was a difficult province. Whenever anything went wrong there, the Jews in Alexandria and Asia Minor sent letters or deputations to Rome, for they never forgot their country. There were armed brigands, too, who frightened the small villages into giving them food and sometimes raided them and even carried away women and children.

One band of these brigands was often in the hills above Beth Zanita, and one winter they raided the community and carried off five children. There was no money to ransom them, and they were taken up the coast to Tyre. Two of them were girls, for whom there was always a market; they were sold at once.

Of the three boys, Josias was a husky twelve-year-old who had fought them till he was beaten and tied down. He still seemed quite stubborn, so he was sold to a dye works where they could do with plenty of cheap boy labor. He would last a year or two.

Melchi was a strong boy too but more easily frightened; he was sold as a house servant.

The third, Manasses, was rather younger, a lovely little creature. He had not fought. At first he had cried a great deal, and then something out of the prayer had come into his head, and he had really tried to forgive his enemies. They knew they could sell him well, and they kept him till they could get their price.

The three boys promised one another, sobbing, that they would try to keep in touch. They would all say the prayer at first and last light and think of one another, and perhaps . . .

After the other two were sold, little Manasses spent some bad days. He remembered the community and tried now to think why it really was that his father and mother and the others were trying to live a different kind of life from the rest of the village. He thought of the stories old Eleazar used to tell, and he turned them over in his mind. He wondered whether it had made any difference, his trying to forgive the brigands who had carried him off and hurt him. Perhaps they had been kinder to the other two. Or perhaps it just hadn't made any difference, but yet it was a good thing to do. Perhaps it made him, even by himself, nearer to the

Kingdom. Though he felt far enough from it now, with no one in all Tyre to be his equal in trust and friendship.

He went on thinking about the Kingdom and never speaking about it for months and months, and twice a day he said the prayer and remembered the other two. He had been bought by a dealer who prepared slaves for a better market, and here he was taught miming and dancing, as well as Greek.

They were quite kind to him, and he learned docilely. He was fond of music, though it often made him cry, even when he was moving in time to it. He had better food and no more fleas than at home. He was not allowed out in case he should run away, but he was not beaten or knocked about, because his body was very salable.

But they wanted him cheerful, and at last someone asked him what would stop his moping. He told them he had two brothers and two sisters—in the community they were always brother and sister to one another—somewhere in Tyre, and he wanted to see them. But he did not know the names of the masters to whom the two little girls and Melchi had been sold, and no one was going to take that much trouble about tracing them.

He did know the name of the dye works where Josias was, and one day his master went over and bought what seemed to him a very wretched, coughing, limping piece of cheap human material, its hands and face covered with the sores they mostly get in the Tyrian dye works.

Manasses fell on his master's neck with an enthusiastic gratitude that made the old man feel quite silly, and set to work washing Josias's sore hands and face.

The sores healed in time but left him slightly scarred, and he was always rather lame where a wagon had gone over his foot. He would never be worth much and could only be used for rough work, but most of the fight had been knocked out of him. Lying in the straw at night with Manasses' arms around him, Josias told about those months at the factory where a new boy was at everyone's mercy, where it was no good trusting anyone or anything, where one was burned with hot irons and splashed with hot acid of the dye base, and worse, much worse, things he wouldn't ever tell Manasses—things that no Jew . . . and he shuddered all over

46

with the horror of it, poor little country boy who had not even heard much evil as a child.

After a time, Josias got well and strong enough to want to run away, but each boy was told what penalties that would involve for the other, and they were never allowed out together.

There was more and stricter mime training for Manasses, and sometimes now he did his dancing to an audience. He might be sent out for an evening, petted and given sweets by Tyrian merchants, and sometimes by their wives, for he was young enough to be allowed in and out of the harems. Sometimes he was petted more than he liked, and once all the women in a harem stripped him and dressed him in girls' clothes and did his hair, which was now in long dark tresses, and painted his face like a bride's, and everyone said things that made him stamp and scream with rage. It was not until a long time afterwards that he could forgive those fat, stupid, cruel women, jeering at him, holding him with sharp nails.

The boys wondered whether these merchants made their money and supported their wives out of the dye factories. Most likely. There was plenty of luxury industry of all kinds in Tyre, as well as shipping, and most of the big merchants had interests in other cities as well. They looked very fine, great, bearded, dark merchant-adventurers, with gold rings in their ears and gold bracelets on their arms, striding about the docks or across the market squares of Tyre, men who could laugh at emperors and legions, who would not bow to a Roman governor or to any traveling king, descendants of the men who had defied Alexander. But that did not make them any nicer to deal with or any easier to forgive if you were a dancing boy hired from your master for an evening's entertainment.

But one day Manasses was made to dance during the morning for someone he had never seen, and then handled and priced and told he was now going to Rome. He said gently that he would kill himself if Josias was not bought with him, for he knew that if Josias was left behind, he would probably be sold back into the factory. After some grumbling, his purchasers agreed, and a few days later the two were on board ship, for the first time in their lives, sailing west.

During the next few weeks they were bought and sold several times, but were separated only once, and then Manasses found Josias again in the Jewish Quarter of Rome, where he had been kindly treated. Of course, Josias was always sold rather cheap, because of his limp and scars, but he was quiet and strong and didn't grumble so long as Manasses was treated properly. Sometimes they both asked in the Jewish Quarter whether anyone had a slave called Melchi, but they never found him. They wondered how long he had gone on saying the prayer.

In the meantime, Manasses went on learning. Sometimes he was one of a dozen or more dancers, but he did not make friends much. The rest were usually Greeks, and somehow he still did not care for the smell and touch of Gentiles.

It was difficult to keep the Law. Often they lost count of the days and never knew when it was Sabbath for weeks at a time, until they met another Jew who knew. But they tried not to eat forbidden food. Ordinarily, slaves got very little meat, but, of course, a dancer was different. He might be as valuable as a race-horse and had to have his oats!

Manasses was gradually saving up a little bag of money, but he knew it would cost him a lot to buy his freedom. He learned to speak bad Latin, but Greek was almost a second language in Rome.

Rome was a great and horrible city. You could not think of the Kingdom there. It had become impossible, something not even to be hoped for. They usually said the prayer still, once a day at least, but mostly it meant no more than, say, touching a charm. They did not talk anymore about Jesus-bar-Joseph.

They were aware of large and evil forces moving over their heads, of masters not all-powerful but themselves terrified. There came a time when Manasses was about fifteen. It was a big household. His master was a senator, a thin, nervous man with an odd habit of jerking his head around. Manasses was to dance as Ariadne to the Bacchus of a rather older boy, a Greek.

He was making up, darkening his eyes and powdering his cheeks and arms, while one of the others tied back his hair with a woman's band and Josias massaged his legs, pushing up the long, flame-colored girl's tunic, which would swirl about in the dance.

"Who's going to be there?" he asked, but the overseer put a finger to his lips.

"Don't you ask tonight, boy."

That made him all the more curious, and when he went in he wondered who was the handsome, rather soft-looking young man, with only the beginnings of a beard, to whom everyone was paying so much attention. It was fairly obvious that it was this young man who was to be danced to and glanced at, and Manasses did his best.

In the end, the young man beckoned him up, gave him a piece of gold, and then explained very seriously that in one movement he had not interpreted the music as he should have.

To Manasses' great surprise, the young man rose, throwing aside a most beautiful purple cloak, clapped his hands for the musicians and proceeded to give his own interpretation of the passage. He certainly danced well for an amateur, allowing himself to be clasped in the most realistic way by the Bacchus, who was overacting through sheer nervousness, and everyone applauded tremendously, including Manasses.

Walking back to the couch, the young man stopped and stroked the kneeling Manasses, who thought he had the usual Gentile or Roman smell of overeating. "I hope the boy is being seriously trained," he said.

Someone else said, "Not so well as he would be at the palace!" And then the host began, "Oh—allow me—if I might offer him as a small gift, the honor would be mine."

It only then occurred to Manasses that the young man was Nero Caesar, the new emperor.

Manasses did not mind being given to Nero, so long as Josias was included, and they were sent off to the palace, where, as a matter of fact, he only saw the emperor half a dozen times. He was one of several hundred slaves, many of whom were dancers, actors, acrobats, or musicians. Sometimes he was part of the background for the great dancer Paris, who did him the honor of kicking him one day.

Usually he had to entertain the more important slaves or freedmen. He trusted no one and was sometimes nasty to Josias, who, in turn, grew sullen. And he got to know some useful things about poisons. Also he got to know by sight the emperor's mistress, beautiful, discreet Claudia Acte, the Greek freedwoman, a little older than the boy Nero, approved of by his friends but not by his mother.

One evening there was a row. Old Pallas, the financial secretary, was beating up a girl who didn't want to sleep with him, and, if you knew what he was like, you couldn't blame her, but still she'd been sent in by her madam, and she was a slave, so she didn't have any choice. But she kept on screaming that she was a dancer and not a whore, and he kept on answering the way that sort of man answers that sort of woman, and at last he got in a kick that knocked her out, and there she lay, bleeding a little, and Pallas stalked out.

Some of the slaves had been watching behind the curtains, but they weren't going to interfere. The girl groaned a bit and flopped her hands, but it was none of their business to pick her up. It was a kind of passage room that you went through if you didn't want to go through the public courts, and by and by Claudia Acte slipped in, with a veil over her head and shoulders. She saw the girl on the floor and went straight and knelt beside her and lifted her head and spoke to her in Greek. Then she looked up and saw the slaves in the doorway and called sharply, "Here, one of you, come and help me!"

Most of them just dissolved away, for they were more afraid of Pallas than of Acte, and anyhow why should they help? But it came to Manasses that he was a Jew and therefore braver than these Greeks and Bithynians, and besides he had once believed in the Kingdom and all that went with it, so he came.

Acte asked him where the girl could be put safely, and Manasses thought of an attic where there would probably be an old mattress. They carried her there between them, and for the moment he did not care if Pallas was told. Then he got water and some rags to wash her. When he came back, Acte was holding the girl's hand and praying, her eyes shut.

Manasses listened and heard words of the kind he knew and a name he used to know very well, by virtue of which Acte meant to put calm and healing into the hurt girl on the mattress. He said nothing, but bathed her head, and soon she opened her eyes and smiled at Acte. There was a cut on the corner of her mouth that kept on bleeding a little, but it was not deep and would not scar her. Then the girl began to twitch and look frightened and tried to get up.

Acte stopped her and said, "He will not get you. Keep quiet."

"But when they hear . . ." said the girl, her voice filled with fear of her madam.

Acte said, "I will see to it. You know who I am."

"Yes, Claudia Acte, we all know," said the girl simply, and Acte blushed and looked a little troubled, but after a time the girl began to fidget and cry again, though there were no bones broken.

Acte laid one hand on her forehead and the other on her twitching fingers. "In the name of Jesus, rest," she said.

And as Acte bent over her, still and intent, the girl calmed down and shut her eyes.

But Manasses, looking at Acte, thought of her not as a Gentile woman but as someone in the Kingdom, and he became full of excitement and a hot desire of worship, with her and toward her. He began under his breath to say the Words, "Our Father who art in heaven, hallowed be Thy name," and for the first time for many months they began to mean something again. He was saying them aloud now, and Claudia Acte joined in, saying them almost the same, and at the end she looked very happy and said, "I did not know you were one of us, brother. What is your name?"

Manasses told her and said, "But I did not know that the Kingdom could happen in Rome. How did you come to it, Claudia Acte, seeing that you are a Greek?"

"But many Christians are Greeks," said Acte, "and a few, even, are Romans. Did you think it was only for the Jews? Are you from the church at Jerusalem?"

"No," said Manasses, "I have never been as far as Jerusalem"—for Jerusalem had seemed a very long way from Beth Zanita when he was a child— "and why do you say *Christians?*"

"Because Jesus was the Christ," she said, "the Redeemer. Surely you know that?"

"I know that the things He said were the truth," Manasses answered slowly, "and that He lived to show the truth."

"And died to show the truth."

"Because the rich would not let Him live. Because the things He said were against the rich and powerful."

"Because He had to die the slave's death to show that He was our brother as well as the Christ."

"But what is it to you, Claudia Acte? He was one of us; we have always had prophets. But the Gentiles never heeded them."

"He spoke for the world, for all who would take what He said. Why should you try to keep Him from me? Paul of Tarsus made it clear that He was for all!"

"Who is Paul of Tarsus?"

"He is a Jew, and it was he and Luke, who is a doctor and a Greek like me, who have been telling the rest of us what you would have kept for yourself, greedy boy."

"I—I am sorry, Claudia Acte. I never thought the Kingdom could be for the Gentiles, and I have heard nothing since we were in Rome, Josias and I. But if you can heal and if . . . if . . . I mean, when you called me brother, Claudia Acte—then you are in the Kingdom, and it was only that I did not understand."

Acte said, "Tomorrow is the Eighth Day and the breaking of bread. Will you come?"

Manasses only looked puzzled.

She smiled and said, "Surely you know about the breaking of bread? No? Well then, you have not yet had real knowledge of the Kingdom. You have heard only half, Manasses. Are you baptized?"

"I was purified in running water when I was a child," said Manasses, and then he thought about all that had happened since and above all about the last months in the palace and some of the things he had done or had done to him, and how he had not even minded, and he began to cry and said, "But now I am dirty again and full of sins, and I have not been able to keep the Law, and I have forgotten about everything, and I did not know that Jesus was the Christ! I want to be purified and born again, Claudia Acte!"

She looked at him very pitifully and said, "I think that can be done, Manasses, for you were only half baptized. Now, will you look after this girl for me?"

"Yes," he said, "I will do anything for you. But what am I to say if Pallas asks?"

"Pallas will not be here much longer," said Acte, and her face hardened. "I know that. Lie to him and tell the others they are to lie, or Acte will be very angry. We shall get Pallas out very soon."

"But the empress—" said Manasses astonished, knowing that Pallas and the Empress Agrippina had acted together in the past and now knew too much about one another ever to quarrel.

"That account may be closed too," said Acte, "but keep your mouth shut. Get the name of this girl's madam and go to her in the morning with this"—she took a purse out of the fold of her dress and gave it to him—"and say that Acte needed the girl." Watching him, she added, "It is good to know that I can trust you. I will send you word about the breaking of bread."

He knelt in front of her as he had done as a child with Eleazar and said, "Give me a blessing."

She laid her hands on his head and gave it, and he forgot that she was a Gentile woman and only felt the blessing of the trust again and knew that the teaching of Jesus was not in vain.

That was the beginning of many things, including his friendship with Lalage, the hurt girl. He and Josias came to the breaking of bread, and they learned how in the love feast all those eating together could be sure of the temporary experience of the Kingdom and got from it enough faith to go on in a world that seemed utterly against them.

But even in Caesar's household and even under the protection of Claudia Acte, it was necessary to be very secret. Because the Kingdom of Heaven could only come—and this was plain to everybody—after the overthrow of the world of success, of emperors and governors, of priesthoods and Senate, of the rich and strong: the world of Rome. And the only thing worth asking for and living for was the coming of the Kingdom.

After a while they had one of the periodical siftings out of the palace, and once more Manasses and Josias were sold, this time to a very respectable household, where Manasses was expected to do other things besides dance. Actually, his dancing did not improve at all after he was sixteen. He grew too tall and solid for the boy parts, and fortunately for him nobody had chosen to take effective physical measures to keep him young. It was not done quite so often to Jew-boys because they made such a fuss and sometimes killed themselves. After a time he was allowed to cut his long curly hair. It curled still, but close over his head.

His present master, L. Flavius Crispus, preferred the old-fashioned comic dancing with masks at his dinner parties, or even recitations. Manasses used to read aloud to him sometimes, when his secretary was busy, and also helped with the ordinary waiting at table, saw to the wines, and so on. It was a stricter household, and for a time he disliked it, but Josias, who worked in the kitchen, liked it more.

It was difficult for them to get away for the love feasts, but by and by they found that they were not the only Christians in the new household, either. There was a little imp of a boy, Phaon, whom Manasses had to teach to dance—he was quite good when he took any trouble. He was a slave, but his mother, Eunice, was a freedwoman and Christian. She had sometimes been to the meetings in Caesar's household, and now there were meetings in her house, which Manasses and Josias could go to. Euphemia, another freedwoman, used to come, and Rhodon the metalworker, and Phineas and Sapphira, and sometimes others. Lalage used to come when she was in that part of the city. She had been baptized almost at the same time that Manasses and Josias were rebaptized, after the meeting had decided that their old purification did not count. And later on Niger, who was black and having a bad time where he was, came, when he could manage to get away.

But the meetings were often in the house of Crispus, in summer always in the unused boiler room, where the furnaces for the hot-water system stood cold for eight months of the year. By that time Argas had come, and Dapyx, and then little Persis.

Sometimes, too, there would be brothers who were strangers, who had only just come to Rome. They were always welcome and always trusted, and usually, but not quite always, the trust was justified. There was one man who prophesied and spoke with tongues, and they lent him money, and they never got any of it back.

More of them than not were Jews, but still quite a number were Greeks or other Gentiles. Manasses hardly even noticed now. And sometimes there would be a new convert, like Sotion, the freedman who lived quite near and who had begun to come to the meetings lately.

It was another life going on all the time under and beside the ordinary slave's life. The two lives did not really overlap. On the whole, the Christians in Crispus's household were good servants, unusually truthful and honest. But none of them would have dreamed of breathing a word of all this to their master. It had nothing to do with the masters.

And so when Manasses looked up from clearing the table and saw Beric the Briton making the sign—their sign—it was like suddenly seeing light through a brick wall. And then, when it was apparent that the Briton did not really know what he was doing or who they were, he had been sickenly afraid. But he had gathered up his courage and spoken gently, and he had seen that the Briton was afraid too, only in a different way.

And then? Was it that he had forgiven the Briton for being one of the masters, or had the Briton forgiven him and Argas for being slaves? They had become each a little in the power of the other. But not this time as he had always before been in the power of his masters. Not in hate, but in some suspended feeling that was halfway to love, that was a reaching out from either side to the other.

Lalage had gone out and left them alone. She had said, laughing, that she would come back and be paid the next day, and the Briton had stood looking after her, one hand out as if he would have stopped her but not finding anything to say. Then he turned back to them, saying, "The words—what was it you meant by 'the words'? Is that how you know one another?"

"Yes," said Manasses, adding, "they are the words of our prayer."

"Your prayer," said Beric. He was stumbling over it, thinking hard and slowly. "To your leader. But he is dead."

"He is risen," said little Phaon quickly, but Manasses said, "Yes, He is dead." Time enough for the other thing later.

"Then," said Beric, "is this to call him back?"

Manasses was thinking what to say, but Argas said, "He will come when the time is ripe and the people have suffered enough. This is to show we are His!"

Manasses said, "He taught us to pledge ourselves to His Father in heaven, who is the Father of us all, with these words and in this manner of praying . . ." And then he hesitated, because it was so queer to be saying the Words in front of one of the masters.

But Beric said, "Go on, Manasses."

And Manasses stood up by the table, which still wanted wiping over, and lifted his hands and said, "Our Father who art in heaven . . ."

Then Argas stood up too and suddenly touched Beric's hand and said to him, "Say it with us, brother." And he and Phaon and the Briton all stood and repeated it line for line after Manasses.

3

Persis, Eunice, and Phaon

Bersabe's eldest girl had been sold three years ago. So now she kept trying to hide Persis, dressing her in old rags and sending her to work in the dirty back kitchen where perhaps she mightn't be noticed. Hoping her master wouldn't see.

If it was to be again as it had been with Roxane, she would die. She had wanted to die then, but she was too tough. Besides, there had been Persis and the little ones—though she hated them for months, hated them for not being Roxane and then for forgetting her. She never forgot Roxane, day or night.

But from that day to this there had been no word of her first baby, the little soft thing she'd nursed through her childhood, stolen milk for, been beaten for, been so proud of, that silky dark hair—oh, all the summer evenings she'd sat on the step combing Roxane's hair and singing to her, happy, oh yes, as happy as a slave woman could be!

And then, she kept on dreaming still of the dealer's agent, the fat Syrian. Bersabe had always thought these things happened in other households, to other mothers, not to her. But it had happened. So now she must never be proud of Persis, mustn't touch her softly or get the tangles out of her hair, never beg a piece of material for a dress for her.

But Persis was cross with her mother. Why couldn't she ever be allowed into the front part of the house, why was she always treated like a baby? On her own she begged herself a dress from one of the daughters of the house, and oh, then, when she put it on, smoothing it against herself, Bersabe couldn't help seeing that the child was a woman, and that she was terribly like Roxane. And Bersabe threw up her arms and howled, flung herself into a corner and cried, as she knew she was bound to be made to cry, some day soon.

But Persis combed out her own hair and looked at her reflection in a pan of water.

It was less than a year since Bersabe had been a member of the congregation of the church at Philippi. Sometimes still she caught herself asking for luck from other gods. But now, more and more, when she was unhappy, her mind wheeled back to the low room, away from the glare and noise and laughter of the street, to that feeling of unbounded kindness and trust that sometimes overwhelmed her into tears and sometimes into singing or the sudden sharp cry of delight, and that stayed with her, at work or asleep, for days and days afterwards.

She had never taken Persis with her. Not taking her was part of the insistence that Persis was only a child. Now she was sure she must take her, and at once.

Epaphroditus, the deacon, was a little doubtful about baptizing Persis, but Bersabe wept and stormed, and Euodia advised it, and Persis had fasted and seemed to know the Words of the Way of Life and to be eager for it herself.

Actually, she was very frightened. Two or three days after she had dressed herself up in that cast-off dress, feeling so grand, her master had called to her as she was carrying a bucket of water through to the kitchen. She left the bucket and ran over, pleased to be noticed.

But after that, it wasn't so nice. He asked her how old she was and what she could do, and a lot of other questions, and tilted up her face with a finger under her chin and looked at her in a way that made her want to cry. She had scuttled back to her mother, and the two of them had cried in one another's arms, and neither had said anything about Roxane, but both remembered her, and for the thousandth time Bersabe wondered if she was alive or dead . . . or just being hurt.

Now in the meeting they were both praying that the thing need not happen, if only the Lord Jesus would take it away! And when Persis was taken to the pool under the waterfall and felt the water of baptism, she thought that perhaps it would be all right. Oh, she was almost sure it would! And when they brought her back she was lifting her arms for joy, and some of the congregation thanked God for letting them see so lovely a sight.

But Bersabe stayed behind to talk to Euodia and Syntyche, the two senior women of the congregation. They talked it over together, while Bersabe sobbed and Persis listened and became every moment colder and more frightened and less able to think that the baptism had changed anything.

Euodia took her aside and told her that in this town or that she might be able to find a church and friends, but above all she now had a Friend forever, the Friend whose presence she had felt when the waters touched her.

But already Persis, swaying from her two days' fast, had forgotten how she had felt then. Only she remembered the names of the towns and the signs that she might look for and repeated to herself the words that could make her known. But she could not bear the rueful looks of the older women and the way they would not let her forget what might be going to happen to her.

That night and for three more nights, she cried herself to sleep, and Bersabe slipped away from work to come and sit with her and smooth her hair and stare at her lovely mouth and soft eyebrows and straight little nose—as she had not dared to stare and love while the thing might yet be averted. As she stared she prayed. And on the fourth day, the same dealer's agent who had taken Roxane came to take Persis.

Bersabe asked him very humbly if he could tell her where Roxane was, but he had no idea. She had changed hands several times. Bersabe remembered what changing hands meant in the way of stripping and handling. She had been a pretty slave girl herself, away in Asia. At least there were some things people didn't want to do to women after they got gray hair.

One of the daughters of the house gave Persis a silver piece, and they were all quite nice to poor old Bersabe after Persis was taken away. She had screamed at the end. In fact both of them had.

Persis was put on board ship and taken to Delos. All the time on the ship she cried and whimpered and did not think much about the church at Philippi or any of the words she had been taught. She thought only about her mother and her little brothers and the warm kitchen and the way to the well, and a certain crack in the wall that she always used to run her finger along, and a certain tree she used to climb, with handholds shiny from children's using.

But when she got to Delos, she stopped being homesick because the immediate things that were done to her, or that she thought were going to be done, were so very horrible that she couldn't think of anything else.

The slave dealers were mostly no worse than other merchants and generally more interested in the price than in any other aspects of their merchandise, but in the hot, steep, crowded little city of Delos, something bad used to get at them—the smells and cries and the foreign voices and the constant handling of foreign and helpless women and boys. So it was a place where human beings asked much for mercy and got little.

The dealers would get bored with their stuff and wouldn't even mind spoiling it; there was plenty more. When they had been drinking they would go down to the warehouse and the docks and knock the chained barbarians about. Anything that was hopelessly spoiled could be thrown into the sea.

Of course Persis was not treated like that; she was too valuable. She only heard and sometimes saw it. She was darker and slenderer than the Greek girls, and easy to teach. By the time she had changed hands a few times, been reembarked and landed again at Ostia, she was still technically a virgin. It did not make much difference when she ceased to be, except that she was hurt in a new way. Sometimes she could hardly remember her mother and Philippi now; the barrier of horror between herself and all that was too strong. It was too much to hope that she would ever find friends or kindness again.

In the first household, the mistress whipped her and sold her, because of what the master did. In the second she was so frightened of the overseer that she dropped her work whenever she saw him and couldn't remember what she'd been told to do for five minutes on end.

It was almost a relief to be resold to the same dealer, who fed her up and was tolerably gentle to her, even let her play marbles and cat's cradle with some girls of her own age, and finally sold her into a decent house, where she was to be trained as maid to Flavia, the only daughter of her new master, Flavius Crispus.

Here there was nothing special to be frightened about over her master; he was oldish and kindly. There was a young master in the house too, but he was apparently not even a Roman. The slaves called him "the Briton," and by and by someone told her that he really did come from an island weeks away in the cold middle of the sea, where his father had been a king.

He was quite well liked. He had asked Persis her name and spoken to her once or twice, but he didn't do anything to her. After a time she couldn't help knowing that he was really interested in her young mistress, Flavia.

The old slave woman who was training her found her quick and clever at doing hair and pleating and pinning. She thought Flavia was very beautiful with her crisp shining curls and brilliant eyes, and she would have loved her if Flavia had been at all nice to her. However, she was safe here; she could look up and breathe again. She could look about the new household and wonder if she would make any friends.

It was very puzzling at first, trying to keep it all in her head. There was no regular overseer, but one or two old slaves or freedmen, and the Briton kept a general eye on things. The head cook was an Italian freedman, good at the traditional dishes. There was the usual amount of scolding and threatening but very little real punishment, and on the whole it was fairly cheerful and the food not bad.

There was no one else from as far east as she was—by race at least—but there were several Jews, plenty of Greeks or Sicilians, some Thracians or North Gauls for the heavy work, but no Britons. Perhaps Crispus had thought it wasn't tactful to have them in the same house as the boy he had brought up.

Nearly as much Greek as Latin was spoken in the house. However, Persis had to learn Latin quickly, for Flavia, although she could read and write Greek fluently, was not going to take the trouble to speak it so as to make things easier for the new girl.

There was a boy about the same age as Persis, one of the Greeks. He was a dining-room slave, clever at dancing and miming and all sorts of tricks and able to get around the old master. He was born in the house.

Eunice, his mother, had been in the kitchen for years and, even now she'd been freed, was still in and out quite often. It was she who had spoken in a friendly way to Persis, asking her to come over some evening to her little bakery, which was quite close. Persis hadn't wanted to at first. She didn't like Phaon, who was a brash, teasing little imp, quite sure he was going to be freed himself soon. And besides, she knew about the house where she was now, the best and the worst of it. She wasn't going to risk looking outside; there wouldn't be anything worth looking at. She knew what a slave girl's life was now. It wasn't any use doing any silly hoping or picturing.

All the same, fat old Eunice asked her again. She said, rather surprisingly, "My boy said you were lonely."

Persis thought angrily, *What right had he to talk about me!* But then, he didn't look as if he cared. And while she was thinking that, Eunice had taken her by the arm, and then Persis found herself crying and sobbing that she had lost her mother—had lost everything—and Eunice stumped straight off to Flavia's old slave woman and said that she was taking Persis along with her that evening and there was to be no fuss. And before Persis had quite stopped hiccupping from her burst of tears, she was out in the street, with Eunice patting her and talking to her.

Persis hardly listened to the words. It was the kindness behind them that mattered. That was like the rich, warm smell of new bread that she breathed in at the bakery, curled up on a rug on the floor at Eunice's feet.

By and by Phaon came tumbling in.

Persis attempted to jump up, but Eunice wouldn't let her, and Phaon curled up on the rug too. He was much nicer now. He didn't tease her at all. *Perhaps*, thought Persis, *his teasing me before was just his way of trying to make friends.*

She stayed there for the best part of the evening and forgot she was a slave girl who had been bought and sold and forcibly made adult at Delos and other toughening places, and remembered she was fifteen and it was still nice to dig one's fingers into dough and play silly games with Phaon and his mother.

After that, she came fairly often, whenever she could get away for half an hour. Sometimes she would find one or two of the others, Manasses perhaps or Josias or Argas, another of the Greek boys. But she didn't pay much attention to them. What she wanted was to be allowed to be clean and a child again. Perhaps, after all, the whole world wasn't hateful.

Sometimes she and Phaon helped with the baking. Most of it was rye bread or some mixture, but there were always a few white loaves for the better class customers, and often Eunice made them up into fancy twists. Phaon was very good at this; he would give the dough a flip and mold it with his fingers, and it turned into a swan or a rose.

"Make something else, do!" said Persis.

He laughed and dipped his hands into the flour and began on another lump of dough. In a couple of minutes it had turned into a fish with beautiful fins.

His mother looked at it, smiled, and then said, very seriously, "I can't bake that, Phaon."

"Why not?" asked Persis. "It's lovely!" And then she saw that Phaon and his mother were looking at one another with a strange sort of understanding, and suddenly remembered something she had forgotten for more than a year and said breathlessly, "Do you mean the fish is—something else?"

"It's only a joke," said Phaon quickly.

And Persis thought, *Oh no, of course not, that would have been too good to be true,* and looked it, for Eunice took her hand and asked, "Did you ever hear of a fish that meant something different?"

"Oh yes," said Persis and knew she was bound to cry in a minute, because remembering that meant remembering everything.

In a blur she saw the piles of cut wood and the round oven and the table with the dough on it, and Phaon looking straight at her, reaching for her, saying very eagerly, "What was your fish, Persis?"

Was it dangerous to say? Hadn't there been some warning from Euodia? She mustn't speak unless she was sure. But oh, in this little room she'd had kindness! "They were the Name letters," she said, and it all came back to her, and she stared at the dough-white fish and murmured them.

"Persis, how lovely!" said Phaon and kissed her but not teasingly. No, like a brother.

"Why didn't you tell us, dear?" said Eunice. "You could have been coming to the meetings all this time."

"But I didn't know," said Persis. "I thought—oh, I thought it was all no use and Jesus had forgotten me."

"That doesn't happen," said Eunice. "Now tell me, what was your church and of whom your baptism?"

"Philippi," said Persis, "and I was baptized by Epaphroditus—but then, you see, I was sold—"

"I know, my lamb, my lamb," said Eunice, cuddling her, "but you've come here. Think if you'd been sold the way my brother was—he was a skilled man, of course, a joiner—right away into Spain. Where there's no church—unless he was able to make one."

"Don't you know about him, then?" asked Persis.

"No, my dear, and it will be seven years, come midsummer. Only I keep on hoping he found what he could make a church out of, with God's help."

"But what could he make a church out of?"

"Why, what I've been trying to give you, all this time, not knowing you were one of us: faith in Christ and poor folks' feeling for each other. Kindliness, as you might say, or, it might be, love. Once you've got it, and you do get it mostly among slaves and that, then you can build on it. You can start telling what He said it was, and how He lived and died to make it plain for those that can't see. My brother could have told all that. A skilled man, he was. But you'll come to the meetings now, Persis. Sometimes we hold them here and sometimes at the house, in one of the back rooms."

"Do any of the masters know?"

"No, nor your young lady. It's no concern of theirs. It's ours."

"But Epaphroditus at Philippi, he was a gentleman, or almost."

"It's not that way in Rome. Of course, one of them might perhaps come. If he'd had a bad time—got in wrong with the emperor, say. But it doesn't come natural to them. A gentleman wouldn't want to share, not really."

"Epaphroditus had a farm. But I know it didn't pay. Mother said he never got any new clothes, and that old mule of his was a sight!"

Phaon giggled. "I don't see the old man putting all his money into the bag, nor yet your Scratch Cat not getting herself a new dress!"

That last was their name for Flavia. Sometimes the scratching was quite literal—on the face. Persis knew already.

Phaon added, "I can bring you into the meeting, Persis, can't I? They'll want someone to stand surety for you, and I never have for anyone yet. May I?"

"Oh, do, Phaon!" said Persis. "Who else is in the church?"

"Oh, Manasses and Argas and Josias, and one or two from other houses. There's always enough of us, sometimes the full twelve, sometimes more. I am glad you're one of us, Persis!"

"If only mother knew," she said.

"Perhaps she'll have a dream," said Phaon hopefully. "Oh, Persis, I'm simply longing for the next meeting! Come on, we can't leave the fish. He's done what he was meant for. Look, you take one end, and I'll take the other. We'll make him into a loaf."

After that she was never really unhappy, even when Flavia hurt her and she couldn't help crying, or when the old woman scolded her. Nothing was bad for long, and Argas and Manasses used to save her sweets from the dining room. And once or twice, when she had done Flavia's hair really beautifully, Flavia gave her an old dress.

She was rather frightened of the Briton, who never seemed to notice whether she was there or not but was always looking at Flavia. She shut her mind tight against what else he might be doing; it was none of her business. Things were different in Rome, at any rate for the ladies and gentlemen.

She had to stay up late, of course, when Flavia kept late hours. She slept on a mattress just outside the door of her mistress's room, ready to jump up if she called. In winter she always had to get up once in the night to refill the lamp, in case Flavia might wake in the dark.

The mattress was her own territory. There was a hole in it, next to the wall, where she kept things. There was a fish amulet there, which Eunice had given her. She didn't dare to wear it, but it was lovely to put in her hand and feel and know that her cheek was resting just above it all night.

She was sitting on her mattress, waiting, half asleep, when Flavia came back to her room after the dinner party. *How beautiful she looks*, thought Persis, and wondered if it was nice being Flavia. Nice being rich and having all those lovely clothes and jewels. Nice being a Roman. Or didn't you notice if you were like that to begin with?

She had jumped up, and now she ran into the room to light all the lamps. The one by the bed was a very pretty, silver, three-necked one, and it burned special oil, scented from Alexandria.

Flavia flopped down to be unpinned, stretching and yawning.

"What a lovely color madam has tonight!" said Persis shyly.

Flavia laughed and looked at herself in the silver mirror and said over her shoulder. "I'm going to be betrothed next week!"

"Ooh, madam!" said Persis, feeling so pleased to have been told.

"Yes, and I shall have to see about a new dress. Candidus is going to give me an emerald necklace. And bracelets. Don't pull my hair, you little idiot! I wish I knew what kind of bracelets the empress was wearing. Well, when I'm married I shall be able to go to the palace and everywhere. I wonder if Tigellinus will give me anything. I like a man to have black hairs on his arms; that's a sign of strength. Tigellinus has black hairs right on to his shoulders. They say that means a man's always going to have his own way."

"Oh, does it, madam?" said Persis and tried not to think about the Briton's arms, which certainly had fair hair.

"Does it! Does it!" said Flavia. "You silly little thing, why don't you try? I believe you'd scream if anyone kissed you. You are stupid! When I'm married I'll see if Candidus hasn't got a big slave with nice, black hairy arms—you know, you'd love it!"

"Oh, please, I wouldn't!" said Persis, terrified.

"You little fool, of course you would! Everyone does. I ought to have emerald earrings too. Open the shutters a little. How intolerably hot it is. You can fan me now, but don't stop till I'm really asleep, or I'll bite you."

4

Argas

All that summer there was nothing to eat but beans and chick-peas and sometimes porridge made out of the sourest sort of meal. The children went hunting for wild berries and roots but came home so hungry that it was worse than if they'd stayed still.

It was the same everywhere. Little Argas and his friends were always talking about food. Sometimes they went into the rich quarter of the town and stole from the shops, but that was getting more and more difficult. And sometimes there was something to be got by hanging around the temples.

There had been bad weeks before when Father couldn't get work. He was a skilled mason, but nobody was building houses, and people were even skimping on their tombstones. Sometimes one of the citizens who was still tolerably well-off would distribute some grain or have an ox roasted, but what you got was hardly worth standing for a couple of hours. But this year the bad time just went on and on. The last baby had been exposed, of course; everybody had to do that. But the older children were so thin. They weren't growing. They looked better than they were because they were all sunburned, but they got tired as easily as old people.

There had been a time when Epidauros was prosperous and full of life. But now Hellas was dying. They were a province, and if there was any blood in it, Rome sucked the blood. The Achaean League still went on; some people took it seriously, dressed up, talked about freedom and honor and all that. Who cared? The Romans let them. They knew they had only to say the word and the whole thing would crumble. And little Argas and the rest of the boys threw chestnut burrs at the processions.

But even the chestnuts did badly that year. It didn't help to think what winter would be like. But winter came, and mother got ill; she just hadn't had enough to eat for a long time. When fathers are out of work, mothers usually give the food to the others and make do themselves on the smell of the cooking pots and a joke or two, and it was the same in Epidauros.

So Father went out with Argas one day and came back without Argas, but with enough meal and dried fish for a month. And when mother cried, he said that at least Argas was going to be fed now.

That was what Argas remembered about the first week of his slavery, crying and eating at the same time. And then being taken away, to Corinth perhaps, and sold again.

For quite a long time he was a house slave in Athens. They were an old family, not so well-off as they had been, always treating their servants well. At New Year they always used to give Argas a little present of money and material for a tunic. And when he wasn't well, the old mistress looked after him herself. Some day, he thought, he would buy himself back and go to Epidauros, but it was no good if he was to go back penniless.

With enough to eat, he grew up into a tall, handsome boy. His master had him taught to read and write and also speak some Latin, as there were often Roman visitors at the house. Sometimes Metronax, his master, used to talk to him, mostly about the old days, when Athens had been the center of the world and his own city, Epidauros, had been something to be proud of too. Those were the days when a single person, a statesman or a soldier, could change the destinies of a people. They were wild, heroic times.

But now all power was in one place, now everything was ordered, and you knew from year to year more or less what taxes you had to pay, and nothing could be done without the leave of the Roman governor. And if the Romans wanted anything, they took it, and you had to stand by and say nothing.

There was a statue that was taken out of one of the temples, carefully and efficiently packed, and shipped to Rome (apparently the emperor loved anything Hellenic). A good many Athenians went to see that being done. From time to time they were elbowed out of the way by a Roman official. Metronax came home and sat down and cried about it.

Young Argas, kneeling beside him, very bothered, tried to understand. The statue was a goddess, the special goddess of Athens. But Metronax didn't believe in the old gods and goddesses; Argas knew that. His master only believed in some kind of very remote god or gods who had really nothing to do with people, only with sun and stars and the progress of the years and justice and virtue and things like that.

So why was he crying? Argas didn't know. He himself didn't believe in the gods of Olympus either. They were all a fairy-tale for rich people, and even they didn't believe in them now. He, Argas, didn't believe in anything, except perhaps luck. It was better not to do anything that was generally supposed to be unlucky. And you could alter the course of things by going to a witch, but that cost money. He thought for a moment above love potions and one of the maids, a girl called Lykainis. But that could wait.

He brought his master a cup of wine. If only he would drink and say something dry and hard, anything except just sit there looking so miserable! Argas began singing. Sometimes his master liked that, and if he didn't—well, it would be something if Metronax would even look up and scold him. His voice had changed and was now very deep. He sang the old-fashioned songs that his master liked, not the melodious ones he liked best himself.

For a minute or two Metronax cried more painfully, and then he straightened himself up and wiped his eyes, sipped at the wine and laid a hand affectionately on the shoulder of his young Hellenic slave. "Can you understand, Argas," he said, "that this statue meant something that people thought worth living for and worth dying for? It was part of a value in people's minds, and now we have all had to see that this value is finished. There is nothing for us worth living for or dying for any longer. Not for an Athenian."

Argas thought he did understand. "It's nice to be proud of something," he said shyly.

"Athens was a very proud city, a very great and beautiful city," his master said, "and then the gods closed their hands on us. Because we did the things which men do carelessly and wickedly in their pride, but yet justice must in time be made manifest. But the justice of the gods is very hard to bear for us who are not immortal but in the flux of time." And he wiped his eyes again.

"But then," said Argas hopefully, "if the gods are really just, Rome will fall one day! And we shall get everything back."

"Perhaps in the gods' time," said Metronax, "but not in mine and hardly in yours, lad."

"Oh no, in *your* time—it might be," Argas said quickly. He couldn't bear Metronax talking as though he might die any minute! "Master, you'll have years and years still!"

Metronax patted his arm and laughed. "Well, we'll see. In your time, let's say. You won't be a slave all your days, Argas. Save up like a sensible boy, and you'll go home, and perhaps you'll be able to help your own city to be a place worth living and dying for again."

"I will," said Argas and bent quickly and shyly and kissed his master's knee.

Argas was happy that year. Lykainis was lovely and smiled at him and let him carry the water jugs for her when she went to the well. In the evenings she would lean against a pillar, spinning, with an easy, steady movement of her hands and arms, and he would sit at her feet and sing to her, sometimes making up the words himself.

But then Metronax died suddenly, and most of the slaves cried like children and mourned after his body and came back to the house wondering who the heir was, for there were no sons living and the old lady was very frail.

It turned out after some days that the heir was a son-in-law who had been living in Corinth, a merchant-shipper and a very different kind of man from his father-in-law, whom he had always rather despised. He opened the will, which had been made years before. According to it, some of the slaves were to be freed, but nothing was said about the younger and newer ones.

Then it became clear that the house was going to be sold and the old lady taken to live with her daughter. And the slaves?

It began to dawn on Argas that he was almost certainly going to be sold again into another household, perhaps not even in Athens, and there was no certainty or even likelihood that Lykainis would be sold to the same owner.

Terribly upset, he went to one of the older slaves, who gave him no hope. This was what you had to expect. And by the end of the week it was quite definite that all the household effects, including the slaves, were to be sold at once.

The old lady gave Argas a present, a little money and one of his old master's poetry books. He promised to treasure it and said good-bye very shakenly. She was crying too, poor old dear, not wanting to be uprooted any more than they did.

But Argas and Lykainis never even managed to say good-bye to each other. They were taken off separately to be stripped and sold. Argas went to a purchaser with an odd accent, who turned out to be the overseer to a traveling Roman official. So Argas was bundled into a big household, friendless, bewildered, missing his old master and mistress, expected to know where to go and what to do, and kicked when he didn't know.

In a little it became apparent that he was even to leave Hellas, perhaps forever. They were all bound for Italy.

It was in the close quarters on shipboard that some of his fellow slaves found his bundle, undid it, and got hold of the book. Seeing him anxious about it, they began to tease him, snatching it away and pretending to read it aloud, making dirty jokes about it.

Suddenly he went wild and began to fight them, struggling for his book. He got hold of one end, but someone grabbed it and tore it right across. And the next moment it had been tossed out to sea.

Argas went, furious and miserable, to complain to the overseer, who only said, "Book? What do *you* want a book for?" And turned his back.

It was altogether a wretched business, for Argas got on badly with all his fellow slaves. Half his money was stolen, and again he could get no help from the overseer.

This, then, was a slave's life—this utter insecurity, dependence on accident. Not worth living. One could, perhaps, kill oneself; there was always that way out. And yet, obviously, he had never had a really bad time, as some of his fellow slaves had. They talked endlessly and sickeningly about things that had been done to them or their women.

Sometimes Argas thought he would be almost happy if he could at least know that Lykainis was back in something like the old life, even if someone else were singing to her and carrying her water jug. But he couldn't even know that. Never.

For some time the household was at Ariminum in North Italy. Argas did his work fairly well and only got into trouble over fighting with the others. Then the overseer would threaten to send him to the mines and tell the cook to put him on bread and water. He didn't mind much, but there was just nothing worthwhile from day to day. He was a dining-room slave and sometimes helped the secretaries, but his master never spoke to him. He was not allowed to read any of the books, even though nobody else seemed to want to. Sometimes he got time off in the afternoon and went swimming by himself in the warm, shallow seawater, thinking that this same sea went on and on till it touched the beaches of Hellas.

Ariminum was full of temples and shrines. Sometimes there would be a big sacrifice and processions going on, and his master would wear his official robes and go. People in a small way went to the little shrines with little offerings. Argas did not go. He thought it would take more than that to change his luck.

There were one or two temples to foreign gods and goddesses, Isis and Serapis and some very queer ones indeed from Asia. All of them had their priests ready to put you right with the gods— if you were ready to pay. At least, that was how it seemed to Argas.

One day he was in the kitchen having dinner with the rest, the usual black bread and stew with sour slaves' wine to wash it down. Nobody spoke to him, and he spoke to nobody. Then he caught one of the undercooks staring at him, a little old man with a pointed beard, some kind of Asiatic, Vono his name was or something of that sort.

"Well?" said Argas angrily.

Vono grinned at him disarmingly and came over, sat beside him, so close that Argas could see a bug walking around his neck. "Things going badly, friend?" said Vono in his bad Greek.

"What is that to you?" said Argas and swallowed a big mouthful of stew and choked.

But Vono was still grinning at him. He said, "We been watching you, some of us. And they tell me to say this—there is a way out."

For a moment Argas was on the point of throwing the remains of the stew in Vono's face. Then he grunted. "Way out? Why don't you take it, then?"

"I have taken it!" said Vono. He went on, apologetic. "True, I do look like dog's dinner! But I'm all right—inside."

"Well," said Argas, wondering if the old man were a little mad, "spit it out."

"There is hope," said Vono, "for us who get done down now. The poor. The slaves. Suppose, some day, we were to have a kingdom of our own, all over the world, what would you say?"

"I'd say you'd had a knock on the head," said Argas.

"But it is true. Our leader said so."

Argas looked more interested. "Got a leader, have you?"

"Yes. Jesus Christ. He said so. He said I was to come to you. To ask you could we help you."

Argas puzzled for a minute. "I think I've heard of him," he said. "Some kind of prophet—rebel."

"He was the Son of God."

"They all say that. Whatever he was, the Romans smashed him up, didn't they?"

"They crucified Him."

"And you ask me to believe what he said!"

"We ask you, first, be friends with us. Don't believe till you see. We got something to give you. To make it—all right, being alive. You come this evening when all are sleeping. Will you?"

Argas thought a moment. Why not? "I'll come," he said.

Little old Vono came for him in the dark, and they went together to the stables and up into the loft.

Five men were there, and two women. They were mostly from the household, and one was Rufus, a secretary whom he had worked for occasionally. Argas wondered why, if any of them wanted to get hold of him, it hadn't been Rufus. But apparently they left it to the feelings of the individual, and it was Vono who had felt called to bring him in. *And perhaps that was right,* thought Argas. *If it had been Rufus, I'd have thought he was trying to trap me into something.*

They began to tell him about this Jesus Christ of theirs and what He had taught and how He had lived, and about this idea of a kingdom of the poor and oppressed. It was new. It didn't fit in with any of the old gods. And it didn't seem to cost anything. You weren't asked to give a beast to be sacrificed; there weren't any priests sitting on top of it. And—well, it was the first time since Athens he'd been treated as a person. Someone with a mind. He said he wouldn't mind if he did join. Yes, he would like to stay for their eating together, and he would take whatever oath they liked to say nothing about it. They did not bind themselves with oaths? Well, then, he would promise.

There were certain rites in which he could not share yet, not till he had become a full member. Yes, he understood. He would wait while he was on trial for them to see what they thought of him. But in the meantime he could come to the meetings and ask questions. Or if he was ever alone in the library with Rufus . . . Yes. Yes.

He went back to bed and slept on it. The whole thing seemed good sense, this idea of a chance and a hope for the ones underneath. The ones—he suddenly thought—that there were more of. And always had been. It took a prophet to think of that. Or a Son of God? Well, the way he remembered, the gods were always having sons.

Things went pretty well for a few weeks. It was grand to go swimming with Rufus, as he did a couple of times, talking about all that out at sea, the sun hot in their faces as they floated. And now when he saw old Vono in the kitchen, he winked at him, and Vono dug him in the ribs or made a queer sign at him if they were alone. Once when he went out on some errand, he saw one of the women, with her big basket, marketing, and wondered if she'd bawl him out—seeing it wasn't at a meeting—and took a chance and spoke to her, a freewoman, and she called him brother, and they bargained together for the chicken and carrots.

He felt himself a living person again, a man, and it seemed to him that everyone recognized it, not only the brothers. There was a kind of friendliness about all sorts of people who had been just hateful before. Perhaps it only was that he was no longer hating himself, but that was how it looked to him. Grand.

He heard a good deal more about what they believed and what they did. He learned the signs. He thought he would like to do everything with them, to belong really, to take what they had to give. To be reborn. It would be fine to throw off all the thoughts and hates that had been getting him down all this time, to have them washed away. He would like to be good. He would fast for two days, and then they would baptize him, and he would be able to share in everything.

And then, of course, the same thing happened. His master's brother was going to Rome and wanted a few extra slaves to take with him. Causally looking around the dining-room slaves for his choice, he jerked a thumb at Argas and said he would take him.

There were five days to go before they left, but Argas bitterly refused to be baptized. Again he was betrayed and hating everyone, half hating even Rufus and Vono and the others who were for the moment secure. For after all, nothing was altered. Life had turned back its devilish face onto him. Nothing counted but luck, and he, being a slave, had bad luck.

Rufus tried to talk to him. Argas knocked him down and blackened his eye. The others caught Argas and held his arms. Rufus, who was, after all, one of the secretaries and someone of a certain importance in the household, sat up dizzily and said to Argas that it was quite all right, they were still friends, he forgave him.

"You do not!" yelled Argas and broke away from the others and ran off.

The next day Rufus met him again and tried to say the same thing, but again Argas bolted. Why couldn't Rufus have had him whipped while he was about it? That would have been the ordinary thing and had made the bad luck complete.

As they left, someone pushed a bundle of food into his hand. When he opened it at their midday halt, he found that one roll of bread had been split and inside, in Rufus's handwriting, was a note giving him the name of a woman in Rome and the street she lived in. If there had been any more nonsense about forgiveness, Argas would have torn it up. As it was, he shrugged his shoulders and kept it. And they went on and up and over the hills for days, and down through dust and thunder, past market carts yoked to white oxen, and ugly little houses, and vegetable fields stinking of city manure, and so to the gates of Rome.

The new household was much like the old. Argas lived in it suspiciously and angrily, working no more than he had to. After a time he thought of the note with the woman's name and address and decided to try and find it. He didn't know what it would be, a witch or a brothel or anything.

It was winter now, and cold, and he had no thick cloak or tunic. His master had gone out, and he had the evening—at least if he wasn't wanted before he got back. He hurried across Rome, staring about him a bit, mostly at the shops. He would have liked to steal something—anything almost.

He came to the street and asked and was at once told to go to the bakery, which he had spotted already by the good smell. He knocked, and a woman opened.

"Are you Eunice, daughter of Hermas?" he asked roughly.

The woman said yes and asked him to come in. When the door was shut, she said kindly, "Who are you?"

He blinked at the bright edge of fire under the oven door and answered his name and his master's name.

"But who sent you?" she went on. "Have you come to buy bread? Cake? No? But someone must have sent you, surely?"

For a moment he didn't want to answer. But if he didn't answer, he would be turned out of the warm room. He muttered that he had come from Ariminum and again said the household.

For a moment the woman seemed puzzled, then her face lit up, and she put her hands onto his shoulders. "From the brothers?" she asked.

He nodded. He wished he hadn't come.

She pulled his head down by the ears and kissed him. She was old enough to be his mother, and she had a round brown face with little veins showing and smelled of dough. "Come and sit in the warm by the oven," she said, "and tell me about them." She pulled him over and sat him down on a stool and gave him a big slab of warm, sticky pastry. "Eat that up first, son," she said, looking at him.

It was nice to be in the warm, to have one's mouth full of the sweet stuff.

She began to tell him that one of the women in the church at Ariminum was her sister.

"She was all right," said Argas, relieved at not having anything more difficult to talk about, "only she had twin boys last May. Did you know?"

76

"Fancy that—twins!" said Eunice. "Did you see them?"

"No. I—I wasn't there long."

Eunice looked at him quickly. "Are you baptized?"

"No," he said. "No fear! It's all lies."

Eunice opened the door of the oven to see her batch of bread.

A sweet hot air came out at him.

After a minute she said gravely, "Then why did you come to me?"

Uncomfortably and angrily he answered, "I didn't know you were one. If you are! Anyway, I'm going."

He felt he oughtn't to have eaten the pastry. Well, she gave it to him—it was her lookout!

"Do you want to go?" she asked. "It's cold out."

"Got to get back," he mumbled. He knew it would be cold.

She said, "Don't you want me to lend you a warm cloak?"

He turned at the door. "Forgiving me, are you?" he said. "Rufus started doing that, and I knocked him out!"

"Did that stop him?" asked Eunice.

Argas came a step nearer. "What do you think you'll get out of all this forgiving? I tell you, I won't be baptized!"

"If poor people can't do that for one another," said Eunice, "there isn't much left for them that's worth doing." Then she said, "Why don't you stop, now you are here, and give me a hand with the dough for tomorrow?"

Well, that wouldn't hurt. It would make up for the pastry he'd eaten. "Well, where is it?" he said.

She taught him to knead properly and thoroughly. He had never done it before. It amused him to be doing something, not because he'd been made to but because he'd been asked to, and with an accompaniment of bad jokes from Eunice, who had dropped all that about Christians. And a good job too.

He finished it off, while she saw to the bread that was baking and then mended a boy's tunic.

Once or twice, customers came. She seemed to be on good terms with them, and they paid cash down. When the dough was thoroughly kneaded, Eunice gave him some delicious ends of fresh white bread—masters' stuff. Then she said he must take the warm cloak and come back another evening and do some more kneading for her.

He looked at her sideways. Was she trying to get at him? Well, if he thought she was when he got home, he'd keep the cloak and never come back!

However, he did come back a week or so later. It would be nice, he said to himself, to have some more pastry, and he didn't mind if he did do some more kneading for the old lady.

When he came this time there was someone else sitting by the oven, a metalworker called Rhodon, a skilled man from Asia. At first Argas thought he was free or at least a freedman, but by and by found he was a slave too but getting a small wage. He would be able to buy himself out some time. He was tired out, and Eunice had made him a hot drink.

When he left, Argas said to Eunice, "He one of you Christians?"

Eunice said quite gravely, "You mustn't ask questions."

Argas felt hurt or thought he did. "So you believe I'm going to give you away!"

Eunice said, "We have to be careful."

"Then you don't trust me," said Argas and went on kneading angrily.

After a time Eunice said, "I'm not sure if you know just how badly we Christians are looked on in Rome. We might have the police on us any time. They say we're atheists. Not respectable, that means! And not respectful either. Not of their things. And you might even get a reward for putting the police onto me."

"Catch me going to the police!" said Argas contemptuously.

"It might be a big reward," said Eunice. "Big enough to— help you get free."

"Oh, come off it!" said Argas, moving along the kneading trough, suddenly aware how very much he would like that reward. If it really—if she wasn't—but, anyway, he wasn't *that* sort! Out of the blue there came at him the image of his old master, Metronax, talking about honor and justice, things that were in the care of the remote gods but yet existed, and existed alike for master and slave. In Athens. His hands were all doughy, but he rubbed his upper arm over his face, so that she shouldn't catch him crying.

Eunice had begun shaping little rolls. She said nothing.

After a bit, Argas said, "Then—could it be really dangerous—being a Christian?"

"Yes," said Eunice, "we're all right so long as things go tolerably well with Rome. But if things looked dirty—well, they might want to take it out on us. See?"

"I don't mind if I join," said Argas.

Eunice answered slowly. "But I'm not sure if we want you, Argas."

"Oh, all right!" said Argas fiercely.

"Don't knead so hard. The bread won't rise even, and I'm not going to lose my reputation for your temper." She went over to him and took on the dough herself. "If you still want to be one of us in another ten days, come back."

It was more than ten days before Argas came back, but he did as soon as he had a chance. It was another bitterly cold night, and the warmth of the bakery made him almost dumb again. He was strictly determined on what he was going to do, even though he knew it meant being forgiven. After all, it *was* sense what they'd told him at Ariminum. Nothing altered that.

Eunice came to him quickly. "Come in, son," she said.

He sat and warmed his hands and feet by the oven.

She offered him a bit of pastry, but he refused it.

At last he said, "Here I am, if I'm wanted."

"Some of the others will be around later. We'll talk to them about it. And then, if you know what you're doing, we'll think about letting you have the baptism."

"I want it now—tonight."

"But, my dear, you can't," said Eunice, "you've got to understand what it's about, and then you must fast for two days."

"I do understand," said Argas, "and I *have* fasted." He looked at the floor and trembled a little. "When it looked like a chance of me getting out tonight, I started. I've had nothing but water for a couple of days. That's all right, isn't it?"

"Have you prayed?" asked Eunice.

"Oh yes," he said, low. "I prayed enough." He still wouldn't look at her. "You see, at Ariminum I was taught everything. What it was about. The Way of Life. It looked like sense to me, even then.

Only everything went wrong." He sat there shivering, his eyes shut. Finally he whispered a little more of what had happened. He felt a bit sick.

After a time he heard Eunice talking in a low voice to a boy. He did not even look at the boy. He was intent on something that might elude him, something deep in him and yet infinitely elsewhere. He shut all the doors of his senses. He only woke, with a jump that sent his heart pounding into his throat and stomach, when somebody laid a hand on his shoulder and said his name.

He saw that the room was half full of people. He didn't know who any of them were, except Rhodon the metalworker. He only knew that this must be the congregation.

Eunice said, "I have told them."

He stood, and they looked at him. It was like being put up to be sold. Their eyes were stripping him. One of them, a young man rather older than he was, began asking him questions.

He knew the answers. They had been in his mind since summer; they made sense. He knew the Words.

When he was through, a woman in a long cloak of good stuff and wearing fur shoes asked him other questions, putting things a different way. He answered her too.

Now they were whispering to one another. He thought he must do the hardest part now; he collected his thought and steadied it. He asked, "Are you the congregation that I am—going to join?"

"Yes," said the young man Manasses.

Argas went down on his knees and said, "Forgive me, then, for I know that I have done wrong, and I know that I have been angry and stupid, and I know I have no right to ask it. Only—out of mercy . . ."

He could not go on speaking. The steadiness had all gone.

But Manasses was kneeling beside him. "What have you done?" he asked.

Argas whispered as loud as he could. "At Ariminum—I wouldn't come in. I knew it was right, but—and I hurt Rufus, and he forgave me, and I wouldn't take his forgiveness—"

"You can take it now, from us," said Manasses.

"I have been angry. I have hurt people. I have lied. I have stolen. Once I went to a witch. And then—oh, this is all worse!—I have denied Jesus and His teaching." Argas was shaking all over with the difficulty of getting it out.

Manasses said, "He has taken you all the same. Even though you denied Him. You are forgiven. Do you also forgive?"

"Who should I forgive?" asked Argas, puzzled. Now that he had said what he had, it seemed to him that there had been a great weight on him and now it was off, and he felt queer and light and a little dizzy.

"All of us," said Manasses.

And Eunice came to him. "You need to forgive me, anyway, son," she said, "for I made you angry."

"It wasn't you," said Argas, "it was my own sin turning on me. But I forgive you if you like. And if I ever get angry again—"

"Well then, we forgive one another again, and that's all there is to it." She said to the congregation, "Well, what shall we do?"

They began talking it over.

Argas was now clinging to Manasses, beginning to remember all the times in his life when he had not done the right and decent thing, seeing all his thoughts and actions lying like a dirty rag in the gutter, wanting to disown them. He could not bear to wait any longer for the hour when he could start fresh.

Manasses was afraid he was going to get into real hysterics and knew that some of it was probably due to the fast and the sleepless night of praying. He knew also that if the boy went too far, he would feel ashamed afterwards instead of glad. So he began praying for Argas, using soothing and complicated words.

Argas became calmer. Manasses left him kneeling in the middle of the floor with his hands over his face and the tears of repentance, which none of them would have dared to laugh at, dripping between his fingers.

"I think we should do it," said Manasses.

"It's out of order," said Rhodon. "Let him wait the ordinary time. Like I had to."

"I don't want to take the risk of refusing him," said Manasses. "He's like someone starving. What do you think, Lalage?"

"I wish he hadn't chosen such a cold night, but I'm quite sure we'd better go down to the river with him. We don't often have a soul tearing its way through the body to us like this. Remember, Rhodon, he went through the ordinary waiting time with the brothers at Ariminum."

"And denied them! And denied Jesus Christ and His Father. Isn't he to have any punishment for that?"

"Look at him, Rhodon. No, look at him as if it was you yourself. You don't cry like that for fun. Do you want to hurt him any more?"

"It isn't that," said Rhodon. "I've nothing against the lad. But I hate favoritism. But, of course, if you've all made up your minds—"

"Favoritism, nonsense!" said Lalage. "Now, Eunice, you're the one that knows him. What do you say?"

"I think we ought to," said Eunice. "Leave the leaven too long, and you will spoil the whole batch. But who'll baptize him? I would if he was a girl, but—"

"You aren't going to get yourself wet tonight, Mother!" said Josias. "Tiber's frozen over at the edges. Maybe we ought to get someone older from the other church."

"We must have a deacon," said Rhodon. "I never saw a man baptized unless there was someone in authority doing it. It wouldn't be in order."

"I think it can be done by anyone through whom the Spirit moves," said Lalage, "that's all. It can't matter what a man's called. Not with us!"

"Well," said Eunice, "are any of you moved to be the one to baptize this man?" She went and stood by him.

He was not crying now, but listening.

At last Manasses said, "If you would all give me leave—I know I am young, but I think—I have tried to live as a Christian should, and a deacon can't do more than that. I will go down into the river with Argas and make him one of us."

After a little they agreed. Eunice said she would stand guardian for him, and the others said that was all right if she didn't go into the water over her ankles, but they weren't going to let her catch cold.

Then they all put on their cloaks, and Eunice found blankets for the ones who hadn't got them. Phaon lighted a lantern, and they all went out into the biting night and locked and bolted the door of the bakery behind them.

It was some way to the nearest part of the Tiber from where they were. They wrapped their cloaks tight and walked quickly, no one saying much. Sometimes they had to stand aside for a litter with torches, and once a drunk barged into them. At last they came to the street leading down to the Tiber. Phaon went ahead with the lantern. "It's in flood," he said.

They all gathered around the edge, and the two young men, the Jew and the Greek, stripped. Josias took their tunics over his arm, and Phaon held the lantern out as far as he could reach over the water.

Here the flooded river was running too quick to freeze, but the steps were slippery, and they gasped with cold as they went in, holding onto one another. They looked white and thin in the lantern light, stepping down into that tearing bubble- and stick-streaked water, opaquely dark with mud. Josias watched anxiously as Manasses, leading, went down waist deep.

The steps ended, and they were on mud, and the river tore at them, and they were almost out of the circle of lantern light, out of reach of the others.

As the icy water bit on his loins and stomach, it seemed to Argas that it was indeed the river of death and defeat. He could have flung himself down onto it, arms at his sides, not swimming. He did not know what Manasses was saying to him. He only felt worthless, sick with himself. There was nothing right about him.

They were breast deep now, staggering in the current. He felt Manasses' hands on his shoulders, weighing on him like sin. His feet sank into the sucking mud. He heard Manasses saying, "Into the name of Jesus." And, with that name in his mind, he went down into the water, dark, choking, over his head and tear-hot face. He struggled up, towards the name of Jesus.

Three times Manasses ducked him. Three times he felt the cold and darkness of death, and each time his body seemed to die a little, until as he came up the third time he felt nothing, but was only aware of the name that had been with him under the water and heard his own voice shouting it.

And then Manasses was pushing him back, out of the mud, out of the pull on legs and body of the black, drowning water. And he was going up, up, into lantern light and among faces, and the water streamed off him, out of his hair and ears and nostrils, taking away with it everything that he had finished with.

Eunice was rubbing him with a blanket, and Josias was rubbing Manasses, who was shaking all over with cold. Gradually Argas began to be aware that he had a body still, that blood was racing in it, that someone had pulled a tunic over his head, that he felt a marvelous warmth coming, even under his wet hair, even in his feet on the wet stones.

People kept on taking his hands or kissing him. He could say nothing because the name was still ringing in his head, still filling him. He belonged with it now and it with him.

Eunice said to Manasses, "You had the Spirit with you." Manasses nodded. He did not say that he had also had a moment of terror when he thought he had lost hold of the man he was baptizing, when he thought the river had got them both. He could not swim, and he did not know that Argas could.

As they walked back, Argas gradually began to reinhabit his body, to like the movement of his legs walking, the touch of his neighbors on each side. Two or three times he laughed out loud. They came again to the bakery, unlocked the door, and lighted the lamp.

Manasses and Eunice gave him bread and salt. The grains of coarse salt were each separate beings; the texture of the bread was beautiful. For a moment he did not want to eat. What did this new person he had become want with eating? And then suddenly it became so lovely to take food from the hands of friends that he bit into the good bread, which the others then ate with him, and so, in the space of two hours, he got three things: repentance, baptism, and the breaking of bread.

He was late in getting back, but the old porter let him in and thought, by the way he looked, that he had been sleeping with a woman for the first time and so, sympathetically shaking his head, did not even scold him.

And he did his work without grumbling, and while he stood, still as a statue, behind his master's couch at dinner, he had something filling his mind all the time, making the mere business of being alive worthwhile.

Soon spring was beginning, and there was almond in light blossom in the courtyards. And then the same thing happened. His master was going to take up a position somewhere in Gaul. Nobody told Argas till a few days before the move.

He told them at the next meeting at Eunice's house, trying not to be angry all the time, trying to let the Will be done on him. Eunice and Manasses put their heads together, and Manasses went straight out, saying he thought he might be able to do something.

He came back in half an hour. Most of them had left, but Argas was staying on, wondering desperately whether he would ever see this room again, trying to pray. He saw that Manasses was not alone, that there was someone with him. Not one of them. One of the masters.

Eunice and Phaon stood up, and so did Argas. Eunice whispered to him it was the Briton, and he knew that it must be the young master from Manasses' household. He saw someone about his own age, with queer blue eyes and a fair, long-shaped head, and the eyes were looking at him as master's eyes mostly looked, remotely and appraisingly. He heard Manasses explaining that this was the dining-room slave whom he had spoken about, whose master was leaving Rome. He was sure he was for sale. And he, Manasses, would guarantee that he was satisfactory.

"That him?" said the Briton. "Looks a bit young."

Argas came forward a couple of steps, aware that his destiny was in this man's hands, not knowing what to say.

Eunice spoke for him too.

"Boyfriend of yours, Eunice?" the Briton asked and laughed. He walked over to Argas and began to handle him, looking at eyes and teeth. Obediently, Argas stripped; there was nothing wrong with him. He confirmed that he could read and write, was well-trained, could do anything about the house.

"You take him," said Eunice. "He wants to come. Knows a good master when he sees one."

The Briton said, "Well, if we can get him reasonably cheap, I don't mind taking him." He turned his back on Manasses and ate one of Eunice's little cakes.

The next day Argas was in the new household, trying to show that he had been a good bargain.

He wanted most of all to show the young master, the Briton. But although Beric was quite pleasant to him, often had a word or two with him and had never lost his temper with him at all badly, he could never speak to his master as he wanted. Never as though they were just two young men living in the same house.

And after the Scratch Cat began her tricks on the Briton, there was less chance than ever. Beric's temper began to fray; he was sometimes unjust, sometimes accused or threatened the slaves for things they hadn't done or actually punished instead of only threatening.

Once he had thrown a roll-book at Argas, cut Argas's cheek with the spike on the end, and torn the book. Argas hated to see a book torn; it reminded him of *his* book. He caught himself wanting terribly to tell the Briton about that book. Fool, he wouldn't care!

But all the same, he used to like to be the one to wait on the Briton, to wake him up in the morning or carry a lamp for him or fill his bath. But now nobody liked that; the Briton might be in any kind of temper. And they all knew why!

Argas had wanted desperately to say something at dinner that day. If only the Briton hadn't been so far! And then afterwards, when he came in with the bucket of water, at first he had not understood, only he felt that something was happening, and he had to start it by speaking to Lalage.

And then the barrier between him and Beric began to crumble. For the first time they looked at each other as one man to another. Some day he would be able to help the Briton, to do something for him, give him something . . .

After they had all said the Words together, and while Manasses was still praying quietly to himself, Beric looked at Argas as though something had amused him a lot and said, "Well, I've said your Words. What are they going to do to me? Going to turn me into a fish?"

That made Argas feel rather uncomfortable, but he saw that the Briton had thought the Words were magic, so he said, "It's not what they do with you, it's what you do with them. They aren't a spell; they only say what we want."

"A kingdom?"

"Oh, it's not like you think, sir! Can I tell you?"

"You'd better," said Beric.

It was really Manasses' place to tell the Briton, since he was by now the deacon and leader of the church in Crispus's household, but he saw that the Spirit had come to Argas. So he and Phaon finished mopping up quickly and took out the bucket and rags, leaving the other two. Manasses knew, just as Lalage, for instance, knew, that there were many ways in which the prayer could be interpreted, but Argas would probably explain it one way only. That didn't matter. What mattered was that he was the one who had been called to do it.

Beric sat down on the couch and motioned to Argas to sit beside him. "This is a mad day," he said. "Well, come on, tell me what it's all about."

Argas was shy, sitting on the same couch as his master, in this equality he had wanted so much. He tried to remember Athens, but by now he'd had too much Rome, and still for a moment he could not speak.

Beric, suddenly wanting to help him, said, "Argas, were you ever free?"

"Yes," said Argas quickly, "when I was a boy in Epidauros! My father was a mason, but there wasn't any work. He had to sell me to get food for the others. That's how it was, sir."

"Rotten luck—brother," said Beric.

Then the Spirit came again to Argas. He said, "The prayer is first, to the Father, who is also Justice and Honor and Freedom and Love. That is, He is for everyone, because these things are the same in Rome and Athens and Alexandria and away in Parthia and Thrace and Gaul—"

"Even in Britain," said Beric, a little ironically, but Argas didn't notice that.

"And we ask Him first, and tell ourselves every day, that what we want is the Kingdom of Heaven. And that's to be the time when

87

everyone is without fear and without shame and without hatred, when there aren't any more rich and poor, masters and slaves—" He suddenly stopped, wondering what the Briton thought. He had spoken of it before only to other slaves or those who had been slaves.

Beric said, "That means the end of things as they are, doesn't it? And that can't come by just wanting it. Only by—making it happen. For instance, here, you could only make it happen by killing Crispus and me and—the others." He didn't want to say her name.

"No!" said Argas. "If we did that, it wouldn't come. Because we mustn't ever do anything wrong to hurry it. We don't murder, we Christians. We don't steal. We—we want not even to hate or envy. And often we don't."

"Clever chaps!" said Beric. "But how are you going to get your kingdom if you don't mean to kill?"

"Well," said Argas, daring, "you didn't want the Kingdom an hour ago, and now you do. Though you are my master."

"What makes you say that?"

"You called me brother," said Argas haltingly, "and now it's going to be difficult for you, ordering me about and all. Not—I don't mean that you've ever been hard on me. I don't mean that—"

"I cut your face open with a book."

"Well, you might feel bad if you did that tomorrow—not that I care, at least, not about getting my face cut, only—"

"If I ever do it again, you can throw it back at me. That's what you're after, isn't it, Argas?"

"Just that. And that's a bit of the Kingdom."

"Equality. That's Stoic doctrine, you know, Argas, only carried a bit further." He puzzled over it, talking half to himself. "The Stoics didn't say anything about having to be poor. Only that if you happened to be poor you could still be free and the equal of anyone. But Lalage said you Christians couldn't be rich."

"I don't see a Christian being rich," Argas said, "or if he started rich, he'd soon be poor, if he lived like a Christian, because he wouldn't be able to keep everything for himself."

"Wouldn't be able? You mean, you wouldn't let him?"

"He just wouldn't want to. You'll know if—if you do join us. Claudia Acte gives away all her money."

"Is she a Christian?" said Beric, startled, then, "No, it's all right, Argas, you haven't made a mistake. I shan't tell the police."

"I didn't think you would, sir. Only—"

"As soon as you get frightened, you start sir-ing me again. Idiot!" said Beric amicably. "You'd better call me by my name. I suppose you've got a nickname for me too?"

"We didn't have any nasty name for you—truly—only 'the Briton.'"

"What did you have for the others?" asked Beric, amused and wanting to hear it all.

But Argas suddenly realized that he must not hear the name for Flavia. That would hurt. That would interrupt. He said, "No, I can't tell you."

"You've got to!"

For a moment Argas was afraid again, with the Briton glaring at him, really annoyed. Then he saw that he needn't and mustn't be. His fear was only something left over. "How are you going to make me tell you—now?" he asked. "I'm not going to do a thing more for you except of my own free will."

Beric suddenly began to laugh and threw himself back onto the cushions in fits of laughter. "Then I shall have to fill my own bath!"

Argas was rather shocked. He said, "I shall go on doing my proper work. Because I choose. Can I go on telling you about our prayer, or are you going on laughing?"

"It makes me feel like laughing," Beric said, "the whole thing. I like laughing. I laugh at things I like. I think I see what you're after about this kingdom, you and Lalage. And you think it'll come?"

"We know it's coming. That's the will of God that we ask to be done. It's—it's *reason,* the Kingdom. It's the only thing that makes sense of people being in the same world with one another. It isn't sense, is it, some people having all the money and others slaves all their lives and never getting a chance of being real people?"

"It's always been like that," said Beric slowly. "I don't know about being sense. I never thought about sense in the way people are arranged."

"That's because you were on top. You didn't have to. I've had to, and I know it's nonsense as it is. It's wasting people all the time. Men and women."

"You want a world, then, where all are poor?"

"Where money and power aren't being used any longer to make nonsense of the way we live with one another. With making friends. A world where you and I can be friends."

"Can't we be friends as it is?"

"We'll see. I—I wanted a lot to be friends with you ever since—well, ever since you bought me. I've read plenty of books and that. I'm not a fool. Only you never gave me a chance till now. You made nonsense of me wanting it."

"I'm sorry, Argas," said Beric, not laughing anymore.

"Well then, God's will must be reason. And that's what the Kingdom is. That's why we ask for the Will to be done, even when we don't understand how it's working. And when we ask for daily bread, that means security. Just knowing from day to day where we shall be. One can't make the Kingdom without that much."

"I don't think I want security," said Beric. "That's a Roman thing. I want adventures."

"You've never not been secure," said Argas, "never been at anyone's mercy for everything. Punished for what you hadn't done. Yes, it wasn't me that broke the wine jar last week! Oh, it doesn't matter. Truly, it doesn't matter now! But they stole half my savings, and nobody cared, and I had a book—and it was torn up, and if you hadn't bought me at the beginning of last year, my master would have taken me off to Gaul, away from the church here and everything I cared about. That sort of thing happened twice before. But you were part of the Will. Don't laugh, no, don't laugh at me! It's true. And then, after that, we remind ourselves to be always forgiving one another. And how we're always doing things ourselves that need forgiveness. That's important. And sometimes it's difficult."

Beric thought about it, lying back on the couch, one knee up, the other crooked over it, swinging. "Not one's enemies? You don't mean you try to forgive them?"

"Yes," said Argas. And then, "You could forgive Aelius Candidus if you tried."

Beric sat up sharply. "That's none of your business!"

But Argas wasn't going to let himself be frightened now. "If I'm your friend, it is my business," he said. "We all saw, and it's no good pretending we didn't. And we were all on your side. Though I knew you'd kick me if I said so."

"I would have," said Beric. "I know I would. And then you'd have the job of forgiving me."

"Of course. You see, it's all in and out like that. People knocking up against one another. But it's one thing forgiving friends and another forgiving enemies. That's two different ways of doing it. Your friends take it, and as like as not they'll need to forgive you too. It's mostly six of one and half a dozen of the other. But with your enemies, perhaps they don't accept it. But you've got to do it all the same."

"Why?"

"It's just part of how we all want to be. We call it the Way of Life. And if you forgive a person, you stop being in his power; he can't really hurt you any longer. And maybe you get to see why he's doing it, and then you can most likely stop him."

"But look here, Argas, if you forgive people, you've got to forgive the emperor and Rome and—and all the masters—and then you won't want to destroy them any longer."

"I can forgive my own master," said Argas, frowning, thinking it out, "for what he does to me as a man, but forgiveness is between people, so I can't forgive all the masters because I don't know them. Together, they're a *thing,* and I hate them, and I want to destroy them. And we shall. And the rule of Rome is a thing, so I don't forgive it. I don't forgive what they did to the people in Epidauros and the people in Athens. And if you become a Christian, you will not be able to forgive the Roman rule that you have been part of yourself."

"I think I see," said Beric. "Did your Jesus forgive his enemies?"

"He forgave the men who were killing Him. But before that He spoke against the rich and the priests and the rule they had over His people. He never forgave their misuse of power."

"And he will be king of your kingdom?"

"He is in all of us," said Argas, "when we are trying for the Kingdom. And the next thing in the prayer is asking not to be led into temptation but to be delivered from evil. Because we all want to be good."

"Do we?" said Beric and added, "I wonder if Tigellinus does."

"Perhaps people with a lot of power don't. But ordinary people do, if things aren't being too much for them. Well, that's what the prayer's about." Argas suddenly looked tired—tired and defeated. "But it doesn't mean a thing to you!"

"Yes, yes, you stupid, it does!" said Beric. "And I'm glad it's sense and not magic. But I want to sleep on it. And it's late. Everyone else is asleep but us." He stood up.

"I'll bring you your lamp, sir," said Argas.

"You will not," said Beric. "I shall get it for myself, and I shall actually carry it along to my own room myself! And we shall put out the lamps in here together." He began doing it. "And whether or not I have anything more to do with you Christians, I shall remember what you said, Argas, and if you come and wake me tomorrow morning—which you'll probably be too sleepy to do—you shall tell me if you still want to be my friend."

Argas wanted to answer but didn't know what to say. Only he felt happier and less tired. It was queer and nice going around with the Briton, putting out the lamps.

Suddenly Beric said, over his shoulder, "Who did break the wine jar?"

"You don't want to punish for it twice," said Argas, a little uncomfortably.

"I thought you were lying," Beric said. He went over, close to Argas. "I sent you off to get a whipping. What happened?"

"I got it," Argas answered casually.

But Beric was thinking about it differently and with increasing trouble. "I never bothered—about it being a person. Someone like me. And you were only a slave. So they tied your hands"—he was speaking with a kind of horror now—"to the ring in the kitchen yard. What did they give you?"

"Ten."

"Cut you?"

"No fear! Old Felix wouldn't try *that* on me. After all, I'm not one of the kitchen slaves! Not like poor little Dapyx; he's one of us too."

"What did you think about while it was going on?"

"You don't think much while you're being whipped. You just don't squeal."

"And then he untied you."

Argas laughed. "Matter of fact, old Felix left me tied for half an hour. He'd got me so that I could only stand on tiptoe. That hurt a bit."

Beric swore. "I'll take it out of Felix!"

"No, you won't," said Argas quickly. "It's nothing to do with you. He was a bit down on me, that's all. But I didn't tell you as a master."

"What did you think about," Beric asked again, "while you were tied?"

"I had my work cut out forgiving old Felix. But I did. That's why you can't touch him now, see?"

"But it was me—I had you punished, Argas. For something you didn't even do."

"Well, I forgave you too. More or less. I knew she'd been at you. It's all right. Don't go getting upset about it!"

"You were hurt, and it was I who did it." Beric could hardly speak, with misery and astonishment at what was having the power to make him miserable.

"But I forgive you." Argas caught hold of the Briton's hand and held it hard, with both of his. "Look—Beric—don't go fussing about this, please! There are some houses where the slaves get it badly, and there are the mines, and . . . oh, this was nothing! Good night and peace be with you—Beric."

5

Lalage and Sophrosyne

In the late afternoons those women who had to work at nights and sometimes into the morning, and who must mend their dresses and sleep in the heat of the day, would come slipping out into the streets and do their shopping or go to the fortune-tellers or witches or temples. They were not made up for the evening, and some of them looked plain and pale or downright ugly. It depended a good deal on how long they had been doing it and what their economic position was.

It was not so bad for those that owned their own bodies, but most of them did not even do that. When they began to wear out, they were looked after so long as they were of any use, but when the cheaper clients no longer wanted them they were lucky if they were given some kind of food and shelter and allowed to do the housework.

But the girl who was going, as she always did, to the little temple of Isis was still young and still so pretty that she must keep a veil close around her and hurry a little.

She did not own her own body. She did not know if she had been born slave or free. She did not remember exactly when she had been a virgin. Things had been like this when she was a small child, and like that when she was an older child, and still otherwise when she was no longer a child. But always there was the same madam, kind if you did what she said the way she wanted. Otherwise not so kind. There would be girl and boy children huddled into corners, waiting for the sharp, pouncing fingers to pull them out, the fingers that made the blue marks on their arms, that took the whip out of the cupboard—children frightened into an adult stillness and stealthiness, alone with their nightmares, afraid to cry.

Sometimes there would be stray bits of kindness from a customer or from some older woman but not enough to break through the shell of fear. Once, the child Lalage had got kindness from a boy dancer with whom she had to do an act. It was a horrid act—she had cried afterwards—and then he was so kind to her, and he went on being kind for months till suddenly he was sold, and she never saw him anymore.

Much later on, remembering it, she knew that at first he must have hated her as she hated him, and that he must have acted with the deliberate kindness of someone who knows what kindness is worth: more than anything else in the world. Kindness of slave to slave.

For the last few years Lalage had been making a little money. The madam of course, was paid for her services, but she usually got a little something too. There'd been one or two regular clients, young married men. She'd been quite gone on one of them for a bit, and he'd given her ever such a nice bracelet—real silver and amethysts. She always wore it. And she reckoned that perhaps in another two years she might be able to free herself.

But two years was a long time. Anything might happen in two years. She'd been unlucky once already, but there was a woman in the establishment who could usually care for that if you went soon enough. It had hurt, and she had been ill for days, but it had been worth it. You weren't always lucky, though. Two years.

Some of her own money had to be spent on little extras, but she was careful. And usually a few coppers went in another way. Either she took flowers to Isis, or she dropped the money in the little niche in the stone. That was the only money she really liked spending, the money she got something out of. She looked forward to going there. Sometimes one of the others came, and sometimes there'd be girls whom she knew by sight or whom she'd got to know a little, and then they'd go back together part of the way, gossiping.

It was a very little temple, a shrine for the goddess, with a wooden door in front that stood open always and a room behind for the priestess. She was an Egyptian, with a brown, wrinkled face. She seemed to speak all languages, for Lalage had heard her talking to girls from the gods know where, the farthest places slaves come from, places you'd never even heard of, and talking to them so that they talked back and came alive again.

Only women went to Isis. In Egypt, the priestess said, she had great temples and feasts and offerings, like any other god. And there was another big temple over on the smart side of Rome. But here it was different. She was not only Isis—she was also Cleopatra-Isis, and the face of the wooden statue was not an Egyptian face but the face of a Macedonian princess. The priestess told them all about Cleopatra one day, talking quietly to a dozen little prostitutes who sat on the steps of the shrine in the spring sunshine, eating raisins and sometimes exclaiming or crying a little, for they laughed and cried easily.

Cleopatra was a great queen. She was queen of Egypt and the East. She led her own ships and men into battle. She was wiser at statecraft than any man. She was too great a queen ever to love, but she had sons by the men who loved her, who were to rule over all the world. For although she had no mercy on the rich or the strong, always she was as compassionate to the people as Isis herself. And so it was, in the end, that she had Rome against her——Rome which meant naked power, Rome with the sword and the whip. She fought Rome for the thing that we all want, for the golden age of peace and joy and compassion when the common people shall at last be free.

"But Cleopatra was beaten by the Romans, as your fathers were, Salome, and yours, Iotape, and yours, Gwinedda, and yours, Lalage. And Octavian Caesar, whom the Romans call Augustus, he killed her sons who were to have taken her golden age across the whole world. And she was to have walked shamefully through Rome in Caesar's triumph, but in the end she escaped him. For Re, the sun himself, sent his messenger to Cleopatra—the asp who rears his head, which is death, from the crown of Egypt. And the asp took her and made her into a goddess, into her in whose image she had lived as queen.

"And with her, of their own free will, also to be taken up into the divine likeness, went her two serving women, Charmain and Iras. And that is why, beside the great statue, you will see two small statues. In the lap of the great statue is a little child, and this is Harpocrates, the Wise Child, whom Isis nursed, and it is also one of the children of Cleopatra. And at the foot of the statue is the dead body of a man, and this is the body of Osiris, who was murdered and torn by his enemies, but it is also the body of each of her own murdered sons.

So, because she suffered all, she is kind to all and welcomes all, but mostly women who are hurt and lonely and mothers whose sons have died or been taken from them. And because she was a great queen, she does not ask for offerings. She is not a taker, but a giver."

The girls on the steps sighed and wriggled and wondered what it was like to be a queen. And one of them thought for a moment about a baby she'd had, only they'd taken him away, and what could she have done with him anyway. And Lalage said her prayer to Cleopatra-Isis, Star of the Sea, Looser of Prisoners, Strength of the Weak, Justice That Is Also Mercy, and asked to become a great dancer. It was more of a life if you were a dancer too. She practiced now, an hour or two every day.

She had been coming now for years, and she knew that the goddess turned her luck for her, often. Some girls were always getting caught. But she—just that one time, and then it was all right in the end. Well, that was luck. If she had a good evening, when other girls were knocked about and she not, she knew who to thank for it.

Or that nice old senator who only wanted to talk about what he'd suffered to someone who'd stay awake and look like she wasn't bored stiff; who always called her "my child" and was so sweet. She'd found out a lot about Rome that way, and those emperors. That was luck too. Only then he died, poor old dear. He hadn't ever really got over having his sons killed under that Gaius Caesar. She wished she could tell him about Isis, only he was a man. Funny, having a family. It meant new ways you could be hurt.

And then one day she came as usual, and the door across the shrine was shut. So she waited. And by and by some of the others came. They all wondered why and talked about it, and then one of them tried the door, and it wasn't bolted or anything, and they all went in together in a bunch, whispering, and there was the priestess lying on the floor at the foot of the statue. She was dead.

You could tell at once, for her arms and all were stiff, and she was quite cold, and none of them knew what to do. So then another woman came and fetched someone from the big temple of Isis, where the rich women went, and men came with a bier and took the priestess away and shut up the little temple.

Though Lalage came back often after that, the little temple never seemed to be open again, and she didn't feel like going to the big one. It was different. It made her feel shy. It wasn't for slaves. It wasn't her own Cleopatra-Isis, the hurt one, but a grand, far-off goddess to whom you had to give expensive offerings. Most of the rich women, too, were initiates and went to special services, and the priests and priestesses always recognized them and gave them a particular welcome and the best seats. And Lalage couldn't begin to afford the initiate fees. So now she was alone again with no one and nothing to bring her luck or stop the bad spirits from coming to her in dreams.

Once or twice she went to a fortune-teller, but she could only afford the cheap ones, and they weren't much good. You didn't believe them, not really. Not the next day.

She moped quite a bit, and the only thing that kept her going was the hours of dancing practice that she put in, whenever she could get anyone to play, or even without music. Then one day she was sent over to the palace. She didn't know what for, not at first. Then, when she was waiting, someone told her. And she knew her luck was gone.

At first she had tried dancing for Pallas. But he was bored. There were plenty of dancers in the palace and plenty of other things as well. He only wanted someone new. But she just couldn't. She did what she'd hardly ever done—she fought him. And then he got her down, and there was some kicking, and she didn't know anything more for a bit.

And then she began to feel the pain here and there, and she opened her eyes and saw a kind face, a woman. And she knew it was Claudia Acte. And then she began to be frightened and tried to get up in spite of the pain, but Claudia Acte laid a hand on her head and spoke to her powerfully, and she went to sleep, wondering in a muddled way how she had got back to the shrine, because the hands that were so kind and powerful were surely the hands of Acte-Isis.

When she woke again, there was a Jewish boy who was kind too, who said that everything was all right, that Acte had taken charge of her, and she must sleep. In two days she was quite well, only a little stiff and dizzy and very puzzled. Every now and then she felt in her dress to see that the money, which she always had sewn into it, was there quite safe. That was reassuring somehow, and she still had her bracelet on.

Claudia Acte came in and sat on the mattress beside her, as though they were just two girls together. Lalage didn't know what to say or do. She wondered what her hair was looking like. She hadn't been able to comb it, even.

Acte said, "Well now, what are we going to do with you?"

"I've got to get back, Lady Acte," she said, "or my madam'll be after me. I hear you've been so kind as to make it up for now."

"It seems a pity to go back, doesn't it," said Acte, "or were you all right there?"

Lalage raised herself a little and spoke in a whisper, though there was no one to overhear them. "I've got a bit of money saved up, Lady Acte. In another year, perhaps, I'll buy myself out. If things don't go wrong."

"And then, my dear?"

"Then—I can dance some, you know. I was meaning to improve on that side of things. I like dancing."

Acte said, "Suppose I make up what you need? We'll call it a loan, but you needn't pay me back till you've got it to spare. Then you can stay here till you're well and perhaps have a few extra dancing lessons. I'll get you started with a little room somewhere."

"A little room," said Lalage, "for me . . ." And she began to cry weakly and seized Acte's hand and kissed it. "What makes you so kind?" she said.

"Don't you think people ought to be kind to one another, Lalage?" Acte smoothed her hair back out of her eyes. "I'm not doing very much, you know. After all, I've been a slave myself, as everyone knows. And now I've got some money, and it's a pity not to use it."

"But lots of people have money," said Lalage, blubbering, "and nobody else ever thought of spending it on me. You're like

Isis, Lady Acte. You're One Who Knows What Is Wanted. You are Isis."

"No, no!" said Acte quickly. "You mustn't say that. Do you go to Isis, Lalage?"

"I used to go, but now the little temple is shut, and the big one's not for the likes of me."

"I could tell you of somewhere else to go," Acte said.

"Somewhere that would bring me luck?"

"Luck? I'm not sure that I believe in luck. We're responsible for ourselves. I expect you've had to believe in it, Lalage, but when you're free, you'll have to look after yourself. Even your own soul. Tell me, did you ever hear of the Christians?"

"They're the ones that don't believe in anything, aren't they?"

"Hardly that. They believe in other people, for one thing. No, don't look so puzzled, Lalage. I'll tell you something about them one day if you're a good girl and get well quickly. Meantime we'll see what your madam wants for you."

Now there were comings and goings in the course of which Lalage got her bundle of clothes and things back. Acte bought her from her madam, and then she bought herself back and was properly and legally released from all obligations and became Acte's freedwoman.

She showed Acte her best dancing, but Acte was noncommittal. A few days later she found she was to have lessons from Paris himself. He raged and stormed at her but taught her more than she had ever known.

And in the afternoons she went over to Acte's rooms and listened to reading aloud from Greek plays. The first few days she was only interested in the story, and, as they were mostly tragedies—Acte had a taste for Euripides especially—she was always dissolving into tears. But later she began to hear the poetry and then, almost at once, began to think of the stories as things that could be danced.

She wondered if Acte would tell her more about the Christians, and one day she took courage in both hands and asked.

Acte told her, and Lalage opened up to it at once. This was what she wanted. She wouldn't be lonely anymore. It was lovely. It was new and yet, she thought, it was what she had always expected. It brought back all the times when people had been kind. The boy dancer and the old senator and the priestess of Isis. And now Acte.

Acte drummed it into her that she must be very careful, must never speak about Christianity except to the brothers and sisters. "But you spoke to me," said Lalage.

"Yes, but I'm an old hand. Some day, Lalage, you'll get to be able to tell when people are ready for it. But not at first."

For some weeks Lalage came to the meetings but went out before certain of the rites. The Jewish boy, Manasses, did so too for a short time, since he had much to relearn, and he and Lalage became very good friends.

Lalage had her little room now, a top room in a tenement right under the roof, hot—and, of course, there were bound to be bugs in summer, if you minded that sort of thing—but it was her own. If she'd wanted to, she could have sat there all day, just sat and wondered or anything else she liked, and nobody could have made her do anything else!

But she was an industrious girl, and she began at once to try and build up a clientele. Acte had a party for her and recommended her to several friends. She did her very best. At that time plenty of respectable gentlemen were glad to do any little favors for Claudia Acte. And Pallas went into retirement on his country estate.

Then came the time when the meeting agreed that she was ready for everything. She was to be baptized and become completely one of them. She had been nervous at first when she heard about it, wondering whether it would mean paying something, but now she had realized that it was free, and that struck her almost more than anything.

This was a religion that nobody was making anything out of. Each church had a fund of its own, and you put into it what you could afford to, or, if you couldn't afford anything, you didn't put anything in, and nobody sneered at you. But you knew exactly what happened to the money. The meeting discussed that—down to the last penny.

Sometimes, later on, Lalage used to watch Claudia Acte fidgeting with boredom while that went on. But all the same it was important, and Acte knew it. Some day, when the Kingdom had

101

come for all time, there would be no need for that. Everyone would be equal. In the meanwhile the needs were there and must be met. Many members of the church were slaves, sometimes with no money at all, nothing to meet age and sickness except the uncertain charity of masters who, in Rome, might hardly know they existed. And an overseer was harder on the sick and old than a master, any day.

And some were free or freedmen living very precariously. In spite of all the luxury in Rome, things weren't always too good for the workers. Food prices were high. That didn't matter to the rich, but it did matter to the poor, especially when they had no storage space, even for flour or meal.

So there were always plenty of hands to dip into the bag, and nobody thought any the worse of you for asking.

The time came when Lalage fasted and prayed, and so did Manasses, who stood guardian for her, and Claudia Acte, who took her down in the early morning before people were about and dipped her in the Tiber.

They came back very happily. It seemed to Lalage as though none of the things that had happened to her were true, or rather as if they had not, after all, been horrible and wounding. There was nothing now that she hated to remember. And when she came in to the breaking of bread, there was such a lightness in the air, an kind of swelling happiness. Was it in her or in the others or in everyone?

For several years she used to go to the church in Caesar's household. According to how many could get away to the meetings, there would be anywhere from ten to thirty members. Very often someone would be there from one of the smaller churches in Rome, usually asking for instructions about something.

From time to time a letter would go from one city to another. Supposing, for instance, a Christian slave or freedman went with his master on an official journey to one of the provinces. That would be the moment to send a letter. And when a letter arrived, it would be read out in the meeting, talked over thoroughly, and prayed about. Sometimes there was action to be taken, sometimes something that had puzzled them was answered, or sometimes it was they who were questioned. Or they would disagree with something that was said, and then they had to draw up a letter to go back, giving their side of it.

From time to time some small groups would get hold of a bright new idea, and perhaps a whole church would take it up. It might be something harmless like vegetarianism, but sometimes visions and practices would turn up from the borderworld of ghosts and spirits and sacrifices. There were those who wanted to be rebaptized, to have the mysterious change made in them over and over again; that was the way of magic.

There was too much magic about in the world as it was, and magic was evil because it was against reason, black streaks cutting across the white light of sense that they themselves had come into. If you believed in magic, then there wasn't any real security that the Kingdom would come. It had just gone back to being a battle, where the wrong side could win. But you knew now that this wasn't how things were, so you wouldn't have anything more to do with bribing or cheating or getting power over the other side. Being a Christian, you had another way. Besides, you could always tell that magic was evil because of the kind of people who did it and the kind of ends for which they did it—and the pay they got. No Christian could have anything to do with that.

Others came in and then got the whole thing wrong some other way. They thought that, once reborn, they could do nothing wrong but might follow all impulses. They didn't see that you'd got to guard and watch the flame in you, which was always being attacked by the outside world. Besides all that, there was often jealousy between Jews and Gentiles. Or someone would have a special revelation, and it was up to the older members of the church to try to decide whether it was from God or just a mistake.

And always there were different interpretations of the many-sided life and teaching of Jesus. Which were right? It was on a matter of interpretation that Lalage was first moved to speak.

She had always sat quiet before, but now she felt she could make clear something that was bothering everyone else. After that, she spoke from time to time and was always listened to. Usually this happened after the eating together and conversation, after the first prayers, when a tide of mutual understanding seemed to flood over the men and women who had met together in the half darkness—for they had usually met at night when workers and slaves could get away.

This was the time when someone here or there would confess a wrongdoing, on his knees in the shadows, and the others would know how nearly they themselves had done the same thing, how well they understood the doing of it, and they would forgive, sometimes with tears. And they would perhaps be able to show the forgiven person some action he or she might take to make up for what had been done. And in Jesus' name the action would be taken.

Sometimes there would be such happiness and understanding, such strong temporary experience of the Kingdom, that one or another must stand up and sing or dance—only they had to be careful not to make too much noise, or they might have been overheard by those who wished them ill. And sometimes several, or all, would be dancing, moving in joy, filled, body as well as soul, with ecstasy.

Sometimes someone would speak with tongues, and all would listen with a queer kind of sympathy, till the taut throat and breast had ceased vibrating and the upstretched face was again the face of every day. Men and women would kiss one another, and often Lalage would throw herself down beside some man, holding to him in delight, and sometimes when it had ebbed away she would wonder how it was that they could have embraced so strangely, without the delight ever localizing or becoming the other thing that she knew so well. But so it always was. The kindness they felt toward one another was always of constant life, not of the little death that comes from the flesh.

She found an old man who had once been a successful lecturer but was now living in a garret close to hers, and she paid him a little to teach her to read and once cleaned up his room for him. He kept a magpie to talk to. He said it was more intelligent than most of his audiences had been. Later on, when he died, Lalage took care of the magpie.

Having learned to read, she borrowed one book at a time from Acte and read so much that she even sometimes neglected her dancing. She found new themes for dances, if only she could have obtained the music. But she was bound to dance to whatever music could be provided by the slaves where she went.

That bothered her, and she prayed about it. And a few weeks later, an old woman whom she had seen sometimes at the love feasts, but had not thought about, came to her and said, "Sister, do you ever need someone to play for your dancing? They used to say I was good in my time."

"What do you play?" asked Lalage, interested at once.

"Harp, double flute, shells, and drum," said the old woman, who was called Sophrosyne. "I have been a widow ten years, and I would like to play for you."

"If only you had your instruments here," said Lalage, "you could bring them along to my room, and we could try out something."

"But I have them, sister." The old woman smiled. "It was laid on me to bring them today." She added, "Sometimes the Spirit tells me quite plainly what to do. And sometimes I cannot understand clearly, but if I were with you, sister, you would interpret."

They came back together, and the old woman played, and Lalage danced and was satisfied and told Sophrosyne to bring her things over. After that they lived together, and Lalage put up her price, because she now provided her own accompanist.

Sophrosyne had been a Christian a good many years. Her own husband had died in the hot weather, and after a very few hours there was no doubt that he was not only dead but decaying rapidly. So when she heard about someone rising from the dead after three days she found that very striking indeed. That was what startled her. She liked stories about miracles too, and when she retold them they had always become slightly more vivid. When she was waiting around, as she did a great deal now that she was Lalage's accompanist, she was telling them to herself all the time, or thinking of new ones. She dreamed about them sometimes too, and then she and Lalage would talk over the dreams in the morning while Sophrosyne swept the room and Lalage did her practicing.

After a while Lalage got a room in another quarter of Rome. It was rather bigger, and she needed the space. She had to make up new dances, and once or twice she took a theme that had something to do with what she was thinking about—the phoenix, for instance, symbol of the soul rising after baptism. She danced that for her clients in a short feather tunic, with her legs coated with some special stuff to stop them from getting burned by the real, though quite small, flames that she lit on a kind of tray and which afterward smoldered as incense. Real flames, real blood, really difficult acrobatics at which you might hurt yourself—those were what the Romans liked.

It was easier for her and Sophrosyne, from this new room, to get to the meetings at Eunice's house or in the household where Manasses was now, but she sometimes went back to the old church.

Acte was no longer Nero's mistress, though, oddly enough, she remained his friend. The old empress, Agrippina, had been murdered by her son. It was the new empress, Poppaea, who now pulled Nero around by his passions.

She was a queer one, attracted since her girlhood by Judaism, shivering at the bareness of it, feeling at the back of it the austere desert spaces filled with a powerful and volcanic God, blazing out of dry bushes, shimmering in mirages, clutching jealously and fiercely at His own, proclaiming that they and they alone were saved in a world that might at any moment break into flames and chaos.

Rome was a world of little gods and goddesses, domestic, official, or of the earth—each, as it were, taking on some different aspect of life. One could believe as much or as little as one chose in any of them. They were bound to be tolerant of one another. There were others as well, the Great Strangers mostly, whom one had for one's own personal use and belief, about whom people felt passionately and gave up time and money and even respectability. But all the same, you would not find that the initiates of Isis or of Cybele hated one another or, for that matter, despised someone who had made a different choice and gone, perhaps, on the pilgrimage to Eleusis.

But Poppaea Sabina had found this one God who would not for a moment put up with rivals. How stirring, how satisfying! And the angry prophets, great, bearded male creatures, stalking the despised cities and the jagged mountains, striking out with their

106

hands, shouting, full of living certainty—Poppaea wanted to be engulfed in all that, longed to feel her soul, tired of perpetual arrogance, at least beaten with the rods of Judaism, bound and quaking in glorious terror at the feet of the Ancient of Days.

So she made advances; she protected the Jews in Rome. They would not worship the Divine Emperor? Marvelous daring! But she could make it all right by him. And she alone. She would show him, and he would understand. Nero, too, had his longings.

Sometimes he turned toward mysteries and blood sacrifices but sometimes away from that toward Hellenism, toward a cleaner, saner world, which had finished with blood—even the arena bloodshed, which the crowd liked so much. He would have games like the Olympic Games—no professionals. He would make Rome into a new Athens! Let the crowd, the filthy sons of Romulus, grumble as they would.

And when he thought of Athens, he would send for Acte again and talk to her. She was never quite out of his favor. He called her when Poppaea was far gone with child, and then it was to console again the wild, half-frightened, half-angry boy. He sometimes called her when something was on his conscience, some evil and horrible thing that he could not always tell her. That matter of Octavia . . . Acte could help, could calm him and make him a little reasonable, so long as she was never a rival to Poppaea. And she never let herself be that, even when Nero tried to tease her or anger her into saying things . . .

She said little at the meetings of the church. They were used to her. She gave them money and visited the sick. They knew that she lived simply, so simply that some people laughed at her or called her a miser, yet not so simply as any of the rest of them. Things being as they were, Acte had to compromise. They understood that, and they had no blame for her.

She had been the one who had brought them together at the beginning, encouraged and protected the little church. They took her for granted. Sometimes, even at the love feasts, she looked very sad, but it was not for them to speak first. If she had chosen to ask for forgiveness for anything she would have had it. But perhaps the forgiveness of the congregation was no longer satisfying. Lalage talked to her sometimes. They understood one another.

Manasses knew that Lalage was wiser about people than he was and probably also a better interpreter of difficult sayings or dreams or visions. He had come to that conclusion after a long time, and reluctantly. So now he thought that almost any action she took was likely to be a right one. He hoped she would come early the next day after the dinner party, and she knew he hoped so. But she had another engagement the next night, and she was determined to get a good rest.

Sophrosyne was careful not to wake her, and it was well on in the morning before she stretched and yawned and remembered the night before. She intended to go to Crispus's house, but before she had finished combing her hair, the cobbler at the bottom tried to murder his wife again, and again the wife got away in time and started screaming the place down.

Lalage, knowing the wife, didn't entirely wonder at its happening, but she ran down and stopped her screeching, or she'd have had the whole of the tenement in, and all, of course, going for the husband, who probably didn't really want to kill his wife or she wouldn't have escaped every time.

If, thought Lalage, I can once get at that little bit of whatever it is that stops him from killing her and get it to grow, then things might be all right between them. She did fix up the cut on the wife's head, listened to them both, had lunch with them—bread and figs—and put up with being patronized by the cobbler, who was a citizen and never let you forget it. Had she been able to help them? One never knew—not till years and years afterward. After all that, she had a word with a girl on the third floor who was going to have a baby pretty soon and was rather gloomy about it.

So it was not till later on in the afternoon, when by rights she ought to have been lying down, for it was another blazing day, that she managed to get over to Crispus's house.

Manasses seized on her. "Do talk to him, Lalage! I can't."

"Netted a lion, have you?" said Lalage. "How's he shaping?"

"He keeps on asking questions."

"That's good."

"But I can't answer him properly. It seems so queer, him asking. And I'm the deacon. It's my place to answer."

"Can't help remembering you're still his servant, Manasses, and he might kick you?"

"Yes. And sometimes—"

"Wanting to kick him now he's down? Balance, that's what you want." She stood on one toe and lifted a leg slowly into the air. "And take it gently. Tell him it's difficult for you. He'll understand. He's soft now, like clay. He's open to you."

"You tell him, Lalage."

"He's a nice boy," said Lalage.

She looked older by daylight, Manasses thought. She was older than either of them. A dancer could go on for a long time—what with makeup and lighting—so long as she kept up her practicing. But Lalage did that.

He brought her through to where Beric was sitting, doing household accounts. "This time of day," whispered Manasses, "he's mostly been up with *her.* Whatever they were doing."

"Ah!" said Lalage. "So that's why you're sending *me* to talk to him!"

Manasses didn't like her saying that sort of thing, even if she didn't mean anything by it. And perhaps she did. You never knew. She made him feel like a baby sometimes. He watched her go up to the Briton, then went away quickly. He wouldn't watch. She was a wise one. The Spirit moved in her.

Beric jumped up. "Lalage! Come and sit here and tell me everything."

"Why don't you ask Manasses?"

"I do. But he seems to be always washing up or something. And Argas is shy today. I like Argas."

"Fun being a Christian?"

"But I'm *not* a Christian!" said Beric, rather shocked. "So far, I haven't heard anything wrong. But there must be something."

"Why?"

"Well—everyone says so."

"Yes, because you've only heard people talking about it who —aren't dirt. Beric, have you said anything to Crispus about last night?"

"No, of course not. He wouldn't understand. He's been kind to me, though." He hesitated for a moment, looking at her deeply.

"I know what else you want to ask me, Lalage. I haven't told Flavia. I haven't even seen her all day."

Lalage leaned over and tapped him lightly on the left side of his chest. "Does it hurt?"

"Not quite as much as I thought it would."

"It will, though. But you're brave. Now, what am I to tell you?"

"Everything."

She told him, then, about the surprising life and death and rising of the Christ. She told him about love and forgiveness. She told him about the organization of the churches, about baptism and fasting and the love feasts.

He kept on interrupting and harking back and understanding things wrong.

She told him about prayer.

"What do you pray for?" he asked.

"Always, I suppose, that the Will may be done."

"Not for real things?"

"That's real. We trust God for money and food and things like that. Yet we try to earn them honestly. And by the way, you haven't paid me yet for last night."

Beric blushed scarlet and suddenly realized how uncomfortable it was to have money relations with people you knew—friends.

Lalage added, "I'd like something extra because of Tigellinus, please, and I think you might give something to Phaon. He had a horrid time."

Beric thought two things—first, that he had glared at Phaon to make him go to Tigellinus for whatever fun Tigellinus wanted to have with him, and, second, that it was going to be extraordinarily awkward being on these terms with the slaves. He said as much to Lalage.

"But think how much more awkward it is being one of the slaves! No, Beric, I'm not sorry for you about that. And you know, you can't just get out of it by being kind to your slaves. A good Stoic is that. Or a good Epicurean. Anybody except a good Roman, really! But it isn't enough for a Christian."

"What does a Christian have to be, besides kind?"

"It's not only what he has to be, it's what he has to do. He can't, you see, tolerate a state of things in which one person is a master and another person a slave. Sooner or later things will change."

"They're Crispus's slaves, not mine. You're making it all very difficult, Lalage."

"It is difficult," she said, "as difficult as walking on your hands when you've never done it before. It's only just at the very first that it seems easy and lovely. Before you know what the Kingdom really means. So don't say you're going to be a Christian and then complain that you haven't been warned."

"Oh, you've warned me." And then he banged his hand angrily on the table. "I wish I was back at yesterday and none of all this had happened!"

"I know," said Lalage gently, "but it has happened. All of it. And you can't get out of it now." She added, "Three days from today, there'll be a meeting at Eunice's house. Do you want to come?"

"Who'll be there?"

"Everyone who can get away."

"Will you be there?"

"Yes, I've kept it. I'm free too! Probably everyone from this house will come. It'll be late, after they're all supposed to be off for the day."

"So that's where they've been, those three. Well, it's funny what one doesn't know about the slaves!"

"It isn't only those three. There are Josias and Dapyx from the kitchen."

"We got Manasses and Josias together. I remember. Josias is a decent, hard-working boy. But Dapyx? That Thracian? He's a bit of a brute, surely."

"He's been treated as if he was," said Lalage. "Do you remember anything about him?"

"We got him straight from the market, I think," said Beric, bothered, "a prisoner of war with chalk on his feet, never been in a house before. The cook thought he could do with a rough boy to train."

"Yes," said Lalage, "and he's been trained all right—with a whip. And the edge of a hot fryingpan now and then. Manasses found he'd got maggots in a sore on his back. Nice thing to have in your kitchen, wasn't it, Beric?"

"Lalage, listen! I don't always see what the cook and old Felix do. They don't like me interfering. I'd no idea—"

"That's the sort of thing you'll have to have ideas about. If you come to the meeting, you'll have to call him brother. And he won't be washed. It's no use looking like that, Beric. I told you we were dirt. And you told me you'd got to get used to being dirt. Remember?"

"Yes," said Beric, low, "I remember. And it did all happen last night." He put his hand up to his face. "Dapyx is going to hate me a good deal."

"He'll be much more frightened than anything else. You'll have to get him over that. If you can."

"Three days from now," said Beric. "She's going to be betrothed three days from now. And I shall have had to be there. I think I shall come to your meeting, Lalage."

6

Rhodon, Phineas and
Sapphira, Sotion, Dapyx

Rhodon was a metalworker in a small Greek-speaking town
in Bithynia. So were his father and grandfather, and, as far as he
knew, all his fathers back to the time when metalworking had
been a secret craft with its rites of initiation and its own prayers.
There were remains of those prayers in the things that Rhodon
said or sang over his work, but he did not know what they meant.
Only they were part of the skill.

He learned his trade from his father, as soon as he was old
enough to handle tools. But he was the third son, so when he was
full-grown he had to leave home with his bundle of tools, the skill
in his hands and brains, his brown-and-black dog, Att, and something else as well, which was going to help him on his journeyings
more than money. He had been admitted as a boy, and was a
member of the Third Degree, a Soldier in the community of Mithras.

His father was high up, fully initiate, a Persian. He had tasted
the honey, had eaten the bread, and drunk the wine. At the most
sacred times, in the middle of the months and especially at the
equinoxes and solstices, he would stay all night in the Cave, and,
though he went back to work next day and his hand was no less
steady, yet he would be muttering strange words, which came
from another language, and now and then he would laugh out
loud with the joy of something he had experienced. Something
that Rhodon too would experience in time.

It would all come. Somewhere, in some town, Rhodon would
find his fellows and settle there as a skilled worker, and after a
time he would be admitted to the first stage of full initiation as a
Lion of Mithras, a fire-bearer. Then certain things would be made
clear that were still hidden. Then he would have the blood of baptism of which his father had once spoken, when the bull is killed

at the altar, and, below, those who wait naked and fasting to be made into Lions take the hot blood suddenly on their upturned faces and arms.

In the meantime he had been through the rites of the first three Degrees. His eyes and his hands had been bound. He had felt the touch of slimy things, heard and resisted the whisperings of the tempters. He had leaped the water and repeated the words, which had at first been strange but now filled him with comfort, so that he knew that even if he died on his journey, he could whisper them again as he died and One would come to his deathbed.

In the last rite he had taken the mark on his forehead, the tiny brand, the touch of fire, unflinchingly and gladly borne. Often, for that matter, Rhodon had got worse burns in his father's smithy, and he had stood very steadily, so the mark was clear and sharp in the center of his forehead. He had only to brush his hair back with a casual hand, and those who knew the mark would see that he was one of them.

He went northeast to Heraclea on the Bithynian coast and then east along the coast road, mostly in sight of the Black Sea. He could have had a mule, but he was young and did not mind carrying his own bundle. A traveler on foot was less liable, too, to be set on by robbers. Yet even so, he might have found friends among the robbers. Besides, he was armed with a short sword and dagger of his father's forging, and his dog would fight for him.

As he walked he thought a great deal about the things he had been told and above all about Mithras, the Redeemer and Mediator, the Bull-slayer, picturing him always as a young man, a companion, going out alone as he was but into a world without even life, except for his dog, which must have been, he thought, a dog like his own Att, and the Bull, which he must hunt over plains and mountains.

The Bull that was also himself. Must every man, then, hunt for his self and, having found it for certain, track it down and at last kill it in the Cave in the mountains? Sacrifice it and make it one with the greater things, which are called Time and Light and Truth?

At midday he sat under a fig tree, sharing his bread and dried meat with the patient, watching dog and wondering what his self

114

was. He was first a worker. Surely at least he must never sacrifice his skill. His father and his father's fathers before that had never done so. He need not think it.

What then? *What, my dog, my Att, looking so wise at me, tell me, what is my self? I have kept the rules; I have said my prayers; I have been brave. I might have stayed at home another year, but I set out without complaining. Yes, I did go one night with the girls, when they went to the woods to ask whoever it is they ask for whatever it is that women ask for, but I didn't know what was going to happen. No, I did half know, and perhaps I ought to have stayed away. But that was only when I was in the Second Degree. Since I have been a Soldier, I have known no women. So that is not my self. And you, Att, you go after all the lady dogs, don't you, old son? But the first dog, he was a better dog than you—he only helped his master. But you'd help me, wouldn't you? And Mithras, whose Soldier I am, he will show me some day what my self is and be with me in the ultimate sacrifice.*

At Heraclea he found friends of his father's, worked for them a week, and went to the Cave with them. But he wanted to go farther. They gave him names at Amastris, four days' journey on, and here again he stayed for a short time and then went east again, always feeling that he was on his hunt.

In Paphlagonia, people spoke a new language, but some of the words were the same. In the towns they spoke Greek as well, and the services in the Caves were in some kind of Greek, so he could follow them, and the things that those in each Degree had to do were always the same.

When he came to the River Iris, he turned south and struck up into the mountains. He was tired of the sea. There were high passes ahead of him. Breathing hard and quick in the cold air, he and Att went up and up along the track marked here and there by the vulture-picked bones of pack mules.

So at last they were across the passes and into Armenia, and he began to think that he wanted to settle somewhere, for the rainy season would be coming on, and one must stop sooner or later.

Sometimes there were rumors of war. Once or twice he had seen companies of Roman soldiers on the march. But Rome had nothing to do with him, either as craftsman or as Mithraist. It was outside. He sat on the roadside, looking at those men in queer clothes carrying their gods, he supposed, on the ends of poles. His dog barked at the Romans, and he himself laughed.

He found a town by a river where he thought he would like to stay. For a day or two he stopped at the inn, watching those who came in and out. He liked the looks of them.

He found out where the Cave was, and on the right day he went up there. It was above the town, where a spur of mountain came down to force a sharp bend in the river away below. And as he got nearer, other men kept on glancing at him, and when he came to the Cave he was, of course, stopped. But when he pushed back his dark hair and showed the mark, they kissed him and made him welcome, and at the right moment in the service he stood up with the others of his Degree and went through the movements. All was in order.

After the service he was asked by the men who could speak Greek where he came from and what he wanted to do. He answered, of course, truthfully, and then another man in his trade who was a Degree higher than himself, a Lion, suggested that he should come in with him.

So after that, Rhodon and his dog shared a room with this man, who was called Addon, and his wife and baby, and worked with him, sharing the profits. The wife spoke only some dialect, but she was a good cook. As he and Addon were in the same community, there was no need for any formal contract between them. They would be honest with one another.

Rhodon enjoyed his work and made friends. He did the right things, drank little, never kept shavings of gold when he was given it to make up, did not go with women, but thought that some time he would get married and have sons. Addon's wife had a young sister that might do. He had learned the native words for different kinds of food and tools and ordinary things; she could be made to understand everything else.

Now that he was working full-time he thought less about his self and Mithras, who would be with him at the time of trial. He thought about it in the Cave, but then it was all made easy by singing and lights and movements and the sense of the other men who were with him. Mithras was the Redeemer; he could be trusted in all ways.

In due time Rhodon was elected an official in the Mithraic community. He was one of those who were trusted with the money. They held meetings about it and decided what was to go to the poor and what was to go to the Fathers, the officiating priests, who had no trade of their own but spent all their time on things to do with religion, keeping alight the fire on the altar and making long prayers at dawn and midday and evening, prayers that were for the whole of the worshipers of Mithras in that town. This business was another thing that Rhodon liked doing. Soon he himself might be initiated into the next Degree.

From time to time news came though from the outside world, talk of kings and queens and battles. That was an affair for the nobles. The only thing that mattered to the ordinary townspeople were the sudden demands for money, usually from Parthia. Armenia was almost part of Parthia; the Parthian kings were Sons of Light, initiated. The tax-gatherers said that the sun himself, in the form of a golden man, had crowned them. But the forces of evil were always close to kings, whispering lies and blood into their ears. So wars came.

And one day, out of the mountains with no warning, war fell on the town. Bad King Radamistus and his army of savage, terse-speaking foreigners were driven back north again with the Parthians after them, hideously determined to take or destroy what they could before they themselves were destroyed. The townspeople fought, defending their homes against whoever these invaders were, whichever side they were on. They barricaded doors and windows, shut up the screaming women, and fought till they were dead or prisoners, their houses in flames, and their wives and children dead too or crying for help that no one could give them.

Addon was killed at his house door. His child's brains were knocked out against the wall. His wife and the girl Rhodon had planned to marry were raped and then thrown back, half dead, into the burning house. Rhodon himself, wounded and flame-blistered, one arm useless, was dragged off after the retreating army with other prisoners in the same state as himself. If they could

117

stand it, they would survive; if not, they died. Most of them were dead before they got down to the coast.

Rhodon was just alive, though not worth much. His dog had tried to follow. He was wounded, too, and limping. Rhodon saw someone throw a stone and break Att's back. He was so hurt and miserable himself that it did not seem so bad at the time as it did afterward.

He did not know what was happening to him, but after a time he was in a city again. He was in Trapezus at the far end of the Black Sea and sold to a dealer who had his raw blisters treated, his arm put into a splint, and gave him some stuff to drink that put him half asleep for days.

When he woke up thoroughly, he was in a ship, chained by the ankles to other slaves, mostly prisoners of war. But he could move his arm again, though painfully. After a time he discovered that they were all being shipped from one dealer to another. When he found they were putting in at Heraclea, he got hold of a sailor, told him the name of those friends of his father's who would certainly ransom him, and promised a reward.

All the time the ship lay in harbor there, he waited with intense eagerness for the voices he knew, for the chains to be struck off, for life to come back. But the sailor had never got in touch. He had spent an enjoyable time on shore drinking, and, when Rhodon reproached him bitterly, said that a good drink now was better than any reward in the future, and anyway it would be a lot of fun giving Rhodon a good hiding.

At one time the ship must have passed fairly near Rhodon's old home, but Rhodon did not really know, and he was so wretched that he could not make any more plans. While he was ill he had in his drugged sleep said his words and seen lights and heard voices. But now he could hardly ever bear to say them. He was alone, and his Redeemer had not helped him. Every now and then he remembered little horrible things out of the fighting, things that stayed with him that could not be exorcised by any prayer.

They touched at various ports. The slaves, still chained, had to scrub the decks. Sometimes someone on the quay would throw them a half-eaten piece of bread or fruit, and they scrambled for it, hurting one another. The ship became more and more filthy and stinking, especially when she was through the Hellespont and out in the open Aegean where she pitched a bit.

At Delos, an agent took delivery of them, and they were taken to one of the warehouses. Their owner scowled at them, as mixed a lot of Armenians and Cappadocians and Phrygians and Bithynians as he'd ever laid eyes on. "Any of you speak Greek?"

Several, including Rhodon and another Armenian whom he had got to know a little, a man called Abgar, from another hill town, answered that they did. They were unchained and taken into a separate building with some moderately clean straw. They didn't know or care what happened to the others.

When their owner came in, Rhodon explained that he was a skilled man. That made a difference at once. He was given the first decent meal he'd had for weeks and allowed to wash and shave. He was taken to a forge and watched while he handled the tools. His arm was a bit stiff, but they decided that what he needed was exercise, massage, and decent treatment. Then he would be the main profit on a very random bunch of slaves, bought entirely on speculation.

Now that he was unchained, Rhodon could pray properly, yet he didn't seem to want to. It was all dead to him. *Surely,* he said to himself, *surely it was he who saved me—Mithras, my Redeemer?* But he couldn't persuade himself that it was. All that had been mixed up with the Cave, with worship together, with doing things in order, and the organization of the community. It had been part of being strong, able to fight and defend himself and what he believed in. It had been part of being a craftsman working regularly every day at something he had been good at. There was nothing to hold onto here.

He wasn't part of anything. Even when they started him on work again, he wasn't working his own way and time, for himself, but was told what to do, for a master. They even made him hold his hammers a different way. It all stopped him feeling the way a craftsman should. But he had been alone before and not working, three years ago, when he walked whistling on the road east. Why had it been different then? Because of the dog perhaps? It wasn't only that. It had been decent and in order, walking that warm white dust, on his way to work and a new home. He didn't seem to be on his way to anything now.

But he was on his way to Rome, the place he had heard of and never thought of seeing. By the time he got there he was nearly well. He was sold to a Jew called Barnabas, whose people had come to Rome two generations before, a tolerably rich man but brought up, like all good Jews, to a skilled trade. He himself worked mainly as a jeweler, but he had several slaves doing coarser metalwork.

It was some time before Rhodon got back to anything like his old skill. Sometimes he was afraid he was not working fast enough and that his master might sell him as he constantly threatened to do during the first year. He could not bear the idea of being sold again, of digging up such precarious roots as he was beginning to make.

He lived in the Jewish household in the Jewish Quarter of Rome and got to like the rhythm and routine of it. The non-Jewish slaves did any work there was on the Sabbath, but even they rested for most of it. And worked better during the week for the rest.

So things went on for a long time. Rhodon still sang in a low voice the words that he had sung over his work at the other end of the Mediterranean. He was fairly happy; he had many of the ordinary pleasures. After a couple of years his master began paying him a small wage, depending on the quality of his work, fairly enough considered. He saved most of it, banking it with his master.

He might have got in touch with other Mithraists in Rome, but the thing had died in him, and, of course, there were very few in the Jewish Quarter. Rhodon had heard that somewhere else in Rome there was said to be a great Cave and worshipers, but it would have taken more of an effort to find it than he was able to make. He could not feel anymore that he was part of the army of Mithras. How can a man be a soldier by himself? Not being a soldier any longer, you shamble along somehow and don't think about it. He would have liked to keep a dog again, but his master would not let him.

When he began to have wages, he would sometimes buy fried fish, which he liked very much, usually from a shop at the corner of the street. Gradually he got to know the owner of the shop, a young Jew called Phineas, and his wife, Sapphira. They had a dog, but it was a watchdog and usually chained up. He offered to take it out for a walk on the Sabbath, explaining that dogs like walking, and that he was a Gentile so it was all right. They let him, and he very much enjoyed talking to the dog.

Sometimes they asked him into the living room behind the shop, and as his hours of work were fairly regular, he could usually go in the evenings. When their two-year-old child was irritable, he gave Sapphira a hand with it or the cooking, and he noticed that they were keeping slightly different fast days from the ordinary one. The evening after Sabbath, Phineas was usually out, and Sapphira too, if she could get someone to come in and mind the child. After a time Rhodon offered to, and often did.

His master asked him where he was going and, when he explained, grunted. "Those Nazarenes!"

Rhodon asked what a Nazarene was and gathered from his master that they had a new prophet, not one of the recognized ones, and that they associated with Gentiles.

That seemed to be so, because when Rhodon was there, others would come in who were obvious Gentiles, and they greeted one another not with ordinary, suspicious politeness, as sensible people do, but with a "Peace be with you!" of a pleased and open kind. When Rhodon came, the watchdog was unchained and came in and bounced around him, and he sat on the floor beside the dog and stroked it and told it about Att. But if he had been doing that, Sapphira always made him wash his hands before he touched the cooking pots or the child.

Sometimes there was a older Gentile woman there, a Greek, brisk and heavyset. He gathered she had lately been freed, and she spoke well of her patron, Flavius Crispus, and his daughter, who was ever so pretty but spoiled, the way only children often get. Rhodon did not always attend to what they said, because often he was talking to the watchdog, telling him about the softness and wooliness of his own dog's ears and throat, which he would hold up to be stroked, and how Att had been faithful to death, as a good dog ought to be.

But one day, when there were several, including the Greek woman, in the room, he heard someone speak of a Redeemer, and it occurred to him that he had already heard words such as Redeemer and Savior, words which once he had known very well, but he had never heard spoken in the presence of women. Nor did he think that any Jew could be a Mithraist.

He looked up, puzzling, and suddenly the Greek woman pointed to him and said, "Have you ever spoken to him, Phineas?"

Phineas shook his head.

"Just because of his being a Gentile! So there he sits with the dog—"

"He likes the dog, Eunice," said Phineas.

Rhodon stopped stroking the dog. "What is it you haven't spoken to me about? Is it the Redeemer?"

"I told you so!" Eunice said.

Phineas said, "If I tell you, Rhodon, you must promise never to tell any outside people."

Rhodon stood up and lifted his right hand. "In the name of Mithras, I promise." It was the most binding promise he could make.

Phineas looked extremely taken aback. "Are you a Mithraist?"

Rhodon answered, sadly enough, "I used to be. At home. But not since I've been in Rome."

They all seemed bothered.

Then Eunice said, "You wanted a redeemer, didn't you? Someone to be with you and in you, to help you to understand the great things—things that get too difficult for a man by himself?"

Rhodon nodded. That was it, though it was disturbing to hear a woman speak of it.

"So you took Mithras for your redeemer. But he was only a story."

That hurt Rhodon. He had to try and defend the remains of something. "That's not the way I see it," he said. "Mithras was my god and my crown."

"Now," said Eunice, "you're saying that, friend, but what does it amount to? You were told about your redeemer. But you never asked yourself who was he really. Did you now?"

"No," said Rhodon, "I didn't need to."

"Why not? Who told you?"

"Well, the priests." It made him feel bad, saying that, as though he had given something away to this woman. Well, he'd done it now.

"Then supposing Mithras was only a story made up by these priests. What then?"

Rhodon looked unhappy. He did not want to think like this. "There must be priests," he said.

"But not between you and God. Not—you know—making up stories for the rest to believe."

Rhodon thought of the sacred things that the priests did, which were in a way not real: the pretended murder, the frightening of the novices. But those in the higher grades knew it was all a pretense, just something that had to be done. And who but the priests would make the great sacrifice, the killing of the Bull? "There must be priests," he repeated firmly.

Eunice said to him, "There's only one human sacrifice which matters, and that's the sacrifice of one's life for what's worth dying for. And that's a sacrifice that any one of us can make. Man or woman."

Or dog, thought Rhodon suddenly, and his eyes were full of tears.

Eunice went on. "Our Redeemer made that sacrifice Himself. And He isn't a story. He was a real man."

"The Messiah," said Phineas.

But Rhodon did not know what he meant. He was beginning to attend to Eunice.

She went on. "He healed the sick, and He taught about the Kingdom and about forgiveness, and in the end He gave His own body as a sacrifice."

"His own body," said Rhodon, thinking of the Bull, which was also Mithras. "His self?"

"Yes," said Eunice. "He let them crucify Him. He gave Himself for us."

But Rhodon was thinking of something else. "Was he really a man," he asked, "an ordinary man like us?"

"More than a man. But He was a woodworker."

"A skilled man," said Rhodon with a kind of relief in his voice. "Tell me some more about what he died for."

That was how Rhodon came into the church. He was rather slow at learning because he got the old and the new prayers mixed up, and besides, he got tired more easily over anything than a man would have done who had not been once badly wounded. So it was some months before he could be baptized.

But he liked it. He liked being in a community again, feeling that there was an organization around him, something to hold onto. He got used to women being in it, and sometimes, instead of going to the fish shop, he went to Eunice's bakery in the evenings after work, especially in winter, when it was so warm and pleasant.

Sapphira was tied up caring for her children, especially when the new baby came. Besides, she found it nearly as good if Phineas went and told her all about it when he came back.

Phineas had been born in Rome. His father, Gedaliah-bar-Jorim, was one of the Jerusalem Nazarenes, intensely patriotic, a friend of James, who had never quite understood his strange elder brother but had always stood by Him in spite of His having obstinately gone to certain death in Jerusalem when He might have been the Messiah. When asked, He had not denied that He *was* the Messiah. And afterward, it appeared that He might be going to be the Messiah after all.

When the dreadful news came that Emperor Gaius was going to desecrate the temple in Jerusalem, shaming all Judea, Gedaliah-bar-Jorim was one of a deputation to Rome. Before they got there, even, the emperor was dead, but several of the deputation stayed on in Rome and married. Gedaliah married the daughter of a respectable, hardworking family and settled down to his trade of carpet weaving. A couple of years later, Phineas was born, the eldest son, much loved by his violent father, who brought him up to look forward to the sudden reappearance of the Messiah, this time visibly a God and a destroyer, and the establishment of the Kingdom. Any time it might happen, while he was at school or out in the street playing. He would be saved, but his companions licked up like one enormous flame.

Whenever there was a thunderstorm, little Phineas began to expect the Coming. But it kept on not coming, and Phineas began to have other thoughts about the Kingdom. And he got into touch with others in Rome—Gentile Christians—and even ate with them. His younger brothers and sister seemed to be able to go on expecting the Messiah in the same way, year after year, never disappointed. He couldn't do that. Yes, Jesus was the Messiah, but not, oh, not just to bring us all back to Jerusalem, to make it another Rome, ruling the world! He did not like even discussing it with his father now. They meant such different things by the same words.

Phineas had been baptized as a boy, and it was intended that he should, in due time, marry the daughter of a neighbor who was also a Jerusalem Nazarene—if the Messiah had not appeared by then. But he fell in love with a slave girl, redeemed her out of his own savings, and married her.

Thank God she was at least a Jewess, though from one of the coast towns, and her father had been free. As Phineas was going now he might even have thought of marriage with a Gentile! And Sapphira was quiet and gentle and very grateful and a good housewife. And she believed everything that Phineas believed. That was good in a wife, but she should have paid attention to her father-in-law, and she did not. She even contradicted him, defending her husband and the foolish beliefs of these new Christians, as they called themselves. She even went to the meetings and sat with Gentile women—yes, and men—but at least she had given her father-in-law two healthy grandsons.

It was Phineas who had brought Sotion to the meetings. He had seen him hanging around several times, and when Sotion asked him point-blank if he was a Christian, he had answered yes, very happily, and brought Sotion in to one of the gatherings at Eunice's house.

Sotion had been very eager to join the church and had asked quantities of questions. He was a freedman, and his job was rent collecting. He was rather small, with bad teeth, and very friendly to everyone. Manasses had baptized him. Once he had gone as a delegate from their church to the church in Caesar's household and had been very accurate and painstaking with his report.

It was just after Sotion's baptism that Rhodon had saved up enough to buy his freedom. He went on working for Barnabas, at a slightly increased wage, and nothing was really altered except that he enjoyed being free. His master had never ill-used him, or indeed any of his slaves, and now he let Rhodon take a little private work and do it at his old bench and forge after hours. Actually, Rhodon worked rather harder than he had done before, but he also put a little more each week into the funds of the church. That was another thing he enjoyed doing. But he still got tired rather suddenly, and sometimes his arm ached.

Phineas and Rhodon and the watchdog walked over together that night to Eunice's house. Rhodon had trained the watchdog to stay on guard outside. On the way they picked up Sotion, who asked about Sapphira. Phineas explained that she couldn't come just now as she was still nursing the baby. He spoke softly and lovingly of her and the children.

When they got to the bakery, they found Lalage and Sophrosyne there already. Then Euphemia came and got them all laughing with a funny story about one of her customers. Then Niger came, looking as miserable as ever, and with him Felicio, the young Italian from his household whom he had brought once before, quiet and intelligent and well-read, a slave. Then they heard Manasses' voice at the door and the voices of the others from the household of Flavius Crispus. Soon it would be the full meeting.

Rhodon wondered why Lalage had stood up, where she could see over Euphemia, who was sitting in front of her, and why she was looking so excited.

Manasses in the doorway said, "Peace be with you." And they all answered, "Peace, peace, brother," and he came in, Josias behind him, then Phaon, then Dapyx with an awful boil on his neck that looked as if it might burst at any moment.

"Persis can't come tonight—her mistress wants her. But—" And Manasses half turned to the door. Argas came in, and with him someone whom none of them knew except Eunice, and she jumped up, one hand at her mouth, with a strange look.

"Peace be with you," Argas said and then turned to his friend. "You say it."

"Peace be with you," said the newcomer, in rather unsteady Greek, with an accent they couldn't quite place.

And as they answered him they all stared at him, taking in his tunic and cloak, which were certainly old, but the stuff—you could tell the stuff! And his sandals that hadn't been mended—hadn't ever needed mending—and then the look of his face, washed and shaved. Well, you couldn't help knowing, and most of them rose, as they hadn't for Manasses, their deacon, their brother. And most of them were half excited and half frightened.

Niger remembered who it was, and he felt sick and wanted to hide.

"But you can't—" Eunice began, her voice trembling.

Lalage spoke to her quickly, across Euphemia. "It's all right, Eunice, it is really! I only didn't tell you because I wasn't sure. I'll be his guardian."

And Beric whispered to Argas, urgently, "Please, *please*, let's sit down in a corner somewhere, or their eyes'll drop out of their heads!"

Argas grinned and pushed him around into the corner behind the kneading trough.

But Eunice said, "Oh, but he must sit in front. Take my chair. Bring him around, Argas!"

"Oh *no!*" said Beric, and Phaon giggled.

"But who is he?" Sotion whispered excitedly.

Manasses answered, with a funny mixture of pride and casualness, "He's our young master."

Phaon giggled again, and then Lalage pushed Eunice back into her chair, and Euphemia walked over to Dapyx and said, "Here, son, let me see that boil of yours." Then she took him through into the scullery with a lamp and began squeezing the boil.

Dapyx said it was where the iron ring he'd had on his neck for months had caught him.

Euphemia made him hold the lamp so that she could see what she was doing, then asked, "Who is he, really?"

"Manasses said. It's him," Dapyx answered.

"Your master? Well, I could hardly believe it. But then, what's he doing here? Don't wriggle, son. It'll be done in a minute. Now tell me, do. Did you know he was coming?"

"No. When I get to the others, he is standing there."

"Weren't you scared stiff?"

"Yes. But he makes the sign. To me."

"There! Now I'll put a nice piece of rag around it. What do you think'll come of it, Dapyx?"

"Don't know. Maybe better times for me."

"But what I can't see is, what one of *them* wants, coming in with us. Whatever can he be after?"

"Maybe he's a fool. But he calls me brother. Me."

"Well, I never. There, that's done. Come on back, son. I want to have a good look at him."

But when they got back, Beric had got himself well wedged into a dark corner, sitting on the edge of Eunice's bed between Argas and Josias.

Everyone was pretending not to look at him, and Rhodon was saying to Phineas that he hoped they'd get started soon—there was a lot of business to get through. In this group, too, Rhodon was one of the administrators of the funds. Only nothing had to go for upkeep here, nothing for bells and candles and robes and sacrifices.

Then Manasses rose for the first prayer.

7

Niger

On the edge of the brown desert there was a village behind a stockade of thorns, with dried mud houses tumbled and piled together and a space in the middle where the young men could leap and yell and fling their feather-tufted spears high in the air and show off to the grave, watching girls at the women's end. Squatting along the sides, the old men commented on the black shining bodies of the boys. They were working up for a raid over the mountains and into the rich country where there were metal and horses and plenty of food.

The raiding party started off, some riding, some running on foot, all dressed for war with ostrich feathers and dangling pieces of metal and the glossy, swinging tails of wild beasts. They crossed the mountains by a pass and came down among crops and fruit trees. They were hoping mostly for horses. In the mountains they had shouted war cries, but now they went silently, looking for hoofprints.

By now the province of Tingitana, farthest west of the North African provinces, was used to these raids. It was not a case for legions, but there were patrols of auxiliaries all along the frontiers, ready to gallop when the message came for them, as it did now.

In an hour they were onto the raiders, had killed several, taken a few prisoners, and sent the rest scuttling back over their mountains. The prisoners, with their hands tied, were made to run beside the horses most of the way into Volubilis. That took the fight out of them completely. Here they were turned over to the regular slave trade, and the auxiliaries left again for the frontier patrol.

The newly caught slaves were kept chained the whole time, fed on beans and water, and separated from one another, so that, until they chose to know the Latin words for things, they could not communicate with anyone. From time to time they were beaten just to show them what was what. Some of them were wounded. The wounds were looked after efficiently but without regard for pain. Then they and some others were marched across Tingitana to Siga, the port from which they were to be shipped to Rome. They had no names now. Their old names were unpronounceable. They had ceased even to be angry and bewildered individuals. They had become part of the silent mass of slaves.

Aelius Balbus had an overseer, an Italian called Montanus, who saw to it that his employer was comfortable. He was reasonably honest, did not flirt with the slave girls much because his wife usually heard of it, and he did not get drunk. Balbus was quite satisfied with him. He went off to the market to get another litter slave for Balbus. It had to be a black one, like the last, who had ruptured himself and was no use any longer. Montanus had proposed to sell him to anyone who could use him up, but Balbus had said he could stay on in the kitchen, which was really very kind of him, as things went.

Balbus had four slaves for his litter: a German from up near the Rhine, who had been taken prisoner in one of those interminable wars that were always going on there—he was a blond, extremely strong and rather stupid; a red-haired, freckled tough called Zyrax, from Moesia or thereabouts, who knew something no one else knew about the overseer and was thus in a better position than the rest of them; a dark-haired, dark-eyed Cappadocian, who would probably be the next to go; and a black to make up the lot into an amusing color contrast.

They all wore iron rings on their necks and iron cuffs on their wrists—by which theoretically, and sometimes on very special occasions literally, they were chained to the litter—and blue and yellow livery tunics. There were a couple of spares who walked behind, but Balbus preferred always to have the same ones carrying him.

Montanus bought one of the slaves who had recently been imported from Tingitana. He was called Niger, like his predecessor. He did not understand at first that this was his name now and for the rest of his life, but he soon got used to it. He could speak a little Latin, and he found that he also had to know some Greek, as that was what Zyrax and the Cappadocian spoke ordinarily, and a good deal depended on being in their good books.

There was nothing very difficult to learn, except actually lifting the loaded litter without tilting it in the least. That was the moment when litter bearers were apt to rupture themselves. And Aelius Balbus was a fair weight. If he was in a hurry, they had to trot, insofar as that was possible in the crowded streets of Rome. And there was endless waiting about, sometimes in the full sun in summer—the German still managed to blister with that!—or in east wind and frost in winter. If they bumped the litter into anything, they were all beaten when they got back, or all except Zyrax, who was very expert at finding suitable excuses.

Niger could hardly remember the village any longer, the tossing spears, and the dark glisten of the girls' eyes and breasts. That had been wiped out. This alone was happening. His predecessor was from Nubia, southwest of Egypt, and they did not even speak the same language. Also, the ruptured and discarded Niger hated the new one and was always trying to get him into trouble.

Sometimes they carried the son of the house, Aelius Candidus, and sometimes father and son together, in which case the two spares gave a hand. Or sometimes Balbus had a friend with him or, if he had much business in hand, one of the slave secretaries, young Felicio, for instance. Several other slaves, also in livery, went ahead to clear the street, carrying torches if it was dark. That was easy.

If litter bearers lived to any age, they often had asthma, and those who could not afford to have a succession of new litter bearers every so many years would have to put up with an accompaniment of unpleasant asthmatic noises as they were carried about the streets. Occasionally, too, a litter bearer would die of heart failure.

Flavius Crispus, the way to whose house they knew well, had nothing fancy about his litter bearers. They were just Thracians or Moesians, all more or less alike, easy to replace. The last lot that had been replaced were sent off to his country estate to do light work. But Flavius Crispus did not have an economical overseer like Montanus.

Aelius Balbus had never actually spoken to Niger. He gave all his orders to Zyrax, who nodded cheerfully, whatever they were. But he once personally ordered Niger to be whipped for letting his pole down too suddenly. Niger was frightened of him but not so frightened as he was of Montanus.

When he saw Montanus coming, he was apt to stand absolutely still, flattening himself against a wall, perhaps, as though he hoped not even to be seen. But this annoyed Montanus, who would give him a prod in the belly as he passed by.

Usually if their master went visiting and was going to be a long time in the house, at a dinner party, say, the slaves would bring the litter into the yard, and themselves would sit with the house slaves. If they were lucky, they got something to eat. They always did at Flavius Crispus's house if the young master there, the Briton, happened to see them. And he would make some cheerful remark to Zyrax who, of course, grinned back.

But one day when they were there, Zyrax was angry with Niger and avenged himself by chaining him to the litter by his iron collar and cuffs and leaving him in the yard. The Cappadocian was probably sorry for him, but the German only laughed, going into the warmth and company of the house. Niger could have loosed himself, but he didn't dare, in case Zyrax did something much worse—complained of him to Montanus.

It was cold in the yard, and he could smell food from the kitchen. Besides, with the litter on the ground he had to kneel in a cramped position beside it because of the chains. He got colder and colder. His mind was like a frozen stone. Occasionally one of Crispus's slaves passed and glanced at him, but said nothing.

At last one of them asked, "Why aren't you in the kitchen with the others?" This was a house and kitchen slave, Josias. Niger had spoken to him once or twice. Now he only pointed to the chains.

Josias came over and began to unhook the chains, but Niger stopped him. "No! Zyrax will be angry. I must stay."

"You poor devil," said Josias and went into the house.

That was all, Niger thought, but in a few minutes Josias came back with a bit of blanket, which he put over Niger's shoulders, and a bowl of food.

Josias watched him wolfing the food for a moment, hesitated, and then said, "I can stay if you like."

Till he heard that, Niger had not particularly noticed how lonely he was. That was just part of it all.

But now he took Josias's hand with a look of such gratitude that Josias caught himself at what he least liked remembering—the dye works in Tyre. He said to Niger, "I'll tell you a story," and sat down on the edge of the litter.

Niger was now beaming with pleasure. He loved being told stories. In the village there had been nights and nights of storytelling. All the old men told stories. But no one had told him a story since he had been a slave.

Josias spoke slowly, using simple words, because he knew Niger did not understand Greek as well as most of them. He told the story of Jesus-bar-Joseph, who was also the Christ, but that wouldn't mean anything to Niger. After about an hour they heard the others coming out. Josias picked up the bowl and blanket quickly. It wouldn't do for Zyrax to see that Niger had been fed or warmed.

Niger, who had been quite silent, so silent that Josias wondered sometimes if he was really listening, said, "Next time, tell me more."

There was hardly any need to tell Niger to hold his tongue about it. There was no one for him to talk to, and he hardly ever managed to get to the tongue-loosening stage of drink. He had no money at all, and nobody ever gave him anything. For a long time he was suspicious of the rest of the congregation. He could not believe they might not suddenly turn against him. But he trusted Josias. It only came to him gradually that there was comfort and joy in the church.

He went there at first just to hear more stories and because it was warm and dark, and he felt safe, and because Josias wanted him to come. But gradually it began to sink in to him. He began to feel that he was part of something that was bringing back his manhood to him. After the first prayers, he would begin to forget that he was only a slave. He had been given a direction, and he took it with all his being.

After his baptism, he came whenever he possibly could, but that was not always. He had nothing with which to bribe the porter into letting him out, unless sometimes when he got it from the moneybag of the church. Sometimes he had to go for weeks without once getting the comfort of the love feast. But he repeated the prayer to himself and told himself again all he had heard, over and over, all the stories.

The litter slaves had to clean and polish the litter and the chains that might be fastened onto their own necks and wrists. One day he was doing this alone, and as he did it he kept repeating the prayer to himself. Once to each of the chains. And when he turned around, the young secretary, Felicio, was standing and watching him. He crouched back like a dog, not even daring to lift a hand to ward off the blow.

Felicio said, "I came to order the litter around in ten minutes. But this is much more interesting. I believe you're a Christian."

Niger said nothing. He didn't know what to say. Felicio was one of the kind that rode in the litter, almost a master.

"Well," said Felicio, "are you?"

No help came to Niger, no way out. "Yes, sir," he answered.

"Caught you," said Felicio. "The litter in ten minutes. Get your livery on."

The others came running up. Niger scurried for his tunic, then ran to the litter pole. They were kept waiting half an hour, of course, and then had to trot. Niger didn't begin to know what might be done to him, whether he would just be punished alone or made to give names or what. Could he manage to knock his brains out on a wall? Once he stumbled, and Zyrax whispered to him viciously that he'd catch it when they got back. He couldn't even pray.

When they got back, he caught it all right. Zyrax saw to that. And then? He kept on waiting. It was the night for the breaking of bread, and he longed most painfully to go. If he could have gone, he said to himself, and just had it all once more, just once, then he could have stood anything. But he didn't dare try to go out. He waited in intense fear.

But he did not see Felicio again till the next day. Then the secretary, coming softly as before, tapped him on the shoulder and beckoned him to follow. They went up into an attic under the roof where old books and furniture were stored.

Niger wondered how Felicio was going to hurt him. So deep was his slavery that he did not even think of killing, which he could easily have done, as Felicio was half his size. But Niger did not even have to say to himself that Christians do not murder. He just stood and looked at Felicio, waiting, and then, as Felicio had not yet done anything to him, went down on his knees.

Then Felicio laughed and said, "I thought Christians were braver than that! Dangerous people. I thought they'd learned not to be afraid of anything!"

Slowly Niger realized that this was an accusation that must be met. He got up and said heavily, "I can stand anything you do."

Felicio regarded him. "You'd be a fine-looking creature," he said, "if you hadn't got the soul of a slave inside it all." He tapped him on the chest. "Why don't you get rid of it?"

"What are you going to do?" Niger asked. Till he knew that, he couldn't know anything else.

"Nothing. What do you think? You don't seem to realize, Niger, that I'm a slave too."

"You? You go in the litter."

"And you go in the Christian meetings. Now then, Niger, tell me all about it."

"Why?"

"Why? Because if you don't, I'll see you get whipped."

"I don't care. I been whipped before." Niger was recovering his balance now, whether Felicio meant one thing or the other.

"All right, then. Tell me because I want to know."

"What you want to know for?"

Felicio began to fidget about the room, neat and light, his hair properly clipped, his young beard properly shaved off. "If anyone comes, Niger, you're moving a desk for me—see?"

Niger nodded approvingly.

Felicio picked up a book-roll, put it down again, said, "That means telling you all about me. Care to know?"

"Yes, sir," said Niger happily, aware that this was going to be a story again.

"You may have heard, I come from the country estate. I was born there. My father was doorkeeper. He was an old man—they wouldn't let him marry when he was young. Didn't want to have a lot of brats about the place. So there was just me. Well, they're often not there for months at a time, and as I grew up I used to hang around the house and look at pictures and finger the books. Then I taught myself to read. I read a good deal; that's been my life really. But reading's a funny business. You don't notice at the time you're reading a book, but afterward you find you've been shifted a bit. In whatever direction your mind's going. That is, if you've got a mind. Some people haven't. I don't suppose you have, Niger?"

"No, sir," said Niger obediently, not sure what all this was about.

"I taught myself Greek, of course. There is no other language! I read the philosophers. Once I heard there was a traveling lecturer staying overnight at the village. I thought he'd be able to answer my questions, but he couldn't. At first he thought I was a young gentleman, and he was very polite, but when he found I was a slave with no money, he threw me out. Well then, once when he was up there, Aelius Balbus found me reading and thought he'd have me trained as a secretary. He's a decent old bird, though you wouldn't think it, Niger. So I came to Rome. And there were more books here. Too many books." He looked around the attic, frowning. You could smell the rather musty leather cases of the old book-rolls.

Niger suggested humbly, "There's plenty more in Rome besides books."

"Oh yes. There are girls, for instance. And boys. Almost everyone has something for sale. And there are lovely circuses with elephants if that's what you like. Or you can always see a few criminals being killed in the arena if you want a nice change. And there are several kinds of mysteries. Or one can go and raise evil spirits with a witch. Ever go to a witch, Niger?"

"Christians don't go to witches."

"Well, they don't miss much. But, you see, I kept on looking about and poking into holes and corners and temples and lecture rooms. And I can't lay hands on whatever it is I'm shifting towards.

And one of the things I haven't gone into is Christianity. I haven't been able to trace it down. Whenever I think I've got it, it's always turned out to be Judaism, and that's a bore—the angry old man up top like a master of all masters. There are some good ideas in it, but a lot of bad ones too, and somehow most people adopt the bad ideas out of any system and leave the good ones to rot. Have you understood a word of what I'm saying, Niger?"

"No, sir."

"I thought not. Now, Niger, I am determined to know about Christianity, and you've got to show it to me."

"I can't make all that explaining!" said Niger anxiously.

"I don't suppose for a moment you can, but you can take me to a meeting of your church or whatever it is. I can pretend to be a Christian."

"You can't do that," said Niger. "Christians can't lie."

"No, but I can! Come on, Niger, take me. I won't breathe a word to anyone."

"I can't take you," Niger repeated, "except you're serious."

"Fool, I am serious!" Felicio's voice rose a little. "I wouldn't have read through all those intolerable books if human life hadn't seemed to me to be extremely serious. And now you, you great blockhead, you can't see!"

Niger scratched his ear. Then he said, "First time I was took to the meeting, I didn't understand. Not a thing. Maybe I could take you in for the beginnings. But I got to stand guardian for you. If you tell—"

"Off goes your head. You needn't worry, Niger. When can we go?"

"By rights we could go next week. But maybe I can't get out."

"Is it at night?"

"Yes, but the gatekeeper—"

"I'll fix the gatekeeper. Now tell me, are there any books about Christianity?"

Niger looked blank. "Books? No. Why should there be books?"

"I see. Tell me another thing: are the rest of your church all like you?"

"Like me? Black? No."

137

"They may be pea-green for all I care. Are they all stupid? Have they all got slave souls?"

For a minute Niger didn't answer. Then he said, "I wasn't so stupid, long time back. When I was free. I could hunt wild beasts—angry, quick beasts. I could make all kinds of things— different things—I don't have the words for them here. I could dance."

Felicio put a hand on his arm. "And they knocked it all out of you and knocked the slave soul in. I know. A nice place, Rome. I understand the Christians are against it. . . . But you were born free. I've been a slave all my life, trying to get rid of my slave soul. Perhaps I shall manage to do that some time."

Felicio found the meeting quite interesting. He had met one or two of Crispus's slaves before, also Euphemia. It was a surprise to see women there at all.

He asked Manasses a good many questions, both at the time and later on when he happened to go over to the house with his master and was there for an hour while the two old men gossiped. They had been fixing up everything about Flavia and Candidus. Felicio would not promise Manasses anything; he would think it over.

At present he did not feel like joining the church. But he would certainly come again.

He was rather angry with Niger for being so upset that evening when Beric came in. The slave soul again. Nor did he himself rise and shuffle and stare at the young master. That was stupid.

The meeting was rather like the first one that he had been at. There was business: the dividing up of the church funds; where the next meeting was to be; what was happening at the other churches in Rome; who had come lately from Jerusalem or Ephesus; how Trophimos, who was due to go on a mission to Gaul but had caught some kind of fever in Miletus, was now better and probably on his way; about the book that the doctor was writing for them all; about Paul of Tarsus, who was held in the Mamertime on an appeal to the High Court from the governor of Judea.

Lalage had been to see him—anyone could who didn't mind the risk of being put onto the police blacklist. He had his own cell, with books and writing material and anything else he needed. Of course, he was a Roman citizen. That made all the difference.

She had asked him, as delegate from the church, two simple questions on what had actually happened at a certain point in the life of Christ.

"But I wonder if any of us really know," said Lalage, "even Paul."

"Did you say that to him, sister?" Manasses asked.

"More or less. And at first he was snappy, said I'd got my answer. Then he asked me if I thought it mattered. So I answered, in the name of our church—and I hope you'll say I was right, friends—that what we really wanted him to tell us wasn't so much how things happened but what was pushing them into happening."

"And what did Paul say?"

"He said in that sharp way he has, 'Now you're talking sense for once. Counting heads isn't for those who know, and knowing is a living, so tell your church to go on living in the Way, and that'll push things into happening all right.' So, you see, you can take it or leave it. I've given you just what he told me, and what Luke is going to write in his book about what happened when they were in the waste ground by Bethsaida. And I've given you what else he said."

Niger had thought it a lovely story, about the magic fishes and bread. He knew what he was going to believe. Rhodon was glad to know the exact number who had been fed. He wrote it down.

Between business, one or another might say something in the nature of a prayer, or as if they were speaking freely about what was in their spirit because they were among friends and it wouldn't be laughed at or used against them. Sophrosyne told them about a dream she'd had, and Phineas capped it with a story about a healing that he had heard from one of the old Nazarenes.

Then Manasses said, "There are two here who are with us but not of us. Not yet. Have Felicio or Beric any questions?"

Beric had been whispering questions at Argas on and off during the whole evening. He sometimes found the slave's Greek rather hard to follow, and there were special Christian words in the prayers that puzzled him. Now Argas told him to ask his questions out loud.

But Beric wouldn't. They'd got to get used to him before he'd stand up in the meeting.

Felicio asked a couple of questions and was answered. Then Manasses said that the two must go. As Beric got up, Argas unexpectedly kissed his bare arm. Beric was hoping desperately that they wouldn't all stand for him again. One or two did, but most of them just stared. *And I put on my oldest tunic on purpose,* thought Beric, *but I suppose it does look all wrong.*

He and Felicio met in the doorway and went out together. It was now so late that there was no one about and few lights to be seen in the houses. Beric wondered what to do. He rather wanted to walk the short way back by himself and think it all out, even to walk alone a little farther. But perhaps it would be better—more what it was all about, more like the Kingdom—to talk to this other person. Who might be lonely. Who might be a slave. With a certain effort he said, "Which way are you going, friend?"

"Up past the Esquiline," said Felicio and added, "You've not got far yourself."

"No," said Beric, a little uncomfortable because this other man knew all about him, who he was and where he lived, while he, on the other hand, had no idea about—what was his name?— Felicio. "I'm in no hurry. Would you care—shall we perhaps— walk part of the way back in your direction?"

"Certainly," said Felicio, "if you don't mind walking back with a slave."

"Of course not!" said Beric, realizing that his voice was rather overcordial but quite unable to get it right. *Silly fool,* he thought, *why does he need to make such a fuss about being a slave?*

"Was this your first time?" Felicio asked after a minute or two.

"Yes. I wish they hadn't all fussed about me so!"

"You can't blame us. It was like seeing—oh, a flying pig! Most of them haven't got steady minds. They're in this through their hearts, not their heads."

"And you?"

"I'm not one of them. I don't know yet if I'm going to be. I'm not sure what their concept of brotherhood really amounts to in practice. After all, it's something which has been put forward before. And not acted upon much."

"I suppose some of them—the Stoics—they talk a lot about poverty."

"But what they'd all love would be a philosopher-king ruling everyone with an iron rod. One of themselves!"

"No, Felicio, they'd be the Council behind him—" Beric was remembering all the talk he'd been hearing at Crispus's house for the last five years. "And he'd be a kind of dressed-up dummy to impress the masses. All for their own good, of course!"

"Even Plato saw that didn't work. When his precious philosopher-king at Syracuse started going the way of all kings. But the Romans are still hoping it's going to work with the next emperor—or the next but one."

"I suppose," said Beric a little doubtfully, "that there was more real brotherhood in the Garden than anywhere else."

"Yes. Epicurus had it himself. And some of his followers. But look what Rome's made of it! Their idea of happiness: eating and drinking and having women!"

"My old tutor," said Beric, suddenly thinking of him again, "was always supposed to be a Stoic. But he had a good many Epicurean ideas. He was a Greek, of course. I liked him."

"You had a proper Roman education, had you?"

"Yes. Look, Felicio, how do you know about me? Because you obviously do."

They were standing at a corner now. There was a full moon, and they could see one another very well. And through the blue moonlight there was a curious reddish glow in the sky to their right.

Felicio asked, "Do you mind?"

"I don't think so. Only I would like to know—"

"Whose slave I am. Well, I was there this morning at the betrothal, helping with the documents. I saw you. I belong to Lady Flavia's future father-in-law."

"You saw me, did you?"

"Yes." Felicio hesitated. "There was one moment when you looked so unhappy that I couldn't help supposing—for whatever reasons—you didn't like Aelius Candidus any more than I do."

Beric didn't answer. He put his arm up against the wall and leaned his forehead against it. He wondered how many more slaves knew what was happening to him! Would it have been any help or pleasure to box the ears of this one? Not actually, he decided.

Felicio went on, impersonally. "I don't suppose there is anyone in that church who has not been hurt. Quite badly hurt. I suppose you need some kind of knock before you're prepared to take it. Before, as they'd say, you were reborn. Or become adult. I'm not quite sure which. They tend to use these words that come from the heart rather than the head. Perhaps it's because I haven't had a knock that, though I like them, I'm probably not going to come in."

Beric had been given time to recover, to get away from himself. He said, "I don't like thinking that all those slaves of ours have been hurt. I know about Argas. Funny, the thing that seems to have hurt most was really quite small—having a book taken away from him. I suppose—I don't begin to know what things are like for them."

"You may yet," said Felicio, "and that will be interesting. Of course, it happened to a good many Greeks. Epicurus himself, for instance, lost everything in a war between states. And Plato was sold as a slave. But naturally his friends bought him back. And I very much doubt if he had to clean the boots even when he was a slave! But it doesn't happen to Romans. They're rather too secure. Except for their Great Big Divine Insecurity in the palace. Only that's different. But perhaps your own slaves will be able to tell you what's been done to them, so that you'll see. I don't suppose they've spoken to you yet as equals."

"No," said Beric, "only just now and then for a minute or two. And then it all goes. How do you manage it?"

"Well, I'm a secretary. I write people's letters for them. Take all their lies down in shorthand and then write them out beautifully. That doesn't leave you feeling so inferior. Besides, it's rather easy to feel morally and intellectually superior to Aelius Candidus."

142

"But all the same he might—hurt you."

"Yes, I know, and as a matter of fact, I dislike pain. But one can't pay too much attention to that sort of thing. For that matter, you might turn around now and beat me up. And you well might, by all the rules, for my speaking as I have."

"You don't think I would, do you?" said Beric quickly.

"No. You aren't a Roman. Perhaps you'll allow me to say I like you."

"I like you," said Beric, suddenly thinking that there was, after all, an element of seduction in it, on both sides. And then he noticed that the glow in the sky was getting wider and brighter. "There must be a big fire somewhere," he said.

"I don't wonder," Felicio said. "The whole place is as dry as tinder. No rain for a couple of months. And then some fool of a woman is a bit careless with a cooking pot. And a whole tenement goes up. And the people in the top rooms are popped off by the flames like so many lice."

"Yes, it's usually the poor quarters that suffer. I suppose the fire brigades aren't in such a hurry."

"Personally," said Felicio, "I shouldn't mind if the whole of Rome was burned down. If this judgment the Christians talk about meant that, there would be something to be said for it. Don't you think so?"

"If it was destroyed forever. With all that it stands for. Then there could really be brotherhood."

"Exactly. But, of course, it wouldn't be destroyed forever. The rich are always covered. And the poor not. So I'm doubtful whether we shall get brotherhood that way. You know, it looks like quite a large fire!"

"Yes. It must be up by the Circus Maximus. The glow's spreading. Oh, well, I expect they'll get it under soon."

8

Euphemia

Euphemia was a freedwoman. She had lived in a more or less legalized way with her old patron, and when he died he left her quite a handsome sum. But that was twenty years ago when she was young and pretty and a genuine blonde. A good deal of the legacy had gone, in the end, on the dowry for their daughter, who had married very respectably. Too respectably, Euphemia sometimes thought, for she hardly ever saw her daughter now or her two dear little grandchildren. They lived at Neapolis, but even when they visited Rome she couldn't help thinking her daughter was really rather ashamed of her and the shop and everything. And as to letters, it took Euphemia a week to write one, and what with one thing and another she never had time.

The rest of the legacy had gone in setting her up in business. Her first venture had been in Pompeii. They had lived near there. But somehow it wasn't quite the class of customer she liked. She wanted to have everything respectable. And at first, just because she was still nice-looking, people thought she was that sort.

So then she had moved to Rome and started in business again. There was nothing like Rome, not really. At first she'd stuck to perfumes, cosmetics, and hair oils, and had a couple of girls in the shop. She was still trying to be a lady, for her daughter's sake. But it didn't do. You'd got to run the place yourself, or you lost money all the time. Besides, she liked doing things with her own hands.

By that time she'd got her daughter's marriage fixed up, very suitably, with an old client of her father's, an official in the municipality of Neapolis. Once that was dealt with, Euphemia sold one of her girls and began to turn to herself. She fixed up a connection with one of the really good baths and would either visit customers there or at their own houses. Hair and nails were what she liked, though she could do a bit of taking out wrinkles and massaging away double chins.

But she never had anything to do with poisons, and as to her tonics, there was nothing in them that would hurt a fly—she really didn't go in for them, only made them up for old friends. And as to abortions, she just wouldn't touch them. There were always plenty who would and did, but not Euphemia.

She made the perfumes herself at the back of her shop, in her cozy little room with the two pictures on wood, one of her daughter wearing a bride's crown and veil—for she'd had everything there ought to be at that wedding—and the other of her old patron with a scroll in one hand and a gold cup in the other.

She used often to look at this picture, feeling puzzled. *He wasn't like that,* she'd say to herself. *I'm sure he wasn't. He was always hopping about after something. If he only hadn't taken his duties as magistrate so seriously, he mightn't have died when he did, nor so sudden. I'd only just time to run to him.*

Euphemia had lots of friends who used to come in and sit with her in that room while she was making up the perfumes and lotions and face paint, and some of them would tell her things. She'd think that she'd kept more of other people's secrets than any other woman in the Quarter.

Then Megallis, the girl who was still working for her, had gone and fallen in love with a decent young man, a tanner, and Euphemia had let him buy the girl out for not much more than half her real value. But there, they were ever so happy, and when Euphemia went over to their little house, it was more like a daughter's than her own girl's ever was.

And after that she didn't buy another slave. It was just as simple to shut up the shop when she went out to her customers with the neat basket on her arm with the clippers and razors and curlers and that. She made enough to live on and give a meal to a friend any day, and what more do you want?

There was only one time in her life that she didn't like thinking about. And yet, in a way, she did too. That was when she was still not so old, still had her daughter living with her and doing fine sewing at home and weaving her bottom-drawer linen, as a nicely brought up girl ought to do. And Euphemia had gone and fallen in love.

It was the real thing. Well, naturally she'd loved and respected her patron, but then he was nearly forty years older than she was, and that makes a difference. This time it was one of her customers. She could still remember those fingernails of his, ever so long, and terribly brittle—broke if you looked at them. What a lot of trouble she'd taken over that one set of nails! She didn't tell him, not for months, but wore her prettiest dresses and a flower and hoped he'd guess. And she kept on going to fortune-tellers, and if she'd had a chance she'd have slipped him a tonic—and not one of her own!—but she never had. And then she just couldn't keep it in any longer, and she told him. And he didn't take her seriously.

Well, that doesn't sound so much. But he said some nasty things. And laughed. And that was the end. Night after night she went to bed crying, and the girls got quite worried and kept on asking what was the matter. Nice girls they were, though she was always having to get after them to make them work. But it got her right down. She kept on wondering who was taking care of his nails now. Sometimes she thought, *If only I could tell somebody!* But she just couldn't. It was all making her feel so ashamed. You can stand getting booted out but not having made a fool of yourself! She tried not to see any of her old friends, even. She was afraid of their asking questions and being sorry for her and then perhaps laughing themselves afterward. It was just luck her running into Eunice. Or perhaps not luck. Perhaps something better than luck.

Eunice was still a slave in those days but knew she was going to be freed soon. At any time she was prepared to leave the house and start in business on her own. She knew she'd have to leave the boy, as he was wanted in the house, but Phaon was sure to be freed too, later on. And anyway, there was nothing in it. The boy could always run around the corner to see her. He was a little Tartar anyway—three or four years younger than Euphemia's girl and such a tease!

Well, it all just came out, and by the end she was crying on Eunice's shoulder like a girl her first time. And somehow she was

146

sure Eunice wouldn't laugh at her afterward behind her back. And then Eunice told her all about everything. Not all at once, of course, but now she couldn't remember how long it had taken. Only she suddenly realized that she'd stopped feeling ashamed and almost stopped feeling unhappy. And by and by she completely stopped. After that she came to the meetings regularly, regularly gave to the church funds, and was always ready to visit the sick or anything like that. Anything she felt she could do.

The only thing she could never manage was telling anyone about it herself. She tried to talk to her own daughter first, but she just didn't pay any attention, and now, with her husband in an official position, it would be ever so much more difficult. Later on, perhaps. And two or three times she'd meant to have a talk with Megallis, but somehow she never could get around to it. And anyway Megallis and her husband were so happy, and you can't have everything.

Of course, she hadn't got it right to start with. How could you? She hadn't realized, not for a long time—but that kind of thinking wasn't her game—how much it meant going against, really, all her old line of business. Because, after all, perfumes and that went directly against the Kingdom, the way they were used now anyway, just for pride and grab. It was a bit upsetting at first, having to see that. There were days she half hoped the coming of the Kingdom wouldn't be in her time. Or that it could all happen some magic way—in some other world or something—and she wasn't the only one in the churches to do a bit of that sort of fancying.

Well, it was all right if you kept it as fancy, but once she and some others began to let it get at them. That was when they used to go mostly to Aquila's house, on the other bank, and when Aquila found what was going on he had them all up and gave them a straight talk and showed them where it was going to lead. One or two dropped out after that, but not Euphemia. She repented and tried to think straight, with God's help.

Coming into the church had meant a whole lot of new friends for Euphemia—and best of all, Lalage. She couldn't always understand Lalage, but she did like listening to her. If one of her perfumes or powders had come out especially well, she'd always keep some for Lalage and put it into her hand after the meeting. Lalage often bought things from her too. Once she had come to the shop with Claudia Acte, and that was something to think about for days, but, of course, she couldn't expect Claudia Acte to buy anything. She didn't stock that class of goods.

At the end of that last meeting she had come out with Lalage, wanting to ask about that young man, for Lalage was the one who knew, and Euphemia had always wanted something like that for her! But they knew there was something wrong almost at once. There were people in the street talking and pointing. The fire had been going a couple of hours by then, and it was quite obviously in the direction of Lalage's room.

And Lalage thought about her dance dresses and her magpie and Sophrosyne's musical instruments and also about the girl on the third floor who was so silly sometimes. She pushed Sophrosyne into Euphemia's arms and ran straight up the street towards the fire like a deer.

Euphemia took Sophrosyne back with her to the little shop, telling her she was sure it was all right, bound to be.

All the others hurried off—Niger afraid he'd have to go a long way around because of the fire and might be late getting back and would catch it. The fire was nowhere near the Jewish Quarter, but Phineas was worrying about his wife all the same.

An hour or two later, Lalage came back to Euphemia's shop. She had scorched one hand, and there were spark holes burned in the front of her dress. She was very tired, and while Euphemia did up her hand, she said, "Everything gone. I'm sorry, Sophrosyne, all your instruments."

"No," said the old woman. "I kept my double flutes on me. I had a kind of whisper. So I'll be able to play for you, dear."

"I don't feel like ever dancing again," said Lalage. "It all just went up in one flame like—like hell. The third-floor girl who was going to have a baby, she tried to jump." Lalage shuddered. "The cobbler got his wife out, but he's lost everything. Well, he's a citizen; he won't starve. I don't know what happened to old Demetrius, and those kids from upstairs are all badly burned."

"What about your savings, dear?"

"They were all behind a brick in the chimney, Euphemia. They're gone. And my magpie. He was such company. And all my dresses. Well, Sophrosyne and I, we'll have to apply for the church funds now!"

"You tuck up on the bed, dear, and get a nice sleep," Euphemia said. "After all, you can stay here as long as you like. And there's all the brothers and sisters and all the love and joy we'll have yet. Oh, I can't say it like you could yourself, but this is what being a Christian's for, isn't it? You've got all of us, and you've got Him. And we'll have a special subscription for some new dance dresses for you!"

"Oh, I'm all right," said Lalage. But she was still thinking of the third-floor girl and how she hadn't quite died for what seemed like a very long time. Lalage had tried to move her, but it wasn't any use. That was how she'd got her hand scorched.

Suddenly Euphemia said, "Do you think it might be the judgment?"

"Yes," said Sophrosyne, "the flames that were foretold! Then He'll come back in a glory!"

But Lalage said, "How could it be? She was such a pretty girl, and there must have been dozens like her burned in the other tenements. That couldn't be the Will. Innocent, ordinary people."

"I've always liked looking on at fires," Euphemia said, "apart from anything nasty happening, I mean. I'd have gone with you now, if I hadn't had Sophrosyne with me. Of course, I haven't been to the arena since I was a Christian any more than any of us, and I never did like all that fighting and killing. But I did like races and sham fires and all that."

"This was a real fire," Lalage said. "It is still."

"I suppose it'll be a real fire when the judgment does come," Euphemia said. "I always thought so. Only it would be a fire up on the Palatine. All those big houses and the rich people running out screaming in their nightclothes, not able to save a thing. Screaming for mercy to us before the judgment gets them!"

"We'd give it, though," said Lalage. "I wouldn't send anyone to a fire. Now that I've seen one. This fire didn't have mercy. You could see through the windows how the staircases just boiled up into flames. They hadn't a chance! Let's pray."

All three of them prayed for quite a long time, and then Lalage dropped on the bed and was asleep in half a minute. Euphemia lifted her over nearer the wall. There was plenty of room for
two, and Sophrosyne shook down on the floor with some extra
blankets.

They expected the fire would be under by morning, but it
wasn't. What was more, it had got at the houses of the rich, even a
new wing of the palace on the Palatine. But Euphemia didn't think
it was the judgment any longer. She was a bit worried about her
own little place. And it wasn't only the fire; people were getting
panicky and nasty. Already there were the beginnings of looting.
Euphemia put up her shutters and prayed.

9

The Sign of the Cross

By the middle of the next day, the fire was blazing in half a dozen new places where sparks had been blown, and water was so low in all wells and cisterns that the fire brigade couldn't do much. They concentrated on pulling down houses so as to isolate the fires and keep them from spreading, especially to the better-class business and residential districts.

But even so, a great many respectable people who owned old houses in the Palatine and Esquiline districts were burned out. And it was here that most of the looting took place. And sometimes in the smell and panic of fire, an owner would find himself uncomfortably and unexpectedly jostled by slaves who were more afraid of being burned alive than of their master.

Most of the big households beyond the fire area sent out working parties to help. Balbus sent a number, including his litter slaves, which really showed that he was prepared to make a personal sacrifice. Actually, his house was on the farther side of the Esquiline, and there were moments when the fire came unpleasantly near. In fact he had a good many of his best objets d'art, jewels, and plate packed ready to be taken away at a moment's notice. Felicio was kept busy cataloging them. But fortunately he did not, in the end, have to do anything drastic. The Praetorians, of course, were out, keeping order. Candidus had dealt with several looters. You couldn't be too squeamish where property was concerned.

Crispus's house, which was just beyond the forum of Augustus, was also unpleasantly near the fire. You couldn't help smelling it all the time, and two of his most tedious old female cousins, whose house had been burned, were taking refuge with him and would probably stay indefinitely.

Here Beric organized the working party and himself went out directing and working with it. He took almost all the able-bodied slaves except Manasses and Phaon; Crispus really didn't want to send his dancing boys. And there must be someone in the house.

The working parties managed to get a fairly large area cleared, mostly slums. They came back filthy from their shifts. Of course they were pulling down people's homes, and often they had to deal with screeching old furies who couldn't be made to realize that the great houses had to be protected at all costs. There were several relief camps for them to go to, not to speak of relatives in the country. Food had been requisitioned for them, they could take any furniture and household goods that they could carry, and anyhow if their houses had been burned they would have been even worse off!

The Jewish Quarter across the Tiber, which was in no danger itself, sent out relief and working parties, and prepared to take in refugees, especially Jewish ones. Phineas and Rhodon both volunteered. Rhodon organized an extremely efficient working party and was at it all day. Barnabas let him off work and had a good meal waiting for him when he got back.

These working parties had to deal with looters too. Sometimes they tied them up and left them for the fire to get them—unless someone else was merciful. Rhodon tried to get his gang not to do that, but sometimes he was so angry with the thieves that he wanted to himself.

But once he stumbled over a man who had been tied up, obviously a thief, and the man called out his name. Rhodon did not recognize him, but it was the Armenian Abgar, who had been on the ship with him. Rhodon loosed him, told him if he was caught looting again he couldn't expect to get mercy a second time, and then decided he'd got to give the man his address—he looked half-starved.

Beric and his party were pulling down the houses in the dip between them and the Esquiline. A good many people had left. While they were pulling down an empty slum shack at the back of a tenement, which would have gone at a spark—Beric had no idea before of what was behind even the decent-looking poor streets, every inch of space crammed and stinking—they came on a charcoal scrawl on the wall. A fish.

One of the men with Beric said, "Look, sir, there's been one of these filthy Christians here. Left his mark, he has," and put his pick through it. He added, "If you ask me, they're the sort that would start a fire."

That wasn't the only time Beric heard something of the sort either. Everyone naturally wanted to blame someone or something for the disaster. Some people even said it had been done by the emperor's orders because he wanted to turn Rome into Athens, make them all into a set of Greek pansies like he'd got in the palace already!

And there was some story about that when he came back from his countryseat at Antium, which he did the moment he got news of the fire, he sent at once for his favorite architects and told them to get out plans for rebuilding Rome. Wanting to change things, Nero was! Even Rome. Of course, that was obvious nonsense, but it showed that the emperor was unpopular with the ordinary man in the street as well as with the Stoic senators. And oddly enough, the admirable way that Nero organized the relief camps and kept down the prices of food made no difference. The people in the camps were so wretched that they had to blame someone, and those who were preparing to make a nice thing out of corn and meal were naturally even more annoyed.

Other people said that the fire was sent as a punishment for neglecting the old gods, the gods of Rome, and was all due to the way the women had gone traipsing off after foreign gods and mysteries and neglecting their duty. They were delighted when the big temple of Isis and Serapis went up, whereas the Capitol remained unhurt. And Beric heard two or three people say that it was the Christians, who were known to have no respect for anything, who had started all this, a pack of Levantine seditionists!

Beric hadn't any time to talk to Manasses or Argas. He'd had his hands full running things. He enjoyed the physical work and was a great deal better at it than the comparatively underfed slaves, who simply couldn't keep up with him. Besides he had the best ax.

Crispus came out to watch what was going on. The boy was on the top of a roof, cutting through the main beam and shouting down directions to the others. *I must send him off to the army soon,* Crispus thought. Indeed, this was what had been planned all along and taken for granted. But he had kept putting it off.

It had been pleasant having Beric in the house, almost like the son who'd never lived. He'd come to depend on the boy for all kinds of little things. But it wouldn't do to go on. Wouldn't be fair not to send Beric off to the army this year. He had found out about getting him his citizenship; that was done from time to time on a senatorial recommendation. He could say honestly that the boy would make a valuable soldier and servant of the State, and the thing was practically certain to be put through. Then he could be started off as senior centurion in a decent legion—nothing too smart, of course, but where he'd learn his job thoroughly. One would have to make inquiries.

And then, well, most likely his next service would be in Britain, helping the authorities there, and there'd be no chance of his coming back to Rome for years. *And I'm getting old,* thought Crispus. But the boy would have to take whatever service was decided on for him. You can't think of yourself in these matters. Well, it must be done, and soon.

There'd been that awkward moment with Candidus. Couldn't blame young Candidus, of course. After all, Beric had no real status in Rome or in the household. Less than a freedman's actually. Perhaps he oughtn't to have let himself get so fond of the boy.

Crispus knew, and Beric did not, that the eldest of Caradoc's sons, Rudri, had proved unsatisfactory and had to be got rid of. You couldn't risk any centers of discontent in the provinces. But the second one, Clinog, who was seven or eight years older than Beric, had been very teachable and had been successfully educated at Arretium in Roman methods of government, so that he could, if necessary, be sent to Britain some day as a good Romanizing influence, with the added prestige of being one of the royal family.

Perhaps he had better arrange for Clinog and Beric to meet some time. Yes, he would see to all that as soon as Flavia's wedding was over. And then he would be left without any young people in the house. And that reminded him, he had kept on promising dear old Eunice that he would do something definite about Phaon's freedom.

Well, at any rate, nothing could be done till after the fire. What a disaster! All those poor wretches. He decided to make a handsome contribution to the fire relief fund. Indeed, all good Stoics were doing so.

But the day he had seen the fish scrawled on the wall, Beric told Argas to come and see him later on.

Argas, who was pretty exhausted with levering and pulling, nodded. He wished he could get into a lovely hot bath, as Beric certainly would, and lie in it. Still, Manasses would probably have got him a basinful anyway. You couldn't get really clean, though, that way, nor the smoke properly out of your eyes, and when he went, later in the evening, to Beric's room, he was neither as clean and comfortable as the Briton, nor had he had such a good supper.

However, he didn't say so. He stood waiting, not knowing what he was wanted for or whether Beric still thought of him at all as a brother.

Beric was sitting on his bed. There were a couple of chests by the wall, a lamp at the headboard, and a curtain over the door space. That was plenty. "Look, Argas, I've got something to ask you. Come on over and sit."

Argas came over, glad of the friendliness in Beric's voice, and sat down on the floor beside him. He was, anyway, not clean enough to sit on Beric's bed.

"What exactly was that fish sign on the wall we pulled down?"

Argas stiffened. "Don't you know?"

"I wouldn't ask you if I did."

That bothered Argas. Beric wouldn't have asked him—wouldn't have spoken friendly. He turned his floundering mind back onto the fish, the immediately calming and strengthening sign. "The Greek letters for fish—they stand for the Name words: Jesus Christ, God's Son, Savior." Merely repeating the words steadied him, steadied his voice. What did it matter even if the Briton was only a master, compared with that?

"Are there any other signs?" Beric asked.

"You know the cross sign, the sign of the poor." He hesitated, then said firmly, "That's been our sign of—of brotherhood—since Spartacus's time, anyway."

"Why?"

"He died for the people too, on the cross. And six thousand of his men. They were crucified all along the Appian Way, drying up in the sun and dying slow for three days. Haven't you heard?"

"I suppose I have. But it didn't stick in my mind. They were just rebels."

"They were. They were slaves rising against their masters mostly. But the masters won. They'd got the arms and the money. They could last out and cut off the food supplies from overseas. They were bound to win. That's one reason against murder. Against me murdering you."

Argas felt Beric's hand on his shoulder, trying perhaps to stop him. But he was going on now! Beric had to know. "So we remember Spartacus. There's stories about him going around. In your own backyard, the whispering you don't hear. When someone's been whipped and can't sleep, lies on his face moaning a bit, and the man next to him wakes and curses him, and then starts telling the stories. For comfort in pain and dark. Spartacus and Eunus and Kleomenes of Sparta and Nabis—and above all, Jesus Christ. They were all of them for the oppressed ones, the common people. It's been going on always for five hundred years. Maybe longer. I don't know.

"Kleomenes was a king, but he freed the slaves in Sparta and divided the land. But the rich got him in the end, and he was killed and flayed and staked in Egypt. And the signs for Kleomenes are a snake and a vine and a cup. Nabis was king of Sparta too, afterwards, but he made the revolution again that had stopped when they got Kleomenes, and he killed the rich. And it would have been all right in Sparta, only the Romans were called in from the outside. The Achaean League—they were the other cities in Hellas that were rich and frightened in case it happened to them!—they made that betrayal. But they brought the Romans down on themselves too. They hadn't thought of that!

"When I was a boy we used to throw stones at the Achaean League processions, and now I know why my father used to laugh when we did it. So then the Romans came and helped the rich against King Nabis, and he was murdered, and all who'd been in his revolution were hunted down and killed and sold. And they thought they'd got it under for ever. The sign for Nabis is an ax."

"I didn't hear it like that in my history lesson!" said Beric, protesting.

"No," said Argas, "you wouldn't. After that, leaders weren't kings. Eunus and Spartacus were slaves themselves, and what they did was from below, from the very bottom. Both of them died for the slaves and died by torture. Eunus was a slave and a prophet, and he foretold the Kingdom. He and his friends Kleon and Achaeus, they held all Sicily against Rome and the masters, and the free laborers sided with them too, for they'd felt oppression on their own bodies. They and the slaves held Sicily for a year."

"But, Argas," Beric interrupted, "they did the most horrible things in Sicily, those rebels. I know that!"

Argas, who had been leaning against the bed, speaking softly, looking rather away from Beric into the shadows of the room, now turned and caught hard hold of Beric's knees, one with each hand, and spoke straight at him. "Wouldn't *you* do horrible things—wouldn't you murder and burn and who knows what else if you'd been a slave like they were?

"Not one of them hurt the girl who'd been kind to them, though she was the daughter of the worst of the masters! But there was no mercy for them. They were nailed and tortured and thrown down the cliffs to die, broken, in the sun. And it was the same for Spartacus. So their sign is the cross, and wherever that goes the thing isn't dead, though the masters may think it is! But we remember."

Beric looked down at Argas with something like horror. He wasn't really clean, not around his eyes and ears, and there was a cut on his hand that was festering. Beric said, "That's only one side."

"But it's our side. And you made our sign."

"I wish you hadn't told me, Argas! You're making me feel—a traitor—to Crispus and everything I've belonged with."

"You don't belong there now. You belong with us."

"I didn't know the sign meant—that."

"You know now. And it means the Kingdom. Because that always happened a little. When Kleomenes and Nabis freed the helots who'd been slaves for hundreds of years. When Spartacus and his men were fighting for freedom. Yes, and when they were all on the cross, dying together. Only we didn't know what to call it before."

"Jesus wasn't a slave."

"No, nor He wasn't a king either! For all that the Nazarenes say, He came from the house of David, and He was called King of the Jews on the cross. Some people say He was a very poor man to begin with. But He wasn't that either. He was in between, a craftsman, the kind that get security from their craft because it's bound to be wanted anywhere. But all the same, He made Himself one with us."

"*And* with the kings!"

"Very likely. But the kings had to suffer too. It's no pleasure being the kind of king that chooses to die for the people."

"It's no pleasure being a king against Rome."

"No. What's it like being a king's son, Beric?" Argas had let go of Beric's knees and was sitting back on his heels, the way he'd been the first time, on the floor in the dirty water.

"It's not like that," said Beric. "It's—it's nothing now. My father wouldn't have died for his people. He would have led them all right and died in battle. But that's not the same thing. He didn't think of them like your kings did. He didn't love them."

"But if you went back now—"

"They wouldn't have me. I can't speak British, even!"

"You don't belong there, then. You belong to us. Like I said."

"But, Argas, I don't know if I'll join. I don't know if I want to join!"

"You must. You're going to, aren't you? You can't go back now. Not after I've told you what—what no other master in Rome—" His voice was trembling.

Beric said quickly, "But surely all the slaves don't know this?"

"No. Not like I've said it. Not clear. But most Greeks know about Kleomenes and Nabis. And about Agis, the other one, the king that was betrayed by a kiss from his rich friend and was killed in front of his mother and grandmother. And most from Italy and Sicily know about Spartacus and Eunus. But the barbarians don't know, not at first anyhow. And we Christians are careful about telling, because we've got the final thing, where it's all made plain at last. Where we know it's not as simple as killing, but something that the masters can't win against. And now you know, Beric. As though you'd been one of us."

Beric didn't know what to say or think. What would a Stoic say? That it was all nonsense, womanish? He seemed to remember that this King Kleomenes was a Stoic. Only he'd heard the story differently. He hadn't bothered much with Greek history anyway. Roman history was bad enough! He'd read about those slave revolts, how for a few years the escaped brutes had definitely threatened order and security and civilization. Till they were put down. Why hadn't Lalage warned him what the sign of the cross meant? She must have known!

He looked at Argas again. Argas was tired out. Beric was a bit stiff himself but not tired like that. And what else? Was Argas afraid now, frightened at having told him?

He got up and began walking about the room and became aware that Argas was following him with his eyes, watching to see what he'd do. Beric kept at a certain distance. He was afraid that if he let Argas touch him, or if he touched Argas, he would commit himself, out of pity, out of a feeling together that was very alarming, that he had never had before. Not with Flavia. Never in any casual encounter. Something that was not of the mind only, that was also of the body, but in some new way.

He said, "Don't be frightened of me, Argas. Whatever you've said, and whatever I say. And tell me when the next meeting is. I'll come."

Argas was now no longer upright but crouching down, his hands on the floor. He didn't answer.

"What's the matter?" Beric asked.

Argas muttered something.

Beric had to kneel beside him, to touch him. "Go on, tell me!"

At last Argas, not looking up, said, "I'm hungry."

"Haven't you had supper?"

"Only what we always get. Bread and soup. No meat. And we've not just been standing about all day! And I thought there'd be something over from your dinner, but there wasn't."

Beric remembered guiltily that he hadn't left a bit of the steak, but he didn't say so. "Those idiots in the kitchen! Go on down and tell them I say you're to have some meat."

"No," said Argas, "they're saying already that I'm your little pet. I won't."

"Fools," said Beric. "Then I suppose I must. No, it's all right. You stay here."

He went into the kitchen and collected some cooked sausages and bread, while the cooks fussed around, apologizing for not sending enough dinner. Beric said, "I hope you're giving meat to my working party when they come back at night?"

"They don't need it, sir. I'm giving them some nice bean soup—"

"Meat, I said."

"The price of meat's gone up, sir. You've no idea! I can't always get it in the market, even—"

"Well, you chase around a bit, hear me? And if you don't, I'll chase you." Beric stalked back with his sausages.

The cook wasn't used to being talked to like that by the Briton, who wasn't even a citizen, whom he remembered as a crying brat who couldn't speak Latin! But he had apparently grown up. The cook shrugged his shoulders and supposed he must give the slaves some meat the next day.

Beric gave the food to Argas, who bit into it hungrily. It was fully as good as bits of lukewarm steak, mostly the fat and gristle from the dining-room. He pulled Argas's hair, gently. "Better?"

Argas looked up and nodded, then held out the half-eaten bread and sausage. "You have some."

"I'm not hungry."

"Have a little. Please—Beric."

There appeared to be something urgent and special about it. "What are you after now, Argas? More magic?" However, he took the stuff and bit off a little piece, carefully biting where Argas himself had bitten. At least he could show him that much brotherhood! He gave it back. "Well, what's that done to me?"

"It's—it's like something—that we want you to know. Later. Soon." Argas finished the rest quickly and stood up. "See you tomorrow on the job."

"That's it. Good night, Argas." Beric yawned, thinking it was time he turned in, ready for tomorrow too. He noticed that the hand he'd had on Argas's hair was grimy with dust and black ashes.

10

The First Sacrament

On the sixth day, when it seemed as if the fire were under and people were beginning to take things easier, it broke out again in two other quarters, and there was worse panic than ever, especially as one outbreak was near the biggest relief camp. Everyone was onto fire duty again. Most Christians didn't even get time for the meeting the next evening.

The churches were buying food and blankets with their relief funds; a great many Christians had been burned out and had to be looked after. There were widows and orphans too. Eunice had taken in several children, some of whom were old enough to help her with the bakery. She was working for a public relief committee, and her oven was going the whole time.

Euphemia would have liked to take in some, but, besides Lalage and Sophrosyne, she now had Megallis and her husband. Their home had been burned as well as the tannery where he had worked.

It had been a bit embarrassing at first, as it meant that the three Christians couldn't pray or talk openly in front of the others, and old Sophrosyne was apt to come out with things. But one afternoon when the young man, Tertius Satellius, was out on a municipal working party, for which at least he got a small amount of pay, Megallis, who was helping Euphemia to cook dinner, said to her, "You're a Christian, aren't you?"

"Whatever makes you say such a thing?" Euphemia answered quickly.

But perhaps not quite convincingly, for Megallis, who was a pretty, dark little Sicilian, said, "You don't think I'd put on an act— not after what you've done for the two of us?"

"Well—" said Euphemia.

"You are, you are!" said the girl and hugged her. "You know, we've often wondered. It wasn't your lot that started this fire, was it?"

"We wouldn't ever do a thing like that. None of us."

"I didn't think so. When we didn't know where to go except you, and when my man started off on that story, I said, 'Well, if they're all like her, it's just flat nonsense!'" She blew on the charcoal under the cooking pot, then, not looking up, she said, "I stole some of your money once. I did mean to put it back some day, I really did, only then I didn't."

"Well, there," said Euphemia, "I did think it went a bit fast once or twice, but I kept putting off doing my accounts. You know I am absent-minded! Don't you fret yourself about it now, my dear." And she began to bustle about and put the vegetables on to stew.

Sapphira and Phineas had taken in a Jewish Christian woman whose husband had been killed. She had a child about the same age as their eldest. Rhodon's old master had a couple of Jewish refugees. And so it went on.

The Armenian, Abgar, had come to see Rhodon. He had been in a fish-curing factory on the coast—hard and sore work during the curing season and not much to eat out of it. Abgar had run away to Rome but found no work and nothing much to live on there. He'd hung around fighting for scraps with others like himself. The fire was a godsend to him and his gang. Then he'd been caught. He didn't much like being a free man the way he was. Could he work for Rhodon?

For the moment Rhodon said he could take him into his working party. He gave him a meal, and then—regretfully, but it had to be done—also gave Abgar his spare sandals and a decent tunic instead of the charred rags he'd got on.

But by the end of the ninth day, the fire was definitely over. There was a good deal of clearing up to be done still, and everyone was busy, either working or grumbling.

Balbus had two friends and their households staying with him, and Crispus had his cousins and theirs. He was thinking of taking them down to his country estate as soon as this was all over. They should stay there till something could be done. He'd take Beric too and have a talk to the boy about his future.

In a few days it was time for another meeting, and Manasses

told Beric. As Eunice was so busy, it was to be at Crispus's house, in the boiler room.

After Crispus and the cousins had gone to bed, Beric went down there by the winding stair from the kitchen. There were three brick furnaces at the back, with lead pipes going up from them. It was an irregularly shaped room, built among the foundations of the house, with rough brick and stone pillars at the sides. In the middle there was a big, round chopping block, the bole of an old tree trunk. Some cut wood was lying in one corner. There were a couple of rough benches, one by the chopping block and the other by the stair, and two small pottery lamps, one by the stair and the other on the block. Beric brought down another with him.

Manasses, Phaon, and Dapyx were there, and Dapyx grinned nervously when Beric came in. Also Euphemia, Lalage, and Sophrosyne—Beric was very glad to see Lalage again. He had heard what had happened and started saying how sorry he was.

But Lalage was quite cheerful again and asked him to try and get her some more jobs as soon as possible after things settled down.

Then Niger came down, but said that Felicio wouldn't come. It wasn't what he wanted, but all the same he told the guards for Niger. Then Rhodon came, explaining that Phineas hurt himself a bit on his working party. It was nothing much, but Sapphira wanted to keep him in bed for a day or two. Manasses said that Josias, too, had been hurt. A beam had crashed and knocked him down, and he was rather badly bruised. He'd be all right, too, in a few days. They weren't sure if Argas would be able to come. He and a few others were still out on a special working party digging about for some gold plate that the cousins insisted must be in the ruins of their house. So the slaves were having to dig by torchlight.

No one else came, though they waited for a few minutes, so they had the first prayer, the main one. Beric knew it by heart now.

Rhodon had begun explaining something else when Sotion came in, saying, "Peace be with you."

Manasses answered, "And with you, Sotion. We've had the first prayer. God is with us." He put an arm across Niger's shoulders. Niger was already beginning to look less unhappy.

"Thirsty work collecting rents these days," Sotion said, putting his bundle down, "with everyone complaining that their little savings have been burned up in the fire!"

"Yes, like mine!" said Lalage. "But you must feel wretched collecting rents these days. I suppose you've got to, though. Working on a percentage, are you?"

"It means I can put a little into the bag," said Sotion and did so.

"It's nearly empty," said Manasses, rather worried, "and we've got so many to see to!"

Beric, who was standing next to Lalage, whispered, "Couldn't I help? Would they let me?"

"All in good time," Lalage answered. "They'll be happier about it after you're baptized. We all know you're with us, Beric. When you're baptized, you'll be part of us."

"Yes, I see," Beric said. She was taking it for granted that he was going to be baptized. He wasn't sure about that, but he did want to help!

Somebody else came in now, carrying a lantern. He was a middle-aged man with a short beard, wearing a cloak with a silver pin over a good, plain tunic. Manasses went to him at once, looking very pleased.

"Who is he, Lalage?" Beric whispered again.

"He's Luke, the doctor, Paul's friend—you know, our Paul who's appealed to Caesar."

Manasses had asked at once for news of Paul, and Luke was answering. "As good news as you can expect of a prisoner. His health's no worse, and there's no question of them stopping him seeing people. They still let me fetch and carry for him, thank God. But he's asked me to go around to all the churches and see how things are. See that nothing's being let down. For we may be in for a bad time."

"What sort of a bad time?" Manasses asked.

"Well," said Luke, "someone's going to be made to take the blame for this fire. And they want to get rid of us anyhow. They say we're a danger to the State, and so we are, of course, though perhaps not in quite the way they think. But the shopkeepers have begun saying that we're dangerous foreigners, preaching sedition against the State and paid for it with foreign money. It won't be difficult to make them believe that it was we who burned Rome."

"So long as it's only the shopkeepers!"

"It won't be," Luke said. "Now, tell me, how's your church, Manasses? Sure your people are safe? We'll have plenty of false witnesses against us."

"I think so," Manasses said anxiously. "You've seen most of them, Luke."

Luke looked around, lifting his lantern. He saw Beric. "Who's that?" he asked.

Lalage said, "His name's Beric. I'm guardian for him, Luke."

"Beric? A Gaul?"

"No. A Briton," Beric answered.

"A Briton, speaking Greek with that accent? Strange."

Manasses said, "He's our young master, Luke. I'll be guardian for him too."

Luke, holding up the lantern, looked very close at Beric, who blushed slowly. "You think he'll do, Lalage? Even in times like these?"

"Yes," said Lalage, "I'm sure."

"When are you baptizing him?"

"We've not got that far," Manasses said. "But he knows the Words and the Way of Life. And I thought, this evening, we might try him on the water."

"Very good," said Luke. "May I stay for a little, brothers and sisters?"

They all said yes, and Luke sat down on the bench by the stairs.

Beric was wondering what was going to happen. He didn't like to ask. He felt them all looking at him, and he very much wanted to do the right thing by them all, to make them feel that they were right to trust him.

Manasses came back with a pottery bowl of water, a small oil jar, and some clean rags.

"What is it?" Beric whispered to Lalage.

"He's going to wash your feet, Beric," Lalage explained. "It's one of the funny things we do, to remind us that we're all one another's servants. Jesus did it."

166

"Sit down, friend," Manasses said.

Beric sat, feeling most uncomfortably serious and tense, and began to take off his sandals.

But Manasses pushed his hand away and undid them himself. "I do this first," he said, "because I'm the deacon and so I ought to try to be most like Jesus Himself."

Beric was finding it unexpectedly moving. Manasses, kneeling in front of him began to pour the oil for the washing. Suddenly Beric half laughed and leaned over. "No need to waste oil, Manasses—I had a bath this morning!"

Manasses looked up. He was half laughing too, and so were Lalage and Phaon, who had overheard.

How nice of them to laugh, Beric thought. *It's all going to be friendly after all!*

"Yes, I know about your bath," Manasses said. "I helped to fill it!" Then he went on, under his breath, "Will you try and help the others to feel easy with you? It's strange for them. You know, you being one of the kind that has a bath every morning."

"I'll try, Manasses," said Beric, "but I don't feel quite easy myself, you know. Do I wash yours now?"

"No, you're the newcomer," Manasses answered and dried his feet on the rags, "but when we've all had our turn on you, you can have your turn on us. If you like."

It made Beric feel shaken up, the idea of that, and yet in a certain way, rather happy. "Yes, I would like to," he said.

Euphemia was kneeling in front of him now. "Very nicely trimmed toenails, I must say. Never mind me, dear—it's just professional."

"What is your profession?" Beric asked shyly but wanting to help, as Manasses had told him to. "Hair and nails?"

"Oh, you are quick, dear!" she said. "You could tell it was the nails, but fancy your guessing it was hair too! There, nice and dry, dear."

"Thanks most sincerely," Beric said.

Sophrosyne came next. She said nothing, only murmured to herself. Then Lalage. It made him feel stranger yet, her hands on his feet.

As she did it, she said, half to herself, "I wonder what sort of bad time Paul meant. What would be the worst things that could happen to us?"

"Separation," said Manasses, standing behind Beric, speaking slowly as he thought it out. "Breaking us up. I don't mean some of us drifting away; that's bound to happen, perhaps. And I don't mean one here and there sold to another master. But if we were broken up altogether, so that not even two or three could gather together—so that we wouldn't be sure He was in the midst. Not just shutting yourself away from the brothers for a time, to be alone and face God, and then coming back. But being cut off from everything. If one was cut off like that and then hurt—badly hurt—alone, tortured and killed. Like He was."

"But at the very last He wasn't left alone," said Lalage, drying Beric's feet, "nor should we be."

Rhodon was the next, and he didn't say anything. Beric wondered what his job was. He had obviously been on fire duty. The others talked a little, in low voices. Luke was watching. Niger came then and suddenly looked up and said, with a lovely wide grin, "Looks funny, don't they, my black hand on your white legs!"

Beric laughed too. He had no idea who or whose Niger was but saw the heavy slave-ring and iron cuff; none of the slaves in their household would have had that. Did this wild, black creature know about Kleomenes and Spartacus? He couldn't ask now. Perhaps later, when—if—he knew them all better.

Now Sotion came. "What made you one of us, brother?"

Beric very much wanted to answer any of them honestly, but yet he couldn't speak of Flavia and Candidus. If it *had* been that. He was beginning not to be sure now. "I suppose it was what Lalage told me. And then everything that's been happening."

"Yes," said Sotion, "the fire! It's so like what we've always hoped for, in a way, isn't it?"

"I don't think so," said Beric, a little upset. "I've been on a working party!"

Sotion got up, and Beric saw Manasses whispering to Dapyx, who obviously didn't want to come. He tried to think of something to say that would stop Dapyx being afraid of him, forever. But he couldn't, and, as Dapyx finally knelt, he saw that his hands were shaking. Beric was so terribly sorry for him that he nearly cried. The boil on the man's neck was practically healed. His hair had been cropped with a kitchen knife and was all in ugly edges.

Beric leaned nearer and whispered, "Dapyx, do you know about Spartacus?"

Dapyx went absolutely still, like a hare so terrified you nearly step on it. His fingers in the water stiffened.

Beric hadn't wanted to do that to him. He said, "They died for you. That's something to be proud of."

But Dapyx never looked up, only he finished quick, dabbing unskillfully at Beric's feet with the now damp rags.

Then it was Phaon, the youngest. He whispered, "I always get the best of it because I wash last! But Dapyx—oh, he was a treat! We had to change the water twice. I say, are you really going to go through with it?"

"I hope so, Phaon," Beric whispered back. "Is there any order I ought to do it in?"

"It doesn't matter, only begin with Manasses. Aren't you going to think it's beastly?"

"I don't believe I am, Phaon, but I can't think why!"

"That's Jesus getting into you," Phaon said. "Oh, Beric, it's going to be lovely!" He looked up with a face of sheer delight. If he could only have done a dance like that, Beric thought suddenly, he'd have had us all after him! "Now come and get clean water and rags," Phaon said and pulled Beric's hand.

They went up the twisting stairs to the kitchen for the things. Beric passed Luke, watching him, and wondered if they were going to talk him over. He hoped they'd like him! He came back with the basin and said uncertainly to Manasses, "May I wash your feet, brother?"

Gravely Manasses sat down on the bench, and Beric knelt and undid his sandals. It was a strange mixed feeling. He'd never be the same again, never able to be a master. A kind of panic caught him, and he stopped, holding onto the edges of the basin, his head down. Then he realized that it was too late to get out of it now and began to touch Manasses' feet, which were reasonably clean, with fairly steady hands.

169

Manasses was the deacon of the church. Doing this for him, he had accepted it, accepted the superior position of Manasses, who was, all the time, the old Manasses who waited on him at the table. There was something not very real about it all. He dried Manasses' feet. He felt dizzy with this unreality. Then he got what he needed, for Manasses laid his two real and certain hands on Beric's head and blessed him in the name of Jesus and this church.

Manasses took his hands away, and Beric stood up, feeling extremely glad about everything, knowing he had done right, looking all around, seeing suddenly wood or human hands or pieces of material solid and real in the live, soft circles of lamplight, seeing the odd-shaped room full of men and women who were his friends. He said in a loud and surprising voice, "Come on now, who wants a wash?"

They all laughed, and some of them came closer and touched him. One after the other sat on the bench, and he washed their feet with a kind of delight that there was no accounting for but that was sufficient in itself.

Lalage had the most beautiful feet, with high insteps and strong flexible toes. Beric kissed her feet as well as washing them. He could at the moment see no reason against doing anything he wanted to do. Sophrosyne's feet were old and white. Rhodon's feet had interesting scars on them; Beric asked him what they were, and he explained that they were from burning metal. Sotion had a corn. Euphemia's feet were well-kept but dull. Niger's feet had a different shape from the others.

Again Beric said so out loud, and Niger laughed and said it came of walking so much.

"Walking where?" asked Beric.

"Between my master's houses and yours."

"Why?" It just seemed a funny thing to do.

Niger said, "I belong to Aelius Balbus. I carry his litter."

"Do you really?" said Beric. How very odd it would be if Balbus knew he was washing the feet of one of his litter slaves! All these feet walking in and out of his hands. The real feet of real people. Some of them had ashes on them, some only dust and ordinary dirt. What was he doing?

170

It was Dapyx now, and as Beric picked up the oil flask this time, he began to lose the feeling of irresponsibility and lightness. He began to see things as they were, and Dapyx's feet were not only very dirty but one of them had a nasty sore place on it. The water in the bowl was dirty too, filmed at the top with oil and ashes. He oughtn't to have gone on using it!

"You wait," he said to Dapyx. "I'll get some fresh water."

"This is all right," Manasses said a little anxiously, but Beric wasn't going to be put off.

"No, it's not," he said and went up to the kitchen for some more.

"What do you think, Luke?" Lalage asked.

"Very interesting," said Luke. "I'll just stay and see it out."

Beric came back with the clean water. He felt perfectly ordinary now, very matter of fact. He rubbed the oil thoroughly all over Dapyx's feet. Had he done that with the others? He couldn't remember. Silly to have to wash one's dirty feet in a wretched little bowl like this instead of a proper bath. But none of the slaves had the use of the big marble bath with the running water. If they'd been caught in it they'd have been very severely punished. Manasses probably went to the public baths sometimes, but not Dapyx. He wouldn't have the money. So, naturally, his feet were dirty. But they were a good deal cleaner now, anyway.

Beric touched a scar on his ankle. "What's that?"

"Chains," said Dapyx, very low.

Beric began drying the feet. He'd made a good job of them, though they weren't very nice feet, even now. But the sore place worried him. He didn't want to put back Dapyx's filthy, broken sandal over it. "I think I'll tie a bit of rag around that," he said, half aloud.

For the first time, Luke got up and came over and knelt beside Beric, looking at the foot in the better light of his lantern. "Wait a minute," he said. "I've got some ointment here." He fumbled about for it in the purse he wore at his belt.

Beric, looking at last from feet to face, saw Dapyx staring at him, in the old bewildered fright. "What is it, brother?" Beric said. Still the man did not move.

It was stupid; it couldn't be left like this! Beric began to talk to him. "Now listen, Dapyx, and try to be sensible. You still think nothing is altered between us except some magic. But everything's altered. I wouldn't be washing your feet for any magic! I do it because of our being in the Kingdom together, and you're stopping me getting into the Kingdom by hating me and fearing me still. I've washed your feet to show you that this is nonsense. Have you got to try and keep me out of the Kingdom?"

Dapyx still looked bewildered but in a rather different way. "You mean that?"

"Why else am I here?" said Beric. "I'm a Christian."

Dapyx gasped and said, "Then—I stop hating you."

"About time too," said Beric and turned to Luke. "Found your stuff, brother?" Luke was no doubt high up in the church, but as far as Beric was concerned, he was a provincial doctor—and a brother.

Luke had at last discovered the ointment. He dabbed some of it on, and Beric tied a piece of rag around the foot before he fastened the sandal on again. He thought he had better have a talk with Crispus about a few little things—like new sandals for the kitchen slaves.

Dapyx had got up, and certainly he looked a bit easier and stood more upright, whether that was the ointment or the brotherhood.

Then it was Phaon's turn.

Beric looked at the water. "I'm not going to wash you in that, Phaon, so don't you think it!" Again he took out the water and emptied it, got fresh, and came down, feeling normal and cheerful, and knelt in front of Phaon.

"Oh," said Phaon, "I wish mother could see me having my feet washed by a nobleman!"

Beric pinched one of his brown toes. "Be quiet, Phaon," he said. "This is serious."

Phaon's feet weren't really dirty. He swung his legs when Beric had dried them. "How's that?" he said.

"I must be going on," said Luke, "but I'm glad to have been here. We're all the better for it. Good night and peace with you, friends."

172

He went out, and the others began discussing business, sitting on the floor or the chopping block or the bench.

Beric stayed where he was, on the floor by the basin, listening. It was remarkable how little there was that really had to be decided. The members of this church and the other churches had merely and simply comforted and fed the widows and orphans and homeless, looked after those who were burned or injured, shared their clothes, money, and other goods, and in general done their duty by their neighbors. It was all quite simple if you were prepared to do it, though it was, of course, harder for the slaves, who hadn't got much to share.

It occurred to Beric that a slave who was also a Christian mightn't even save up enough to buy himself out. That could only be done by strict economy, which wasn't compatible with the giving that was part of a Christian life. Argas, for instance, who so much wanted to be free. He probably had less savings than any of the other dining-room slaves.

While he was thinking that, he heard feet on the stairs, stumbling a little. Persis came in. She was sobbing, not very loud, but quite hopelessly.

Lalage ran up to her. "What is it, darling?"

Phaon tossed his head back and said, in a harder voice than Beric had ever heard from him, "There's no need to ask her that. Flavia's been using the child as a pincushion again!"

"Oh yes," said Persis, coming into the lamplight, smeary with tears, and held out her arms, red and swollen, with the telltale little blood dabs on them. "And I can't help squealing, and she slaps me so when I squeal!"

Beric got to his feet, staring, and saw Manasses put his arms around her, saying in a voice that was both kind and angry, "But you're with us now, Persis. You're safe."

It was being most horrible for Beric. He said, "Persis, why didn't you ever tell me?"

She was still crying. Manasses sat her down on the bench, and Phaon began rubbing his cheek, very softly, down her hurt arm. Her mouth twisted with sobs, she said to Beric, "You wouldn't have believed me if I had, would you?"

173

He knelt down and spoke in a low, rough voice, "This won't help you, but it'll help me if you'll let me do it." He began to unfasten her sandals and wash her feet, with a determined gentleness. He said, "That's something I never did for Flavia."

Persis began to stop crying. She wiped her eyes with the overfold of her tunic and smiled a little.

"It is helping her, you see," Lalage said.

While Beric was fastening her sandals again, Argas had come down, just as he was, straight from the working party, smudged all over with ashes and sweat. He was carrying a full pottery bowl, which Manasses took out of his hands and put down by the pile of chopped wood.

"Peace be with you!" he said, out of breath. "Here's the wine," and he flopped down on the bench by the stairs and shut his eyes, which were red and smoke-sore. "I thought I'd never be here in time," he said again, "and, oh, I didn't want to miss it!"

Beric got up and carried the water and oil over and knelt and began to wash Argas's feet. Euphemia brought one of the lamps so that he could see what he was doing. Argas had got his feet into an incredible mess. Beric began to wash up towards his knees. It would have been much more to the point, he thought, to put Argas straight into the big bath. How on earth any of the slaves kept even moderately clean!

Argas opened his eyes and saw Beric. "Oh, it's you—your first time, isn't it?" He grinned. "Lucky for me. Look at the mess I'm in!"

"Yes, Argas," said Beric, "this is good for your feet as well as for my soul!"

Argas leaned nearer to him. "Do you hate doing it?"

"Not a bit," said Beric, "though I can't think why. Yes, I can, though. You've got some tar or something on your heel. I'll see if I can get it off with the rag."

Argas suddenly said, "It feels very nice having one's feet washed—apart from anything else."

"Yes, I expect it does," said Beric. He hadn't thought of that himself, while his were being washed. But then, he wasn't tired and dirty. "Argas," he said, "I'd like to be baptized. Will you tell the others?"

Argas put a hand on his shoulder. "Are you sure? No, look up and tell me."

Beric looked and nodded.

"You can't be just yet. But I know what it's like wanting. Only everyone takes it different ways. Won't you tell the others yourself?"

"No," said Beric, drying his feet, which were at least cleaner than the rest of him. "You tell them. Please, Argas. Now let me have your sandals."

"I won't put them on yet," Argas said. "You know, Beric, my feet were pretty sore. There's a lot of hot ash and grit about still. Now they feel grand. I wonder how nearly ready you are."

"I think I'm about ready."

"Well, we'll see. You'll have to go now, Beric, because we're going to have the love feast."

He pointed, and Beric saw for the first time that, besides the cup of wine, there were two baskets of food by the wood pile.

"Can't I stay?" said Beric.

"No," said Argas, "not this time. Next time—if you want to."

11

Second Sacrament

During the next week Beric was increasingly happy. He was able to do a good deal for their own house slaves and for stray Christians. When he asked Crispus for anything, he could almost always get it. This was partly because he had thought out what he wanted beforehand, and he discovered that he could now deal with the cook and old Felix, and partly because Crispus was a bit fussed about everything and in the mood when it was simplest to say, "Yes, yes, my dear boy," and get it over.

The wedding had been fixed for the following week. Beric managed to avoid Flavia, almost instinctively, and this annoyed her quite a lot. She couldn't go on having that lovely feeling of achievement if he didn't go on being hurt and angry, or at any rate if she couldn't see whether he was! And he'd been in her power that evening, but now he seemed to have slipped out. Perhaps that dancing girl had tried a little consoling on him!

But she had plenty of other things to think about. The presents—yes, and Tigellinus had sent her something, a ruby bracelet, a beauty, a big one!—and the clothes and the new household. She was going to take a few slaves with her, including, of course, her maids, Persis and the Italian. She would leave the old woman behind. Between times, however, she made up her mind that Beric wasn't to get off so easily!

Balbus was constantly coming and going. The two old men had so much to fuss over, and Beric had often to be there with the secretary, Hermeias, a Greek who had been in the house for twenty years. Hermeias knew that he was to be freed and left enough money to buy himself a cottage in the country, under his master's will, which he had written out himself. In the meantime he was content and silent and knew what was to be done, though he preferred Beric to give the orders.

Apart from the wedding plans, Crispus and Balbus were both even more worried than usual by the state of things in Rome. The fire was, of course, completely over, and there had been no epidemics in the refugee camps. There was talk of some of the property losses being partly made up from the Imperial Treasury. But all the same everyone was jumpy.

And it was not at all tactful of the emperor to have sent at once for his two special architects, who apparently had plans for a new Rome already drawn up. It was as though he wanted to get still another thing gathered into his bundle of power: *Urbs Roma*, the city. Men are shaped by their circumstances, including even the circumstances of brick and stone. Would there be any liberty left?

Flavia went out in the litter, accompanied sometimes by her maid and sometimes by the old cousin, and always by a suitable retinue of slaves. When she stopped, half a dozen shop assistants would scurry out and bring the best of everything for her to choose. Sometimes the narrow streets were quite blocked. She didn't mind! Nor did she bother to ask the price, except occasionally when she had a fit of bargaining.

It was not the affair of any of the slaves if the prefect of the Praetorians happened to turn up. No one could be more surprised than the Italian maid! And, of course, if Tigellinus chose to help a young lady leaning out of her litter, greedy and light-hearted and excited, like some game bird in best condition, no one could object.

Sannio, who had been out with her, told Argas, "Proper refined little lady, isn't she? Suppose when it comes to the night, her hubby finds her not quite—?" He made an expressive gesture.

"It's always a surprise packet," said Argas.

"I would half like to have a look in," said Sannio. "Stuck her arm right in my face, she did, grabbing for a bit of flimsy she was after. Like a bit of cake it was."

"You look out!" said Argas. "She's cake for the gentlemen."

"What sort of bit did the Briton have? You're thick with him, Argas. You ought to know."

"Not so thick as that, I'm not."

"He was as sick as muck that evening. Got over it all right. Who's he after now—you?"

"What do you take me for?"

"All right. All right. I only asked. I wouldn't mind having a spot of fun with him myself. Treats you decent, he does. You bet it was him got us meat for supper those days we were on the working parties."

"Yes, it was."

"Thought you'd know, somehow! Listen here, Argas, who started that fire? I keep on hearing things. There's some say it was the Christians began it. Know anything about these Christians, Argas?"

"Why should I? All I know is, setting fire to houses isn't their game. Who was saying that, Sannio?"

"Oh, it was about. If these Christians want to have a spot of change, I'm all for them. Suppose you could burn Rome. And all."

"Burning Rome's not going to get you anywhere. Look what happened when they tried that game on the masters before."

"The cross every time. But it wasn't half bad going out with the Briton. Remember when that fool Josias got the beam onto him? You'd have thought they was brothers, the fuss the Briton made. Good job if he was the old man's son. Instead of a barbarian. D'you know where Britain is? I sure don't."

"Up north of Gaul somewhere. Always wet, Britain is, nothing but mud. His father was king near where the best oysters come from—you know, the big ones that come in barrels with seaweed."

"Two a penny, those kings are. If you ask me, it's a bit of luck for him, getting quit of the Scratch Cat. Whoever it is he's onto now!"

So the slaves thought. Occasionally, also, Felicio thought of the Briton, wondered if he'd got involved with the Christians. He also wondered, as far as he himself was concerned, whether perhaps he ought to have given it another chance—or was it as stupid as it seemed, as small-scale, made up of the pettiness of individuals? Well, at the moment, what with the wedding and the postfire complications, he had his hands full.

Once Beric, walking through the back part of the house, saw Crispus's litter slaves waiting about and, being brave, made a quick sign of the cross to Niger.

But Niger, standing in sight of a master, made no acknowledgement, just stood and stared sadly.

"Was that to you?" Zyrax whispered to Niger.

"What?" said Niger blankly.

Zyrax pinched him. "You know—that sign."

"I don't know," said Niger. "Nothing. He was a master."

"You black bonehead!" said Zyrax, but Niger just stood. The Cappadocian glanced at him and wondered. He had an idea about that sign. And also he was beginning to get curious sharp pains inside his chest.

But after Beric had finished telling the cooks about some of the wedding arrangements, he heard feet after him in the passage, turned, and saw Josias, who was up and about again. "Well?" he said cheerfully.

Josias said in a whisper, "You mustn't go making the sign, sir—not open like that! Not just now. He didn't answer, did he?"

"No—I only did it to cheer him up a bit."

"You'll go getting him into trouble. And yourself. And all of us, you will!"

"Oh, surely not!"

"But you will! There's every kind of thing being said. And what's more, it looks like stories being put out—on purpose. You know, sir—from the top. Like as if someone had got orders that we're to be blamed. Well, I don't know about that—how could I?—but Manasses said we was all to be extra careful. You will too, sir, won't you?"

"Well, of course," said Beric, "but I think you're all getting a bit overexcited. I don't believe anything's going to happen. Not yet, anyway, Josias. But I'll remember."

When the day came, Beric asked one of them to come and fetch him when it was time.

Argas came along to his room. "As soon as the house is quiet," he said, "we'll go down. They'll all be in bed soon."

"What will it be like?" Beric asked.

179

"You'll see," Argas said and sat down on the floor by the bed head. "This is what's best. This is when the Spirit comes. This is what none of the others knew, not even Spartacus, but only Jesus. He showed it to His friends."

"But is it—difficult?"

"No, it's so easy that nobody else thought of it. Like the prayer."

"That's not easy."

"It is, and it isn't. It is if outside things aren't stopping it. Only they do usually."

They waited, listening for complete quiet in the house. Beric had been sitting on the bed. Now, in the increasing silence, he leaned over on his elbow and half lay along, his head and Argas's head close together. He bit Argas's ear.

When Argas turned his surprised face up, Beric kissed him. It was meant to be a light kiss, but turned out to be hardly that. Both of their hearts had been set beating.

After a moment Argas said in a hard voice, "That's the first time I've ever let any of my masters do that to me."

"You beast!" said Beric.

"Well, aren't you my master?"

"Have you got to say so all the time?"

"Yes."

"Oh, very well." He added, "You'd better be going along to your love feast. I don't think it interests me."

Argas swung around at Beric blindly with his fist and hit him in a rather harmless way on the chest.

Beric jumped up, shoving Argas in a sprawl onto the floor as he did so. He held him down, one knee between the shoulders, his right hand ready to hit.

Argas did not defend himself. No slave does! Then the complete stillness of the body under his knee horrified Beric with its unlikeness to the gymnasium. He had never been one to knock slaves about; it was not amusing. He stood back.

Argas picked himself half up. "Well, hit me!" he said.

Beric had never seen him like that, white and unsmiling, the Greek-shaped bones of his head clear under skin and muscle.

"No," said Beric. The whole thing was over. Yes, the whole thing. "Now get out," he added and shut his eyes and put his hands over his ears.

When he looked up, the slave was still there, saying harshly, "It was my fault. I spoiled the evening—for both of us—your first time."

"It doesn't matter in the least," said Beric. "Please go."

The hardness of Argas's face changed into misery. He went on slowly, "It was my sin. I can't go to the love feast like this."

Argas came and knelt in front of him and caught his knees in the oldest gesture of conquered to conquering. "Don't send me away!" he said. "Not unforgiven! Beric. Master."

Beric jumped. It was the one word he couldn't stand at the moment. He wanted Argas to go—go quick—as an equal but not sent out of the room like a dog.

"Master," said Argas again.

"Oh, stop it!" Beric half cried, and then, "What has happened? What have we gone and done, Argas?"

"Forgotten the prayer," Argas said slowly.

"All right," Beric answered, "let's say it. Quick, before anything else happens." They did so, standing, and then looked at one another. "Can we go after all?" Beric asked.

Argas answered shakenly, "I think we can if we forgive one another."

"I expect we do," said Beric, "but what for exactly?"

"As far as I'm concerned," said Argas, speaking in a casual kind of way, looking at the far corner of the room, "it all started when you kissed me, and I liked it and couldn't say so. There wasn't any harm in the kiss, but it set off everything else—pride, lust, and anger. They woke up. My own pride partly, and partly— oh, the pride of being one of the underdogs. It wasn't going over to *you*. And at that I didn't think of you as a person—as Beric; you'd turned into part of a thing—part of the masters. And I was a thing too—part of the slaves. It wasn't till we were fighting, and you had me down that I remembered—anything. Then I stopped."

Beric interrupted. "Tell me one thing. I thought you weren't fighting because slaves don't fight. Was it that or because you are a Christian?"

"Because I am a Christian. Truly. But for that I'd have fought. I—I used to be always scrapping. I didn't care *who* you were! And then—then I knew what I'd done. Me—a Christian for a year and a half! It was my doing. And just before the love feast."

"That's all right by me," said Beric. "I'm glad you'd have fought. As for me, I suppose you've got to forgive me for kissing you."

"I do forgive," said Argas, "really."

"Well," said Beric, "it would have saved a lot of trouble if you'd explained the sin earlier."

"What I've also got to forgive you for was thinking like you did about the love feast. As if you didn't care. That was *your* pride, wasn't it?"

"I suppose so," said Beric. "It just came into my head. I meant to hurt you."

"That was what made me angry. Instead of forgiving you at once like I ought to have. Why, you've not been to the love feast yet, so you didn't know what you were doing when you spoke of it that way! Oh, I've got a lot to learn yet!" He spoke ruefully. After a moment Beric said, "Is it always so bad to be made love to by the masters? I'm thinking of all the fellows I know who've got a pet slave boy or girl."

"Most of them don't mind," said Argas, frowning and considering it. "They've accepted being slaves, and, of course, they're bound to make something out of it. And a good many like it; they're that way. But we—we Christians don't stand for that. Even the ones that can afford it don't buy women. But if a man and woman fall in love, why then they get married and equal in love. Phineas needn't have married Sapphira; she was a slave. But he did."

"But why couldn't you have taken it from me?" Beric asked. "Let's sit down. I shan't kiss you again!"

"But suppose you did," said Argas, "and you got kiss for kiss from me, and more. What would it do to the both of us? We'd want to grab one another, wouldn't we? We'd be apt to get angry and jealous. And it would come between us and the rest of the church, being two instead of being all. It would come between us and the words of the prayer and the remembering of Jesus."

"Manasses seemed to think," said Beric, "that your Jesus said we'd got to cut out all this if we wanted the Kingdom. Have we really got to?"

"The Jews don't hold with it," Argas said, "as between man and man. It's against their Law. They're always wanting to have children. Even Manasses really wants that. But I'm a Greek, and what I think is that Jesus wouldn't let Himself get tied up with love for any single man or woman because He meant His love to be for all.

"There was an old woman—I can't remember her name, only she was in Rome last year; she stayed with Claudia Acte. All of us went over to the other church to hear what she'd got to say. She came from one of those little towns on the sea of Galilee, but she spoke Greek, so she must have been someone in her time. She was on her way north, telling about Jesus in the new churches. She'd loved Him, and He'd been kind, the way it still made her happy thinking about it, but not different to how He was to all who were in the Kingdom with Him. I think that old lady must have been very beautiful then; maybe it was difficult for Him not to love her more than others. But there it was.

"Now I'll tell you something. I think you only kissed me because you've felt full of love to us all ever since the feet-washing, and it was only me because I happened to be there."

Beric gave a start. It was a disquieting echo of what he had said to Flavia and forgotten but now remembered. Perhaps it was always true of all love-making?

Argas went on. "You wouldn't have kissed old Sophrosyne or Dapyx, say—it wouldn't have fitted. But Sapphira or Phaon or Lalage? Wouldn't any of us have done?"

"Yes," said Beric. "I think you're right. I don't know myself just now. Oh, I wish you'd all let me be baptized soon!"

"I expect we shall," said Argas. "Come on down, or we shall be late."

Actually they were almost the last to get down to the boiler room, and most of the business discussion was over. They gave one another the peace greeting. Manasses was there, and so were Euphemia, Lalage, and Sophrosyne.

183

Lalage had one dinner engagement since the fire; she wouldn't let the church open a special fund for her dresses, but she'd borrowed a couple from Claudia Acte, who had seemed, she thought, to be sadder than usual. Her little house was full of refugees, and she was cheerful enough to them, but something was wrong underneath. Lalage wondered if she'd ever be told what it was.

Persis, Josias, and Dapyx were there from the house, though Persis was a little worried. Supposing her mistress wanted her? She knew that the Italian maid assumed that she slipped out to meet a lover and would be correspondingly sympathetic and helpful, but still—if Flavia woke and for some reason wanted *her*. . . Well, it would be worth it.

Beric found that all of them met his eyes now and smiled.

Niger said, "I'm sorry I couldn't get to answering you that day, brother. Things was just so I couldn't."

"I know," said Beric. "Next time I'll just look at you, and you'll know I'm thinking it."

Rhodon and Phineas were there too, but again Sapphira hadn't been able to get away. She and the Christian widow, and perhaps one or two other women, would be praying now. Rhodon explained that he had begun to tell Abgar, who was now working with him for his keep. But not enough, yet, to bring him. Beric couldn't help supposing that Rhodon was bound to take a long time to get that far with anyone.

On their way down, Argas had gone into the room where the oil jars were stored. He brought out their cup and filled it from an earthenware wine jar that was hidden in a hole in the wall. He said to Beric, "We bought it ourselves. It's not good wine. But—"

"I shall like it," Beric said.

Everyone who had come in from the outside had brought food, except Niger. Euphemia and Lalage had fried a nice piece of fish. Rhodon had brought a small pot of honey, and Phineas some lettuce and a couple of hard-boiled eggs, which they cut up into slices. He couldn't bring much because of their refugees.

They hadn't any bread yet, but Beric recognized that what the house slaves had brought was part of the remains of dinner, the usual privilege of the dining-room boys. Yes, there were the extra slices that had been cut off the roast kid, and some mixed vegetables—he knew he hadn't finished what was on his plate, nor had Crispus. And there were some bits of the almond cake. The food was all being put out onto chipped pottery bowls and laid on the tree bole between the lamps.

Tactfully, Beric looked away, but Manasses said, "It's only what we'd have had anyhow. We're just eating it later instead of at once."

Beric believed that; they all looked rather hungrily at the food, especially Niger.

The two benches were brought up to the tree bole. Manasses began to pray quietly. "Our Father," he said, "we know we shall have our bread. We ask You for it, and we always get it, this evening and at other times. Give us the daily bread of the Spirit. Let us always stay certain of You and of Jesus and of the Kingdom. Even if we are separated from one another, let us keep hold on that. Let us not even need the love feast or the feet-washing to make us certain. Our Father and Jesus, when danger comes, be our strength, be in us, let us feel You strongly. And give us knowledge of the Kingdom tonight."

Phineas added, "Come to us, Jesus, when You are ready. We are ready for You. We are always ready. We are thinking of You and the love feast You made for your friends. Messiah, may Your time come soon."

Some of them sat down on the benches, waiting, but not impatiently.

Beric whispered to Lalage, "Is that another meaning of the Words—the daily bread of the Spirit?"

"Yes," said Lalage. "Daily certainty, daily knowledge, living and stirring in us all the time. Lifting our hearts. We ask for that in the prayer, and mostly we get it."

"I wish you'd let me have the baptism soon," he said. "I feel ready."

"What do you think, Manasses?" she asked, leaning over.

"He's untried," said Manasses. "It's different with most of us. What do the rest of you think? Argas?"

"I'm not fit to judge," Argas said. "I quarreled with him earlier this evening."

"Have you forgiven one another?" Manasses asked quickly and very gravely.

"Yes. We wouldn't have come otherwise. It was my fault mostly. I think I like him too much to know about him."

Beric was startled and uncomfortable at all this coming out, but nobody seemed to notice much, except Lalage, who said, "We all like him. We want him to be one of us. We'll see if the Spirit comes."

Niger said thoughtfully, "I can't see just how it feels for a nobleman to want our baptism."

Then Phaon came running down the twisting steps, his arms full of long loaves. "Sorry I'm late!" he said. "Oh, sorry, Manasses, peace be with you! Here's the bread."

"Peace be with you," said Manasses, taking it. "Where's your mother?"

"Mother said she was terribly disappointed, but she simply can't come. She's got an order from the relief office for every last loaf she can bake before tomorrow morning."

"Well, then," said Manasses, "I think we're all here. We won't wait any longer for Sotion. He may have been kept. He seemed a bit upset and strange about something last time, but he wouldn't say. Perhaps he's got something on his conscience and doesn't feel he can ask for forgiveness yet."

"He's bound to soon," Euphemia said. "There's nothing like forgiveness, is there!"

Manasses looked around, counted, and said to Beric, smiling, "Twelve, and you, brother."

Niger picked up one of the loaves and smelled it. "Fresh white bread. There's nothing so good in the world. And some folks eat it every day."

He put the loaf back on the chopping block, and they all came closer, in a half circle.

Beric, shaking with excitement, was between Manasses and Lalage. Looking at the food, he wondered if it wasn't going to turn suddenly into something strange and other.

Manasses said, "Let us take this bread and break it, friends."

"In the name of Jesus," answered Euphemia and Rhodon

from the two ends of the half circle, and they, too, picked up a loaf each and broke the bread and handed it around.

Each man or woman had a big piece of bread and something to go with it from the table, giving one another what seemed best. Manasses gave Niger one of the two whole slices of meat. Leaning over, their hands and fingers met on the food in the light and slight warmth of the three little lamps set among it. Beric had his bread dipped in honey.

Then they all sat down, either on the benches or on the floor. Manasses sat on one bench, and Beric sat at his feet, beside Lalage. But all were close to one another, in touch. After the first few bites even the hungriest ate slowly. They were quiet, waiting, letting pain and anger and anxiety drop off them. Obviously they had learned to do this, but Beric was strung up, wondering what would happen next.

Lalage put her hand on his. "Breathe deep," she said, "watch the lamps, think of others. We are safe here."

And after a time Beric felt that too, only he wanted to be completely one of them. Gradually he became filled with a mist of sadness because he was that much outside, and this sadness hardened into sharp thoughts of all he had done or not done, of unkindness and injustice and time wasted. For a moment he thought of his mother and Britain and a child's burrow in the bracken among bright hill pansies, in Wales perhaps, and he was ready to cry.

He may have moaned a little, because he felt Manasses' hand on his head once more, as it had been that other time in blessing, and then he thought of all the oppressed people, all slaves and prisoners and hurt, all the men and women who were people and might be in the Kingdom but who were at that moment and always being treated as things by a thing. And his sadness was changed into indignation at this great sin of which he had been a part but which now he hoped he would never be part in again.

As he thought that, he looked away from the lamps, across Lalage to Dapyx and Rhodon on her other side, and on the opposite bench Niger and Josias and Persis, Argas at their feet, Phineas and Euphemia beyond, friendly and trusting—across the low table of the love feast. Old Sophrosyne behind him was dreaming; Phaon sat next him with his face lifted up and his lips moving.

Phaon said softly, "Oh, I'm so happy." Manasses and Niger from the two benches each reached out and touched him. His hands fell on their arms, and he began to sing, low, almost wordlessly. For a time he was the focus. Then he stood up, slipping away from the arms of his friends, picked up a lump of chalk, went over to the middle furnace, and with two sweeps of his arm drew a fish across the brickwork. The others turned towards it and murmured the Name words: "Jesus Christ, God's Son, Savior." With a dancing step, Phaon came back to the half circle, joined again in the nearness.

From the far side of the table, Phineas spoke in a low voice. "I have sinned against Jesus and the Kingdom. I have not been kind to the widow who is staying with us."

"Why not?" Manasses asked.

"I didn't want anybody else in our home. I let her see it."

Manasses said, "You can be kinder now. You will be."

Lalage said, "Where there are two together, they have to be very careful not to cut themselves and one another off from the Kingdom."

Euphemia said, "We understand, don't we, friends?"

"When you are kind to her, you will know our forgiveness," Manasses said.

Again there was peace. Beric saw Niger's broad, black hands stroking Argas's cheeks and neck. It was very odd, but he did not feel disturbed at all. He himself leaned back, the taste of honey and bread crust in his mouth, his head against Manasses' knee. He used to dislike and distrust Manasses—disliked because distrusted. He remembered Saturnalia last year and the great harming of the Jewish slaves in which he had joined. Where had Argas and Phaon been in that abuse? Probably, he thought, from his present knowledge of them all, Manasses had told them to keep out, not risk either hate and anger or saying something that would give them away; not to help him even though he was the deacon. Manasses would say it did no good for more to be hurt than need be.

It was strange how much it amused people to hurt others. Most amusements seemed to depend on pain of some kind. He had often been to the arena with Crispus. Now he didn't think he'd ever want to go again. All that, the blood on the sand and everyone yelling for more, and in a small way the humiliation of Manasses and Josias and the other Jews, the activity that he had been part of—the thing whose weight was on him, that he would lose only at baptism. "When are you going to baptize me?" he whispered again up to Manasses.

"Are you so sure, brother?" Manasses asked.

"Quite sure," Beric answered.

"You'll have to fast and pray," Manasses said. "You'll do that, I know. And you'll have questions to answer, from all of us, perhaps."

"The Way of Life?"

"Yes. You know all that. I only wonder if you're as sure as I hope you are. It means finishing with a great many things that mayn't let you go as easily as you think now. That's something that'll be harder for you than if you'd just been a slave. You see, you may have to take action for the sake of the Kingdom. Or refuse to take action, which may be more difficult and more dangerous too. You're young."

"I'm nearly as old as most of you. Older than you were when you were baptized, Manasses."

"Yes, but I'd been through it already. So have most of us. We've known what it is to be without the Kingdom—wanting it, though we didn't know what it was we wanted—for months and years, almost physically painful. You just know when the Kingdom enters your heart."

"Is there anything more I can do to be sure—and to make you sure of me?"

"I don't think so, son," Manasses said, and Beric felt how extraordinarily kind he was, trying to face a new difficulty not by rules but according to what it really was, allowing them all to be individuals, different and separate and yet all to be gathered into the same association.

Lalage said, "But perhaps you'll find something. Usually

things turn up, if one's looking for them." Then, speaking across him, she asked Manasses, "Shall we have the wine now?"

"Yes," said Manasses and took up the full wine cup. "In Jesus' name," he said and drank, then gave it to old Sophrosyne, next him on the bench. "You have it last," he said to Beric.

They passed it around, all drinking and saying the name of the One they followed. Beric watched with the same kind of excitement he had got out of the feet-washing. All these mouths were coming to his mouth. He had never thought deeply before about eating and drinking, about his mouth taking food and giving love and wisdom, the gate in the face opening and shutting, the lips that no animal has but only humans. All those lips on the cup and at last his own.

He took it with hands that shook a little, and himself said the Name and set his mouth where the others had been and finished the wine that Argas had said was rather bad wine. What had it tasted like? He didn't know. Only he was suddenly surprised at this eating and drinking, which had been going on with nobody standing behind to wait on him.

"This is a party," he said, "that's for everybody at last!"

Manasses and Argas both laughed.

"Nothing but joy!" said Lalage, sighing. She sat very close to him, looking into the flames of the lamps, her face stretched and intent. It seemed as though she were becoming an instrument for some unknown and unmeasured power.

Manasses knew that look on her and thought that soon the Spirit might come to her, and she would speak and tell them something that would stay in their minds for all the coming week.

Niger said happily, "And I'm at this party too!"

Euphemia said, "Not like *their* parties. Nothing but good for everyone."

And Josias said, "Why do they want to hurt us Christians? We do no one any harm."

But Argas said, "Our being able to be happy is harming them. Or will harm them some day."

"Happy," said Phaon, "happy. Oh, I do love you all!"

And then suddenly Lalage spoke, "I think there is something wrong." Her whole body was trembling. The others stayed very still, startled and listening, but hearing nothing. She said, "Beric, you are with us but not of us. Go up quick and see!"

"What is it?" asked Beric, staring at her.

"Quick," she said, "quick—go!"

"Go!" cried Manasses.

So Beric ran across the room and up the twisting stairs and through the kitchen and along the passage into the front court and the flare of torches and saw suddenly the thing that Lalage had got the sense of down below. "What are you doing here, Aelius Candidus?" he shouted.

"Hold that man, corporal!" said Aelius Candidus.

But Lalage had risen to her feet. "Let us pray," she said, "brothers and sisters, let us pray."

"What for, sister?" asked Manasses.

And Lalage answered, "For the strength Paul warned us we should need. Father, Thy will be done on us!"

So all were on their feet, close together, praying aloud, led by Manasses and Lalage, and that was how they still were when the Praetorians came down the stairs into the boiler room with Sotion pointing the way.

And they prayed still as the chains were locked on, coupling them, except when one of the soldiers slapped a face or shoved an elbow into someone's mouth to stop it. But none of them did that to Lalage. Mostly it was to Josias and Niger and Dapyx.

Behind them Sotion was pointing out the drawing of the fish on the wall.

I ought to have seen what he was, Manasses thought. *Oh, my little church! What have I done wrong that this should have happened?* And the misery of this began to stop his praying, and he knew he was being no use that way, so he tried to do something else. He said to Sotion, "I forgive you. You can't have known what you were doing."

Sotion ran at him and hit him furiously.

Manasses didn't even lift his chained hands.

"Go on, hit him again, knock his teeth out!" the soldier said.

And Sotion hit once more, but after that he couldn't.

In the meantime Beric was doing some hard thinking and acting. He said to the two Praetorians who were holding him that

191

Crispus would be extremely displeased and that he, Beric, was the young master in this house!

The soldiers said, rather apologetically, that they had their orders, but they wouldn't keep hold so hard if he wouldn't do anything stupid, but, after all, they were only doing their duty and routing out a nest of Christians!

Beric answered that he was interested in this too, as he had reason to suppose that dancing girl he was after was mixed up in all this, and when they smiled fairly respectfully and eased their grip on his arms, he got at his belt.

At his right was a sharp, rather fancy knife that he often wore—a present from Crispus—and a purse at the left. Luckily he had a couple of pieces of silver, enough to be worthwhile for a Praetorian to accept. He slipped them over, adding that he thought it was all nonsense and they weren't Christians, but only playing at it, and anyhow what was the point of arresting these miserable Christians?

"But it was them set fire to the Circus Maximus!" said one of the guards.

"You don't believe *that* story, do you?" said Beric contemptuously.

"Well," said the man, "that's the charge they're being arrested on."

The prisoners were brought through.

"Remember," said Beric, "I've got to have a word with my little wench."

"That's all right, sir," said the guard.

He banked, and rightly, on their not knowing Greek. "What can I do, Lalage?" he whispered.

"Tell Crispus," she whispered back. "If he goes to Tigellinus and only claims his own slaves, that's six of us. Tell Sapphira and Eunice."

"What's going to happen?"

"What we want is a public trial," she said, "not just to die in prison."

"Oh, Lalage, it can't be that!"

"We'll see. I told you something would turn up to test you,

192

Beric! It's the power of the Will over us all, working out on our bodies."

"Hurry up, sir!" said the guard.

"I told them you were my mistress," Beric said. "Say good-bye!" He found it very peculiar kissing a woman in chains and difficult to press her convincingly against himself. He couldn't think of anything but the chains, nor, for the moment, could she. The others who were chained too, having overheard, looked on and said nothing. All was in God's hands now.

12

The Tempting of Beric

The prisoners were marched out of the house, Manasses and Argas especially taking care not to look directly at Beric in case anything showed.

Aelius Candidus said to Beric, "You may think yourself lucky not to be under arrest too!"

"It's all a complete misunderstanding!" Beric said.

"But you may join them yet, Mr. Briton!" Aelius Candidus added. Then he beckoned Sotion, who was hanging about, and paid him. Sotion followed the Praetorians and the prisoners out into the dark street.

Beric followed him.

Sotion tried to stick close to the soldiers, but the corporal growled at him and finally kicked him off. He slipped into a side alley. But when he peered around, he saw it was no use. He began to run, which was hopeless, because Beric caught him in two street lengths. He had hardly breath to whimper.

"How much did you get?" Beric asked in a horribly calm voice. Sotion held out his shaking hand with the silver in it.

Beric wrenched it around, and the silver tinkled away into the gutter.

Sotion went down on his knees in utter, dribbling terror.

"Did you give the other names?" Beric asked.

"Oh no, sir, not yours, sir, oh, I swear it. Don't kill me. In Jesus' name, don't kill me—"

But Beric had drawn the little knife, and, while Sotion clung to him, stabbed him behind the collarbone, saw that he'd got the artery, and kicked the dying creature away before the blood got all over him.

He was back at the house by the time the doorkeeper and a couple of other slaves, all of whom had been held by the guard during the arrest, had picked themselves up and tried to decide what to do or say. He walked past them and straight to Flavius Crispus's room.

Flavius Crispus was most upset. Why had he not been told at once? Because everyone had been held under temporary arrest. But that was a most extraordinary procedure! However, he quite understood that there might be a case for arresting all Christians. In his own house, though!

"You ought to have been more careful, Beric!" he said, very reprovingly. "We might all have been murdered in our beds! I ought to have got rid of my Jewish slaves. Always giving trouble. That fellow Manasses had entire charge of the wine cellar, and I've no idea where my Falernian is! Really, the thing's a menace."

"It wasn't only the Jews. Argas and Phaon are Greeks. And—"

"You know, Beric, those dancing boys were treated like—like my own children! And this is all the gratitude one gets for pampering them. If you ever have slaves of your own, my boy, don't make the mistake of treating them like human beings. They don't deserve it."

Beric was thinking quicker than he'd ever done in his life. "About those dancing boys," he said, "if they're put to the question, the usual way, they'll be spoiled for life. It seems a pity."

"Of course it's a pity. But if the little brutes go off with the Christians behind my back, that's what they've got to expect!"

That made it very difficult to know what to say next. Beric wasn't used to this kind of lying. He began to feel a most uncomfortable and urgent need to tell Crispus the truth, to be sent to prison himself, to possible death and torture—only to be under God's will with the others!

Crispus sat up in bed, frowning, drumming with his fingers on the sheet.

And Beric was already in imagination on his knees beside him, saying that he was a Christian too, explaining everything, making Crispus *see*. But if Crispus didn't? Well, it had to be tried!

But then Flavia came storming in, in a cloak caught up over her nightgown, a lamp in her hand. "Father!" she cried. "What's happened? I want my maid, and she's not there! What's all this nonsense about Candidus arresting our slaves?"

Beric just couldn't help saying, "Candidus has simply been doing the dirty work that is expected of Praetorian officers."

But Flavia snapped at him, and Crispus answered her very solemnly. "What seems to have been going on in our house, my child, was a Christian meeting. We may think ourselves lucky not to have our throats cut."

"It's Tigellinus we have to thank for that!" Flavia said. It was all being as exciting as the arena—throats cut! "He must have had them arrested just in the nick of time. He's so splendidly efficient!"

Beric cut her short. "But there's no suggestion that they were planning anything against you or any of us. What they were supposed to have done is to have gone along with candles and oil and set fire to the Circus Maximus!"

That seemed to have some effect. Crispus said, "But that's preposterous! My slaves accused of that! I shall have to find out exactly where they all were that night."

Beric remembered the night very well—and remembered that the Christians were all out of the house except Persis. "I happen to know," he said, "the boys were all over at Eunice's. They often go. She's a nice old lady."

"But it's her son who is accused of being a Christian! They may have gone there to practice their filthy rites!"

"Well," said Beric, "I was in there myself part of the time." He had a new idea, and the household would no doubt confirm it to Crispus! "As a matter of fact, I was there with Argas. Actually I and he—" He coughed and looked in an embarrassed way at Flavia.

Crispus quite understood. "Dear me. Well, that makes it tolerably certain. Where was your maid, Flavia?"

"How should I know? Anyhow she's too much of a little fool to do a thing like that. I've never seen a girl who squealed so easily at the least thing! But she'll have something to squeal for tomorrow. I've got her trained to do my hair decently, and I must have her back at once. I can't imagine what Candidus was thinking about, arresting my maid two days before the wedding! I shall go to Tigellinus myself and insist on her release!"

"Flavia!" said Crispus. "I absolutely and categorically forbid you to ask Tigellinus any favors. Do you hear? I shall go to him personally and stand on my rights. If Candidus had more experience, he would have known he could not possibly arrest anybody in my house without referring to me first. I shall point that out to Tigellinus myself!"

"But won't that be dangerous?"

"Dangerous, Beric? Frightened? I see you're a barbarian still! Danger, indeed! The man simply comes and takes my property without your leave or by your leave! There are certain decencies that must be observed, even by Nero's friends. I shall go the first thing tomorrow morning. You and Hermeias are to come with me. I shall want a small chop for breakfast. Early breakfast. Now take the lamp and show Flavia to her room. Christians indeed! You certainly ought to have known there was something going on."

Beric dutifully took the lamp and lighted Flavia to her room, past the empty mattress that was Persis's home. He said nothing.

Nor did she till she was at the door. Then she turned and looked him up and down. "So it's little Argas! Not very interesting, I should have thought. But everyone has their own tastes. Which of you is which?"

"Shut up!" said Beric.

"How dare you speak to me like that!" Flavia said. "Trotting around with the slave boys—"

But Beric had caught hold of her arm. "I've got something pretty to show you, Flavia. Look!" He pulled out the knife.

"Blood!" she said and pulled him quickly into her room. "What have you been doing? Who is it?"

"You want to know, do you?" said Beric. "Makes a man of me, doesn't it! Well, I'll tell you, Flavia. After the prisoners had been marched off, there was a little cowering money-grubber left, counting the silver pieces that handsome young officer of yours had thrown him. You see, he was the informer—the man who was paid by Tigellinus and his friends to get friendly with the Christians and then betray them. I don't like that sort of person. So I killed him. It was very easy. I can't make out why some people say it is difficult to kill a man."

Flavia gave a little gasp of pleasure and excitement, then suddenly caught his wrist. "You've got blood on your hand too! And on your tunic! And there at your knee!" She pressed her face quickly against the hand. "Yes, you are a man! You know, Beric, you look different. Come and talk to me. We shan't be able to talk when I'm married."

It was the first time Beric had been in her room since the afternoon of the party. Deep in his mind was all that had happened since. But here were the familiar things, the couch, the silk hangings, the little tables, the silver mirror, the carved chests and cushions, the smell in his nostrils. Flavia's hand after all in his. He was still holding the sticky knife.

She pointed to it. "Did you do it in one stroke?"

"Yes," he said.

"Kiss me, Beric!" she said.

He turned on her and kissed her as she'd never been kissed yet. He didn't care whether she liked it or not.

But she did. She gasped and gave a few little cries—she didn't know what he might do next, but she half hoped he'd do it all the same! She was beginning to go soft in his arms, and then he suddenly stopped. "Oh," she said, "it's lucky my maid isn't here after all!"

He moved slightly away from her. "Yes. It was your maid I began thinking about just now. No, not what you mean, Flavia! I was only thinking that you'd seen blood on steel quite often already."

"What *do* you mean?"

"Those pins. Persis."

"Why shouldn't I! She's mine."

"She can feel things, though."

"I should hope so! You can't train slaves without making them feel. Anyhow, it's no business of yours. How did you know? Had the little rat come squealing to you?"

He made a great effort and spoke very gently. "Do you really think of her like that, Flavia? Not as another girl—someone who'd like to be fond of you if you gave her a chance?"

"What on earth's come over you? Talking in the same breath about me and my slaves! Fond of me indeed!"

"Wouldn't you like her to be fond of you?"

"No, it would be disgusting. All my slaves have got to be afraid of me! Of course, it's different with you and little Argas!"

"That's nothing to do with it!"

"Well, where else did you get your ideas from? Beric . . . why are you so interested in what happens to these Christians? Why did you want to kill the informer? He was probably a valuable police agent! I believe—oh, I believe you're mixed up with it yourself!"

"Believe what you like!" said Beric roughly. "I'll tell you one thing, Christians don't murder. And that's what I've done." He went out of the room very quickly, leaving her all excited and wondering. *Could* he be one of these Christians? Weren't they all murderers? Oh, he'd never kissed her like that in the old days!

But he was on his way to the bakery to find Eunice. It was the opposite way from the street where no doubt the blood was still not dry on the stones. No one had heard. Perhaps it hadn't happened. If he forgot about it, it wouldn't have happened.

He told Eunice about the arrest.

She took it very well. "Most likely Crispus will get our people back," she said, bringing him into the bakery and shutting the door, "and I'll tell Claudia Acte."

"Will she be able to get Lalage out?"

"If anyone can, she will. But this looks like the beginning of what we've been afraid of."

"They don't really believe any of us started the fire, do they?"

"Oh no. But they'll try and make everyone else think so. It's like this, Beric. The way things have been till now, we haven't been hated—not by ordinary people. You know, little shopkeepers and householders, folks in a small way, the ones that make up most of any city. They've *said* things about us, but if a good neighbor happened to be a Christian, well, they just looked the other way, or else sooner or later they've come in. There's churches in Rome that have grown up that way, slow and steady. But that didn't suit those on the top. They want to get rid of us, and they'll only be able to if they can work up a strong hate among these ordinary folk, so that my neighbor, say, will want to see me burned alive. And *like* seeing it.

"No, Beric, don't look like that. It's all in the game. I've known a long time now what we might be in for. I only keep on hoping my boy—well, I just can't help it, me being his mother. But they think they'll be able to finish us that way. Stop the Kingdom from coming. If they can get ordinary people against us too."

"Eunice, who exactly do you mean by 'they'?"

"The emperor and Tigellinus. And all that group. The ones who want everything on earth, yes, and want to be God, though they know in their hearts they can't be—but they'll try and make us all say they are, so they can begin believing it themselves!"

"And you're going to fight them?"

"Yes, and win. Through God's help and will in us. Now, Beric, go over and tell Sapphira, and I'll find Claudia Acte." She gave him directions for getting to Phineas's house, woke one of her orphans and told him to see to the ovens, picked up her veil, and went to the door. Looking out into the dark, she signed herself with the cross. She went one way, he another.

It was half an hour's walk, plenty of time to think. He supposed it was true, what Eunice had said. Yes, it was what they'd all been saying really. Only nobody believes a thing till it happens. He hadn't. Well, he wasn't a coward!

And suddenly, in the middle of the bridge across the Tiber, he thought, *It is terrible for a man to have nothing he can die for. I have been taken away from Britain, my fatherland, which my own people died for, my uncle, my cousins—no, they didn't die for Britain. Who wants to die for a lot of trees and mud? They didn't die for the people in Britain; they only died for their own power and rule over those people.*

And I don't want to die for that, and I don't want to die for the rule of Rome. I haven't had anything to die for till now. But now I have got something, and I'm glad. And the slaves have got something. Even Niger and Dapyx. They've got something the masters can't take away from them. So they're one up on the masters. No wonder the masters hate it!

Having located the house, he knocked, and a woman opened at once but, seeing a stranger, half screamed and tried to shut the door on him. But he made the sign quickly, saying, "In Jesus' name, let me in!"

She held the door still but asked, "Who are you, friend?"

"I come from the church," he said. "They have all been arrested."

Her hold on the door slackened, and he pushed past into the strong fish smell of the shop and shut the door behind them both. He picked up the lamp she had put on the floor and saw that she was crying quietly and steadily. "You're Sapphira?" he asked.

She nodded. This was the girl Phineas had fallen in love with and married, although he might have had her as a slave. Her hair was dark and wavy under her veil. Tears kept slipping over her dark eyelashes.

"Don't cry, sister," he said. "It's sure to be all right. Phineas didn't look afraid."

Her Greek seemed to have deserted her. She spoke a few words in some language he didn't know and pushed him toward the inner room, where another woman sat with a child asleep in her arms. Outside, a watchdog barked. Another sleeping child woke and saw him and began to cry.

He made the sign again to the second woman; it was all he could think of.

At last Sapphira dried her eyes with the edge of her veil and said haltingly, "What can I do?"

"Go to the Mamertine prison tomorrow with as much money as you can to buy him out. If you can't raise it, I expect I can."

She shook her head. "No, friend. His father will have money. Will they hurt him?"

"Not tonight, I'm sure. What about Rhodon?"

"I will see. Will ask. God bless you for coming to me, friend. Are you one of us?"

"I'm not baptized yet. But I will be."

They would have given him milk to drink, but he suspected that it was the children's, and he didn't want it, anyhow.

He left, trying to be as gentle as he could. But once outside the house, he walked quickly, more and more angered at all this hurting of helpless, innocent people. They. The hurters. The ones on top in this tyranny. If they could be eliminated. It was no use killing a creature like Sotion. The person who needed killing was Tigellinus.

At the house, the doorkeeper, who had been drowsing on his bench beside the door till the knock came, let him in. He said to Beric, "You'd know about these Christians, sir, wouldn't you?"

"What do you mean?" asked Beric quickly.

"I've been here since you were a baby, sir, so you don't need to be angry about me knowing. I couldn't help seeing the way you looked. You've heard of the cross sign, haven't you?"

"Well—yes."

"I thought so. I thought, he's been hearing some of the stories. I don't go further than stories myself, stories of some and others that got the cross. I don't go doing things in cellars. No, not me. But you got me this cushion for my bench, didn't you, sir?"

"Well, you're too old to lie on a hard bench all night."

"Nobody thought of that before. Though I've been here all these years. Look, there's the ring I used to be chained to."

"I can't remember you ever being chained."

"Oh, that was away back, when you weren't much taller than my elbow, sir. There was an older man on the door then. When he died, they knew they could trust me, and I was unchained."

"Why did they know they could trust you?"

"Why? Because I'd been chained so long. And so they could. So they could. And so can you, sir. I won't tell about you and the Christians."

"When did you hear about the cross stories?"

"Oh, first in the years when I was chained. Times I was loosed for food and sleeping. I heard then. And now I tell myself the stories. They keep off the ghosts and the little noise of the chains rattling. They aren't real chains now."

"Oh," said Beric, "I hate all these chains and crosses and whips! I'd like to kill everybody who hurt anybody else!"

"You'd have to do a lot of killing then, wouldn't you, sir? You go to bed, sir."

"And you?"

"Me? Oh, I've got my new cushion and the stories I tell myself, and I'm not chained now. You can trust me, sir."

Before breakfast Flavius Crispus sent over two messengers, one to Gallio and the other to Balbus, after Beric had explained that one of the prisoners was Balbus's litter slave. Then he put on his toga, started out, picked up Gallio in the Forum, and marched over to see Tigellinus. Beric and Hermeias walked behind.

The two old men discussed the illegality and impropriety of the arrests, which had, apparently, been general. Everyone was whispering about them already. It was early still, but the sun was blazing and bringing out the unpleasant smell of ashes, and as they walked they got hotter and hotter in their formal clothes and more and more annoyed with Nero and Tigellinus.

Tigellinus indeed! Some people were hinting already that nobody knew more about how that fire started than Tigellinus! But when a man's lost his home, he's got something more immediate to worry about than misgovernment and corruption in high places. And if the authorities round up a few hundred Christians, put them through a solemn trial, and find them guilty, then they'll get all the curses, and Nero will only have to appear on his balcony in uniform to have all Rome lining up below and shouting, "Hail!" Beric and Hermeias glanced at one another. Could *that* be true?

Tigellinus gave them an audience at once and was most affable. Almost too much so. They couldn't be as indignant as they wanted to be. Tigellinus told Flavius Crispus that of course he might collect his own property—he would give them a note to the governor of the prison. By the way, he was going to have Candidus appointed under-governor, a responsible position these days. And he would personally reprimand him for the informality of the arrests.

"By the way, Crispus," he said, looking up from his tablets, "you will, of course, see to it that there is no more suspicion of Christianity in your own household?"

"Naturally! Although I am still certain there must have been some misunderstanding. It is almost incredible that in a household like mine—"

"The information came from a reliable agent. Who, by the way, has been found murdered. However, I think we are in possession of all the facts he may have had."

"Can't trust informers," Gallio said. "Never used them in my time."

"Ah. Well, we do now. It's remarkable what one finds out. Most remarkable. Here is the order for the return of your property, Crispus. I hope you will find it undamaged."

"I should hope so indeed! Two of them were valuable dancing boys. You'd better go straight off, Beric, you and Hermeias, and claim the slaves."

"Ah," said Tigellinus, sticking a handful of nuts into his mouth and crunching them. "Yes, send him along. We shall not begin any systematic questioning for a day or two, but the men get excited sometimes when they have a degraded type of criminal, such as these Christians, to deal with. Now, won't you gentlemen take a glass of wine with me?"

Gallio and Crispus stayed, but Beric and Hermeias went hurrying off to the Mamertine prison. Beric was wondering just how many of the facts Sotion had given. Was all the church in danger? And Tigellinus just waiting? Or, if Sotion hadn't given the names, were the men and women who had been arrested going to be tortured to give them? The whole thing was full of the most horrible possibilities. And Lalage?

In the meantime, did Hermeias suspect something? Beric asked him.

"No," said he, "I had no idea that there was anything of the kind in our household. I find the whole thing rather disgusting!" He hesitated. "As a matter of fact, I am initiate in one of the mysteries. As far as I hear, these Christians have merely imitated some of our ideas and methods. Some of our most sacred ideas. They have, naturally, debased them, putting in crude meanings of their own."

"What sort of ideas, Hermeias?"

"Largely about the life to come. You're too young to want to worry about such things. But as death approaches, we must begin to consider it. And some of us have found a way through."

"A redeemer?"

"Well, no, I should be inclined to call it a process of personal redemption. If you are interested—but here we are."

They handed in the note and were told to come and identify their property. They were taken through barred doors into a courtyard that was crowded with prisoners, standing or sitting, who all turned toward them. Some were singing, but most were talking and praying in low voices.

It was very hot by now, and only a few at a time could get into the shade. The place was beginning, inevitably, to smell very foul. From time to time someone fainted. Here and there a boy or a young woman would be crying with discomfort and anxiety, but enough looked brave and steadfast to encourage Beric. A few, even, looked very happy.

He found their lot, but not Lalage and Sophrosyne, or Phineas. While Hermeias was getting hold of a prison guard to unchain them, he asked quickly and was told that Sapphira had come already. So had Claudia Acte, who had bought out quite a number and was coming back. Lalage had wanted to stay, but her old accompanist seemed ill. Euphemia was really only worrying in case her daughter got to know. Perhaps Eunice would get her out.

"It's mostly a matter of money, then?" Beric asked.

"This time, dear. And surety for good behavior. But they've got our names for next time," Euphemia said. "Well, it's one of the blessings coming to us at last—He *said* we'd be persecuted."

The prison guard took the irons off the others. Beric tipped him and asked him to get some water for the ones who were left. "Do you think we should have their hands tied," Hermeias asked in an undertone, "if they are Christians?"

"Oh no!" said Beric. It was all being very difficult.

None of the house slaves would look at him, except sometimes Phaon. It was the sensible thing to do, but all the other prisoners looked at him and talked about him.

At the last moment Niger knelt in front of Manasses with a look of utter fear and wretchedness. "Give me strength," he said. Manasses laid hands on him in blessing and said low, "Keep your mind on Jesus. He will give you strength, Niger. Don't ever forget. Don't kill yourself. Remember you are one of our witnesses; you are the salt and the light. Your church will be thinking of you and praying for you. We will all be brave for one another and for Him. We are in the Will, Niger. Bless you."

Hermeias was shaking Beric's arm, saying that this must be stopped, and Beric was trying to distract him.

Manasses kissed Niger and said, "We're ready."

They pushed their way through the crowd and out.

Nobody said anything, except when they came to a fountain at a street corner. Manasses asked Hermeias if they might stop and drink.

Here, Beric managed to touch Argas's hand, as though accidentally, and felt his fingers close and grip. Otherwise the six slaves kept very close together, their eyes on the ground. Beric walked to one side, Hermeias at the other.

At the house, Beric went straight to Crispus and said he had brought them back, and what now?

"Send them in," said Crispus, "and Felix."

Beric knew very well that Felix was in charge of punishments. "Do they have to be punished? They've all been badly frightened. Besides—"

"Do what you're told, Beric," said Crispus. "You don't want me to begin to suspect you of this foul thing. Quick now!"

The slaves were quite well aware that it wasn't all going to be forgiven and forgotten. They had discussed that during the night but not at great length. What was the use? It was much worse for Niger; if he was taken out of prison, it would be by Montanus, to get a worse flogging than he'd ever had yet—and alone. Perhaps not able to come to the others for weeks and weeks. Perhaps not ever again.

Manasses thought of his church with a desperate tenderness. If only he could take it all on himself! It must be like this being a father. Lalage was in a way the most important one—much more important than he was—but all of them were his children, for whom he would give his life. He had known now for quite a long time that this might happen, but not in detail. Besides, it is no use knowing things in the future; you have to experience them. He was in the middle of that now.

How cool and sweet-smelling the house was after prison. If one could stay here always, leading the easy life of a dining-room servant, content with little things . . . too late. If one had been having knowledge of the Kingdom all this time, one could not go back to the little things.

Now they were sent for. It was no use making a plan. Their master was sitting in his armchair and old Felix beside him, looking delighted. He did not often have a chance of taking it out on the dining-room boys. Beric was there too; it was his testing time, a different kind of test to theirs.

Manasses went down on his knees. So did the others.

Crispus looked at them. "What is all this nonsense I hear about your being Christians?"

"We are Christians, sir," Manasses said. "I am the leader."

"You wretched little Jew! Admitting it! So you were actually holding one of your filthy meetings in my house. A nice way of repaying me for all the kindness I've shown you. Have you or haven't you been well treated here?"

"Always, sir."

"Then what do you mean by joining this miserable sect?"

Manasses just didn't know how to begin to answer. At last he said, "Perhaps it isn't as bad as you think, sir."

"Indeed? Are you or are you not, as Christians, enemies of society? Answer. Do you or do you not wish to destroy civilization?"

"Not the way you mean, sir!"

"I'm afraid I'm not interested in how you propose to do it, Manasses. Whether by burning Rome or in some other way. You admit to treasonable intentions. You admit that this sect of yours is against law and order. Do you? Answer."

As Manasses hesitated, Argas answered, much less gently. "We've got something better to put in its place!"

"Indeed, Argas? And what is that?"

Argas would have found it easier to answer violence than irony. He said angrily, "Brotherhood," and looked away. His master had made it an impossible word, had withered it!

When Beric tried to say something, Crispus simply told him to hold his tongue. Then he regarded the slaves. At last he said, "There will be no more Christianity in this household. If any of you are caught having meetings, making signs, or talking about it, you will be sold at once. Or possibly sent back to prison. In the meantime, Felix will deal with you appropriately. Ah, yes, and double the amount for Manasses, as he is the leader. You admitted to being the leader, I think, Manasses?"

"Let me take it for the others, sir," Manasses said.

"That would impair your value as my property. No. Ah, and one other matter. There can be no question of your release, Phaon, until I am quite satisfied that you are no longer in any way connected with this wretched business. You may go."

They got to their feet, backing out from under their master's eyes.

He called after Felix. "By the way, the dining-room slaves are to be back at their duty this evening. See to it." When they were out he looked at Beric in a way that made him very uncomfortable and said, "You began to interrupt me just now. Well, what was it?"

"I know all these slaves. They're some of the best you've got—even the kitchen boy. Whether or not they're Christians, don't let Felix do what he likes with them! They'll be spoiled."

"What do you mean?"

Against the cold tone, Beric floundered on. "I mean, instead of having trust and affection from them—because I know they like you—there'll be hate and . . . oh, suspicion and fear! They've been honest, they've worked well, there's nothing against any of them—"

"You call this nothing? I see. Well, go on."

"When Argas said 'brotherhood,' what he meant was the Stoic thing, what I was taught—what you wanted me to learn. They only put it a different way—"

"You seem to know rather a lot about it. Do you?"

"Yes," said Beric, "I do."

"You had better forget it as soon as possible. Immediately after the wedding we shall go to the country. In the meantime . . . yes, go down to the yard and stay there during the whole of this punishment. It will be beneficial for you to see it. You are not to speak to any of the slaves. Do you understand?"

"Oh, very well!" said Beric and walked out with his head in the air, looking like a young savage. As if he had never had a Roman education.

Flavius Crispus was horribly worried about him. Surely he couldn't have been getting among the Christians? If so, it was quite obvious that the Christians were going to be exterminated. Whatever else he was or wasn't, Tigellinus was efficient. Really, Crispus felt, he was doing the greatest possible kindness to his slaves in getting them out of it now, while there was still time.

Beric went very quickly to Flavia's room and called, low, "Flavia! Your father's told that old fool Felix to whip your maid, and if you don't go and stop him she won't be fit to do your hair tomorrow."

That was quite decisive for Flavia. She came straight along and pulled Persis away. No doubt Persis would get slapped or have a few pins stuck into her, but at least it wouldn't be as bad as a flogging from Felix.

But Beric stayed. It took a long time, and no cloud came over the August sun. They all yelled except Argas, and the kind of quivering grunts he gave were very near it before the end. There was no nonsense about not cutting the backs of the dining-room slaves, and Phaon, who had never had more than the lightest flick before, was twisting and squealing like a pig in three minutes. Manasses stuck it the first time, but he was taken before the others and then had to watch them all before his second go. By that time his back was swollen, the bruises were coming out, and the edges of the cuts drying, and it all hurt that much more—as Felix intended it should.

In the end they were all lying on the ground in a very complete mess and stink, and Felix threw a few buckets of water over them. Manasses had fainted. After a minute or two Josias shifted a bit and began to stroke Manasses' forehead and whisper to him.

Beric was merely crying. In a little he went back to the house. He sat in his room till dinner was ready. From time to time he tried to say the prayer, but he couldn't make it mean anything.

Before dinner was quite ready, Mikkos and Sannio came along to remind him to wash and change, which otherwise he would have forgotten to do. They had both been in his working party.

"You cheer up, sir," Mikkos said. "They'll be all right."

"Oh, are you sure?" Beric asked. It seemed very unlikely.

"Yes, yes. In a week they'll have forgotten all about it, sir."

"Will they? I shan't!"

"It's just you not being used to it, sir," Sannio said. "Argas is doing fine. He was asking about you."

This was quite untrue. Sannio had been looking after Argas a bit, but he hadn't said a word about Beric. However, Sannio thought he'd try it out and see how the Briton took it. Beric was obviously delighted—which only showed what a liar young Argas was, thought Sannio, wishing to himself that he could have the Briton fussing over him like that!

Beric put on a clean tunic and went in to supper. There was only himself and Crispus, so, while the meal went on, Hermeias read aloud from an edifying volume of Panaetius on the so-called good. During dessert Crispus usually asked Beric questions about the chapter to see if he had been attending, but this evening Beric did not listen to one sentence in ten.

The slaves were all in attendance, including Manasses and Argas. Even if one hadn't known, it would have been quite obvious, from their faces and the way they moved, what had been done to them. The others did most of the waiting and stooping, but Crispus ordered Manasses to pour the wine as he usually did. Manasses managed it, but his hands shook and there was a greenish look about him.

Crispus disliked having pain thrust at him, but he was certain that he had been right to inflict it. Where was Phaon? He was to be fetched and made to stand against the opposite wall. Unfortunately Phaon seemed unable to stop crying. He did it quite quietly except for an occasional sob, but these began to get on Hermeias's nerves, and he read badly.

Crispus frowned at them both, also at Beric, who was not eating. "Are you ill?" Crispus said to him sharply. "You'd better be bled if you are. If you are not, control yourself."

Beric made an effort and bolted some food. He was trying to catch Argas's eye, to thank him for the message. But he didn't seem able to. It was horrible to be eating and drinking in physical comfort with those other three in the room. Again Phaon sobbed.

"If that boy can't behave," said Crispus, "I shall sell him."

Everyone felt it like a blow. Beric dropped a bunch of grapes. Hermeias lost his place. The slaves all drew themselves together and looked at one another. Phaon went completely still, only his face wrinkled up, and Beric had an awful feeling that he was going to scream, but couldn't think of any way of stopping it. Then Argas went, stiffly but very quickly, over to Phaon, took him by the shoulders and whispered something to him. It seemed effective, for he became quite quiet and stopped crying. Argas still stood beside him, his hands at his sides, his shoulders twitching occasionally.

Crispus beckoned to him with one finger.

He came closer. At another finger gesture he knelt, always looking straight past Beric at his real master. "What did you say?" Crispus asked him. "Answer. Answer."

Argas at last muttered, "It was some words of ours."

"Did or did I not say that if you used Christian words or signs again, you would be sold?"

"You said that, sir."

"Well?"

"He only did it to stop Phaon from screaming!" Beric said eagerly.

"Hold your tongue, Beric. Just for this once, I will give you the choice, Argas, between being sold tomorrow or being beaten again now. Choose."

After a moment Argas said, "Not to be sold." But as he said it, his body quivered and shrank with anticipation.

"Very well. Hermeias, take him at once to Felix and say he is to have as many strokes again as he has had already. No. Beric, you are to take him. Go. Come back when it is done. Not before."

Beric stood up, his fists clenched. He did not know what he was going to do, only not that.

But Argas turned to the door and went out, and Manasses signed with his head for Beric to follow. He caught Argas in the passage and put his arms around him, but Argas cried out. Any touch hurt now.

"If I can stand it," Argas said, "you can."

"But you can't forgive—"

"No. This is the *thing*."

"Can't we get out of it somehow?"

"No. It's nothing to what some of us are getting. Niger. And the women—if they're questioned in prison. It's not the cross yet."

"What's going to happen?"

"This. Come on. We can't hang around."

"You don't hate me, do you?"

"You, no. You're caught too. Anyway, I'm not hating anyone. I'm only angry. That's different. No, Beric, don't touch me!"

They went through toward the kitchen, and the forbidden room below. As they'd gone only the night before. Both of them thought of that.

Beric said, "I've got to stay and see it."

"It's better if you stay," Argas said, rather shakenly. "I can show off to you!"

They found Felix and, whatever Argas did, Beric hated him so much that he could not give the order.

"Another of the same!" Argas said, showing his teeth. "I liked it so much!" And he pulled the pins out of the shoulders of his tunic with tightened fingers. Under the tidy dining-room tunic, his back was a sight.

It was dusk now. Felix slowly lighted a lantern and methodically chose his whip, then jerked his thumb at the yard.

Again Beric stood watching and counting. But this time Argas couldn't bear it. He threshed about at every stroke, banging his hands against the ring and his head against the wall. Suddenly he began to scream.

Felix, pleased, stopped a moment and grinned, then went on. For two or three strokes Argas was able to keep from screaming, then he began again. When it was finished, and the rope slipped out of the ring, he dropped onto the ground and lay doubled up, his teeth chattering.

Felix held the lantern low to look at him. He and Manasses would now probably be scarred for life. Dapyx and Josias were anyhow. Phaon, not so far. Then Felix held the lantern up again and politely lighted Beric back into the house.

Beric came back to the dining-room to find all the slaves dismissed except Hermeias, who was still reading, apparently about the relation between the soul and some kind of divine essence.

"Sit down and listen, Beric," said Crispus. "This will do you good."

Beric listened for a few sentences extremely unsympatheti-cally. He then said in a loud voice that it was all nonsense.

Hermeias stopped reading and gaped at him.

Crispus said, "You must apologize for that, Beric."

"For speaking the truth?" said Beric. "My tutor told me a good Stoic always speaks the truth."

"Now you are being insolent, Beric. You will be sorry for this tomorrow."

"I'm past feeling sorry for things like that."

Crispus motioned to Hermeias to go, then said to Beric, quite gently, "We'd better have this out. I suppose you are angry be-cause Argas was your pet boy. It was a bad choice, and he must certainly have been far from truthful if you never guessed he was a Christian. But that is not important. What you must realize is that I have to do this so as to guard against something much worse."

It was curious how disconcerting Beric found even this much reasonableness. He couldn't simply answer back. "What could be much worse?" he said heavily, his elbows on his knees and his head in his hands, in a clumsy, barbarian-looking way.

"Supposing a thing like Christianity were allowed to spread, unchecked, undermining the roots of society. Wouldn't that be worse than whipping a few slaves?—which is all that has hap-pened so far. Really, Beric, you have lost all sense of proportion. There is nothing to upset you if you were in a rational state of mind."

Beric lifted his head for a moment, looking hard at Crispus. "I lied to you last night. Argas isn't my pet boy."

"Why on earth did you say so, then?"

"To make you believe the other things I was saying. To make them sound right. It wouldn't have meant anything to you if I'd said he was my friend. Would it?"

"I fear it conveys no clear meaning to me now."

"Surely a good Stoic would say that slavery is no bar to friendship? I read that in some book."

"Yes, but that was meant in a philosophical sense. Between adults. And—how can I express it?—not the kind of friendship that would induce passion and loss of self-control such as you have shown."

"I'm sorry. It made me lose control to see my friend do something brave and then be whipped for it till he screamed. And not to be able to help him."

"You seem to interpret all this in a most peculiar way, Beric."

"Well, wasn't it brave of Argas to risk his own skin to stop Phaon from screaming when you threatened to sell him?"

"Phaon was behaving like a sniveling little fool, and Argas was deliberately disobeying an order I had given three hours earlier!"

"It was the only way to stop Phaon. I ought to have thought of it myself."

"Do you know what he said, then?"

"I think I do."

"By the gods. This seems to be very much worse than I thought, Beric. You've been here with me since you were a tiny boy. I've let myself get fond of you. Probably you know that. And now—"

"Yes. I owe you the truth. Shall I go on with the other lies I told you last night?"

Crispus held up a hand to stop him for the moment. There was the boy turned into a man under his eyes, fearless in a kind of wild, emotional, personal way, as barbarians were—as his father had been before the emperor, when Crispus had first seen the little yellow-head staring boldly around him and decided to ask for him.

And it had come to this. Running his wild head deliberately into the future instead of allowing the future to come and accepting it calmly. "No, Beric," said Crispus, "not now. Just tell me one thing. Was it a lie that you knew where the slaves were on the night of the fire?"

"That was the truth. And I know for certain that no Christian started the fire."

"I see. But Manasses admitted that Christians were enemies of society."

"*You* don't like the way things are in Rome. Nor any of your real friends. You're all enemies of Nero and Tigellinus."

Crispus interrupted nervously, "That's something quite different. Better not talked about, either. Even at home."

"Is it really different?" Beric said slowly, trying to puzzle out in his own head the half-formed idea. "It only depends on how far you go with thinking that things are wrong."

It surprised Crispus very much to hear Beric talking this way. "You used not to be interested in such things, Beric," he said.

"They didn't seem to matter to me. Now they do. So I have to think about them. Real philosophy is asking questions, isn't it?"

"Acquiring wisdom, Beric."

"You can't do that without asking questions. That was what Socrates did."

"But he knew the answers, my boy."

"Well, did he? Isn't that only how it seems in the book afterward? Wasn't it different when it was really happening? But how it looks to me is that getting wisdom about anything must be always by questions if it's to be fresh wisdom. And that's the only kind I want, anyway! That was why I said Panaetius was nonsense. He only made clever sentences about what other people had found out.

"But please, I am sorry I said it the way I did. And once you start asking questions you can't stop. You go, and the questions begin to break up the kind of life you're used to leading, and then you're an enemy of society. As Socrates was."

"One should always know when to stop asking questions," Crispus said uneasily.

"Then someone else will ask the questions, as Socrates said they would after he was dead. That's in the Apology, I know. Killing him didn't stop his kind of questions being asked, because they were half in peoples' minds already. Because the things that were happening to people in Greece were making them ask that sort of question!"

Suddenly Beric realized that after all he had got something out of his Greek history lessons. "Christianity is only asking another set of questions, because things are different now, so they must be different questions, mustn't they?—and killing all the Christians in Rome won't stop their kind of questions being asked, either!"

"But if all questions were allowed, nothing would be safe. We can question too much, just as we can eat and drink too much—or be too happy. We must not try to be gods. All the legends of the gods—not that one believes them, of course, but they were made up for our guidance by wise men—tell us that there are certain things which must not be touched or questioned, or it will be the worse for everyone. We can ask questions about practical matters and about metaphysics, but if we start questioning the principles on which society is founded, then . . . then . . .

"My dear Beric, I am arguing with you as if you were my intellectual equal! Wait till you are my age. You will realize then the danger of these enthusiasms. These plausible enthusiasms. I wish your tutor had never let you read Plato. He is always a disturbing author. But I must say I never thought you were taking him in! When we are in the country you will have plenty of other things to think about. Hunting. Yes, nothing like a good day's hunting to clear one's head of ideas. You will enjoy hunting again, won't you?"

"Not if I know my friends here are being knocked about."

"What nonsense, Beric! You know quite well that I am not having the slaves whipped merely to amuse myself! I have to save them from this wretched business, in spite of themselves."

"Save them from Christianity?"

"Yes, yes, quite."

"Or save them from Tigellinus?"

"You seem to be implying that I might condone the Christianity if it were not officially condemned. But of course—naturally!— I should do nothing of the kind. No. In any case, they are my property, and I shall act as I think best, both for myself and for them."

"By thrashing them till they scream?"

"My dear boy, you talk as if I did it myself!"

"Well, it isn't very different, is it—for them?"

"It is an unfortunate necessity. The whole institution of slavery is bound to involve a certain amount of . . . well, possibly injustice. But only in a material sense. I grant you that in theory the essence of a slave's soul may be as fine as his master's. If so, he can disregard his bodily circumstances."

"I don't think anyone can quite disregard being whipped by Felix. I couldn't begin to myself."

216

"I wish I hadn't sent you to see it. You took it quite the wrong way!"

"It would have happened just the same if I hadn't seen it. You know, I obeyed you. I didn't talk to them—only a word or two to Argas the second time. But I'm going to talk to them now."

It was quite obviously no use forbidding Caradoc's son to do what he had said in that tone he was going to do. "If you insist on doing anything so foolish," Crispus said, "at least remember that anything you say will be overheard. And that rewards will no doubt be offered to informers later on."

"Thank you for letting me do it!" said Beric, embarrassingly grateful. "Can I have some money to get some of the others out of prison?"

"I can't have you going to that prison and—and getting involved," said Crispus, "getting your name taken for all I know!"

"Then I'll give the money to someone else. If you'll let me have it."

"Oh, Beric, I wish you were a little older! This is all intolerably dangerous. Now listen to me carefully. You know you are not a citizen. That means that you have no legal rights. If you were arrested there would be nothing to stop your being tortured or killed in any foul manner they chose to devise. I take it you are not being stupid enough to suppose that being the son of a king makes any difference.

"Your father was an enemy of Rome. Your survival was the merest accident of the imperial clemency. Your present position is equally the accident of my affections, and that again is partly due to the accident that my only son died as an infant, with his mother. You have taken advantage of these accidents. No, I am not blaming you, Beric, merely stating facts. But you have less rights—less legal existence—than if you were actually my property."

Beric slipped over and knelt beside him. "I always supposed myself to be—in a way—yours."

"Then surely you might have realized how deeply all this would go against my wishes?"

"It was part of something else. Oh, I've got into a tangle. Two different kinds of good. It never said in the books that they could go against one another!"

"Metaphysics was never your best subject, Beric. Perhaps one never appreciates it until after one has had experience of life. Now, attend to me. I have forbidden the slaves to have any more to do with—what we have been discussing. And I have enforced this prohibition. I would be perfectly within my rights to enforce it on you in the same way. Do you understand?"

"Yes."

"However, I shall not do so. I shall merely leave it to your good sense."

Beric dropped his head down on the couch. This made it difficult. Clearly, he ought to go halfway to meet this kindness, this reasonableness. But he had seen the slaves whipped. The community of which he had been one also demanded his loyalty. The sense of the prayer. Was this being led into temptation?

"Well?" asked Crispus.

"The ones in prison," said Beric, sticking to that at least, "it's only a matter of money. Just two or three of them anyhow—"

"You are not to go to the prison yourself. But I will let you have a reasonable sum. I think you had better take it at once. Then you will be able to start fresh tomorrow. We will go along to my room now and find it. And the wedding tomorrow too! Really, it is all most awkward and annoying."

He got up, and so did Beric. "It is quite bad enough, my mother insisting that she is not well enough to come to the wedding. She ought to have come. After all, Candidus is her side of the family! And my cousins fussing and flapping at me. And now you, Beric."

Beric took the money over to Eunice's.

She was crying a little, having been to the house since Phaon's whipping. She told Beric that Niger had been fetched, that she herself had got Euphemia out, and that they were holding Rhodon.

On the whole they were making a practice of keeping at least one member of each community in the prison, so that pressure could be put immediately. And if the police thought they could get anything definite on a man or woman, then they were not released either. And some of the slaves had not been claimed. Nobody quite knew when the trials were to be. If at all.

"We'll keep the money," Eunice said. "It's sure to be needed later on. Oh, it is good of you, Beric!"

"The least I could do," Beric muttered, not wanting to stay.

"Those poor boys!" Eunice said, "and little Persis, not much older than my Phaon. I wonder when they'll be able to come to a meeting again."

"You know what Crispus said about that, Eunice."

"Oh yes, I know," she answered, rubbing her eyes. "It was bound to come sooner or later. They'll depend on you now, dear. We'll keep up the meetings here, and by and by, when Crispus isn't so angry . . . Unless we're all arrested again before that. But you'll be able to come."

"I've got to be away from Rome for a bit, in the country."

Eunice looked dismayed. "We'll miss you."

He was just going away, when Lalage came in from the street. "Beric!" She held up the lantern to see his face. "What's the matter?"

"He's brought us in some money," Eunice said. "Isn't that nice of him! But I say keep it till we need it more."

"What we're going to need," Lalage said, "won't be money, but courage and faith. And nobody to stay with us who wants to go. Do you want to go, Beric?'

He did not answer at once, but Eunice said, "Whatever can you be thinking of, Lalage, to ask that? Hasn't he just brought us all this money?"

"Money's easy. If you can come by it at all. Eunice thinks it's wonderful, all those silver pieces, because she only makes a little herself, don't you, old duck? But I've done enough dancing in good houses to know about money. It was easy, wasn't it, Beric?"

"Yes," he said gloomily, "I suppose it was easy." She knew too much about it. "Easier than being whipped. But you won't ever allow anything to be easy, will you, Lalage?"

"No," she said, "I like to know where I am. When the Kingdom comes, it will be easy. Till then, we have Jesus and one another. But everything else is against us."

He spoke almost enviously. "You're sticking it, Lalage."

"Of course. I've nothing else that's worthwhile."

219

"But supposing it gets stopped. Tigellinus intends to wipe it out completely, and he's got the power. You know he has."

"Power to do that? Oh no! All he can do is torture us and kill us. He might catch every Christian in Rome and do that, but all the same the Kingdom would come. Faith is like ships' rats, Beric. At the last moment of the last agony, faith will jump from one heart to another. It's quite astonishing how that happens. It was what happened between Stephen and Paul. And somebody has to be Stephen. It was what happened between Jesus and all of us. So, if we die, we are that much in His image. That is, if we die His way." And she made the sign on herself.

"How?"

"Fighting against evil through love and forgiving the people. Difficult, isn't it? Poor Beric! But you'll see for yourself. On us, I hope."

"Oh, Lalage!" He caught her hands. "Don't go and get killed on purpose!"

"I don't want to die," she said. "It's lovely to be alive if one's a Christian. Isn't it, Eunice? But if I'm needed to die, I shall. Now, Beric, go along. I've got to talk over some things with Eunice, and I don't want anyone outside us to hear."

"Don't you trust me?" he asked, hurt.

"I don't want you to hear anything that later on you might find it awkward to have heard. If you are still with us, but not of us."

"I asked to be baptized last night!"

"And we're not baptizing you today. Never mind, Beric. If you're to be part of it, your time will come."

Beric went out, dismissed. Although he had wanted to go before Lalage came in, yet, when she told him to, he had wanted to stay. What had she seen wrong with him? Was it his talk with Crispus?

Or was it killing Sotion? There had been so much to do and think about since then that he had hardly bothered about it, but now he began to remember that the man had cried for mercy, had invoked a name that should have made Beric very unwilling to murder. Nobody else knew that. But oughtn't he to confess, to ask forgiveness? Christians don't kill. But he could only get forgiveness from the others. From God and the others. Not from Sotion.

Sotion was dead, finished, over, would never come to the feet-washing again. Having been alive, was dead. Was Sotion a ghost?

Ought he to do something about it? He began vaguely to think about rites of propitiation. He began to be rather frightened, though he didn't quite know what of.

In the hot attics under the sloping roof tiles, the slaves who were the property of Flavius Crispus slept on straw mattresses or hay infrequently changed and scratchy blankets. Hermeias had a cubbyhole to himself, near his master, but the others were over-crowded now, because of the cousins' household. That was par-ticularly unpleasant in hot weather. It meant more quarrels, more of the constant heavy stench from other people's bodies, more bugs and cockroaches in the dark and flies as soon as it was light, and never any real quiet. In summer the quarrels were worse over love affairs and sleeping by the windows, less over blankets and candle ends, though the latter were useful for vermin. The women in their attics quarreled too and stole one another's things rather more than the men, and screamed and cried more. But most of them were at the far end of the house, from considerations of con-venience and morality.

The dining-room slaves had claimed a bit of the attic for themselves, with a partition of sticks and blankets. Lamprion, who was rather older than the others and an expert carver, had the best place, by the window, and a locked box where he kept his things. He had an understanding with one of the house boys, a pale little Illyrian, and paid him mostly in dining-room food. Mikkos liked a girl when he could get one. The other dining-room boys were a Spaniard who spoke very bad Greek—a thief when he got the chance—and a Coan, not much older than Phaon, who was al-ways seeing ghosts.

The others had spend the last hour or so cross-questioning the Christians, but now Lamprion was bored and had gone to sleep. The three had got out of answering on the grounds that they had been forbidden to say anything about it and weren't going to risk their skins again, but it was sometimes possible to ask a question sufficiently irritating to make one of them snap some-thing back.

Phaon was crying because Pistos, the Coan, had been teasing him so much. Argas was crying a little too; he couldn't get into any kind of tolerably comfortable position, and he was trying to begin forgiving his master but could not make the necessary mental effort.

It was a difficult readjustment for the Christians. Always before, there had been this thing between them, this clean, live hope and practice. Now the others had got hold of it, were asking these horrible questions, not because they wanted to know but because they wanted to hurt. And it would be worse for Josias and Dapyx. In another moment Manasses meant to pull himself together, get up and go to them. He had warned them not to answer, but it might have been too hard for them.

Sannio and Mikkos were both in a way rather sympathetic, but it wouldn't do to be serious. However, they had got hold of some oil and rags to cover the cuts and stop them getting flies on them and drying sore. They had laughed at the Christians, of course, but had handled them kindly. Sannio saw that the water was finished and took the jug to get some more. If he could sneak some wine to mix with it, so much the better. The water tasted rather foul in summer and wasn't cold.

He felt his way down the ladder and into the kitchen. There was someone there. The Briton. Sannio said, "Were you looking for anything, sir?" And then, "I'm getting some water for Argas, sir. I was wondering if there was any wine left to mix."

"Of course there is," said Beric, glad to find something practical he could do. He had come in and had wanted to go to bed and forget about everything, but nothing let him—not the porter's face, turned to watch him; not Hermeias hurrying past him with a book in a shocked way; not a small occasional sobbing, from the direction of Flavia's room, that must be Persis.

That was what did it finally. He wanted to go and stop Persis from crying. But it was too near Flavia's room. She might come out and find him, and she was marrying Aelius Candidus tomorrow. So he had gone off with his lamp toward the kitchen, wondering where the others were. He did not know exactly where they slept. He had been glad to see Sannio and, when Sannio suggested that he might like to see Argas, he agreed eagerly and climbed the ladder after him.

For a moment the sickening slave-smell and heat of the attic choked him, and he could not see who was where. His coming had hushed them all, breaking off sentences or sobs. Then Sannio pulled his arm and pointed to Argas, lying on his face, naked, his back dabbed with the oily rags.

But now, among the slaves, there was nothing Beric could say. He did not even like to touch any of the three for fear of hurting them more. He knelt beside Argas, patted his hand clumsily, and asked if they were all right.

Argas didn't respond at all. *Silly fool,* Sannio thought. Manasses said they were getting along. No, there was nothing he could do for them, but it was kind of him to have thought of it. He went away again.

He sat down on the kitchen table, feeling wretched, trying to think it out. The cockroaches on the floor rustled about their business, no more remote, really, than the slaves had been in their underworld.

Presently Manasses climbed slowly and painfully down the ladder. Beric went over and asked where he was going. He answered, to see Josias and Dapyx and later, when he was sure everyone was asleep, Persis.

"Better not," said Beric. "If you're caught going to her you might be whipped again."

"But I'm the deacon," Manasses said. "I must comfort her if I can. And you," he added suddenly.

"Me? Why?"

"You need it, don't you, son? You're alone. You haven't got the sense of Jesus or the sense of the community, not like we have. And Argas didn't answer you just now. I expect that was because if he'd said anything he'd have said too much. But it was hard on you when you wanted to help."

"You're a queer sort of bird, Manasses, thinking about me just now!"

"But I'm the deacon," Manasses said again. "That means I'm the servant of you all, or it doesn't mean anything. It means trying to be like Jesus, and I don't often get the chance to be."

"Will you at least let me go and see Persis for you?"

Manasses hesitated, at last said, "Yes. Tell her I sent you. If you don't mind saying that."

So, after waiting another hour or two, reading, Beric went up toward the room where Flavia was lying in her last maiden sleep. He saw by the light of his lamp that Persis had cried herself out and now her eyes were shut, her hair tangled and plastered down on to her sticky cheeks.

He wondered whether to wake her, but suddenly she stirred, saw him, and cowered. He made the sign, and almost immediately she stopped thinking he was going to rape her and made the sign back. "Manasses sent me," he whispered and sat down beside her on the mattress.

"Please," she whispered back, "what's going to happen to us?"

"Nothing more now. Did she hurt you, Persis?"

"Oh, not very much. And I forgave her. I can bear it better when I manage to. Do tell me about Manasses and the others."

"I think they're all right. They're being very brave, Persis. You will be too."

"I'll try. Only, when she takes me away to the new house, I shall be all alone."

"She's sure to come back here often and bring you. You won't be so far." He wondered what Manasses would have said, how he could have comforted this child. "We'll miss you, Persis."

"Oh, will you?" she whispered back.

He put his arm around her and kissed the top of her head. She snuggled against him. For a time they sat like that, almost in darkness. He began to think a little about Flavia, but somehow the thinking was blurred by the soft weight of the slave girl leaning against his shoulder. He did not seem to mind any longer about Flavia's being married tomorrow.

13

Compromise

The traditional flame-colored veil was not very becoming to Flavia, but she was too excited to notice, and nobody else paid any attention. The wedding was an occasion for much more than that. It was something that Balbus and Crispus had planned goodness knows how long ago. So often plans went wrong. But not this one. It had not even been put aside by the fire.

Crispus was delighted with everything. One of the cousins acted as presiding matron. The sacrifice was made in due form. Almost all his friends had come, also his wider family—freedmen and freedwomen, including, for instance, Eunice, and also Beric's old tutor, Nausiphanes, who now had a little school of his own. There were tables of food and wine, not only in the dining room but along the sides of the main courtyard, where silk hangings between the pillars kept the sun at bay yet glowed in all their colors with percolating light.

Beric went around seeing that everybody had all they wanted. He was pleased to see Nausiphanes again. He found he wanted to discuss with his old tutor certain points that had definitely not interested him a couple of years ago.

For a minute or two Nausiphanes thought the boy was merely being polite in a rather heavy-handed way but then discovered to his surprise that Beric was genuinely interested, that something had penetrated his British head after all! Why was it, though, that Beric wanted to know about the theory of the State and its rights over individuals? He himself disbelieved profoundly in the State and all its manifestations, whether civil or religious. But these things weren't meat for boys. He answered cautiously, suggested a few books to read, including one in Latin by an Epicurean author, Catius. "But perhaps I shouldn't suggest that," he said. "Some people consider him subversive."

"I'll be careful," Beric said, speaking as someone who was not unused to subversive thoughts.

"One begins asking questions about the universe," Nausiphanes said, "and ends by asking questions about particular institutions. And the answers may be rather startling."

"But we must always go on questioning, mustn't we?" Beric asked.

"That depends," said Nausiphanes. "It was never a Roman vice."

Beric very much wanted to ask his tutor if he had ever heard of the Christians, but it was difficult in the crowd.

However, a few minutes afterward, Lucan, who was being rather greedy about the lobsters, brought up the subject himself, asking Beric if he'd ever heard of them.

Beric admitted cautiously that he had.

"Is it any good?" asked Lucan. "Could I get anything out of it?"

"Not for poems, I don't think," Beric said, adding that he really knew next to nothing about it.

"Probably all hysterics," Lucan said, taking another lobster.

"They certainly didn't set Rome on fire."

"No one in their senses thinks that." Lucan then asked in an undertone if it was true that some of Crispus's household had been arrested.

Beric said it was so.

"Low types, no doubt?" Lucan asked. "Asiatics? No Greeks?"

"Two were Greeks," Beric said, "and they were some of the best of our boys. They are still!"

Lucan raised his eyebrows and moved away.

Did I speak too passionately? Beric wondered. *But I can't stand the way he talks! These drawing-room Stoics. I hate poetry, anyway.* Then he saw Felicio, who was waiting about with the marriage contract. He whispered, "Where's Niger?"

Felicio said, "Having it knocked out of him." He shrugged his shoulders. "Our respected overseer has been having lots of fun with the poor devil. It's amazing what these blacks can stand. But he wasn't fit to carry a litter pole today."

"If you've a chance, Felicio, tell him I—we—asked about him."

"That'll cheer him up. He needs it!"

"Felicio, I suppose you aren't going to—take any more interest, now?"

Felicio shook his head. "I don't think so. I've got the wrong sort of mind for it." Then someone called him to bring over the contract.

Beric kept out of the way of the bridegroom. For whatever reasons, he disliked Aelius Candidus. He could not see any place to start forgiving him from. But he had so little practice. Perhaps Lalage could tell him how to.

There was plenty to do all that evening, bustling around arranging the procession that took the bride to her new home. There were always a few guests who got a little too excited, and you had to stop them rushing about with torches. And then there was all the clearing up of the house. Besides, Beric felt very much that Crispus was keeping an eye on him.

He did not talk to any of the slaves. They seemed all right. He would have liked to know what was happening to Phineas and Sapphira. Eunice had whispered to him that neither Rhodon nor any of the others had been questioned by torture—so far.

But they started off for the country quite early the next morning, and he could only say a friendly good-bye to the three others, nothing secret. At the city gates the horses were waiting for him and Crispus, and a bumpy ox-carriage, curtained and well lined with cushions, for the cousins and their maids. Two more cartloads of slaves and baggage followed, in charge of Hermeias. The only dining-room slaves who were taken were Lamprion and the Spaniard. Domina Aelia had her own staff, and Crispus, of course, intended to live simply.

For the first few miles they rode at the same pace as the carriage, past fenced market gardens and intensively cultivated farms. Here there were refugee camps, and the road was never empty of animals and carts and hurrying people, all kicking up an intolerable amount of dust.

Beric kept thinking back and worrying and wondering how long Crispus would make him stay in the country. He wished he had gone over to Phineas the night before. He had allowed himself to be too much influenced and embarrassed by what he had supposed Crispus was feeling. He ought to have managed somehow to see Argas alone. He ought to have found Lalage and shown her that she was wrong not to trust him.

Then they all stopped and picnicked in a piece of woodland by the road. The slaves put down rugs and cushions. The cousins complained. Crispus was bitten by an ant. The wine had not been kept as cool as it should have been.

Then the riders went on ahead, leaving the carriage and carts to go at their own pace. The country was more open now. The dust was less irritating. There were fewer people, and as often as not they were just sitting by the roadside or amiably lazing along at an ox's pace. They called greetings in country voices to the riders. Rome had dropped behind. Their road discreetly dipped under a great, clean, powerful stretch of arches—one of the great aqueducts that converged from the hills onto the capital, marching its way across country like a legion.

And now Beric was beginning to enjoy his ride, was beginning to say to himself, *Well, no use worrying about it for the moment.* It was pleasant to get the smell of ashes right out of one's nostrils at last!

Soon they were in the foothills, among vineyards. In most, the grapes were not quite ripe for picking, but in some the vintage was on, and there was noise and laughing and pleased squeals. They were offered ripe, sun-hot bunches of wine grapes, and Crispus paid in small coins.

Now every one knew him, and soon they were on his own land, and he was looking about him, telling Beric to remind him the next day of this or that which needed doing.

They made the usual detour to the rocky corner where the forest came down to the edge of the fields and the shrine of Silvanus, a low wall surrounding an old, shapeless stone altar. Here the farmer and his sons and most of the farm and house slaves were waiting, also a young ram, suitably garlanded with leaves. Crispus dismounted and proceeded to sacrifice.

Beric was given the bowl of meal to hold. He wondered what Christians were supposed to do about this. Manasses had said that no Christian ever joined in worship of the old gods, who were powers of evil and fear. But Crispus, who actually had to stick the knife in the sheep's throat, didn't for a moment believe in, still less fear, Silvanus, the God of Boundaries. It was just one of the things which, as landowner, one had to do, or the farm workers would be upset. Partly because not doing it would be unlucky; partly because they would miss a good square meal of best mutton. By custom the carcass, after due inspection of the heart, was handed over to them.

There were various small shrines on the estate. More of them would have to be visited sooner or later. But was this something that Beric oughtn't do? Well, anyway, he wasn't really a Christian! He held the bowl of meal in the right manner, and the sacrifice was properly consummated, the omens declared good, and everyone looked pleased. Must that pleasure, that sense of things going well and customarily, be taken away from the country workers?

A little farther along, out of reach of Silvanus and his influences, which were inimical to women—or they to him; one never quite knew which—the grandmother, Domina Aelia, was waiting in her litter. She looked very sprightly under her white hair and veil and could obviously have come down to Rome for her granddaughter's wedding if she had chosen! She was delighted to see her son and also Beric, who had always been a favorite with her. And, as he kissed her hand, and then she touched his forehead, welcoming him into the protection of the household gods, he felt an intense and definite sense of security and realized how much he must have been missing it all these last days in Rome.

Their horses were led off, and they walked on to the house for a cool bath and change of clothes and a supper of chicken and the crispest of fresh salads. Later on in the evening the carriages with the cousins turned up, and there was chatter and bustle till bedtime. Beric, in his old room, slept soundly and dreamlessly and woke in the morning with the birds.

The country house was very pleasant. The clean blaze of the noon sun was tempered by pine-scented hill airs. In Rome, a house must be a fortress against the smells of garbage and ashes. Flowers must be brought in. Human bodies must be scented. Here there was no need. The house could stand open to nature;

the flowers could be left to grow. There were riding horses in the stable, pigeons on the roof. The slaves were not overworked. There were cheerful faces everywhere. Old age was full of merriment and wisdom. And the rural sacrifices were always an excuse for dancing in the evenings and straying off into the cool woods under the full moon. So what?

Well, that was fine for three or four days, and the others in Rome would be all right. Perhaps when he got back he'd find nothing had been quite as bad as he'd thought. Or as disturbing. And there was a boar hunt arranged for tomorrow.

And then he dreamed about Flavia. In his dream everything was as it had been, and she had whispered to him, "King's son." And he woke up with a heaviness and acute realization that it was all over forever.

And at intervals the next day, during the hunt, he kept on imagining Flavia's shape and texture of body, imagining elasticities and movements and smells and sounds, until his body and mind were wretched, all zones of feeling tense and jumpy, and his heart bumping heavily. He was tired out at the end of the day and had missed his boar, which had got clear away after goring one of the hunters.

The same evening, Crispus had a long talk with him about his future and that was worrying too. Going into a legion and ultimately perhaps to an administrative post in Britain meant very definitely becoming part of the rule of Rome.

But if he did that, Crispus would manage to get him citizenship and status. And if one didn't have these things? He looked down into a shocking gulf of precariousness, which Crispus had illumined in detail. Could one be expected to live like that? And there was something else. If he became a citizen, and, indeed, an important one, wouldn't he be of much more use to the Christian community? Wouldn't that help to dispel the view that they were all hysterical slaves trying to get back at the masters and citizens?

Crispus, in any case, took it for granted that Beric would fall in with everything completely. And Beric, assenting, couldn't think of an alternative. Nor could he be anything but very grateful to Crispus and glad of his luck. He knew he would enjoy being an officer. He would like learning that particular kind of skill. He liked danger well enough. Obviously he hadn't the kind of brain to be a lawyer or a poet or a philosopher or even an architect or doctor, none of which professions opened an avenue for citizenship, as far as he could see.

After dinner he went to his room and said the prayer, but, uninterpreted, it didn't hold his mind. In three minutes he was back on Flavia. Tired of saying a Stoic and rational no to the image, he lay down on his bed and let himself go to it. Let himself imagine this or that.

He had an upper room with a balcony. Outside it was blue dusk, which he could see whenever he opened his eyes. The blue deepened, and a nightingale was singing like something inside him, and the image in his arms was almost tangible.

When he opened his eyes again, the blue was velvet black and prickled with stars. He heard whispers outside his window, went and looked, and saw there was a couple clasped in the shadow under the balcony. Probably two of the slaves, but he couldn't recognize either of them. He only knew jealously that they were mutual flesh and blood, went back and found something in the room to empty over them, break up the couple into squeals and swearing—spoil their night for them!

Then he remembered that he had an ivory box with a curl of Flavia's hair in it. If he gave that to a witch? He thought now that it would be even more satisfactory to hurt her than to have her in his arms. The witch would make a figure with the hair in it, and he could stick pins into it.

And then suddenly he couldn't help remembering that Persis had forgiven the pins that were stuck into her. Oh, he didn't want to think about Persis or any of them! But suppose a master or mistress had done to Persis and—whoever it might be—what he'd just done to that couple of slaves under the window. Would she forgive that too? And would this couple be bound to know it was he? Would he see it in the eyes of one of the slaves tomorrow?

The next day there was a spot of trouble in the houses because old Domina Aelia complained of a ghost in the passage between her wing of the villa and the main building. It mewed at her. Somebody must have been murdering someone! Various rites were performed, much to Crispus's irritation, but Beric was worried in case he had brought the ghost with him. Suppose it didn't go, and they got hold of someone who was really good at smelling out ghosts, and it was traced to him?

He had heard Crispus saying there would be one extra for dinner, and he wondered who the guest could be. One of their country neighbors perhaps.

He had been down to the swimming pool for a rapid, angry swim and was coming back to the house when he saw someone he did not know riding up.

At the house, Crispus was talking to the rider, who then turned to him, held out his hand, and said something that he didn't understand but that yet was familiar, which made him forget all he was thinking, and he seemed to know the answer though he didn't understand that either.

"You know, Beric," said Crispus, beaming, "you and your brother look very much alike. Yes, I should have seen it anywhere."

During dinner, Beric listened to the talk between Crispus and Clinog on municipal government. His brother seemed to know a great deal about roads and aqueducts and how to build main drains and conduct municipal sacrifices. It was rather intimidating. And also rather worrying, because such things were generally useful. They weren't a matter of pride and power and therefore obviously evil, but they were certainly part of the rule of Rome. Would they even be possible if everyone was poor? Didn't this prove that there had got to be riches and order?

But now Clinog was discussing the high price they had to pay for public-work slaves, unless there were criminals or prisoners of war to be had cheap. And they were sometimes more bother than they were worth in disciplining and didn't always last. Yes, it was always an effective threat to the household slaves to say they'd be sold for roadwork. Everyone knew what that meant. Discipline, yes. Worked to death and not a chance of getting out of it. And that was what public works meant. So one would have to do without them. Drains and baths and all. Dropping civilization. Unless they could be done some other way? But he couldn't think how.

The next day he and Clinog went for a long ride. At first they talked about the old days, but it wasn't much of a success, because Beric remembered so little.

Crispus had asked Clinog to have a steadying talk with his younger brother, so when the conversation about Britain had petered out, he began to discuss the machinery of running a city so that the citizens should be secure, healthy, proud of themselves and their own civil and religious institutions, and yet unquestionably loyal to the central authorities. He talked about magistracies and the difficulties of always finding the right man who was willing to take the job, about public contracts and the necessity of getting them into the proper forms and words, and about guilds, which were extremely important for keeping the artisan class suitably employed in their leisure time, as well as being pleasing to the gods.

All the time he kept on using lots of technical phrases and words, which he liked very much, and finally said that he hoped in time to be sent back to the province to help on the civil side of government. He'd like to get one or two British towns properly organized, as an example to the rest. Rivers bridged, swamps drained, streets cleaned, markets policed, weights and measures inspected, first- and second-class baths provided for all citizens. He knew already where the best building stone and brick clay were.

"And there would be no labor difficulties," he said with enthusiasm. "There would always be cheap slaves coming in from the north and west, wherever we happened to be going forward."

"Clinog," said Beric slowly, "suppose things had gone a bit differently, you and I'd have been cheap slaves from the west."

Clinog stared at him. "Well, we are not!" he said. "And it's a very ungrateful boy you are to be thinking such things! Considering poor old father, we've been in luck, yes! What are you looking so black at me for, Beric? Is it the truth I am speaking or not?"

"I don't feel like you do about Rome," Beric said.

They were walking their horses up a field. Clinog said nothing for a minute, then, rather carefully, "Most likely you will not have heard, Beric, but—remember Rudri?"

"Only the way he used to pull my hair. What's happened to him?"

"He's dead. Myself, don't know the sense of it, but it seemed to them he wasn't loyal. It's dangerous to think any way but one about Rome. I like to live."

"But Rudri didn't—*do* anything!"

"No. Only thought. And talked. It doesn't do to talk. No indeed."

"But, Clinog, aren't you really keen on these drains and roads of yours?"

"To be sure I am. But I'm not the kind to go leading revolts. That gets nowhere."

"So you'll use the chain gangs of Britons who have revolted to make roads for the legions!"

"They would be used for something by someone, Beric. No use having silly thoughts about slaves, even if they happen to be Britons. Ah, they'll knock all that out of you when you're a soldier or whatever it is, indeed yes. I suppose you will get a fine command later on. You'll be a governor yet. You will be taking your patron's name when you've been made a citizen. Flavius Bericus. Look you, my good brother, what is it now?"

But Beric said nothing, only gave his horse a kick, then after a time let Clinog draw level with him again and asked, "Have you ever killed anyone, Clinog?"

"Yes. Have you?"

"Yes. Did it get you down?"

"No. It was no one that mattered. Certainly not. I had every right to kill him, as a matter of fact."

"Mine didn't matter either. But perhaps one never has a right to kill anyone."

"It would be impossible to have an orderly world without the right of killing."

"I'm not sure. But—I was thinking of killing someone else."

"Don't you go killing a citizen, Beric. Is it?"

"Yes. You'd know his name."

"I don't like the sound of it, no! Are you jealous? Or what?"

"He has—injured some friends of mine. He's likely to go on doing it. If I kill him, I don't intend to get caught."

"I should hope not, indeed! You've got to look out, young Beric, because if any of us who are not citizens do get caught—"

"Yes, I know. I am wondering how I can do it."

"Now, think, couldn't you just leave it alone? Who are these friends of yours? . . . well, if you won't tell me! But we can't always

234

go running into danger for the sake of friends. That was all very pretty in our stories of heroes—you won't remember them, though, nor the music that went with them!—but now we are in Rome. A man can't so much as have a blood feud here.

"Mind you, Beric, I feel for you, I do indeed, for it is hard not to be able to take revenge, but it is no good here. And it may be the Romans have the right idea. You can't have that and also these fine aqueducts which do not leak at all. Must you do this?"

"I won't if there's another way."

"That's right, boy. There's a way around as often as not."

"I hope there's going to be for me."

They turned their horses for home now. Beric was thinking about the practical difficulties of killing Tigellinus, the man who stood for the rule of Rome. One had to do something against that. Yes.

Clinog naturally went to pay his respects to Domina Aelia.

She always wanted to know what was going on, and she particularly liked talking to young men. One day when she was sitting out on the terrace, she made Beric sit beside her and describe Flavia's wedding, which he did rather uncomfortably. "You'd have liked to be the one, wouldn't you?" she said suddenly. "Come, own up, boy!"

"Yes," he said sullenly, as she laughed.

"You're well out of it," said the old lady energetically, smacking his hand. "That girl was spoiled! Catch me going to her wedding. I told Crispus how it would be, but he's as stupid as the rest of you. That girl's been allowed to think she can do as she likes. *You* won't know, but her maids will, that's certain. She's had everything except the thing that matters. Do you know what I mean by that, boy?"

He shook his head.

"Something to serve. And if there's no something, then someone. That's what marriage is for. And how it used to be. But now! Catch any of these young couples serving one another!"

"Aelius Candidus isn't worth serving, anyhow."

"No. Nor's she. Ah, you'd have found that out quick enough! I shan't be surprised if she finds someone else. Though her poor father will be. You men! I like you, Beric. Always have, ever since the days I used to tan your bottom for you. Wish I'd done it oftener to her. Have *you* found anything to serve, Beric?"

He hesitated, and she pounced on him again. "A thing, I said. Not a girl, Blue Eyes! Nor yet a boy." She laughed at him again. But he didn't mind. He was wondering if he had.

"I think I have, Domina Aelia," he said at last. "Only, is it a thing? You can't serve a thing."

"Rightness is a thing. The gods are things. Rome is a thing. Or was—before the emperor."

"What I want to serve is people. All men. All free."

"Oh, you Stoics! You'll get over that. I know you, talking about equality. Freedom of noble souls! What does it amount to? I'll tell you something, Beric. There's only one kind of equality that makes sense, and that's equality in something you can measure— land or money. How do you like that?"

"You're quite right, Domina Aelia," Beric said.

"I'm glad you've got the grace to say so, boy! That was the kind of equality Tiberius Gracchus and all those Stoic friends of his tried to make for the Roman people, and what happened to him?"

"He had to die for it."

"And no one said thank you, and no one was a penny the better. But at any rate Tiberius Gracchus had the sense not to talk about doing it for all men! He did it for the sake of the race, so that the poor citizens could afford to bring up their sons to be soldiers. That was sense. But you and your ideas!"

"All that was nearly two hundred years ago, Domina Aelia. Ideas change. They take in more."

"And mean less! I shall be pleased when you're a Roman citizen yourself, Beric. You shall come and choose yourself a sig- net ring from my box. Yes, one from my side of the family. The big sardonyx, if you like it, boy. Better you have it than young Candi- dus, for all those ideas of yours."

She reached for her stick, got up, and nodded wisely at Beric.

But Beric was finding he had to start thinking about it all over again. If he had found something worth living and dying for, he wasn't doing much about it now! Could he write to Argas and ask what was happening?—say something friendly, anyhow?

Every two days or so Crispus sent in a slave with letters, who came back with the answers and news from the capital. Beric tried to find out if anything more was being done about the Christians, but Crispus wouldn't say a word to him on that subject. And if he wrote to Argas, what could he say that wouldn't be a giveaway in case somebody else read it, as they were almost sure to do? Crispus would be certain to get wind of it too. Above all, he didn't want to get Argas into trouble again. Perhaps he ought to try to make friends with some of the slaves here. It was difficult with the country boys; they just grinned and said, "Oh yes, sir!" to anything. Their own lives were tucked away underneath somewhere; you couldn't get at them.

Hermeias definitely avoided him, felt that something had happened that was not at all nice.

Beric wasn't sure how much he liked or trusted Lamprion, who was a regular, slick young Greek, ready for anything. It was he, Beric remembered, who'd been Manasses' chief tormenter in the cruelty to the Jewish slaves, had held his nose and stuffed pork into his mouth. And he, Beric, at the time had thought it funny, though he stopped them breaking Manasses' teeth; he had good teeth. But if Manasses had forgiven Lamprion, that was good enough. Beric set himself to try to be friendly with him, talk to him as an equal, not a slave.

Lamprion talked back all right, and in no time was on terms of a cheeky familiarity that Beric disliked very much but couldn't do a thing about now! He had asked Lamprion to call him by his name when they were alone, but every time he did, it made him squirm. He was secretly delighted when Crispus scolded Lamprion for carelessly letting the roast get cold one day. But he felt a beast about it afterwards and prayed and tried to get it right.

The slaves always seemed to get hold of the gossip from Rome, so it was from Lamprion that Beric first heard that people were saying that the prefect of the Praetorians had been visiting at the house of Aelius Candidus at hours when the master of the house was quite definitely away on duty at the prison.

Beric was aware that Lamprion was watching him for a word or a wince, that in a moment he would be making a sly remark about Flavia. But just before the remark came, Beric turned on

Lamprion, saying shortly that he had no business to repeat stories of this kind. And Lamprion slid off his perch into frightened submission.

Beric looked at him fiercely. He was glad it was over, glad the man was frightened back into slavery again! It was a good thing he could do that so easily still. He hoped coldly that Lamprion would do something silly soon, so that Crispus would order a whipping for him. Unfortunately, it was not at all likely; Lamprion hardly ever got punished. He wasn't that sort.

And so Domina Aelia had been right about her granddaughter. Tigellinus was coming . . . in the hot afternoons, no doubt. And if Aelius Candidus found out, it would be extremely difficult for him to do anything effective. It was nice to realize that, at any rate. But Beric carefully did not say a thing to Crispus about it.

Clinog stayed with them till near the end of August. They had some good days hunting. Beric did not speak again about killing, and Clinog hoped he had got over it. Better not raise the question again.

The meeting between the brothers had been a success, Crispus thought. Beric was settling down. Probably the whole thing had been exaggerated. At any rate, it had been taken in time. And then one afternoon, Sannio turned up, to say that Manasses had been arrested again and taken to prison.

Crispus was very angry. With Beric standing by, he questioned Sannio, who said that there was nothing fresh against Manasses. No, there had been no more meetings, nothing had been said or done. It had all just come out of the blue. A squad of Praetorians had turned up at the house and taken him off.

But was Sannio telling the truth? Beric followed him out and took him along to his own room. "What else happened?" he asked.

"They didn't take Argas, sir," said Sannio, looking at Beric sideways.

"Why should they have? Beric asked sharply. "It's all nonsense!"

"Yes, of course, sir. Just as you say. Argas seemed a bit down about it, all the same."

"Has he—talked to you much—these last weeks?"

"Oh no, sir, not about what he wasn't supposed to talk about. Not a word, sir."

"If you weren't such a blasted liar," said Beric, "it would be easier to talk to *you*. I believe you've been decent to him—and the others. They must have said something."

Sannio looked uncomfortable. "I don't want to get into trouble, sir. Nor yet to get any of the rest into trouble—"

"You won't with me."

"That's what Argas said—to start with."

"Doesn't he now?"

"Well, sir, he was upset. You going away, without saying much. And not sending any word. Not that you could have most likely. I kept on telling the young fool—"

"Drat," said Beric. "I ought to have done something. I'm a coward." He made the sign of the cross, slowly and deliberately, at Sannio, who blinked.

"I know it, sir," he said, "but I'm not one of *them*. You're not, sir, surely?"

"I nearly am. Enough for you to tell the police, Sannio."

"Don't you go putting it so awkward, sir! I couldn't help thinking there might be something—well, what I mean is, if it was just you being a bit gone on young Argas, the way I thought at first, you'd no call to fuss about the others the way you did. Only what I never did see was—"

"Well, what?"

"You being decent to me too, sir," Sannio said, floundering. "When I was in your working party. Spoke to me like you'd speak to a free man. And then, you seemed to know what was wrong in the house—not big things, kind of little things a nobleman wouldn't notice, not in an ordinary way. What I mean is, I don't see why, even if you do know that sign—"

"Why I'd do things for the rest of you as well as for the Christians? Is that it? Because if one's a Christian, one's bound to think of you all as persons. Not just slaves. Not just things one owns and makes work."

"I see, sir," said Sannio and scratched his head.

But why, thought Beric, *hadn't it worked with Lamprion?* Perhaps it just didn't take on everyone. Only on people who're ready for it, who wanted to be in the Kingdom, more or less. Fairly decent people. He just didn't have the experience to know about it.

Sannio said, "They've been arresting a lot of the Christians this last week. Everyone says now it was them started the fire."

"What's going to happen to them?"

"Well, sir, it's being said they're going to be made an example of. In the arena, like. Or burned in the emperor's new garden."

Beric rubbed his hands across his face, then asked in a queer, calm way, "What do you think of that, Sannio?"

"Seems silly to me. If they're no worse than our people. And you, sir. If you're so near being one." He hesitated. "Excuse me, sir, but don't you go trying to go back. You won't do any good, and you might get into it yourself."

"Would that matter?" said Beric.

"It would to me," said Sannio, obviously not lying.

After a moment Beric said, "Can you tell me the names of any who've been arrested?"

"No one you'd know, sir," Sannio answered and then realized that perhaps, things being how they were, that wasn't so. He gave a few names, mostly of slaves from other households, but Beric shook his head. Then, "Oh, and Euphemia from the little scent shop—" And he saw he had hit it this time.

Then Beric remembered that Lalage had been lodging with Euphemia. "Was anyone else arrested at her house?" he asked quickly.

"I don't think so, sir." Sannio would terribly have liked to do something for the Briton, something big, something to show that he, Sannio, was as good as young Argas any day. Only if, after all, what he'd thought about him and Argas wasn't true—the Briton looked like he'd done that evening when Aelius Candidus hit him, when they'd all been on his side. They'd all been hit themselves, one way and another. Sannio had dodged it pretty often. He wished the Briton could dodge it now, think of something else.

What did noblemen think about? Sannio had been in the house five years, since he'd been a boy. The Briton had always been friendly to him. He ought to have known what to say. Only he'd never felt like this toward one of his masters before.

Beric said heavily, "What did Manasses do when they arrested him?"

"Nothing," said Sannio. "You see, sir, he wouldn't want to get anyone else into trouble."

"They'll have a note of who was arrested before. Or if they haven't they'll—question him."

"Yes, sir." Sannio put his hand, gingerly, on the Briton's shoulder. Would that be all right, or would he be snapped at?

After a minute, Beric jumped up, took his hand and shook it, then said, "I'm going back to Rome tonight. Pack for me at once, will you, Sannio?"

Then he went out, leaving Sannio to put his things into the saddlebags. There was some money loose on the top of the chest; one piece had rolled onto the floor. Obviously the Briton wouldn't have noticed if that piece hadn't rejoined the others. But Sannio carefully picked it up and put it back with the rest.

Beric went through and found Crispus explaining the situation to Clinog, who had never even heard of Christians. "I'm going back," said Beric, "to see what's happening."

"You are doing nothing of the sort," said Crispus. "I absolutely and categorically forbid you to leave this house."

"I'm sorry," said Beric, "but it's my duty."

"I shall keep you here by force if necessary," said Crispus. "Clinog, stop your brother from being a fool."

Caradoc's sons regarded one another.

Clinog said, "It will do no harm to talk things over, surely now, Beric?"

"No," said Beric, "but if you try to hold me, I'll knock you down."

Clinog turned uncertainly to Crispus. "Could you tell me, sir, why isn't he to go?"

"Because he has been mixed up with this Christianity. You had better know, Clinog."

"But," said Clinog, shocked, "if it is what you have been telling me, he would never have been in it. No!"

Beric said, "You've heard about it all wrong, Clinog."

"Well, Beric, aren't they enemies of society?"

"Enemies of things as they are. Are *you* happy with things as they are, Clinog? Are you doing what you want?"

"I have nothing to complain of, indeed no! Nor have you. Remember Rudri—"

"What's all this nonsense!" said Crispus. "I have forbidden you to go to Rome, Beric, and that's that. I shall find out for myself what charges have been laid against my slave, and if they are well-founded, the law must take its course."

"That's what I'm going to find out," Beric said.

"Unfortunately I can no longer trust you to do it in a sensible way. I shall not be able to do so until I am certain you have nothing to do with this sect, even in thought."

"What do you suppose I would do?" Beric asked.

"Get yourself killed, for one thing, you silly little fool! I shall use force if necessary to stop you going. You agree, Clinog?"

"Of course, yes. Beric, you will be reasonable?"

"If you let me go, I will be reasonable. If you keep me by force, I shall tell everyone it was because I am a Christian. Whether I am or not. You can't keep me forever."

"Suppose," said Crispus, "I don't choose to put my family into shame and suspicion because of the disobedience of a barbarian boy?"

"Yes," said Beric, "you could kill me just as much as Tigellinus could." He went over to where Crispus was sitting and knelt beside him. "Kill me then. Tell Clinog to kill me."

"Idiot!" said Crispus and boxed his ears.

Beric wriggled and shook his head but still knelt there. He said, "If I go, I give you my sacred promise I won't go to a Christian meeting or do anything the police could get me for, till you are back yourself. But I must find out what's happening. I want to go with your consent. Please give it to me."

Crispus took him by the shoulders, looked at him hard and long. "Beric," he said, "you're not a Christian, are you? Surely you haven't committed yourself. Tell me."

"No," said Beric. "I haven't committed myself."

"Don't," said Crispus and kissed him on the forehead.

"I—I won't," said Beric shakenly, "not yet."

"Then go," said Crispus, and Beric went out quietly.

Crispus turned to Clinog. "I shall have to go back earlier than I intended. I had a number of things to see to here. It will be most unpleasant in Rome. It is all extremely annoying. You Britons! I wish I'd never set eyes on you."

14

The Comrades

Eunice had mixed and kneaded the dough, which she now left to rise during the night, and she was waiting, with one small lamp on the table beside the rolling pin. She did not know if any of the others would come. In case they did, she had food. None of them might have dared to bring it.

She thought of Euphemia in prison. There was to be no buying her out this time. Euphemia had gone through a preliminary questioning, apparently to make her confess to revolt, witchcraft, and poisoning.

She laughed about it when Eunice saw her, but her face and arms were blotched with red and purple bruise marks, and there were patches of hair rough and loose where she had been dragged around by it. Eunice had wanted to send and tell the daughter at Neapolis, but that was the one thing Euphemia asked her not to do. Why had they picked on Euphemia? Nobody knew.

Eunice had seen Rhodon too. He had been knocked around a lot the last week or two but not very systematically questioned. He kept on talking about how badly made his chains were. That seemed to have got on his nerves. But what could you expect from government material?

She had not been able to see Manasses. He was thought to be in another prison. People said things were bad there.

Paul was often with the other prisoners in the Mamertine. As a citizen, and one not without honor in the rich Jewish community, he could have had a room to himself and need never have had anything to do with the rest. At first, in fact, he had not even been in the prison but nearby, under house arrest. However, things were different now. Paul was a criminal like the rest of the Christians.

Luke could still go in and out of the prison fairly easily. There had been no sign of his being arrested. He had a wide practice as a doctor. Perhaps some of his patients were protecting him. He was lodging with some very respectable Greek merchants. They knew what he was, but not officially. He had cured the daughter of the house, who had some kind of fits.

As she waited, Eunice began to pray. She had always half expected this, but it was taking so long. Not knowing from day to day! Having to go on with ordinary life. Pretending.

Sometimes she felt that if only they could all go out into the streets, catch hold of the passersby, and say, 'Look at us, this is what we are, this is how we live, how we believe, isn't it just plain sense?"—then everyone would see. Would stop being afraid of them and hating them. Ordinary people. Of course, the ones on top would still try and get them, but it didn't matter being hated by Caesar if you weren't hated by the woman around the corner. *O Father, open my neighbor's eyes, so that she may stop hating me!*

There was a knock on the door at last. She opened it, her face prepared either for a late customer or for—but it was her son. "Oh, my darling," she said, "is it all right, you coming—sure?"

"Of course it's all right," Phaon said. "I'm not going to be frightened out of this."

She brought him over near the lamp, looking closely at him. She hadn't seen him for a few days. It seemed to her that he was hardening, getting older, not her baby any longer but a man and a Christian. After that whipping, he had been frightened and jumpy for days, crying and wanting to be petted. Now he'd got over it, gone forward. So she mustn't pet him or mother him, mustn't in any way break down what he was growing into. "How are things in the house?" she asked.

"The Briton's back. Did you know?"

"I'd heard. Is he going to come tonight?"

"Don't know. Argas was to tell him. Anyway, he's been over and seen Manasses. Says he's all right—more or less. Going to be transferred to the Mamertine."

"Was Manasses—questioned?"

"Yes. You've got to expect that. First of all. Oh, don't be silly, Mother. I'll stick it all right! If it's me. I just know I can—now. We're getting a bit of practice in the house. At nights mostly. They've been trying to make us say things, Argas and me. But we don't. We've got strength. I didn't know what it was before, being a Christian, but I know now, and I'm glad."

"I'm glad too, my son. I suppose poor Dapyx won't come?"

"No. Won't even let us speak to him. And it isn't as though they'd knocked him around that much. Only the poor old lad couldn't stick it. I believe the only one, God willing, who could get him back would be the Briton—if he would."

"Why shouldn't he?"

"Well, he's odd. I don't exactly know what it is, but perhaps a nobleman can't ever be one of us. I tell you what, Mother, the one I'm worried about is Josias."

"But he's been in the church for years. You don't ever mean to say Josias is a coward!"

"Ever since Manasses was taken, he's been down. We've got to be steady now, but he's not. The way I see it, he was getting strength from Manasses all the time, and now he's stopped thinking of all we've had and got. He's stopped thinking of the Kingdom. He's only thinking they're going to do in Manasses, and that's got him right down."

"You think—it's that for Manasses?"

"Yes. Don't you, Mother?"

"I do, son. Only I keep on sort of saying to myself—well, there, I'm nothing but a silly old woman. I know well enough it's not any of us that matters. Not as a single life. They can't stop the Kingdom."

"It's going to be made strong this way. So that it'll spring up at once, anywhere, anytime. Whenever there's a chance. Whenever the lid's lifted. Understand? Manasses and me, we've been working together day after day, all these years, ever since I was a boy. Maybe I'll never see him again. Well, that's all right. We've faced that. Talked it out. Got to die some way, some day, Mother. This way it's worth it. I couldn't not die myself, now, not after seeing what it's all about. But it's no use chewing it all over again. It's so. It's certain. Here's someone else, Mother."

Eunice went to the door. It was Phineas and Sapphira, standing very close together, she carrying a basket. At least they were prepared for the love feast.

They waited till the door was shut before whispering the peace greeting and sitting down together. Phineas asked for news of Rhodon, saying that the watchdog missed him. It was always whining now. He added, "You remember that Armenian Rhodon found? He came to me. Rhodon must have spoken to him, and he wants to join. What do you think, Eunice?" Phineas was still very uneasy because it was he, first, who had made friends with Sotion. And if he could make such a mistake of judgment as that . . !

"Does he know what it means—well, what it's almost bound to mean?" Eunice asked.

"Yes. But it seems he was kind of . . . struck . . . by what Rhodon did. He felt it binding."

"When one gets the privilege to do anything that's a copy of what He might have done, it's binding all right," Eunice said. "Does he know the Words at all?"

"Not really. He speaks a funny kind of Greek."

"Well, you send him on over, Phineas, and I'll teach him. If I'm still here." She went to the door again. This time it was Lalage and Sophrosyne.

Lalage was in a dance dress, straight from a party, and Sophrosyne was carrying her double flutes around her neck, and her new harp, done up in a cloth, under her arm. Lalage took the cloak off and began rubbing the makeup off her face.

But Eunice stopped her. "Don't you do that. It'll look better— if we need to pretend."

Lalage agreed and laughed. "Don't mind my silly clothes," she said.

"It's a good one," Phaon said, regarding professionally her semitransparent dress, painted here and there with eyes and flowers. He added, "Wish there was a chance of Persis coming. I've not seen the child for weeks."

"Nor old Niger," Phineas said.

"You can't expect too much from Persis, son," Eunice said.

"I expect everything," Phaon said in an odd, hard way, "from everyone who's had—this." He looked around.

Lalage nodded at him. She was fairly certain to be arrested, especially since Euphemia's arrest. She and Sophrosyne had only just moved into a room of their own when that happened. But it was possible that Phaon might be regarded as harmless. It was important that he should be filled with the Spirit. He would have to go on.

The next knock was Argas and Josias. Again the peace greeting was whispered and the door shut and bolted behind them.

Eunice was half wondering, but it was Lalage who asked, "What about Beric?"

"Well, I'm not his wet nurse!" Argas snapped at her.

"You told him, didn't you?"

"Oh, I told him all right. He didn't seem to take any notice."

Lalage said quickly, "What exactly do you mean? Is he out of it?"

"He saw Manasses. Talked to them sharply at the prison, so I heard. And he's been—finding out. Going to see people. Doing things maybe. I don't know. But he's not said anything to me, not really. And I wanted him in . . . so badly." Argas dropped his face into his hands and muttered again. "Wanted him in . . . before . . . it's all smashed."

"It won't be smashed," Lalage said. "Only perhaps we shall be. That's different."

"We ought to have baptized him," Argas said, "when he wanted. At once. Then he'd have been here."

"Only if he thought he was bound in honor, or some boys' game. Not good enough for us. We've got to be in the Kingdom *for* the Kingdom now, not bribed or forced."

"Perhaps it's too much to ask them to give up," Eunice said. "If you've been one of the masters all this time, you can't want it the same way as we do—not enough to make everything else look silly."

"He did want it," Argas said. "Only something happened."

"All the other things have been pulling him," Lalage said. "He may be strong enough to make them let go in time. We'll see. And he may think there's another way, Argas, and until he sees there isn't, he'll try. You can't be in a thing like this unless you're sure. And you've got to be sure on your own, with God's help."

She went over to Argas and pulled his hands gently away from his face and whispered, "Stop crying, Argas. If he's in it, he's in it with you—and all of us—whether it's now or years on, perhaps later. Whatever's going to happen to us. In Jesus' name, Argas, get steady, or you'll shake us all."

In the dim light she was watching Josias. Something was wrong with him, more wrong than with Argas, who now, rather ashamedly, sat up and shook himself and began to think of Jesus and the others.

They began to talk business, discussing what was the best line to take with people who said that the fire had been the work of the Christians but who knew nothing about them.

Lalage, in the course of making her living, heard a good deal. She had noticed how those who had at first been inclined to blame the fire on the emperor—not personally, of course, but saying with dinner-party irony that it was a peculiarly fortunate accident for those who wanted to change Rome or to take men's minds off the loss of their political liberty!—now said that it was an excellent thing to use it for getting rid of these Christians. They were inclined to approve the emperor for having thought of it. Here was something in the old Roman manner—there'd be no Greek pansies or Olympic Games nonsense about the games in the arena next month! They'd be the real thing. Blood.

Both she and Sophrosyne had heard it from the other side too, waiting about among the household slaves for their turn to come on at a party. Here again the forthcoming games would be discussed. The kind of show you'd only see in the capital of the world. Not just half a dozen murders, victims who might be all killed off and eaten in ten minutes at the other end of the arena, but tens—hundreds!—and women as well, girls. You'd see them ripped up, everything torn off them, and with so many there'd be bound to be some close for you to see properly.

These slaves, or again, the small shopkeepers she dealt with, were much more inclined to believe that it really was the Christians who had started the fire, and they had no end of stories, which someone must have taken some trouble to make up and circulate, about the kind of monsters the Christians were, wanting to smash up everything that had always been held sacred, holding horrible orgies!

Here and there someone might have known one of the men or women who'd been arrested, and would say you'd never have

249

thought it to look at them; decent, they'd seemed, quiet-spoken, but there, you never knew!

And sometimes Lalage had been able to put in a word, enough to make them feel a bit uncertain and uncomfortable about it, to make them wonder. Eunice could do that too, sometimes.

The Jewish community was very much divided, Phineas said, and some of the old Nazarenes, his father, for instance, kept on insisting that this was the beginning of the wrath and judgment before the Second Coming. The emperor wasn't a man at all but Satan himself. Those who'd been near to him, at nights, said there were flames coming out of his mouth all the time! "You don't believe that, do you, Lalage?" he asked anxiously.

"No," she said. "It's all nonsense. You don't have to make things up and talk big to show why this is happening. It's all plain. They just want to get rid of us because we've got something so much better and stronger than anything of theirs that it's bound to win unless it can be stopped."

"I think this is all of us," Eunice said. "Shall I get the food and wine, Lalage?"

"Please, sister," said Lalage and then looked around them. "Remember, friends, if they come, no panic. I start dancing, the rest of you drinking and clapping. You throw your veil back, Sapphira dear, and laugh. It mayn't work, but it's a chance, and we may as well go on living as long as we can. Anyway, I don't think they'll come tonight."

Eunice was just getting out a couple of loaves and a jar of salt fish, when they heard another knock.

Phaon went to the door. "Oh, Persis," he said. "I knew it was you, somehow! Oh, good." And he put his arms around her and kissed her.

"I can't stay long, or I'll be missed," she said, breathless, "but I had to see you—and get news to Niger. He's chained at nights now, so he can't come. But whenever my master and mistress go to see his father, I go too. And somehow I always manage to see Niger." She gave a small giggle. "Aren't I clever, Lalage? But you see, he's only got me."

"You shall take back some of the bread, with our love and blessing, Persis," said Lalage. "You're just in time. Brave girl. When will you see him?"

"Tonight, after I get back. They're going over quite late."

She took off her veil and laid it nearby, and then all of them came close around the table with the bread and the fish and the little meat rolls that Sapphira had cooked, and they held one another's hands.

Argas, too, had kissed Persis, feeling curiously glad and satisfied at seeing her again. Every time they met together was something snatched by them from the powers of darkness, something solid that could never be taken from them again. He had a consciousness of the two-way flow of time, anchoring them in eternity. If you had this, after all, what did it matter about dying? Death could not alter things that had happened.

One after the other, Lalage looked at them, gathering them together, holding their minds and faces with hers, so that they were not aware either of her painted cheeks or of her dancing dress.

She knew how much it mattered to encourage the others. It was critical to make it worthwhile for the slaves to risk the most horrible and disgusting punishments, for all to risk prison and probable death. Perhaps this might be the last time for some or all of them. Their last supper. That thought must be in more minds than hers. That dizzying identification with their Jesus, the One who had made it plain.

The solemnity in her heart turned suddenly to violent joy. *What luck, oh, what luck for us!—to have this moment.* She saw that they were picking up from her, most of them at least, themselves feeling the joy, knowing themselves blessed. "Lift up your hearts!" she whispered, taking hold of the bread.

"He is with us," Persis said, knowing it certainly, knowing it had been worth it to come across the terrifying night in the streets to this.

"Now we will say the Words together, friends," Lalage said. That would be better than any prayer any of them could make up. They all said the Words. It was amazing for a few slaves and freedwomen and quite poor, unimportant persons to have been given

251

this thing, to be able to be part of the Will and the Kingdom. It was the sort of astonishing event you just couldn't get over. It was too much for you. You could only and simply be boundlessly grateful for it.

Lalage broke up the loaves. They handed around the pieces, smiling and murmuring, in this state of clear and simple gratitude that they were in. You weren't anybody, and yet you were this. They sat or stood around, eating perhaps, or not bothering to eat. Going to live perhaps, or going to die. In a state of personal humility combined with utmost glad pride about what you were part of.

Now Lalage lifted the wine jar to fill the cup. And again there was a quick knocking at the door. But everyone was in the room who could possibly be coming. Unless, she suddenly thought, *Beric?* Anyway, it didn't sound like the Guards. But just in case, she held herself ready to dance—yes, to dance with the wine jar a Bacchic dance. She signed to Sophrosyne, and the old woman felt for her double flutes.

Eunice went to the door, opened it a crack, was speaking to someone, then said, "Come in!" and again shoved the bolt across. They all looked up, but only two or three recognized the veiled girl. It was Megallis, the little Sicilian whom Euphemia had freed, the one who had taken refuge with her after she and her tanner husband had been burned out. She came uncertainly into the ring of lamplight, then threw herself onto the floor at Lalage's feet.

"What is it?" said Lalage, bending over, seeing that the girl's hair was rumpled and her eyes red and swollen. "Why have you come, dear?"

They were all watching and listening by this time.

The girl sobbed. "I want to be one of you. Please. Please. I want to be a Christian."

"What do you know about it, sister?" Lalage asked.

"I know what it's for. I know what you all do. I know the way you are, and I know it's right, and I want to be that way too!"

"Why, my dear?"

"I'll tell you," she said. "I'll tell you all!" And she shifted around on the floor, still holding with one hand to Lalage's dress and sometimes sobbing as she spoke. "You know my Tertius. We've been married two years now. He bought me out—I'd ought to be grateful, oughtn't I?" She wiped her eyes with the edge of her veil.

Sapphira, listening, pressed closer to Phineas, holding his hands in hers.

The girl went on. "Well, we got burned out, lost everything, we did, all our little special things and his tools. But I knew where to come. If you've ever belonged to someone, like I'd belonged to Euphemia before, well, you know what type they are. And she took us in, treated us like we'd still got everything, fed us on the best, gave me this dress I've got on now, oh, I can't tell you! But if that's being a Christian—well, it's all right, isn't it?

"Only my Tertius—I don't know what it was, but he'd been used to having a place of his own. He didn't like to owe anything to anyone, leastwise not a woman. He got angry. Kept on finding fault. Then he started listening to all these stories that's about. Oh, I told him it was all lies! But he was set on believing something bad about Euphemia. And he got it into his head she'd bewitched me, got it into his head she'd been bad to me before, sold me out to customers—you know—as if she would! Said that was why I hadn't had a child, though God knows he hadn't wanted one before! Oh, he was just plain silly!"

She broke into wilder tears, and Lalage knelt beside her, soothing her, trying to remember what she'd noticed of the young man when they'd all been lodging together in Euphemia's two rooms.

Megallis dabbed her eyes and went on again. "So he went off to the soldiers and told them a pack of lies, only he believes them himself, and they came and arrested her and pulled her across her own shop by her hair and broke her bottles of scent and tried to pour hair oils down her throat, and I don't know what all else. Oh, beastly it was! And all because she'd been kind. And I didn't know, not till this evening, it was my Tertius's doing. But I'll never go back to him now, no, not if he swears black's white! So I've come to you."

"Does he know where you are, my dear?" Lalage asked.

"No. I said I'd drown myself. I meant to, I was that ashamed, and then I thought of you and came here instead."

"How did you find it out?"

"He wanted to steal Euphemia's shop and her room, and me to carry on the business. Then, when he got talking about that, I thought there was something funny going on, and then it all came out, and oh, he was so nasty, and we had a row, and then I ran. Oh, I did used to love him so before he went and did this!"

Lalage said, "Perhaps he'll see he was wrong."

Megallis shook and said, "Not even if he does see, I'll never forgive him, never!"

"But Euphemia would forgive him if she knew."

After a minute the girl said, "She told me about all that forgiving. But not an awful thing like this. You couldn't."

"If Tertius finds out that you've come to us, he'll start thinking worse things of Christians, won't he?"

"Yes. What's more, he'll try and do you all in. I didn't think of that. I'd rather not be one of you than put you all into danger. Oh, look!"

Lalage, followed her stare through the heavy-shadowed room, saw Josias at the door, slipping back the bolt, and Argas suddenly after him, snatching his arm away.

Lalage went over quickly. "We're going to have the wine now, Josias," she said. "Stay with us."

"I can't, I can't!" Josias sobbed. "That man'll be after her—get us all too. Oh, Jesus, give us grace!" Josias groaned and twisted his hands about, frightened out of all words.

She and Argas held onto him. Whatever happened, he mustn't be allowed to run out like this. In the state he was in, he might say or do anything.

Then the girl Megallis got up and pulled her veil tighter around herself. "I'll put it right," she said. "I'll go back, and I'll try to forgive him. If you're sure Euphemia would have. Then he'll see, like you say, but it looks to me that's too good to be true. Oh, I don't want to go!"

"Come back to us later," said Lalage, "tomorrow if you like. You shall be one of us, dear, but not while you're hating. Not even for this. You know where to find me, Megallis."

"Yes," she said sadly. "Oh, please do something to make me feel like I can go back!"

Josias had calmed down now. Lalage let go of him and laid hands of blessing on Megallis and then kissed her. The girl clung to her for a moment, then Lalage opened the door and let her out.

Eunice said, "Someone'll go and say we've broken that home up."

"Yes," said Lalage. "Our enemies are in our own households. The ones we love best. That's how it's bound to be. He knew." She turned back to the room. "Brothers and sisters, you see what we're up against. We need all our strength. All the strength we can get through one another and through Jesus. Shall we have the wine now?"

It was Phaon who said, "Wait. We've got to think out first what's been happening. Why we couldn't just take her."

"Because she didn't really understand," Lalage said, "though she will."

"Yes. We've got to be dead certain now." Phaon stood beside the table, gripping it, his face flushed, his lips a little open.

Lalage stood back. There was time still. "Interpret that, brother," she said to him quietly.

Standing straight he said, "I believe when we ask for daily bread we don't ask only for security but also for certainty. Oh, we can't want to die except for that! Listen, friends, it's like the poems I've had to learn, Homer and that lot. All about princes and heroes, those poems are, and they went out to fight in the war around Troy, wherever that was, and they weren't *sure,* none of them. It wasn't going to matter really, which side won; it wasn't going to mean something new—a fresh chance for the whole world—but only one old rule or the other coming out on top. The kings of Troy or the kings of the Greeks. They didn't want to die; they only fought because they couldn't stay always young, and besides it's part of the old rule to fight and kill and to make other people do it for you too!

"This that we're doing is a sight more dangerous than any old Trojan war, and more of us will get killed. But it won't be the same way they were, angry and proud or showing off or just shrugging their shoulders. We'll know every step of our way."

Argas, who had also learned dining-room songs, said, "We're more like those other Greeks that fought at Thermopylae, holding

Hellas against the Persians. They died for something they were sure about."

"They were getting nearer," Phaon said eagerly, seeing it all in his mind. "They did have something new. They'd thought of the rule of all the citizens instead of just the rule of a king or a few of the rich. That was getting closer to our brotherhood. But it wasn't there yet! Same with Spartacus. That was something new. They'd thought of equality. But it wasn't right yet. We're right, though. We've got the first chance there's ever been of living and dying for something that's dead sure. Isn't that the truth, friends?"

"Yes," said Lalage, "we're soldiers who fight because we're certain and with a new kind of sword—the sword of the gospel of Christ."

"Brothers and sisters, let us drink this truth with our wine!" said Phaon, suddenly louder, and he took the cup—he was the youngest still—and lifted it. "In Jesus' name!"

They had drunk their wine in joy and brotherhood before. They drank it now as a more sober but no less passionate pledge. It seemed to Lalage that when the time came, as it must, she would be able to leave the church to Phaon, the boy who had once perceived the truth of Christ in terms of drawing and dancing and singing, the Kingdom as it might be some day, but who now realized them as reason and history and danger, the Kingdom as it actually was.

And Eunice thought, *Oh, if he is killed, it will be not only my loss but the loss of all of us.*

And Argas suddenly thought how extremely glad he was that he'd stopped the little scoundrel from screaming that time, that he'd taken the beating for him. Phaon wouldn't scream now! Oh, they could be proud of one another, as the cup went around.

But after they had drunk it, saying the name that was the seal of their certainty, they could not stay any longer. All went out separately, the slaves first, looking about them to see that no one was spying.

Eunice walked back with Persis, who carried a piece of the bread for Niger tucked into the fold of her tunic. They didn't speak much, but it was nice being with another woman.

Persis was wishing somehow that she could let her mother know that it hadn't been for nothing, that she was faithful. She wondered which way Philippi was from here, under which star. But even if Bersabe was never to know, they'd have been together over this. When she got near the house, she saw the litter waiting at the door and ran, in a sudden panic, in case she was late. But all was well this time.

Eunice had been making sure in her mind that she'd left everything in order at the bakery, in case—anyone came. No, there was nothing in writing, no signs, no marks, only the leaven steadily working in the kneading trough all through the night.

Lalage and Sophrosyne walked back together and were arrested at the door of their lodgings. Lalage protested that she'd been on a job, but it was no use. One of the men pulled the harp away from Sophrosyne, threw it on the ground and stamped his foot through the strings. They made a strange little complaining tinkle as they snapped. The two women were marched off to prison.

It was fairly obvious to Lalage that she was likely to have a worse time during her first examination because of her painted face and professional dress. That would put ideas into the heads of the prison officials. Well, there was nothing to be done about it now. She had become part of the Will and the plan for the Kingdom; whatever happened to her body. And that was good.

15

The Bosses

Tigellinus had in the most gentlemanly way waited until after the marriage. He was not vastly partial to virgins, even willing ones. And now it was all very satisfactory. Aelius Candidus, as deputy governor, had definite hours. No awkwardness was likely to occur, although, as a matter of fact, Tigellinus did not really mind if it did. At present he and Flavia were not at all tired of one another.

With some surprise, he found himself standing all sorts of things from the girl. She liked presents but was not grateful for them. What she really liked was inventing physical tests that he, the prefect of the Praetorians, had to pass. And very peculiar they sometimes were! Oh, she was live and tough, not like these sticky little Greeks and Persians! And a proper little aristocrat. It still gave him great satisfaction to know that. She took the toga as a matter of course, had been known to snub him thoroughly about his own ancestors. And he even took that from her! Of course, when he was tired of her—unless she got tired of him first? He was exceedingly anxious to avoid that.

Flavia was intelligent about politics. All that Stoic nonsense of her father's had slipped off her. She saw the essentials—that you'd got to go on hard with any course of action; you couldn't stop. Still less could you go back, to Augustus or any state of things, historical or imagined. That would dislocate every joint of society. People were living differently now. No one could change the flow of the current. Some of those idealistic old fools even thought they could go back and farm, live on what they grew and made for themselves, like the middle Republic. They'd forgotten where their money came from now, forgotten imports and taxes and all you got out of the provinces, forgotten the rise in the population. You'd got to feed new Rome and new Italy as well as a few senators and their families!

There was no standing still either. It was like the chariot you'd put your money on skidding around the bend at the top of the course on one wheel—that could be done if the horses went at it full speed, but not if they were reined in, not if you played safe. So with government. It had to go thundering on, swinging around the corners of difficulty and danger, balancing on that one wheel, striking out sparks! No good trying to slow it down, or there'd be a smash for everyone in that golden chariot. On the contrary, you had to give more and more oats to the team.

Here Tigellinus slapped himself on the chest and made a man-size joke about the habits of horses—and you mustn't thwart the Divine Charioteer.

Flavia interrupted. "When do I get asked to meet him?"

Tigellinus looked at her a shade warily. What exactly had she meant? "The emperor has his hands full just now. What with the old gang—your father's pals, Flavia, my pet. And now these awful Christians."

"Oh, them! But isn't that just the moment he'd like a bit of consoling?"

"Not by little girls like my Flavia."

"Funny, I thought he liked little girls. You know, I think I must meet him, all the same."

The worst of it all, felt Tigellinus, would be if she got it into her head that she wanted to meet him and managed it on her own—as she was quite capable of doing, blast her! He mightn't ever know, till it was too late.

So he took to tipping the maids heavily. He would have been surprised to know how rapidly some of his money got around into the hands of the prison warders in the Mamertine, materializing as food and drink for Christian prisoners. Persis was a pretty, quiet little thing and never spoke above a whisper when he was around.

The rounding up of the Christians was going on very well. The prisons were nearly full; everything was ready for the great September games. The various stage managers were in touch with the authorities and had been authorized to take out as many prisoners as they needed for each show.

The propaganda had taken well, and now the authorities had comparatively little to do. Information was coming in from all

259

sides; everyone was eager to exterminate the brutes. Sometimes Tigellinus himself almost believed they had burned Rome! Of course, some of the information simply came from people who had a grudge against their neighbors. It was easy to finish off a private quarrel that way. Sometimes the person accused turned out not to be a Christian at all but a reputable follower of Serapis or Mithras or the Great Mother, none of whom had anything against them at the moment. They were all officially recognized and fitted suitably into the structure of the State.

And, of course, plenty who were in one of the Christian churches denied everything the moment they were arrested or had been through a spot of questioning. Usually they were let go with a caution and the knowledge that the police had their eye on them. If they were caught at their tricks a second time, there wouldn't be another chance for them.

At first the arrests had been on the definite charge of arson, but that might be difficult to prove satisfactorily at a public trial. The accusation had certainly had its effect on people's minds, and now the arrests were merely for the practice of the Christian superstition.

"Why do you make such a fuss about these idiotic Christians?" Flavia asked. "They haven't really done anything, have they?"

"They've no right to exist."

"How ridiculous! You look as if you wanted to eat them, darling! Why shouldn't they exist?"

"Because they're against the State. That's good enough for me. If they didn't actually burn Rome, they might do something as bad or worse some day. You'll see if we leave them alive! They're against property."

"Slaves always are! But who cares? A lot of wretched little Jews. You're only drawing attention to them with all these arrests. What does the emperor think?"

"Same as me. You can take that for a fact, Flavia."

"Oh, can I? You know, I don't believe in facts I can't see for myself." Flavia jumped up crossly.

She'd had another of these quarrels with Candidus the night before. She could say things that hurt him, and she knew he wanted to kill her—and Tigellinus—but didn't dare. That was all very fine as a situation, and one got a lot of kick out of it once or twice, but it didn't get any further. It stuck.

And then her father had come back from the country and trotted along to pay her a visit and bleated about the home and the family. She'd picked up her embroidery—the same piece she'd been doing last month, but he'd never notice!—and sat and ached with the tedium and stupidity of it, half longing for the crash—to tell him and see what he'd say. Dig it in and hurt! See them wriggle, him and Beric—if only she could! It would serve him right for talking about grandchildren.

So now she was irritated and impatient, and all she wanted at the moment was to see Nero. Somehow she couldn't believe he was just an echo of Tigellinus!

And Tigellinus was thinking about Nero too. If only he could be sure that the emperor agreed with him wholeheartedly! For instance, this business of the execution of the Christians in the arena. It was good policy; it would go to show there wasn't, after all, to be any nonsense about turning the games into a wretched amateur Greek business, with nothing but races and singing and wrestling under a set of rules that stopped anything funny happening! If you got the sand well-soaked with blood a few times, it would get all that out of people's heads.

The emperor had seemed to agree. He'd thought up new ways of dealing with the criminals—got an imagination, he had. Yes, too much. An imagination like a showman's, so that however a thing turned out in the end, it couldn't be as good as you'd figured it. So the emperor was always getting disappointed. Upset. And he'd look at you with those strange eyes of his as though he were looking right through you. That was nasty.

Having said a tender good-bye to Flavia, Tigellinus went straight to see Nero. He had started worrying again about the master of the world. Supposing, after all, the prefect of the Praetorians didn't understand him? Then? Well, then you had the Praetorians anyhow. For what they were worth. You would probably get enough warning if the emperor—changed his mind about you.

He counted over the number of freedmen and the slaves in the palace who were in his pay. So long as they weren't still more

261

heavily in someone else's pay. It was awful not being able to trust a soul, he thought. Not even little Flavia. And he pitied himself heavily.

The emperor received him almost at once but insisted on his looking at the architect's models for the new palace, the Golden House.

"What's it all going to cost?" Tigellinus asked, poking at the pretty little wax and ivory things. "But don't you worry, Majesty," he added, "that'll be all right. There's money about in Rome. You trust me, and I'll get it for you."

Nero looked sideways at Tigellinus with that veiled suspicious glance that made him seem so much older. He was only twenty-six, and he could have done anything in the world he wanted, if only he'd known what.

"Some of the old senators," said Nero, "have more than they deserve. Ugly old devils. They oughtn't to be allowed to live, as ugly as that. Plotting. Calling themselves Stoics. With as much idea of philosophy or anything Greek as—you!"

Tigellinus laughed. "I don't need to. You do all that for me, Majesty. That's why we're such a good couple. Husband and wife, as you may say." He passed one hand around the Emperor's narrow shoulders and squeezed his arm. "They talk treason too. And they're such a pack of old fools, they get themselves overheard by my boys. They don't mean half of it, but they like making noises about Brutus and that. Then they get into trouble. But we're always prepared to believe they're loyal subjects again when they fork out a nice little present to pay for these pretty palaces of yours."

"They ought to be proud," Nero said, looking somberly at his models. "I am giving Rome the most beautiful buildings in the world!"

"Old Gallio must have made pots when he was governor of Achaea," said Tigellinus. "We might catch him at it." He wondered what Nero would say to that, whether the emperor was still half-afraid of his old tutor Seneca, in spite of Seneca's having been safely banished to the country, and wouldn't have Seneca's adopted brother touched.

But Nero seemed aware and acquiescent, enough to move on. Tigellinus added that everything was ready for the next games. These Christian atheists would then get what was coming to them. It would be the finest show there'd ever been yet. "All Rome's going to be crazy over you for that," he added.

"They ought to be," said Nero, "they ought! When I consider what I do for them. Things that none of the others ever thought of doing. The music. The spectacles. Strength through joy! They ought to be crazy about me. To love me. They ought to do more than love me!"

"They'll honor you," said Tigellinus. "Your name will live forever. Things will be called after you. Solid things.

"My Golden Palace."

"They'll remember Nero's reign long after old Augustus is forgotten."

But Nero was fidgeting.

Tigellinus made a great effort of the imagination. "Towns will be named after you. Cities. Altars will be dedicated to you everywhere." Ah, that was better. "A god, that's what you'll be. A regular god."

"I feel like a god," said Nero, "sometimes. Coming into the arena, slowly, grandly, at the head of the great procession serpent-stretching behind me, lifted on the voices, the closing, rising cheers, the love, lifted above the sand that is so soon to take the blood, lifted and floating."

He raised his arms, moving about the room on the balls of his feet, hovering around his models. He went on, his voice rising a little. "I am the will of Rome, and the people know it, the ordinary people who love me. For whom I make the great blood sacrifices. You said they loved me! It is only the hideous old men, the senators, who refuse to know I am the will. Some day I shall make them. I have been merciful, but my patience will not endure everything. Heads must roll! If they thwart me, they thwart the will and voice of Rome. They become enemies of society. Isn't that right, Tigellinus, isn't that right?"

But before Tigellinus had time to think of an answer, the emperor began again. "The Epicureans as well, they are enemies of society. They want to thwart the natural wish of the people for

263

gods and the gift of the gods, the natural wish of a leader! I have read some of the books of the Epicureans. Why have they not been suppressed?"

"Most of them have been, Majesty."

"All must be. Atheism is as much a crime against men as against the gods. Men need gods."

"They need the divine image on earth, Majesty," said Tigellinus, getting his cue. "They need to see it walking among them, doing the things they like doing themselves."

But Nero was not listening. He was leaning now on the marble sill, looking down and out over Rome, screwing up his eyes so as to see it less blurred. Even here, even still, there was the faint, sour sultry smell of an August city, the remains of an ashy taste in the air. "Roses!" Nero cried out suddenly. "Oh, my roses! Will someone be quick?"

After the room had been filled with flowers, Tigellinus took his leave. He understood Nero; it was all right. But sometimes rather exhausting. He had made up his mind to catch Gallio out. Old fool, coming around in his toga, grunting about justice! He'd have had Flavius Crispus too but for the fact that he was a certain little lady's father. Not that she'd mind most likely—grand little witch! But you never knew. Besides, it might look bad.

Nero had asked for a particular singing girl. Two boys had dashed off to fetch her. She was Asterope, the daughter of one of his old nurses, Alexandra. She looked like a pure Greek, spoke a rather affected Attic, and knew all his poems by heart. He treated her exquisitely. At the moment he was making a wreath of buds for her with his own hands, as Apollo might have done for a favorite muse. With her he would be able to be good, to escape from one of his selves into the other.

It all went back to childhood, that split between the selves. It was his mother's doing, mostly, that tough and able and unmoral woman, Agrippina. She was forever forcing him, a sensitive, short-sighted, pretty little boy, to be what she wanted: the Roman, the leader, the emperor-to-be, character-building him into the Roman pattern.

And he would run away from her, back to his two nurses, Greeks, both of them, Ecolage and Alexandra, and they would be gentle, petting and praising him, listening to his stories of what he'd been doing, and giving him sweets and soft talk when he cried instead of scolding him or smacking him. Till he was quite a big boy, they would take him on their knees and sing him Greek baby-songs about a lovely, lovely world where delightful and affable godlike creatures would spring from tree or fountain with handfuls of presents.

So still he was caught between his mother and his nurses, even though Agrippina was dead. And how hard she'd been to kill, but murdering her couldn't get her out of his mind, nor yet the longing she had planted there for the little boy who cried to turn into the will and voice of Rome, to become the super-Roman of all time.

Ecolage and Alexandra had retired to the country. It was months since he had seen either of them. But there were successors. There was Octavia, his Roman cousin, whom he had been made to marry, the girl so full of Roman virtues that it terrified him to sleep with her—so that he had to drive her off, divorce her, kill her . . . just as Britannicus too had to be killed, the virtuous Roman youth, the snob, the rival. Yes, had to be stamped out. But Seneca had known about Britannicus, the old hypocrite, talking down his nose about philosopher-kings. He must have known, all those interminable weeks before the poison actually worked!

And there had been plenty of Greeks, Acte herself, his own first choice, and probable virgins like this girl Asterope, and others. Boys too, virgin Greek boys such as tempted the delightful gods in the other dream, the dream in which the little boy became the will and voice of Hellas.

But perhaps Poppaea would be an escape from both: not Rome, not Hellas. She was not out of a dream. She was living for something else, for the individual, herself and him. She had leaped straight from her first husband into his arms. She had the same fears as his and the same elations. Some day they would have a son, a wonderful child . . .

Asterope came into the room, with her smooth hair smelling of winter violets, and knelt at his feet. He crowned her with the wreath he had made himself.

When she spoke them, his poems sounded purest classic. Perhaps after all he should have been a poet. Only a poet. Innocent. Living in a rush hut in some wild glade. Under the red, echoing cliffs of cloud-browed Parnassus, watching the gods stepping enormously about their business between earth and heaven. He leaned back, shutting his eyes. No, it was nobler to be a god than even to sing about gods! To assume the difficult, divine mantle, dispensing life and death.

He began now to think slowly about the methods of death for those who affronted and refused the gods. Christians and Epicureans and such. Superb wild beasts, beautiful as panthers of Dionysos, would be his ministers. And fire. Flames in the night. What a marvelous sight Rome had been, burning . . . that wonderful sky, pulsing with reflection. He had given himself one supreme moment to regard it as an artist, although he had been so immensely energetic, sane, and statesmanlike—everyone said so, everyone!—in dealing with the fire, both at the time and afterward. The Roman virtues. He had them after all. His mother might have been proud of him! His mother . . . He shook his head angrily, chasing away these thoughts.

Watching him, the girl Asterope threw herself back a little and put increased spirit and sensitivity into the poem she was chanting for him.

16

Ends and Means

Crispus came back from the country early in September. He had not intended to do so. Balbus was still out of town, and so were many of his friends. The country was at its best. He had intended Flavia to come out and spend a nice week with him and his mother. It would have been good for the two young people to learn to miss one another. But as things were, he was too uneasy. Anything might be going on in Rome.

He came back to find Beric anxious and not very communicative. Manasses was in the Mamertine prison, charged merely with being a Christian.

"But that was dealt with last month," said Crispus, "and finished with. I shall go and explain that, although the boy was suspected of this thing at one time, it is no longer true. You see how necessary my preventive measures were, Beric."

"No good," said Beric somberly. "Manasses himself didn't deny that he was a Christian."

"But I can't make this out. The boy must have known that such an admission was—as things look just now—tantamount to a death sentence."

"Yes, he knew that."

"Then, *why?*"

"Oh, can't you see," said Beric, "it was the one thing that counted in his life! He was proud of it! He'd got to show it was worth dying for."

"I see," said Crispus and added, "Manasses appears to have had more courage—of a misguided kind—than one expects of a dancing boy. But I trust the others have been warned by his fate."

"Perhaps," Beric said. He knew well enough how things were in the household and particularly that, if Dapyx were arrested and tortured or even badly frightened, he might say anything about any of them or else perhaps on his own accuse them of the sort of fantastic crimes that Christians were being accused of.

He knew that Argas wanted him to speak to Dapyx, but he couldn't. In some ways he didn't want to speak to any of them. He wanted to stop and think. He wanted events to remain static until he knew how he fitted into them. But they wouldn't do that.

Crispus was not only worried about Beric and what had been going on in his own household, but also about public matters.

He had been talking to his cousin, Flavius Scaevinus. How long could the present state of affairs be tolerated? A tyrant only considers himself safe among slaves. Nero was getting worse. Perhaps the time had come to end this phase of emperors. Or again if it appeared necessary, in order to please the common people, to continue with the title, it might be possible to restrict the imperial power vastly, to have one of themselves wearing the purple but strictly under the control of the Senate, which would come into its own again. Take, for instance, a man like Calpurnius Piso . . . So the talk went between the two cousins.

It was all extremely serious. The only relaxation that Crispus allowed himself, and which he could really enjoy, was his visits to his daughter. There she sat with her embroidery, the pet. And soon, no doubt, there would be hope of a grandchild.

But now Balbus too came back to Rome. The evening of the day he arrived, his son and daughter-in-law duly came to pay their respects, and after she had left Candidus suddenly blurted out everything. The next morning Balbus went over to see Crispus and tell him. So that much of Crispus's happiness came to an end.

Niger was there with the rest of the litter bearers. He was living through a bad story. Everything went wrong in it. Everything was against the man in the story. There had been other stories before, good ones, but they seemed to be over. This house had been part of one. He didn't see now how he could ever get back into that story.

Waiting in the yard, he saw Dapyx come out of the kitchen carrying two garbage pails. Another of the kitchen slaves, going by, gave Dapyx a lighthearted kick. He stumbled, tipping over one of the pails, then went down on his knees, scrabbling hastily and awkwardly for the odds and ends of muck that had slid out, looking around for the next kick or blow. The lobe of one of his ears was torn a bit. He saw Niger and looked at him with extreme hate. He was in a bad story too. The expected blow for his spilled pail came. He squealed and held onto his torn ear.

Niger looked away. Beside him, the Cappadocian coughed, his hands on his chest. Zyrax was whistling and chewing something. The German was watching Dapyx being hurt. It was a kind of pleasure when other people were hurt, not oneself.

Niger shut his eyes. He refused to let the good story be entirely taken from him. Last night Persis had slipped away from her mistress and out to the shed where he was chained and whispered a few words and closed his hand over a piece of white bread. Hard in his mind Niger began to remake the good pictures.

Josias came by. It was Josias who had talked to him that first time. Now Josias did not look his way. He was hurrying, his old limp catching him as it always did. But he had to hurry now, to be always doing something or looking as if he were.

Josias saw Dapyx and Niger. He was frightened of them both, in different ways. If only he knew what was going to happen; if only they would stop hurting Manasses. If only Manasses would come back. If only he could do anything to save Manasses. If only he could speak about these things that were tearing and terrifying him. Shriek them out loud. It was so difficult even to see Argas alone, and Argas might be angry with him. He would never dare to go to another meeting again, not after that last one and the panic he had been in. That girl! He forgot how he had been assuaged for moments during the love feast, how he had felt for a little time as though he and Manasses were together again, as though he had accepted what was being done to Manasses. He had dreamed again, after the love feast, of the dye factory in Tyre. But there was to be no getting away from it this time, because Manasses wasn't there anymore to save him. Because they'd got Manasses too.

The litter slaves were shouted for and jumped to their poles and trotted around to the front entrance. Balbus came out and regarded them blackly.

Zyrax, aware of nothing wrong, awaited directions with an expectant smile but got instead a fist in his face.

"Home!" snapped Balbus, bundling himself in, and they knew they'd got to do it on the double. Actually, the Cappadocian died that night, and Montanus had to get a new one. The others only had sore shoulders.

Crispus was very much upset as well. He walked about the room, trying to sort it out. His little girl. It was like all those stories he'd heard but not attended to much, about Nero and his friends. Tigellinus must somehow had frightened her into it. Poor little Flavia!

But why hadn't she told her father? He would have protected her! Why had she looked so sweet and comfortable? If Tigellinus had corrupted her to that extent, then . . . then . . . well, then it was time to consider very carefully the proposals about Calpurnius Piso. To get in touch with Seneca . . . and no doubt Gallio would have heard from his adopted brother . . . to take all risks so as to end this monstrous thing.

Sannio, who had peeped into the room and seen Crispus pacing about, frowning and twisting his hands into the folds of his gown, came and told Beric that something was wrong.

Beric went along. He knew Balbus had been there. Suddenly he wondered if anything was wrong with Flavia, if she were ill. Yes, it must be that. From one end of the corridor to the other he'd had time to forgive her for anything and everything . . . these summer fevers that struck and killed in three days! And she had no mother; it would have been all different if she'd had a mother. She would have been kind and gentle as well as so beautiful!

Crispus looked up when he came in. "My boy," he said and hesitated, then, "you will have to know. It is about Flavia."

So it *was* that. "She's ill . . . " said Beric, trying not to let his voice shake.

"I wish she were," Crispus said. "It would have been better. No. No. She . . ."

And then Beric remembered Lamprion's story. And found he had not forgiven Flavia after all. He put his hand on Crispus's sadly groping arm. "I know. It's Tigellinus. Isn't it?"

"Yes," said Crispus. "How did you know?"

"Slaves' gossip. I told them to hold their tongues. Thought it was lies."

"It should have been. My little Flavia. She can't have known. And now it appears that this vile thing is being talked about. Rhymes being written. What shall I do?"

"What is her husband going to do?"

"He is in a most unfortunate position . . . considering that this brute is his superior officer . . . on whom his whole fortune depends . . . and the emperor's friend! And I had been hoping . . . grandchildren. You and she were brought up together. You were fond of her, I think. Weren't you, Beric?"

"I was."

"My poor boy. You will feel it too. What times we live in. I must see Gallio. I must send a letter to him. Tell Hermeias to bring his tablets. No, I shall write this myself."

"Can I write it for you?"

"No. You are in quite enough danger as it is. Give me my pen. I trust, Beric, you have not become—in any way—any more involved?"

"I kept my promise."

"Don't make any more difficulties for me, boy. I shall have—enemies. Ofonius Tigellinus is the key man. Now, leave me. I must consider what to say. What to do."

Beric felt too much worried to talk to anybody, yet when he was alone he kept thinking about Flavia—in ways he preferred not to think. So he went over to the gymnasium and spent most of the day there, practicing various movements and asking anatomical questions of the pro. How far under the ribs was the heart? What length of dagger, for instance? He tried to make it all sound very casual. But supposing the key man was wearing armor of some kind under his tunic—well, one would have to find him at some moment when that was unlikely.

When he came back, he found Argas in his room, putting the week's clean wool and linen tunics, all nicely ironed, back into the chest. Beric wasn't sure how much he wanted to see Argas. Christians don't kill. Yes, but this would be different. This would help the Kingdom. Help to destroy what was stopping the Kingdom from becoming actual and universal. But if Argas didn't think so . . .

He sat and watched Argas, a slave putting away his master's clothes. What did that feel like? Did you take it as a matter of course? Well, a Christian wouldn't. He didn't even know, himself, exactly how many tunics he had. But there'd been a row if he hadn't found a clean one when he wanted it!

Argas turned his head and said in a whisper, "Why didn't you come last night?"

Beric was annoyed. He didn't want to have all this out again. But he answered gently enough. "I told you. Crispus asked me not to."

"Asked you!" said Argas. "You know what would happen to us if we were caught. That doesn't stop us."

"Quite," said Beric coldly.

"What's going to be done in the arena next week doesn't stop us either! Not even Tigellinus can stop us," he added in something above a whisper.

"Don't say so at the top of your voice then," said Beric and walked out of the room. Tigellinus *would* be able to stop them, though, sooner or later, unless, unless . . .

In the middle of supper, Crispus suddenly remarked to Beric that in view of his official position he would have to sit through the next games, which would be starting in three days, including any execution of Christians or other criminals that there might be. He added that it was disgusting to have such things thrust upon one. He liked a good sporting fight as well as anybody, but it was intolerable to see one's fellow human beings, however depraved and however much without status, being torn to pieces unarmed.

"I have always been against it," he said, "but, of course, it has generally taken place during the lunch interval . . . when only the riffraff stay . . . and at any rate in small numbers. Now it will be under our noses."

"Isn't there any chance of its being stopped?" Beric asked. Somehow he hadn't thought it would ever really happen—not to men he might have spoken to. Surely they couldn't be thinking of doing *that* to Manasses?

Crispus shook his head. "Not with the individuals who are at present in power. No doubt they enjoy it. Persons without education or philosophy!"

"I suppose the emperor wouldn't take any advice from Seneca now?"

"Not the least chance. Though the gods know there was a time . . ." He drank a cup of wine and snapped at Phaon to refill it quickly.

So Crispus was helpless in this matter, he and all his decent, respectable, Stoic friends. And what was it Lalage had said?—that something would turn up for Beric to do . . . if he looked for it. There didn't seem to be any other way. How many more times would one have supper here in comfort and privacy? *May as well make the most of it,* Beric thought and held out his cup for Phaon to refill too.

The next morning, Crispus sent for Beric and gave him the letter for Gallio, asking him to take it over. "I'd sooner you took it than any of the slaves," he said, and that made Beric feel curiously happy, as though he were repaying something.

He went off at once toward the Esquiline, crossing some of the fire areas, with the new buildings going up already—and a good bit better than the old ones, Beric admitted to himself, rather grudgingly. Many of them had been started with Treasury grants. As he came to Gallio's house, Beric hesitated. Perhaps he was growing more suspicious, getting the mentality of an enemy of society. He felt there was something odd and, instead of going to the door, he went into a sweetshop, bought some honey drops, and began to gossip.

In no time it came out that there had been an arrest at the big house. Yes, the master of the house, the old gentleman himself—in his toga—early that morning. And the guards were still there, searching.

So Beric took the letter straight back and was hurrying to see Crispus when Hermeias stopped him. "Lady Flavia is with her father."

"My news won't wait, Hermeias."

"Well, just as you like, of course." Hermeias shrugged his shoulders slightly. If the Briton insisted on putting his head into a wasps' nest!

Beric pushed the curtain back and walked in.

They were sitting opposite one another. She was looking exceedingly pretty. Doing her hair a new way. You wanted to get it in your hands.

Crispus frowned at him, motioning him to go, but he said quickly, "I have some bad news."

"The gods avert it!" said Crispus mechanically, then, "What —more than I know already?"

"Gallio is arrested," Beric said, not even glancing at Flavia now. "They're searching his house," and he slipped the letter back to Crispus, who gasped and went rather pale. "Is there nothing I can do?" Beric asked.

"No. Nothing." He held onto his letter. "Thank you, my boy. Thank you. I shall have to see what I can do—later. I shall have to see the authorities."

"Perhaps," said Flavia sweetly, "I could do something, father?" Then she turned to Beric. "You're not being very amiable this morning, are you?"

"Flavia!" said Crispus.

"That maid of mine that you used to be so interested in is waiting about somewhere, Beric," she went on, curling her back in her chair like a soft kitten. "Wouldn't you like to see her?"

"Thanks. I shall go and kiss her at once!" said Beric savagely and walked out.

So that was what she was like now. After Aelius Candidus and Ofonius Tigellinus. To start with. It suited her. And Crispus? What had her father done that she should want to hurt him? Not brought her up properly, he thought, remembering what Domina Aelia had said, not shown her anything worth dying for. So she's taken to power, power over people, because she's a woman. But if she'd been a man it would have been power over money and politics.

People, too, in the end. He almost bumped into Persis.

"Please," she said, "could I speak to you a minute?"

"Of course," he said and suddenly wondered if perhaps she had a private message to him from her mistress, then hated himself for thinking it, for being such a fool, for wanting to eat carrion. He gave her a little push. "We'll go along to my room, Persis."

She followed him and, half-way, whispered, "Please, could I see Argas or Phaon too?"

"Oh, all right," he said and called across to a slave, "Here, Mikkos, tell that fool Argas to get me a clean bath towel!"

She slipped into the room after him.

He sat down on the bed and pulled her down, gently, beside him. "I told Flavia I was going to kiss you," he said, "and you can tell her I did if she asks you. There, silly! What do you think one asks a pretty girl to come to one's room for?"

"I thought . . . I thought . . . oh, aren't you one of us any longer?"

"Yes, of course I am. Persis, you're such a little goose. Why did you shove me away?"

"I . . . I didn't know . . . if you were a friend still."

"I'm a friend." He picked up her hand and kissed the fingers, one after the other. "There. Not frightened? You are a pretty girl, you know, Persis. Would you rather not be?"

"Not till the Kingdom's come. I'd like to be then. When we're all free."

"I'm not thinking of you as a slave, Persis. You know that?"

"I know, brother."

Argas came in quickly. "You wanted me?" And then to Persis, very low, "Peace, sister."

"She wanted you," Beric said. "Now then, Persis, what is it?"

Persis said, "After the last meeting—Lalage and Sophrosyne were arrested."

Argas made the sign of the cross, jerkily. That was that. "On the same charge?" Beric asked.

She nodded.

"Getting close, isn't it?"

"I keep on hearing," said Persis, "when that man—when Tigellinus is in the house—about the things they're going to do to us. Oh, he keeps on talking about it! The things they're going to do to the women. I think I could bear being killed. But . . ."

"Who's to be deacon now?" Argas said.

"You, Argas?"

"I can't be. It's all I can do to get away for a meeting. I'm not even sure of that." He glanced at Beric. "What about Phineas or Eunice?"

"He said he didn't want to be. He didn't feel sure enough. It had better be her; she's not suspected yet. At least, we don't think so."

"They've got her name as like as not. Persis, are we going to talk about this in front of him?"

"Go and talk in the passage if you think it's safer," said Beric and let go Persis's hand.

"Don't be silly, Argas," said Persis. "He's one of us."

"Is he?"

"Look here, Argas," said Beric, cold and quietly, getting to his feet, "I don't think I'm going to stand for this. You can go to the arena your own way. I shall not help you."

The two men stood very close in the small room, each face a few inches from the other, tense, enemy face.

Persis had jumped up too. "You can't—you're Christians! Oh, stop looking like that, Argas. Remember Manasses. He wouldn't—remember Jesus!"

Argas gave a kind of gasping cry and jerked up his hand in front of his mouth.

Persis whispered to him, "Say you're sorry, Argas. It was your fault. Oh, do make it right!"

But Argas couldn't. It was not fair—not fair—that the masters should be able to say such things!

Then, from out in the courtyard, Sannio was calling for Persis.

"Oh," she said, "I must go. Oh, you are unkind to me to quarrel. Both of you!"

"Wait a minute," said Beric and pushed through the curtains with his arm around her and kissed her in front of Sannio—whatever he thought this time!—before she ran off.

Then he went back into the room, and Argas was still there, Argas who was a Christian and had been whipped for it, who had a right to be angry—as he would have been angry if he had been a whipped British slave, with the Kingdom always being taken out of his reach. He looked gently at Argas and said, "Why did you want me so much at the love feast?"

276

Again Argas gave that little cry of war against himself. He looked away and down, past Beric, and muttered, "We're so few now. We don't know what's going to happen to us. Nor to anything. We can't look forward to the next time now. Maybe there won't be any next time. I can die all right. It's been worth it. If I knew it would go on."

"I can't help you to be certain of that, Argas," Beric said.

"No. Not really. Only . . . I wanted you in. Then our church would have gone on. Even if all the rest of us got killed."

"I might be killed too."

"You. They wouldn't kill you."

"Why not? I'm not even a citizen."

"You're—different."

"Am I? Am I, Argas?" He took Argas's hand and held it against his own chest, over the heart.

Argas at last looked up and met his eyes.

"Aren't we brothers, Argas?" he said again.

"Then why won't you—take our baptism—now—be one of us? We wouldn't feel so few then."

"Listen, Argas," said Beric, "I wanted to be baptized last time. Before all this. It's not because I'm afraid that I'm not asking for it now. You know that, don't you?"

"Yes," said Argas, "I know that, Beric."

"There are two things. First, there's Crispus. Well, I've got to decide sooner or later how much I've the right to hurt him. I expect I've got to. And then. I haven't told anyone this. I killed Sotion."

"But—you know we don't kill. Ever. You can't be in the Kingdom if you're a murderer."

"I know. So you see why I can't come to the love feast. But— do you think it really counted about Sotion? He was only a miserable little thing. I killed him like you'd kill a beetle on the floor."

"Sotion was our enemy, and we forgave him. It wasn't easy, but we did it. All of us. Manasses forgave him almost at once, and then he showed us how. We had to see what it was like for Sotion to do it. He did it for money; he was a poor man."

"Not so poor as most of you."

"Well, we didn't let ourselves be tempted, and he did. That's all. He was stupider than the rest of us too. He didn't see what he was missing. Most likely the police had got something on him, besides, and so they made him do it. We thought out all that when we were in prison. And you spoiled our forgiveness by killing him."

"Then I'm out of it." Suddenly Beric felt very much upset. This was much worse than having a ghost after one!

"Not if you're sorry for killing him, Beric. Not if you'll see you had no right to kill him, if you'll take the weight of having done it. Then we can forgive you in Jesus' name, and you can be baptized. Shall we, Beric?"

Beric stood silent. He was sorry for something—something to do with them all and the Kingdom—but was he sorry that Sotion was dead? The man was certainly better out of the way, wasn't he? If they'd all forgiven him, would he possibly have become different? Would he not have given any more names? It was so very unlikely that anyone would change that much that you couldn't take it into account. Or could you?

The prisoners could forgive him because it was the only thing they could do about him, the only action they could take. But he, Beric, he'd had a choice of actions. He couldn't put himself into the man's place, as Argas apparently could. Because he'd never been poor himself, never had the beginnings of that temptation. You don't understand other people's temptations when you haven't had them yourself.

And there was Argas, wanting to baptize him so much! Into danger. Into death. If that mattered. He couldn't quite think about it, couldn't yet picture death affecting him. If he let Argas do it, then Argas would feel as if he were free . . .

Persis came slipping back between the curtains. "She didn't want me after all! Oh, is it all right? Have you forgiven one another?"

"We didn't even need to say so," Beric answered her.

But Argas said, "Persis, he's our brother. But he killed Sotion."

"Oh!" said Persis. "Then it wasn't because you're a nobleman that you wouldn't come to the love feast, but because you're a murderer."

"I'm sorry if you want me to be sorry," said Beric, "but he had to be got rid of."

"You're pretending to be God," Persis said.

"There's someone who needs to be got rid of much more," Beric said low, "and that's Tigellinus. And I'm going to do it. I'm going to deliver you from evil. I'm going to be God's instrument."

"Tigellinus . . . " said Persis. "Oh—not because of her?"

"No," said Beric "because of you. All of you. And you've got to help me, Persis. You've got to be God's instrument too. You've got to let me in when he's with *her*. He won't be armed then."

"You're trying to tempt me," said Persis. "How can I? You're wicked, Beric. You mustn't."

"But think, Persis, it's for Lalage and all of them in prison. Manasses. Euphemia. If I do this, then those things at the games won't happen. The things you were afraid of. They won't happen to you."

"I'd rather they happen than you do this sin—and make me help you—to stop them. If they're God's will."

"Why do you say they are? I think they're the will of Tigellinus."

"The God will strike him."

"Yes, through me. And you, Persis. If you don't help me, I'll do it myself, but I'm more likely to be caught."

"Oh, Beric, you're twisting me—Argas, help me. It's getting so difficult!"

Argas had been listening, trying to sort it out. The difficulty had been that when he first heard Beric say he was going to kill Tigellinus, he had felt a most disconcerting hope and excitement. He had first to fight against this in himself, to think what Manasses would have said, how Manasses would have been able, quite easily, to think of it. Or Lalage. He stood there, fingering the bath towel he had brought at the beginning, praying, thinking over his direct instructions from Jesus who had understood everything— the Way of Life. Sense, it had been.

And Persis was pulling at his arm, and Beric, who was at last being friends with him again, was standing there, certain of what he was going to do. Seeing ahead of him. And had to be stopped.

"Well," said Beric, "isn't it sense?"

He had to answer. "No," he said, "not so much sense in the end as the Way of Life. I'll try and tell you. Give me a minute, Beric. It's not too easy. You want to do something good in the end, good for all of us. Right. But to get there you're going to do something bad. Something directly forbidden."

"If I could do this for you, it wouldn't matter me being out of the Kingdom. I'd do that. I'd lose my chance of the Kingdom. I'd go back to where I was. I'd die too; perhaps I'll have to. Jesus said if you took the sword you'd got to be killed by the sword. I think someone's got to be that now, and I will be."

"But it's not so easy. We can't let you buy us out that way. If we did, we'd be murderers too. You can't get out of having to be good. Having to look after your own soul. What you're trying to do is to get behind what's plain and rational. To say you know best. Better than Jesus and everyone else who's thought about it.

"Listen, Beric, if you do this wrong thing, it will spoil the good thing it was meant to help. Like your killing Sotion spoiled our forgiving. You'll get us all mixed up in it, in our minds I mean, making us feel our Kingdom and our love for one another is happening because of a murder. Because of a sin. Which it can't be. It's got to be founded on faith and love and just nothing else. It isn't like ordinary things that are founded on hate or money or some kind of rule. It's a different kind of thing. You know. You felt it yourself. It didn't have anything to do with murder. Did it?"

"But Tigellinus is part of the *thing*," said Beric, "the thing we're trying to get rid of so that the Kingdom will be able to come on earth. So that there'll be the kind of equality that we'll be able to love one another in!"

"We can't get rid of the thing by killing people who're in it here and there. We've got to put a different kind of force on it. A new kind. So that it'll alter itself and break itself up. Oh, it's difficult to show you, Beric, when you've got this old way into your head! But we've got to do it by living differently ourselves. Thinking different. Acting different. That's why we're going to the arena if we've got to—to be witnesses for our new thing. They'll know it's real if we die for it. See?

"But if we start killing our enemies instead of forgiving them, then it's no different. We'll be like everybody else. And we'll be beaten the same as Spartacus was beaten, because he didn't know the last thing—the thing we do—the faith and love that make it all different. So if you do this, you'll really be helping to beat us. You'll be helping the other side, Beric. People won't think we've got anything different, and you'll spoil our dying for the new way. Our dying won't do what it's meant to do. See?"

"If I do it the way I mean," Beric said, "no one will know who did it."

"I'd know. It would be my sin. And—you might be caught."

Beric answered slowly, "But even then people wouldn't know it was a Christian who killed Tigellinus. If I am that still. They'll think I did it because of Flavia. Even Persis thought that."

"But we'd know."

"If I do it in spite of you telling me not to, then you won't be to blame. And I won't be a Christian."

"Oh, Beric, don't leave us! You did see once what the Way of Life was about. *Why* we're different. Why we just have to be once we've got the hang of it. You saw it was sense then. It's sense still, isn't it?"

"Yes, it's sense still. And I want it to be possible for everyone. Not smashed and stopped. As it may be. You know it may, Argas."

"It couldn't be," said Persis. "It would go on in other places." And suddenly she thought of her mother and the church at Philippi going on. Epaphroditus on that old mule of his, helping anyone who asked him. People being happy there. And she'd be able to die for them. She'd be able to die for her mother. Then they'd be together again, as they'd never be now, any other way.

"That's pride," said Argas. "You think you know the Will and the plan, Beric. But you don't. Nobody can."

"We've got to try and know," said Beric. He looked at the two slaves. He wanted desperately to protect them. That was what being a master was for. But if they wouldn't be protected . . ?

And then Phaon dodged into the room and whispered to the three of them, "Phineas is arrested."

"Then Eunice must be deacon," said Persis quietly. "But it'll be all of us soon."

"They may leave the slaves," said Phaon, "for their masters to deal with." And he grinned at Beric with a touch of malice. "We're supposed to get our beating up privately."

"We oughtn't all to be here together," said Argas, suddenly nervous, "in case . . ." He broke off and began hurriedly to fold the towel.

But this time it was Sannio. He looked a bit shy at Beric and said, "I thought . . . maybe me being here too, sir, it wouldn't look so awkward, not . . . not if anyone began to have their suspicions. Like they might. I won't listen, sir, not to what's not meant for me."

"If I'd happened to be a slave," said Beric, "if the emperor hadn't pardoned my father . . . and all that nonsense . . . I wish I could be sure I'd have been as decent as some of you."

17

The Individual and the State

After the litter had come around for Flavia, Crispus sent for Beric. He was very much upset about Gallio but extremely pleased that his letter had not got into the hands of the police. The next thing to do was to see Gallio if possible, find out if it was a matter of money, or what. Most probably it was official blackmail in some form. But perhaps some other and still less discreet letters had been intercepted.

He was putting inquiries into motion. By the evening he found that Gallio was in the Mamertine prison. The charge appeared to be rather indefinite. Very likely it would be just a matter of money. If possible he would see him the next day.

Beric asked if he could come too, adding that he might perhaps take something to one or two of the other prisoners. "Manasses is there, you know. Perhaps Gallio will have seen him."

"Dear me, dear me!" said Crispus. "To think of Gallio being in the same prison as these criminals. If you come with me, Beric, you must be careful. They may be in a different part of the prison. I certainly trust so."

However, as it turned out, Gallio was not in the decent segregation he might have claimed. Aelius Candidus had received him with every show of politeness and regret for this distressing, this no doubt temporary, misfortune. "All a misunderstanding, no doubt, sir," he said.

Gallio grunted. "I doubt it. Our friend Tigellinus understands perfectly well what he's about. Got some light irons, Candidus?"

"Certainly, certainly," said Candidus, seeing to it. "A necessary formality, I'm afraid." He took him through, showed him his cell, quite a tolerable little room really, and then the exercise yard. "Rather a mixed crowd, sir," he said. "Still, I can have the women removed."

"Let the poor creatures be," Gallio answered. "No need to drive them back into their cells for me. Getting much jail fever?"

"An occasional case," said Candidus. "Some of these wretched Christians come from the worst slums in Rome. They bring it with them." He looked at his prisoners with distaste. "When I joined the Praetorians, I never supposed I should be promoted to be a menagerie keeper!"

Gallio looked around too, then nudged Candidus. "Who's that fellow?"

"That? Another of these Christians. This one's a citizen at least. From Tarsus. However, I think you would be well-advised not to speak to any of them, Gallio."

"Thanks for your advice, Candidus," said Gallio coldly, "but I'm afraid I shall be bored if I don't. Can't stand being bored." He turned his back on the deputy governor and shuffled off towards the rest of the prisoners, who had edged away from him at first. He found the irons uncomfortable but no worse than that. And he thought he remembered the face of this citizen from Tarsus. Though where could he have seen him?

Aelius Candidus made a note on his tablet. It would interest the authorities to hear that Gallio had actually chosen to mix with the Christians. It would be nice to see Gallio crash. Comforting. To know that not even a great name, honor and education, and honest service to the State could save a man if his luck was out!

Some of his prisoners were praying or whatever they did, wriggling about on the ground, turning their eyes up like hens. Disgusting little Jews and Syrians, ugly, half-starved, gutter-smelling—you could believe they'd done anything!

Aelius Candidus deliberately walked across the yard in their direction, through them, and got a few kicks in on the ones who didn't scuttle fast enough. He wore heavy boots.

But Gallio went up to his fellow citizen from the farthest end of the Empire and said, "Morning. I know your face. What's your name?"

"My name is Paul, Paul of Tarsus. I didn't remember your face, but now I hear your voice, I know you, sir. You're Lucius Junius Gallio. You bought some tents from me. I hope they wore well."

284

"So you were one of these Christians after all?"

"Certainly. Did I deny it?"

"The other fellows did most of the talking. What are you doing here?"

"I am here on appeal to Caesar from the governor of Judea."

"Didn't you get justice from him?"

"Yes. But I needed a public trial in Rome."

"Why?"

"To clarify the position. We shall either get leave to preach and teach here, and then we shall be able to go anywhere, unhindered, or else we shall be declared public enemies."

"Looks like that now."

"I think not. I believe this is a phase. Not that it really signifies, because we shall certainly win in the end, but it might be quicker if we could do it peacefully. This killing won't go beyond the next few weeks. And why? Because the men and women who are killed are all going to be witnesses of the truth of what they are dying for. On a big scale too."

"What sentence do you expect yourself—frankly?"

"Oh, a death sentence, as things are just now. Obviously."

"Not worrying, are you?"

"Why should I? It is necessary that some of us should die. One must take the long view, as the farmer does when he buries his corn and knows he won't see it again until spring. Does what I say shock you, Gallio?"

"A little, a little. But never mind. Better be shocked than bored. And I'm bored mostly. Go on, Paul. What made you take up this Christianity? You were a respectable man, weren't you?"

"Yes, I was respectable once. A good Jew. I thought these Nazarenes were as dangerous to us and our established rules as you Romans think they are to yours. It hurt me to hear them talk! I thought they could be got rid of, as Nero thinks now. I tried to do it myself with my own hands.

"I helped to kill one of them. Stoning him. Filled with blind, screaming hate against him—as one must be to kill an unarmed man. And, you see, Gallio, he met that hatred and mad rage with something else. You could see it in his eyes up to the last. Till they were blind with blood. It was love he was fighting us with. Love.

"I went on to Damascus, feeding my hate and rage with words, the way one does. I had to find others to hurt and kill. As I killed them I would also be convincing myself that they had been wicked! But somehow I could never get that man Stephen out of my mind, nor what he had said about his Master. There was sand and dust and rocks, and sometimes a few scraggy, dark palm trees, and the jogging of the mules under the hot sun. And I could never stop thinking about Stephen. I kept on seeing him, half smashed by the stones, his back broken, lifting himself on his elbows and crawling a little like an animal. I kept on smelling his blood.

"You see, it was not as though I had ever killed. I had always been interested in things of the mind, indoor things. Even when I was a child I never threw stones at the dogs in the street. And now I had witnessed this thing done to another person, and this other person had loved me. He had died showing me his love. And suddenly I saw that this was the whole truth about everything, the light in the heart of the universe! Love and blood. Have I made myself plain, Gallio?"

"Not in the very least, I'm afraid. But never mind. Probably my stupidity. All this blood. Got on your nerves, no doubt. Gives me the feeling of a sacrifice, somehow."

"Exactly. The sacrifice of the victim who gives Himself out of His great love. Who sheds His own blood for all of us. That was the mystery that I saw."

"Hm. And that's something to do with this Christianity?"

"It is Christianity."

"Odd. If that was all, it would be no more dangerous than all the rest of these Eastern religions. Saw a lot of them when I was governor. What's different about yours?"

Paul looked at him suspiciously, frowning, then said, "Jesus died for me. And for every man or woman who has the will to accept Him, singly and separately. His love passes to them as Stephen's passed first to me. We believe in the value of the individual human being, his right to be bought by the blood, his right to choose for himself, his right to be in brotherhood. We cannot give consent, even formal consent, to any principle which denies this."

"Ah," said Gallio, "I begin to see. If you believe in human beings, in the importance of the individual person, whoever he may be, then sooner or later that is an attack on the State, which is bound to claim a superauthority and a supervalue. That right, Paul?"

"We allow the human authority of the State," said Paul definitely.

"Yes, hairsplitter, coming here to appeal to Caesar! All of one kind, you Jewish intellectuals. Pretty penny it must have cost you too. You may think you can allow the State's authority. Don't know if you'll go on doing that; not if you're logical. Perhaps you aren't though. But you can't allow the State's value. Now, I'll tell you. What you're up against is the State shaping the lives of these individuals of yours any way it pleases. Making them part of a thing, so to speak. Using them for its own ends."

"We must be against that. Persons are ends in themselves. Under God."

"So that's what this atheism charge is. You won't assent to the worship of the State or the State gods."

"Or the State's emperor."

Gallio gave an abrupt laugh. "I see your point. So even if they wanted you to make a formal admission of the supreme value of the State and its claim over those who live under it, you would refuse to do so?"

"That is so, Gallio."

"You wouldn't even drop a pinch of incense on the altar flame?"

"Certainly not, Gallio."

"Die sooner than do it?"

"Naturally."

"Doesn't it seem to you a bit silly? Bit exaggerated?"

"No. It is a point on which there can be no compromise. It has not arisen yet in the form that you suggest, but it may do so."

"Very probably. Well, well, I've always believed in compromise myself. Up to a point. No doubt all of us stick somewhere. And you say all these—" he looked around at the yard full of odd-

287

looking creatures, undersized, dirty, scarred, obviously uneducated and without taste, dressed in odds and ends of rags "—all these are really valuable as human beings, that it matters what happens to them?"

"Jesus gave His life for each of them," said Paul, "and so would I."

A tall woman, with a cloak pinned over a very torn dress, came across the yard. Again Gallio seemed to think he knew the face. Really, all this might be quite interesting. Quite a change.

The woman spoke to Paul. "My friend Sophrosyne has the fever, and I don't think she will live very much longer. She's old and not strong. They knocked her around a lot at the first examination. Would you mind coming and giving her a blessing, Paul, while she's still conscious?"

"Of course, Lalage," said Paul in an oddly different tone of voice.

Ah, thought Gallio, *now I know.* "So you're one of them too, Lalage! Well, well. Last time I saw you, I think you were dancing Phaedra. Bit of a difference, isn't it?"

"You're not—accused of the same thing, sir?"

"Dear me, no! Certainly not. I fancy I shall be out in a few days. They merely want my money. Not my life at present. Well, we shall be seeing something of one another in the next few days."

Paul and Lalage went over toward the row of women's cells. It was all horribly overcrowded. The buckets weren't emptied more than once a day, and there were a good many sick. Luke came in constantly and did what he could, but there was really no help for the jail fever cases unless they were very strong. A doctor was more useful in dealing with the aftereffects of an examination by the authorities. There were, in any case, several freedmen and slave doctors, Jews for the most part, among the prisoners.

Gallio went back to his room for a time. He had brought a change of linen with him, a few books, and some writing materials; also, of course, enough money to pay for service from some proper prisoner. He considered writing some letters but thought it might be better to wait. One must do nothing injudicious at this stage.

He read for a time, gratified at his ability to do so as calmly as this, then went again into the yard. Lalage was probably in the cell with her dying friend, and Paul was now sitting on a bench, dictating to Luke, and there was a ring of men and women sitting on the ground at his feet and staring at him.

It was remarkable how patient Paul, the educated man, was with these beasts of burden who had never followed out a train of reasoning and kept on interrupting to ask stupid or fantastic questions. He answered them with images and in a vocabulary they knew, so that they could get the feeling that they understood. Only very seldom was he impatient either with the denseness that came of never having been trained in words or the nervousness and violence of the prisoner who is not quite facing what is likely to happen. Sometimes he would stop his letter to tell them a story of something he had seen or done himself, another piece of the great proof of which they themselves were part.

And all the time, under it, Paul was thinking about his churches overseas, trying to foresee the difficulties they might be getting into, considering personalities and possible jealousies. Just sometimes the fact that he could not himself get to them and put things right in a few hours of understanding and patient disentangling and ordering, and the further fact that he would never now be able to do so, that in a measurable time he would be dead and not able to write letters, even, to help his brothers, made his mind hesitate and swerve and occasionally put curious emphasis into the written sentences. But on the whole he went on steadily, managing seven or eight hours' dictation in the day, either to Luke or another.

For a time Gallio watched him. It was interesting to see another man's methods. He also had done much organizing, needing much patience, in the same quarter of the world for the most part.

Then he moved on. He was now getting used to his chains and managed to walk fairly easily about the yard. Again he saw a face he knew and recognized it almost at once as one of the dining-room slaves belonging to his friend Crispus. He went up to him. "Think you know me. Care to come and be my servant while I'm in prison here? I'll pay you, of course."

"Thank you, sir," said the slave and hesitated.

"What's your name? Ah yes, Manasses. One of these Christians, eh?"

"Yes, sir. I'm afraid you wouldn't find me much use, sir. They did something to my hand." He held out his right hand, which was swollen and streaked with red, and had some long, festering grazes on it. "I can't move the fingers properly, sir. I think something's broken."

"Better get it seen to, hadn't you?"

"One of the doctors put on some stuff, but it wasn't much good. It didn't seem worth bothering, sir. I'm sure to be sent to the arena."

"Not so bad as that, surely, Manasses? Isn't Crispus getting you out?"

"He did the first time, but they aren't letting our masters claim us now. I was the deacon of the church, you see. I expect they must have got some information. There was someone who was a police agent, sir."

Gallio grunted and looked at the hand again. "What did they do that for? Want you to give names?"

"Yes, sir. And agree to all kinds of lies about us. Things they'd made up."

"Stuck it, did you? Why?"

"I'm a Christian, sir. We've got to try and show we've got something new. It wouldn't be worth much if we couldn't bear a little pain for it. Jesus showed us the way. He took on our pain and our death. And dealt with them. By loving everyone, even the ones that hurt Him, sir. So I was bound to try and do that too."

Gallio regarded him thoughtfully. "I get the feeling," he said, "that this Christianity of yours means one thing to one man and another to another. Am I right?"

"I suppose we've all got a different idea of what's best, sir. At least we see different sides of it, according to how we've lived. And the Kingdom is a mirror of that; it has all the many kinds of good in it."

"Handy. Well, Manasses, sorry about the fingers. Anything else wrong?"

Manasses smiled a little. "They kick us, you know, sir. A good many of our people can't lie down on their backs, not comfortable. And we go on passing blood for days after."

"Got any kind of fund? You have? Good. Here's some money for it. Go on, take it, man. Better you have it than Nero!"

"But, sir, don't leave yourself short. You're not used to this sort of place."

"That's all right. I shall get some more. Hope that hand's going to heal, Manasses."

Sophrosyne went into the usual coma and died that night. All corpses were removed in the morning. Lalage burned various herbs that the doctors advised to prevent the disease spreading. The smoke made her cough, and by and by she went and sat out on the bench, beside Euphemia. She felt as though she were in the current of a very swift river, which was taking her past everything, the known landmarks of jobs and dancing practice and day-to-day living. In time she would come to the falls at the end and go over.

In the meanwhile she and Euphemia sat in the early morning sunshine and mended their dresses as best they could and talked quietly about clothes and scents and people they didn't know well, people that weren't part of all this. There was something very soothing about surface talk just now, and they both rather needed soothing after the things that had been done to them.

Once Rhodon passed them, and they gave one another the peace greeting. One thing about being here, you could say that openly now! Rhodon was worrying, of course, but not more than usual. He would have been more comfortable if he'd had anything to do with his hands. He'd never been so long without working at his trade except that time he was taken prisoner, before they got to Delos.

The two women sat there most of the morning. From time to time Euphemia was bothered in case, when the time came, she did not go with the Spirit. It would be so terrible to die like an animal at the end, not be a person and a witness! And not everyone died well.

But there was one thing that did please Euphemia. That was Megallis's coming to see her. Brought some food with her. Very nice that was! Megallis hadn't talked much, seemed almost as if talking choked her. In fact, she'd cried a bit. She couldn't stay long, of course, but she'd promised to come back.

After a bit, Paul came and sat with them. It had been one of his bad nights, when he had spent hours struggling with himself, praying aloud and walking up and down. The other prisoners had seen the light in his cell. Later on he would begin to work again, but now for a time he was exhausted, and gentle to the women.

They were laughing at him a little about the letter he had been dictating to young Timothy about his difficult and excitable church at Ephesus.

"These women are plaguing the life out of the boy," he said, "but he's the leader in that church and the only one they'd all accept, and I've got to send him a letter that'll stop them running after him all the time with their fusses and points of procedure and who's to do what!"

"Take care, Paul," said Lalage, "or you'll write once too often. I tell you how it'll be. You write a letter for some particular church that's got its own difficulties, but that letter's going to get kept just because it was you that wrote it, and some day someone's bound to find it and say you've left directions for how all churches are to be, always, everywhere!"

"Nonsense!" said Paul. "People aren't such fools as that. Besides, when the Kingdom comes and the churches are everywhere, there will be no need for directions. We shall be freed from the natural man in us that makes us act foolishly and selfishly."

"And the natural woman," said Lalage. "But suppose the Kingdom takes longer than we think coming—a hundred years, perhaps?"

"It cannot take so long. When there is such a blazing light, people cannot shut their eyes for a hundred years."

"Perhaps I've seen more of the blind people than you have, Paul. The ones who have built up around themselves a kind of dark tower of possessions. Shutting out the sky."

"Words, words!" said Paul. "All you women get tangled up in talking and what you think you see!"

"I've known *you* to get into a tangle of words sometimes, Paul!" Lalage said.

Two new people had come into the yard. Visitors. Respectable looking ones—Flavius Crispus and Beric.

Crispus retired with Gallio into his little prison room. It was really remarkably convenient and private. Gallio had found a decent, civil young Christian, who had been a slave in a good house, to be his servant. The room had been scrubbed and sprayed with his usual bath scent. A shelf had been put up for his book-rolls. Really, the only inconvenience was the set of irons that he was wearing, and, after all, a Stoic should be able to disregard such things.

For some time the two old gentlemen discussed methods of getting rid of their emperor, in the pleasant certainty that nobody was overhearing them. According to Balbus, the soothsayer in the Suburra who always charged such fabulous prices had given Nero another four years. But Piso would shorten that.

Crispus had told Beric to bring a jar of his special potted shrimps, a few of Eunice's best rolls, and some fresh cream cheese for Gallio.

Beric had also brought over some other food, a couple of his own tunics, and also three women's dresses. If the prisoners had a change of clothes they had at least a possibility of getting what they had on washed. That could be done with a little bribery.

When he went to the bakery to get the rolls, Eunice had asked him if he would take the dresses to Euphemia, Lalage, and Sophrosyne. "There's two of my own," she said, folding them small. "They're about the last and a bit mended. And one I bought cheap."

Beric gave her some money at once. It was always so difficult to remember that he was part of this world in which people had only one or two of the things he was used to having in dozens, as part of an ordinary, decent life. He had put all the stuff into one basket with the things for Gallio on the top.

Crispus raised his eyebrows slightly but said nothing. He had told Beric that Lamprion was to carry the basket across to the prison for them, but Beric said Lamprion had got a splinter in his foot—could they take Sannio? Whoever carried the basket would be left outside to gossip with the prison guards, so it might as well be someone more or less on their side. Sannio knew and would almost certainly say nothing, but if Lamprion knew—and you couldn't be sure that he didn't—he might say a lot.

The things for Gallio having been taken out, Beric went along with his basket to see if he could find Manasses. The prisoners could smell the food in the basket and several of them came up, begging for it. For a moment Beric seemed to see nothing but broken teeth, scars, and squints, slave faces and hands, the sickening smell they were apparently unaware of themselves. They frightened him, and he hastily handed out some bread and sausages, hoping they'd go away, but they didn't.

Then, very deliberately, he thought, *These are my brothers and sisters. If they are like this, then it is the thing—evil and the rule—that has made them so.* He tried to put all the kindness he knew into his voice, speaking to them in his rather pedantic Greek, but not to give himself away. Not yet.

Then he saw Manasses and called him. He wished they could have spoken to one another without all the other prisoners crowding around. There might conceivably be police spies among them, and any of them might be babblers. "How's the hand?" he asked. "No better?"

"It doesn't matter," said Manasses. "I shan't be pouring any more wine."

"Manasses—are you sure?"

"The games start tomorrow, you know. They go on for a fortnight. The prison's going to be empty at the end."

"I *must* stop it."

"You can't, Beric. Nobody can. It's out of our hands. We've just become part of something happening. Because of a new leaven that's got into the old world but hasn't finished working on it yet. We're like in between past and future, Beric. We're making what's going to be, just the way Jesus made what was going to be." He spoke in a whisper. Neither of them wanted the others to realize that they were anything but master and servant. A kind master, surely; those existed, even in Rome. But nothing beyond.

"You sound almost as if you were happy," Beric said.

"I almost am, Beric. If only I knew what was going to happen afterward. But perhaps I shall know somehow, or perhaps it won't seem to matter then. I'll have got so mixed that I'm part of it for always, or else, once I'm free of my body, I'll be outside that sort of wondering. Even being in prison where you can't alter anything or hope anything for yourself is in a kind of way freeing." He hesitated. "Does that sound all silly, Beric?"

"No, Manasses. It's wise. It makes me think of all the wise men I ever read about. But when I read about Socrates in prison, I'd never been inside a prison myself, so I didn't know if it was true. Manasses, Phineas was arrested yesterday."

Manasses said nothing for a minute, then, "He's got those two little children. It must be wonderful to be a father. What will Sapphira do?"

"I shall have to try and see her. Look, here are some things for you and Rhodon. Eunice gave me some for the women."

"There's Lalage, over there in the corner. Thank you for the things, Beric. Now, you shouldn't talk to me any longer. There's a lot I'd like to say."

"I know, Manasses."

They couldn't even give one another the peace greeting; it might have been reported. Beric went over to the bench where Lalage was sitting, feeling a bit shy, followed again by a trail of prisoners. He remembered the last time he had seen Lalage, when she had turned him out, and the time before, in the hall of the house after the arrest.

Lalage apparently remembered that too, for she jumped up, saying, "My lover!" And then she begged the other prisoners to leave them a little.

This was quite successful, though rather embarrassing for Beric.

"That'll clear you," she whispered, "and I'll make up a story. Anyone who visits here may get his name taken."

Beric took out the dresses. "They're from Eunice for you and Euphemia and Sophrosyne."

Lalage fingered the dresses. "Sophrosyne won't need anything ever anymore. Yes, she's dead. She wasn't very strong, you see. But someone will wear the dress. I'll be glad of one myself. You'd better have a bath when you get home, Beric. This place is crawling."

"What did they do to you, Lalage?" he asked.

"Nothing much—this time. It wasn't very nice, all the same. Well, all we've got to do now is to keep faith for a few days and then we shall have done what we're here for."

"Unless something happens. If Tigellinus were to die . . ."

"It's silly to make up stories. God doesn't do little things like that, not to cut across a big thing like our all dying. Besides, the ordinary people wouldn't like being done out of their fun now, whatever the ones on top thought! We aren't hoping about our own little lives any longer, Beric. We've got a bigger hope."

"Isn't there anything I could do for you, Lalage?"

"Yes. You could kiss me. It'll help to clear you, and—I'd like it. Take care of my right shoulder, though. It's bruised."

He put his arms around her, taking care of the hurt shoulder —had they beaten her like the slaves were beaten, or what?—and kissed her as well as he could. Without her makeup he could see the lines around her eyes and mouth, but she had been very pretty once, and she was still good-looking.

She did not cower away, as Persis had, but kissed him back. Then she laughed a little. "That was nice," she said. "I'm not likely to be kissed again before—it all happens. And everything helps. Everything that's a sign of what we want to be toward one another. Oh, Beric, I would like to have been going to live, all the same."

He kept one arm around her. She blinked and wiped her eyes with the back of her hand. "I didn't hurt you, did I, Lalage?" he asked, worried.

"No, Beric. Only it was so nice to be kissed. Silly sort of a deacon I am! There, that's all right. Look, Beric, there's just a chance they mayn't get all of us. Depends on what names they've got and whether they're going to take all the slaves. If they've too much respect for property to do that, well, we win. Beat them on their own ground too! So they just mayn't pick on all the slaves. If that's so, Beric, do what you can. Phaon's received the Spirit. If you can look after him a bit—stop him being broken?"

"I'll do what I can, Lalage, I promise. But—supposing I'm in it myself?"

"Is there a chance, Beric?"

"Yes. Lalage, lean back on my arm. Lay your head down, dear. I may be with you yet."

"But because you're really thinking clear about it? Because of the Kingdom for all time? Not just because of a few people that happen to be living and dying in Rome now?"

"I don't know, Lalage. I can't separate it up." And he began stroking her cheek, pulling her around a little toward him, cupping his hand under her chin, then kissing her again.

The deputy governor, making his rounds, walked up to them. "This is a prison, not a brothel," he remarked coldly.

Lalage jumped to her feet, away from Beric. She knew the prison authorities; he didn't. She whispered to him sharply, "Don't interfere!"

Aelius Candidus looked her up and down, considering vital spots, finally gave her a hard flip under the nose, jerking her head back and bringing tears into her eyes.

Beric was on his feet beside her, but her fingers gestured to him urgently. Perhaps she was forgiving Aelius Candidus; perhaps he mustn't spoil it.

"Get back to your cell, you filthy little Christian whore," said the deputy governor. "Don't let me see you in the yard again today. You know what'll happen to you if I do. Now then, you—eh, it's my old friend, Mister Briton! What are *you* doing here? Trying to get it cheap, are you?—cheap and nasty!"

"Is this how you always treat your prisoners, Candidus?" said Beric, his eyes narrowing.

"I have very full powers," said Candidus, slowly and heavily, "Very full. You have no idea what I can do—yet. If any of my prisoners prove less than cooperative, I have my methods. They have not failed so far."

"A very dirty job!" said Beric.

"I represent the State," said Candidus, "and you had better remember that, Mister Briton. If it means anything to a creature like you, which I doubt. A little yelping savage picked out of the bucket like a half-drowned puppy—yes, we all know where you'd have been if Crispus hadn't pitied you, you little rat!"

"You represent the State, do you!" said Beric. "And the Roman hearth and home too, no doubt. I hear Flavia's been seeing to that. Not so Roman as it was—is it?"

297

"I'll get you for that!" said Candidus, his fists clenched. "And that little Christian tart of yours too. I'll make you both squeal, by the gods, I will!" He turned on his heel.

If he means that, thought Beric, *and he probably does, I shall have to do anything I'm going to do rather quickly. I wish I could get him too.*

He went back to Gallio's cell and sat down outside it, waiting for Crispus. It didn't seem possible now to avoid all the consequences of his actions, whatever they might be. Somehow he had got set toward death, unless he was more lucky than he could suppose anyone would be. Yet, sitting there, he still felt like a visitor from outside, not one of the doomed ones. Not yet. He hadn't got out of the habit of imagining himself to have a future as well as a past. He couldn't take things quite seriously. He liked having got in one on Candidus—after that supper party. *It's nothing new, anyway,* he thought, *if he and I hate one another!*

Inside the women's cell, in the half-dark and stink, Lalage was saying to Euphemia, "I will forgive him. I *will!*"

"The dirty beast!" said Euphemia.

"He thinks we're wicked," said Lalage, twisting her hands with the difficulty of getting it out of herself, of standing apart from her own anger and injury and seeing her enemy in another light. "He thinks we're a kind of horrible thing against Rome, and I suppose Rome is a kind of god for him. Because he hasn't seen anything better. When he hurts us, he thinks he's being useful and good. I've got to start forgiving him. Jesus, show me, show me!"

She stood quiet, with her eyes shut, and Euphemia prayed too. Her nose was still bleeding a little. The dark drops crawled down her chin, over her lips. She went on, "He doesn't think of us as separate people. That's making it so hard thinking of him as a person. He's sinned against us. But he didn't know, he didn't know . . ." She tore a piece off the edge of her dress and held it pushed up against her nose. "If only Beric didn't get angry."

"Was Beric really the son of one of those kings?" Euphemia asked.

Lalage nodded.

"There was another girl in my old patron's house—she always said she was some kind of a princess. A bit of a devil, she was. None of us didn't pay any attention to her. Must be nice in a kind of way, being someone. Even if she wasn't really. Unless it kept one away from Him. And from one another."

"It isn't keeping Beric away."

"He's such a nice boy. Wish you could have seen more of him, dear. He was just your sort."

"When I'm thinking about him," Lalage said, "I can start on forgiving Aelius Candidus. Funny, isn't it?"

After a time, Euphemia said, "Lalage, I don't suppose—well, Claudia Acte isn't going to be able to help, is she?"

"I saw her when I was out," Lalage said. "We made a kind of agreement, she and I, that if they got me, as it looked like might happen, she wasn't to try and get me out. You see, Euphemia, I can take it. I know I can. And there's some that can't. That don't all get our blessings. Don't get strength. Well, those are the ones Claudia Acte ought to save, the weak ones, that wouldn't be any use as witnesses. Don't you think that's right, Euphemia?"

"Yes, I do. Lalage, dear, you don't think I'm one of the weak ones, do you? What I mean is, I wouldn't like being. Only, if I was to let you down . . ."

"You won't let us down. You'll be a witness. You know, Euphemia, you might even be able to show the way to your daughter. Like you couldn't just in living."

"Oh, Lalage, wouldn't that be lovely! Now you say that, I can't help thinking—well, it's not pride, is it? Not wrong pride? But I do think I'm one of the strong ones too."

18

Stamping It Out

The other prison, in which Manasses had been before his transfer, was a smaller and nastier place, mainly underground. There was a double set of barred caves cut into the rock of one of the Seven Hills, with a gutter running between them. The caves nearest the outside got more light, and those who were able to pay the warders were put into them. The ones at the back were darker and dirtier, and the rats scuffled and bit more openly. At present they were mostly full of Christians, with a small proportion of ordinary criminals among them.

Whatever happened at the Mamertine, it was quite certain that everyone in this prison was going to die within the next few days. They all knew exactly how, because one of the stage managers had been talking to the governor and had taken no trouble not to be overheard. This particular batch was to be used during the firework display and chariot racing in the Imperial Gardens. There would be high posts at intervals along the route of the chariot race and on each post, roped or nailed, one Christian or other criminal wearing a tunic soaked in pitch. These would be set alight at the beginning of the race, and the calm, star-filled September night would immediately burst into flames and hoofbeats and screams, speed and terror, galloping and punishing, and the ending of enemies. The stage manager wanted them in two batches, one for the first evening of the games, then the other later. Nothing of the kind had ever been done on such a scale before.

Continuous consideration of this had driven the prisoners into a state of tension that led some of them into screaming fits and others to complete dumbness and despair, a kind of lethargy. Some had tried to recant, but it was not usually much use at this stage, unless with more money behind it than most of them had.

But a few of them were in a state of extreme preparedness and clarity. This was their chance. They were in the Will. Sometimes Phineas attained to such a clarity, but sometimes he was shaken and breathless with apprehension. When he was calm, Sapphira tried to be calm too, tried to slow down her breathing to his, to wear the right face for it, whatever was in her mind. But when he was in terror she rose beyond it; she was his mother and protector and builder of security; she pointed the way to the Kingdom. Then, in time, he recovered, and his recoveries were her triumph.

The only person who had seen them was the girl Megallis. It was safer for her—she was not a Christian. In fact, she still thought some of it was nonsense, and, if her case had been taken up, it would have been found that her husband had actually denounced a Christian witch and poisoner. Not that she cared much at the moment whether she was safe or not. She was too angry and hurt—angry deep down—so that her husband was only just beginning to realize how serious it was. Eunice had asked her to go and see what was happening.

Eunice herself had gone over to the fish shop the evening of the day Phineas was arrested, but already Sapphira was gone to the prison with food and clothes. And after Eunice had waited an hour or two, talking to the widow who was still lodging with them and helping to get the babies to sleep, it had become only too plain that Sapphira must have been arrested too. Probably, thought Eunice, the prison guards had been having their fun with her first, most likely where her husband could see it all from behind the bars. That was just what they did. *Oh, Father, why do they hate us so?*

The next day, after Megallis had come back and told her how things were, Eunice made up her mind that she must go over and see Phineas's father. She was a bit shy about it, because the Jerusalem Christians were a bit different—kept themselves to themselves. Made you feel as if you didn't belong.

She knocked and asked for Gedaliah-bar-Jorim. The Jewish slave who opened the door looked at her sideways and didn't give her a straight answer. Then she was let into a big room, with a woman cooking on a stove at one end, who must be the mother, and two girls weaving carpets at the big looms. One of them she had seen once or twice at the fish shop. She was the young sister

Noumi, a quiet sort of girl, very strictly brought up. Wouldn't even speak to a Gentile! But Sapphira had talked about the family sometimes. Sapphira knew the rest of them didn't like her much.

The other girl must be Joanna, the sister-in-law, daughter of a weaving family too. They went on with their work in quick, steady, arm-and-body movements, but they kept watching her past the loom posts, made her feel strange.

Lovely carpets they were. Phineas used to say all the best houses in Rome had one of his father's carpets. The old man and the two younger brothers used to set up the webs, and then the girls would get to work on them. Neither of the slaves could weave—they were only kept for rough work.

Whatever the mother was cooking smelled good enough. Eunice wished they wouldn't keep her waiting too long; she had orders for almond cake and pastry shapes for the next day. One had to keep one's mind on the job, times like this.

Then an old man came in—that must be the father Gedaliah; behind him two young men carried bundles of fine, dyed carpet yarn.

A bit tentative, Eunice gave the peace greeting and got it back, rather distantly, from the old man. His sons only murmured it. These Gentiles who called themselves Christians could never know the true meaning of the Messiah—how was it possible for those who had neither read the Books nor kept the Law?—and it was only by an extraordinary act of mercy, of which there would scarcely be certainty, that they might in the end be saved and even given a place in the Kingdom.

But now the woman was speaking, telling them about their brother Phineas, the one who had left the trade he had been brought up to for his fish shop and the woman without a family whom he had lusted for and married.

Eunice finished speaking. She felt them all looking at her—oh, not like brothers and sisters, not really! She could have cried. "Can you do anything for them?" she asked.

"He is my son," the old man answered her. But what did he mean by that?

The mother had come over from her cooking pots. "We will

go," she said, "and bring our grandsons home." Then to her daughter: "Noumi, my cloak!"

Gedaliah-bar-Jorim thanked Eunice for bringing him the news, took her to the door, barred it after her, and turned back to the family. What should they do?

The two girls had come into the group now, though they did not speak.

Noumi, the youngest, was white with horror. She could only think of burning, of the pain in her hand when she had scalded it with boiling soup, spread all over. Why should being a Nazarene mean that? Could it mean that for any of *them?* Or was it only because Phineas had mixed with Gentiles? Or could he have sinned somehow? For a moment she held her long hands over her ears and eyes so as to shut out everything.

Phineas did not mean so much to Joanna. He had left the household before she had been married into it. She felt the excitement of horror, yet it was all part of the same excitement she always felt when the men were talking in the evenings, when the voices rose and swung and the texts hammered out of her father-in-law's mouth.

The time was coming, was bound by all the prophets to come, when the daughters of Israel would rejoice. There would be no more weaving of carpets for Gentile money to buy and Gentile feet to trample, but instead you would leap and sing through the streets of Rome. You would be like a harlot, but yet right, yet envied and not despised! And so it would be wherever the People were, in Ephesus and Corinth and the Greek cities, in Alexandria, and all through Judea, until the great final gathering in Jerusalem itself.

But this that was happening now—was this the Coming, or was it only an accident, something that God had not intended? Was Nero Caesar truly not born of woman but the anti-Christ who must rise up as the last form of the old world before his final defeat? Phineas must be saved from the anti-Christ, or their household would not be whole for the Coming. Joanna thought that, and her husband, young Jorim, said the same thing.

But Sapphira, who had only been a slave, who went willingly among the Gentiles and sat in the same room as Greek and Roman men, was she really part of their household? Even though she had borne sons to them, as Joanna had not done yet. Perhaps Sapphira had sinned and brought down anti-Christ onto herself and her husband. Perhaps she had sinned before her marriage. The wheels of God grind slowly, and you think you will escape them; but they have you in the end.

It would be difficult to get him out. It would mean money and courage. It was not certain if they could do it. But fortunately this was a small prison, and the worse conditions also meant more likelihood that money would talk. Each of the guards would have to be bribed separately, and there was more than a risk that Gedaliah and his sons might be arrested themselves—with the money.

Hearing this, the women glanced at one another but said nothing. It was for the men to decide. Amariah, the middle son, went out to borrow the money. It would take the household months of work to repay it. They would live that much worse. But Phineas must be with them again for the Coming, he and his sons.

Eunice shelled her almonds and measured out her honey and mixed and shaped the cakes and put them in to bake. It was no use thinking too much. Two or three customers came in; you've got to put a cheerful face on things, with customers. One of them kept on talking about the games.

In the evening she did some spinning. That kept your mind off things too. If only someone would have come in, as they always used to in old days. She went on spinning till she was tired out. The next morning Beric came for the rolls. She didn't like telling him about Sapphira; he'd got enough to think about with the ones in the Mamertine.

Then, later on, Hadassa, the widow who had been lodging at the fish shop, came over, carrying her little boy astride her hip. She put him down to play in the corner by the kneading trough and looked around, in the way one did, before saying a word to Eunice. Then she said, "Their granny came for the two children yesterday. Poor lambs, they did act up. Well, I went around an hour ago with some things of theirs I'd been washing over, and do you know what they've been and done?"

"Just you tell me, dear," Eunice said. She couldn't even bear the ordinary give and take of women's talk now.

"They've bought Phineas out—somehow."

"But not her?" Eunice crossed herself.

"Not her. And now they've had to lock him into the store-room because he keeps on crying and screaming, and I don't blame him. But it seems he didn't understand at first, and then when he did, he started cursing them. Even his own father."

"I suppose they didn't have the money to save her. Let alone, you can't always do it. They won't take money at the Mamertine. And I've no more—not that sort of amount. Not even if I sold everything."

"I wonder if they wanted to get her out all that much. She was always a stranger somehow. Oh, well, I suppose it was him or her, and you'd be bound to take your own kin. Noumi told me they'd be more than a year working it off. There was her dowry money too. Still, she's young. And anyway, it looks like we could expect the Coming any day now."

"This isn't the Coming, Hadassa. It's only a tyrant doing what they always have done."

"But this is different, surely, Eunice!"

"It's not different. Only worse. Because they're cleverer, and this is Rome. Oh, Hadassa dear, don't you go thinking he's Satan! I almost wish he was. Why, Manasses was in the palace all that time, and he ought to know. Tell me, aren't the Jerusalem church getting arrested as well as us?"

"Not so bad. You see, Eunice, it's not so easy to tell who's in the old way and who's in the new in our community. And the empress, she favors the old way. No one would lay hands on them; if they did there'd be trouble everywhere, wouldn't there? Not only in Rome, I mean. So it's only the ones like Phineas that went to a Gentile church that had their names taken. Of course, I didn't see it that way, Eunice, but Gedaliah-bar-Jorim said to me that if his son had kept to his own people—well, there, he was angry, and he didn't think it right to have his son cursing him."

Hadassa looked very unhappy. She didn't know who was right. Her people and her husband's had been Jews from Miletus —they'd only come to Rome after they were married. Somehow they'd never felt themselves so different from their Gentile neighbors, who'd always treated them fair. They'd paid their temple dues every year, but they'd never thought much about Jerusalem, and they hadn't lived in the Jewish Quarter in Rome but in one of the tenements on the other bank. And it had been burned. And if they'd lived in their own quarter, she wouldn't have been a widow now . . . She didn't know what to think about it all.

There was a knock, and Eunice went to the door.

It was Beric, with Phaon behind him, carrying his cloak like a well-trained boy. Once inside, Phaon nodded at Hadassa, who had pulled her black veil around her, and gave her the peace greeting. So did Beric.

It made Eunice feel proud, Beric being so nice. She remembered how he used to come around with that tutor of his when he was a boy—ever so fond of sweet things, he was, and, of course, she being Crispus's freedwoman, he took what he liked. And now—she could have kissed him!

"I wanted to ask if I should see Sapphira," he said.

"You'd better tell them, Hadassa," Eunice said and began slowly grinding down some spices, while Hadassa, stammering on it rather, told what had happened.

The whole room smelled of strong country herbs, as Eunice crumbled them fine, and then of imported cinnamon and nutmeg. She was careful of these; a little went a long way, and she baked her spice bread once a week. You'd got to think of it like that, even if there wasn't going to be a next week for you.

When Hadassa had finished speaking, she picked up the child again, saying she must go.

The other three said nothing for a little. Phaon sat on the edge of the table, frowning, pleating Beric's cloak between his fingers.

"But to burn her," said Beric at last. "I can't—I can't see why!"

"You're looking for reason on the other side," Phaon said. "It's not there."

"But—people don't do things without a reason!"

"Don't they?" said Phaon. "You wouldn't think masters always went by reason if you were a slave!"

It was odd, Beric thought in a passing way, how easily young Phaon was speaking to him as an equal. It wasn't with the kind of passionate brotherhood that Argas felt, yet it wasn't insolent—supposing he had any right to mind that . . . Only there was something a bit stinging about it.

"It must be the Will," Eunice said, "but I can't bear thinking of her, poor little woman, all alone—"

"She won't be alone," Phaon said. "She was one of us, and she's got that still, whatever happens; it's part of her now. Bound to come back suddenly and give her strength. Bound to."

"But if it's the Will for Sapphira to die," said Beric, "what about Phineas? Did his father go against the Will when he bought him out? He wasn't trusting in the Will anyway."

"And I went to them, wanting them to do something," Eunice said. "But only—oh, only in the direction of the Will, if you see what I mean. We know what direction that is, Beric. We're pointed in it; at least we hope we are. It's what we're trying to learn all the time we're being Christians—thinking about being, I mean—it's the Way of Life. So long as we act along that way, you see, we're part of the Will."

"Everything can't be the Father's Will," Phaon said, "or we wouldn't need to pray for it to be done. We do pray, because mostly things go against it. See, Beric? Not things really; people. Only it looks like things when you're a slave. Oh, I've thought about this a lot."

"Lately?"

"Ever since Argas got that beating for me. You've got to have some kind of a knock before you start thinking properly. That was mine. I've kept on going over what our Words really meant. And when we ask for the Will to be done—that doesn't mean just asking, it means living, but you know that, Beric—well, we ask for strength to make things happen in the way that'll bring the Kingdom. We ask to be able, by what we do ourselves, to change people around so that they want the Kingdom too. And one way we're going to do that is by dying for it."

"But about Phineas," said Beric, groping back, for all this seemed somehow related to what was in his mind, "was it in the direction of the Will and the Kingdom for his father to rescue him?"

"He didn't seem to think so," Eunice said, "not by what Hadassa was saying. As I see it, Sapphira was part of the Kingdom for him. They'd had experience of it together. I know, because I've watched them at the meetings. So if she dies, he's lost. Anyway for a time."

Phaon said, "If two people love each other beyond the love of neighbors, well, that's dangerous in a way. They think of one another the same way most people think of themselves, cutting out the rest of the world. So for them the Kingdom is bounded by a single human life, and when that's over the Kingdom's over. That's why Jesus warned us about it, saying we mustn't love anyone better than we loved God. And you bet He knew."

"It's difficult," said Beric. "You can't help liking some people more than others."

"You can like them all right, but you oughtn't to overmuch love them. Not deep as God. Not beyond what's due to a man or a woman. You mustn't want to give your life more for one than for another. That's what's the matter with Argas; he's too set on you."

"You brat!" said Beric. "No. Sorry, Phaon. You've got a cold mind, haven't you? Anyway, Argas hates me too, sometimes. I know that much."

"Yes, when he feels you're his master. But I don't care if you are or aren't. It's all part of the same thing. Aren't I right, Mother?"

"I expect you are, son, but you're young. And I'm old, so I see it too. And I keep on praying not to love you too much—not to keep you from whatever it might be."

Phaon slid down from the table, went over to his mother, and kissed her. "It was all right you trying to save me from things when I was a child and didn't really know what it was being a Christian. But now I'm on my own feet. Though it was you helped to put me there. I'll always remember that, Mother. See?"

Then he said to Beric, "So what's happened about Phineas and Sapphira is against the Will, to my way of thinking. But most of all for him. When she dies, she's got a chance of being a witness—showing people. If she dies as a Christian."

"If only she *can* die that way, not just thinking about her husband and her babies!" said Eunice. "You don't know how easy it is to slip off into that, son."

"If she's really a Christian—"

"But to be burned alive!" said Beric. "When you begin to think what that's going to be like—could any of us bear it?"

"Not by ourselves. But just because we aren't alone any longer, we can bear it. We're all with one another in this pain and this death, and Jesus is with us all, showing us how."

"But if none of that were to happen, it would be still more part of the Will."

"If the Kingdom could come without our dying for it, yes. But it doesn't just happen on its own, like magic or a flower growing. It's made out of people's lives—and deaths!"

"I don't see why it's got to be deaths as well as lives."

"Because the other side isn't reasonable. So they can't be touched by a reasonable thing like living. We haven't much power in our lives, we slaves and poor folk. We only have it when we dare to risk everything. When we go beyond reason."

"Yes. We've got to risk everything. I, too." Beric was silent for a moment, walking up and down the bakery, smelling spices and flour. "And a young mother's got to be burned alive tomorrow night—"

"It's not only her," Eunice said, "and we can't save them all. Not if we had all the money in the emperor's treasury. Only if we could stop ordinary people from wanting to burn us alive." Then she added, "I suppose you'll be at the games tomorrow with Flavius Crispus?"

"Yes," said Beric, "but there'll be none of this the first day. Only the processions and the races. No killing till the evening. And then—"

"Flavius Crispus doesn't have to go to that, does he?"

"No. It's not official. Just a new stunt. Nero getting the people of Rome on his side! Nobody decent will go."

"Meaning none of the good Stoics?"

"Not one of them, Phaon."

"Not one of *them* burned alive! That's left to us. That's why it's we who'll win and not the good Stoics."

"Will you come to the next meeting, Beric?" Eunice asked.

He shook his head. "No."

"Won't you? It would help us if you would. All that's left of us. In four days, Beric."

"Four days!" said Beric and laughed abruptly and shortly. "That's a long time. I never knew before how long four days was. That may be after our days and times, Eunice. It may be nothing to do with us. I'm going back now, for there's something I've got to see to before that." He hesitated, then knelt in front of her on the floor of badly laid bricks. "You might give me a blessing, Eunice."

She, being a deacon now, gave him her blessing, and the two went out together, and she wondered what it was Beric needed to see to and whether it was in the way of the Will. Perhaps her blessing might help to make it so. At least she was sure of her own son.

That night Abgar came to see Eunice. He seemed to be very hungry, so she fed him. He talked a lot about Rhodon in a kind of gabbling Greek dialect that she found very hard to follow. He seemed to want to make some kind of sacrifice for Rhodon, a blood sacrifice, his own blood.

Eunice wasn't certain how much he really understood the Way of Life; you didn't get killed in the arena or burned alive as a blood sacrifice but as a witness. Could she make him see that? She wasn't sure. But she couldn't feel he was ready for baptism. He didn't seem to have the right idea about that either. He looked at it, somehow, as a kind of magic drowning that would make him part of a god. After he left, she prayed for him to be given understanding and for herself to see just how to give it to him.

You would have known it was the beginning of the games next day. Most of the shops had special displays, and everyone wore their best. It was still free seats for citizens, and citizens only, except by special privilege and request, and the citizens took care to let you know. Though, of course, that made some who weren't anything of the kind pretend to be! Naturally, rich men and women too brought their attendants in with them. But even so, there was no nonsense about slaves getting into the citizens' free seats. This was the one time of all when you felt it was something being a Roman citizen—even a slum-Roman.

Tertius Satellius would be there with his wife, Megallis. He would, in fact, be there every day of the games. And if the silly little witch wasn't in a good humor again after that, he'd like to know what would make her! Free dinners were provided on most days for citizens and their wives, and sometimes there was the chance of a lottery ticket.

You would hear the noise right across Rome as the procession wound along from the Capitol after the sacrifices had been made. There were trumpets and cymbals and the shouting and cheering that ran in waves along the crowds.

Eunice stayed indoors and began to cry. This was the beginning. And nothing had stopped it. God had done nothing. As if it didn't matter. As if people's lives were no more value than animals' lives. And you knew you were right, and you knew the Kingdom was on its way, and this was only the last struggle of the old powers against it.

But all the same, the triumphant, dreadful noise kept going on all the morning; and all the afternoon too, you could hear it bursting up in great sickening lumps of noise. It was the horse-racing today. But tomorrow you'd hear the shouting going on again, and you'd know what it was for—you'd know.

So Eunice's hands as she kneaded were shaky, and her spice bread didn't rise as light as it should have, and when she opened her door, thinking it was a customer, her smile wasn't quite what it should have been, either.

She didn't know who this thin, heavily veiled girl could be but asked her in. Perhaps she had come to give an order. Eunice could have done with a few special orders. There wasn't any silver and not much copper left under the loose brick now.

But the girl said nothing for a moment, only leaned against the wall, still holding the veil tight over her face with one hand. With the other she made the cross sign, though in a rather odd way.

Eunice answered it. The girl might be a spy, but it wasn't very likely, and what was one risk more or less now, anyway? "Who are you, sister?" she asked.

In a low voice, the girl answered, "I am Noumi, daughter of Gedaliah-bar-Jorim. You have seen me before—sister." And she loosed a few fingersful of the veil, showing her dark eyes and fine, narrow eyebrows. She went on: "My brother Phineas tells me that I

311

must go to Claudia Acte and that you will be able to show me where her house is."

"To see Claudia Acte—why?"

Noumi's whisper answered. "Sapphira."

"If you're thinking she can help," Eunice said, "well, I'm afraid you mustn't set too much on it. I know Acte's been doing all she can. Did Phineas think she could?"

Noumi said, "Our father locked him away, because he was saying things that should not have been said. He might even have run back to the prison after all we have done. It was I who took him in his food. He says that if Sapphira dies he will go away from us for always, and he will not hope anymore for the Coming, nor keep the Law, nor believe that Jesus was and will be the Messiah." She shivered. "So I had to come."

Eunice took out her own veil, ready to go, and saw to the oven fire. There was a batch of bread in, and she might get back in time. Well, if it was burned, it was burned. One's business didn't get much chance these days.

The girl was watching her. She couldn't be more than fourteen. And brought up with all that about being God's own people and the rest of the world lumped together as so much dirt, not counting somehow. She knew what the Jews said. And she felt, herself, a bit coarse and used beside this delicate young virgin, fawn-eyed and soft-voiced.

She thought of all the years of her slavery, and Phaon's father, a Greek slave in another household and not much catch, really, and it had all been in street corners, with half an ear open in case the overseer was after you. And when Phaon was born they nearly took him away and sold her as a wet nurse.

But she had found what made it all right, made her able to hold her head up, yes, and behave decent and bake as good fancy rolls as any in Rome, and not mind if she was just a stupid old freedwoman who would never be young or pretty again. She had got hold of something so much bigger than all that, which yet took account of her as a person. As an equal.

So she and the young girl went over towards the Palatine and across, taking shortcuts and avoiding the big streets and squares. "Do you know this part of Rome, dear?" she asked.

But Noumi shook her head. "I have never been outside our quarter before." After a time she said again. "Once I burned my finger against the stove at home. And people do that to one another!"

"Didn't you ever think before of the danger you were in— being one of us?" Eunice asked.

"No," said the girl. "Why should it have been dangerous? I cannot understand why this is happening. We have always tried to be good. We have kept the Law, even in our hearts, and we have believed that Jesus would come and set up His Kingdom. You believe that?" she asked suddenly.

"We keep the Way of LIfe, and we believe that the Kingdom which Jesus showed us will come," Eunice answered.

The high brick walls of the palace grounds were on their left now. Here and there heavy creepers hung over them, dark and dusty, leaved or with late blossom. The little houses at the farther side of the narrow street were mostly in the gift of the Julio-Claudian family. Here lived an old nurse, there an old cupbearer or valet. And here was the home of yet another faithful servant, Claudia Acte. As with the rest, the outer wall was clean and newly whitewashed but without windows.

Eunice knocked.

When the doorkeeper opened, she spoke timidly. He might be one of them, but she could not count on it. At least he seemed more friendly than in most houses. They were told they must wait; Lady Claudia Acte was not at home just now. But at any rate, they had not been turned away.

The porter took them through into a tiny, pretty courtyard with blue-painted wooden pillars and a round marble basin with fish in it. They were put to wait in a small room off it with low benches around the walls and cushions.

Eunice leaned back in a hunch; she was tired. But Noumi sat up very straight and still, looking out through the door space into the courtyard, and the sunlight gradually tilted out of it, pulling a line of shadow after it up the pillars as the first day of the games drew on towards evening and that much-advertised fireworks display.

After a time, Noumi asked, "What is she like?"

"Who? Claudia Acte? She's so nice and kind. But, of course, she's had a different kind of life from us—from me, I mean." For Noumi, the daughter of Gedaliah, had never been whipped or sold or half-starved or any such commonplace things.

But the girl looked startled. "And very different from my life! I could never have imagined—oh, never!—that I would have to go and beg from this palace woman. Yet I will do it."

Now and then someone passed through the courtyard. It might have been one of the Christians that Acte had taken in after the fire. They'd be safe here. Or wouldn't they be?

Eunice thought of her bread. It would be hopelessly spoiled. Well, that couldn't be helped. But it wouldn't be so nice if all her money ran out, not when she was a deacon and there was so much to see to. She had given most of the money Beric had handed over to what remained of another church, to help their people in prison.

But at last there was the sound of the outer door, and a voice that Eunice remembered from meetings where she had been as a delegate. "Here she is!" Eunice said and picked herself up, ready to go out into the courtyard.

But Noumi had sprung out of the room and in front of the woman who had just come in and had fallen at her feet.

Eunice watched. Better if the girl could do it by herself. Noumi, on her knees, told Acte what had happened and begged for her help.

Acte listened very patiently, her forehead wrinkled with dismay at one thing more that she had got to try and do. She looked exhausted, and, indeed, she had slept little for the last week. She had done what she could: here and there a prisoner freed; here and there a person or family saved, for the moment, from arrest. But it was very precarious. She did not know how long she herself would be left unmolested. Tigellinus and the police must certainly know about her.

And she had not been able to see Nero for some weeks. She had tried to, but nothing seemed to come of it. Perhaps the channels that she had thought friendly and trustworthy had been blocked. Once or twice she had spoken to Asterope, and the singing girl had faithfully and tactfully given her message but told her afterwards that the emperor had pretended not to hear or had passed it over with a casual word. Nero was not looking Acte's way just now. Asterope had herself got an order for the pardon of a couple of criminals and had handed it on to Acte. She was no Christian, but Acte had been good to her mother, Alexandra, and Greeks should stick together when possible.

Eunice thought Acte's dress was just lovely. It was made of a very fine, gray-green wool and showed her figure where the veil had slipped as Noumi's hands pulled imploringly at its edge. *Most likely,* thought Eunice, *she wears one of those fine muslin shifts under it, the ones made of imported stuff.* Her sandals were white leather with gilt buckles and little decorations over the middle toe. She had long earrings that set off her neck and shoulders so well. It would be nice to know who she got them from. But if one had thought about her the way Noumi thought—from above as it were—well, then, it must feel very strange indeed to be kneeling at her feet. It must hurt. Oh, it must be a rotten feeling!

Acte said, "You see, dear, the stage managers ask for a certain number. If we manage to get your brother's wife away, someone else will be taken from that prison or another."

"Oh, no!"

"I'm afraid it's certain."

"Then—oh, what am I going to say to my brother, Lady Acte?"

Acte said nothing for a minute, then, "I think perhaps I see one very small chance, and it means waiting till the last moment."

"Oh, tell me!"

"If I can get one of the under-managers to put her somewhere at the end where the crowds haven't come yet, and rope her instead of nailing her—no, child, you must listen!—and then at the last minute before the torch, take her down and put a bundle of straw there, so that by the time the people are along they won't know if it was a person at all . . . My dear, it's not much of a chance, and it means that you and I will both have to see things which we'd give anything not to see. You'll never be able to forget them, Noumi, dear. They'll . . . no. Shall we try it, Noumi?"

"Yes, please," said Noumi and kissed Acte's hands and stood up.

They had to wait a little. It was no use doing anything yet. Now the prisoners would be being pulled and kicked out of their cells, given to the stage managers, forced into the pitch-soaked, stiff tunics. In the little house on the edge of the palace grounds, the three women ate together, but none of them could swallow much. Eunice was coming too; it was only sense. They might have to carry Sapphira. If they got her at all. Neither Acte nor Eunice was really very hopeful, but Noumi hardly realized that.

At last Acte said it was time. Dusk was beginning. It would be a fine night; not even a chance of rain. They walked along the street a little way, and then Acte let them through the palace wall by a narrow door of which she had the key.

When they came out about an hour later, it was really night. Behind them the fireworks were flaring and shooting up, and there were other blazes, yellow, throbbing horrors on the lovely darkness. And there was continuous screaming, getting fainter as they left it but, even after the house door was shut, only too audible to those who could not help listening.

Acte called rather sharply for wine, but when the slave brought it and knelt in front of her, she spoke to him with a kind of abashed, shaken kindness, laying her hand on his shoulder and calling him brother.

He was a big, tawny-eyed North Greek, with a silver-gilt collar on his neck, a present from Nero. He smiled at his mistress, but he, too, knew what was happening. He had not been long enough in Rome to have any friends among the people who were being killed. He only wished it wasn't happening, because it made her so bothered and unhappy.

He offered the wine to Eunice, who felt rather embarrassed, but took two cups for herself and Sapphira, who lay along the couch, her eyelids half shut, the whites showing a little, dropping her rope-bruised arms and wrists over the cushions.

Noumi refused the wine, even though Acte urged her to take it. It was as the Greek woman had said; she was remembering all too well everything she had seen and heard in that devilish garden.

Acte drank off her wine, and the watching slave refilled the cup at once before she could speak. As he knelt by her with the jug she rubbed her hand, gently, in his hair and over the back of his neck. He had, of course, been made safe as a lady's slave before he was given to her. The curtain over the doorway swung a little, and the thin screaming was still going on. He had screamed then too.

As soon as possible the woman must get the cutting, pitch-soaked tunic off Sapphira. Abruptly Acte jumped up and left them, to find a dress of her own to put on her.

The screaming had dropped out of the night. The blazes that were not torchlight or firework flares had died down. Eunice, Sapphira, and Noumi left the house and walked back across Rome.

Acte turned away into that pretty supper room with the light-colored hangings and cushions, the smiling marble child in the niche, and the elegant, tall wine jug of flecked glass. The pitch-soaked tunic still lay stiffly on the floor. Acte picked up the jug and drank off one cup of wine after another. At last the pictures in her head began to swim and blur.

In a little, the tawny-eyed slave came in and saw his mistress lying asleep on the couch, her mouth desolately half-open, her hand dropping over the edge. He put her arm back on the couch and covered her with a light rug. Then he picked up the pitch-soaked tunic and took it away to burn—better not to have that kind of evidence in the house.

The others walked slowly. Sapphira was still very weak. She clung to Noumi, and the girl guided her along with an arm around her waist. It was only when they were over the bridge and into the Jewish Quarter again that Sapphira spoke. She looked up and around her and said, "My babies?"

"They are well," said Noumi, "at our house. You will see them soon."

"Am I going to your house?" Sapphira asked dazedly. "To your father's house?"

"You are going there, Sapphira," Noumi said.

"But they don't want me," Sapphira said. "They never liked me. They said I should not have married him. They said I had sinned."

"I want you, sister," Noumi said, "even if you had sinned all the sins in all the books. We have all sinned."

They came to the house. It was her father who answered the knock at the door and took them both in his arms. And the babies were safe and asleep in soft blankets, and the younger brothers ran to unlock the storeroom and tell Phineas.

Young Noumi said to Joanna, "Will you bring me a lamp, please? I want to go on with my carpet. We must hurry with our weaving and pay the debt." And she sat down behind her loom, hoping it would shelter her again.

Eunice had left them at the corner of their street and gone back to the bakery. She could smell at once that the bread was burned. The bread. Bread doesn't scream. Nor is bread ever terribly, horribly brave, silent or calling the Name, as the pitch flames and crackles.

She prayed for a time, then got into bed and was nearly asleep when again there was a sharp knock, breaking through the beginnings of her nightmares. She jumped out of bed and ran to open, her hair tousled and a blanket snatched around her.

Of all people, it was Mikkos. What did he want? He pushed past her and put his lantern down on the table. "See here, Mother," he said and then hesitated.

He was a decent sort of boy. Phaon liked him. *Had something happened to Phaon?* "What is it?" she asked urgently.

Mikkos said, "The Briton's been arrested. Thought you'd want to know, somehow."

"He can't have been," Eunice said, her hand at her throat. "Not Beric! Whatever for?"

"Tried to kill the prefect of the Praetorians. Near pulled it off, so I hear. And he won't be the only arrest. They'll get some of us. Blast him."

"What for? To give evidence against him?"

"Yes. All that. Slaves' evidence—torture, see? And I was on his working party! Oh, well. See here, Mother, they'll get the others who were in prison before. Your child and all. Put them through it hard this time, they will. Make them say he was a Christian. *Is he?*"

"No," said Eunice, "no. No. Oh, I can't seem to believe it! Christians don't kill."

"I've heard they was all a pack of murderers. Isn't that so? You know all about it, Eunice. Don't you know?"

"Mikkos," she said, "if you think that, do you still think all Christians are murderers?"

"Well, I'm not squealing anyway," said Mikkos, "not on you nor yet on the Briton."

"Is anyone at the house arrested yet?"

"No. Not had time. I'd best get back. You come around in the morning and ask to see the old man. Then you'll know. But when you come around—oh, don't have anything silly on you! In case the guards are there. 'Night, Mother."

Mikkos took his lantern and went out again, and Eunice on her knees began to wrestle with her own fear and her own temptation.

Phaon, Phaon, Phaon.

19

Difficulties of a United Front

Flavius Crispus was having a small and quite intimate supper party with his cousin Flavius Scaevinus and his old friend Aelius Balbus. They had all been to the games, but none of them, naturally, would go to the evening display. There was to be no elaborate dancing, but Phaon would sing two or three serious songs during the roast.

Crispus had asked Beric to have his supper in his own room or out with a friend. As things stood now, he would not have minded in the least if Beric had been present, but it might have embarrassed the others.

Beric said yes, he would have a tray in his room and read. It was funny, but he didn't want now to see any of his old friends, not even to say good-bye. The self they had been friends with was not at the moment inhabiting his body. Was unlikely ever to do so again.

He looked at the bookshelves, fingering the tops of a few rolls. There were books that had interested him and that he had not finished reading. But he could no longer want to finish them. Not even that book by the Epicurean author Catius, which he had borrowed from his tutor, badly written on cheap parchment, full of jibes and jabs at an imaginary Asiatic state, which was obviously Rome. If he had luck, very great luck, he might yet finish Catius and talk it over with Nausiphanes and do a number of other things that he could not now clearly envisage since they were beyond some boundary in his mind. Beyond some tomorrow, which might have nothing at all to do with one Beric, son of King Caradoc of East Britain.

His brother Clinog had said he was going to try to get down to Rome for the games. He'd like to see old Clinog again, but that, too, was past the barrier.

He opened his chest and took out a dagger, which he had sharpened himself to a beautiful point. It was about three inches longer than the little knife that had got Sotion out of the way so satisfactorily.

Argas came in with his supper tray and looked at the dagger. "Don't," he said.

"I saw Tigellinus today," Beric said. "He'll be there tonight. Enjoying it. Laughing at it. Decent, innocent men and women, and he—"

"This will pass," Argas said, "and the Kingdom will go on."

"But not for them."

"They will be part of it forever. Oh, Beric, I'm not saying this without meaning it! It may be me any day."

"I know. And I want to stop it being you. Funny, I wouldn't have cared two months ago if you'd been killed. No more than if you'd been—oh, one of the dining-room vases smashed!"

"I wouldn't have minded about you either. Yes, I would, though. But I'd have thought it served you right for being part of the thing." He put the tray down on the end of the chest and spread the napkin and poured the wine, carefully, as he had been taught.

"They'll be having supper at the palace," Beric said, "and looking forward to all this."

"Tigellinus," said Argas, "will be looking forward to something else. I saw Persis today, and she told me her master would be at—the Gardens—and Tigellinus would be slipping back to have his spot of fun. He'd get more kick out of it after seeing women—!"

He covered his face with his hands. He didn't want Beric to see at this moment he couldn't do any forgiving. Sapphira there, and men and women from other churches, hands he'd held in his. But pain and death were only spots passing in time. The Kingdom would be forever. So that there would be an end of people hurting one another.

"Interesting," said Beric. He took up a piece of bread from the tray, broke it, and gave half to Argas. "Remember when we did this before? During the fire?"

321

Argas took it. "Beric," he said, "I'd mind very much if you got killed now."

"Perhaps none of us will get killed, after all," Beric said.

Niger was waiting in the kitchen yard with his master's litter. They'd had some food brought out to them and were munching it.

The Briton came out of the house. He nodded at Niger, and Niger smiled a very little. Then the Briton went out of the yard by the back door into the street behind. The new Cappadocian looked at him wonderingly. He would ask Niger about him in the night. He slept next to Niger and sometimes, when he was lucky, Niger used to tell him stories about Someone who had done magic and extraordinary things—but things that also fitted into life as he knew it. Into work and pain.

Niger wouldn't tell him the name of the Person, but it wasn't a king or a chief nor yet really a magician, but apparently a woodworker. The Cappadocian thought about this Person and these stories whenever there was a gap, and Niger had promised, some night, to tell him the name.

When supper was cleared away, Crispus sent the slaves out of the room. The wine and nuts and sweets were handy on the little table between him and his guests.

They were discussing their emperor, whom they had all seen that day at the games, first in the chariot at the head of the procession, then in the imperial box, watching the races. Was there any alternative to what they were intending to do? And, again, how much support could they count on from the masses? Had these shows of his bought over the people onto his side?

"There's a new song that's going around," said Balbus, "all about this marvelous emperor of ours and all he's done for us! Seems to be catching on. Got a good tune—they'll be singing it at us from the cheap seats every blessed day of these games. For what that means."

"Young Lucan has written a very fine poem about freedom," Scaevinus said. "Very fine indeed. Dignified. But, of course, it doesn't go to a tune."

"I suppose he can be trusted?" Balbus said. "Never quite know about poets. Nervy devils, some of them."

"Seneca says we can trust him absolutely. And his own uncle ought to know."

"What I ask myself," Scaevinus said, "is what safeguards we can devise to stop this happening again. Supposing we put one of ourselves at the head of things. After all, the Divine Julius made all kinds of promises and apparently intended to keep them. But perhaps Brutus saw more clearly than the man he assassinated."

"It should be possible to avoid a tyranny," Crispus said, "if there is an aristocracy which choose to serve the State and to understand what it is doing. They can share both powers and responsibilities, evenly. But with a democracy it's not possible. Most of the common people are too lazy to take responsibility, so they'll shove it all onto a leader if they can."

"What do you call us—the State and people of Rome—aristocracy or democracy or what?"

"We're something that would have made old Aristotle shut his eyes and think again! Fact is, Crispus, we've spent our lives serving the kind of State no decent man ought to serve. And we're old enough now to see what we've done."

"It's very hard," said Crispus. "The wise man should no doubt keep aloof as far as possible, as Chrysippus himself advised, but that has never been found possible in Rome, at least, in our class. Philosophy, although such a necessary part of one's life, does not always provide a positive guide for action, even when it shows us the causes of things. And I am sadly afraid, my dear Balbus, that none of us has lived up to our ideals."

"At least we've been able to stand things without allowing them to affect our souls," Balbus said sharply.

Was he thinking about Flavia, Crispus worried to himself, or about more general disasters and disturbances?

"And we have a way out if tyranny becomes intolerable," Crispus went on, the wine slightly affecting him towards pomposity. "If it reaches a point where it is bound to affect the soul. We must all of us have in mind the noble example of the younger Cato. I am proud to be sure that any of us three would open a vein sooner than submit to be forced into an unworthy action."

"Yes, I take it we'd slip out by the back door," Scaevinus said. "But that's all it is, in spite of the philosophers. And we have singularly little idea of what's on the other side . . . if that matters. Now, I'll tell you how it is, Crispus. Let's take the thing historically. Go back to the Republic."

"I wish we could," said Crispus, sighing.

Balbus added, "Those were the days. A man was a man then. There wasn't any of this modern corruption." He jammed a walnut between his teeth and cracked it viciously.

"No," said Scaevinus, half to himself, slowly, "go back three generations further. To the Punic Wars. Why did we have to destroy Carthage?"

"Carthage was our enemy," Balbus said. "It had to be done."

"You say that, Balbus—"

"Most certainly I do. And what, my dear Scaevinus, has Carthage three centuries ago to do with Rome now?"

"A great deal, I think," Scaevinus answered. "You know, Balbus, I've been thinking about this. Started off, I suppose, the year I had my province." He laughed to himself a little, annoying Balbus, but the memories were by no means unpleasant. "I amused myself finding out what was going on in the procurator's office. A governor has to have his relaxations, and there was one of the secretaries, quite the Praxiteles type, those rather heavy eyes . . . yes, yes, he had most of the accounts through his hands. And I began to realize how much my side of things, administration and justice, were being influenced, without my knowing it, by their side—the imperial taxes.

"I was shocked at the time to discover how powerful money was and how much it altered people's lives. I found out a little too much about the imperial accounts, and, as you know, I was recalled. That score won't be wiped out till we do our cleanup of the Treasury—afterward.

"But it made me think. Since then I've had to look up old decisions of the Senate from time to time in the course of my duties. And I know that the destruction of Carthage was necessary to our forefathers for reasons of money rather than of honor. There was an empire shaping, and it was going to be ours. We weren't going to allow anyone else to go about in it, making money without our leave—or our taxing it."

"We had to step in because the rest of the world was decadent," Balbus said. "All those Greeks and Easterns squabbling! That was what made the Empire."

"That was what we said," Scaevinus answered. "Oh, yes, we went in to keep order or because some king who'd been turned out asked us to send a legion along! Or to clear the high seas of pirates—but they had to be *our* seas. With no Carthaginian ports opening out of them. It was the Punic Wars that ended the genuine good old days, Balbus, the days of man-to-man, small-scale dealings, when every family had its own gods at its own hearth and the men came back from the wars in time for worship and the autumn plowing."

"Empire was laid upon Rome," said Balbus sullenly, "and the greatness that takes a man far from his own gods and his own cornfields."

"And that greatness had to go on growing, Balbus, and men had to fight farther and farther from Rome. We couldn't go on talking about defending our homes then, and above all we couldn't go on sharing up the land we'd conquered. We couldn't divide up the shopping streets of Smyrna or Antioch among respectable Roman veterans who wanted a yoke of oxen and three acres! But since cause produces effect, the grandsons of these veterans who were done out of their land went on deputations to Tiberius Gracchus."

"I always found the family estate in Sicily most troublesome," Crispus suddenly remarked, following up his own line of thought. "Only went there once myself. I sold it, of course. Monstrous great herds of cattle. I ask you, what is an educated man to do with ten thousand bullocks?"

"There would have been little farms there once," Scaevinus said, "and families of Sicilians cultivating the land. In the good old days Balbus likes. Before *we* came on the scene. Not that they could have gone on in the modern world probably."

"But when we stopped dividing the land into veterans' small holdings, we took—those of us who were clever at catching a new idea—to these large-scale farms and ranches worked by gangs of prisoners, and worked so that the heart was out of the soil in a generation or two. But the profit had been made by that time.

"And we'd got our provinces then, and we took to taxing them because it's more satisfactory to get the money out of someone else and that at a distance. And we took to writing out figures on bits of parchment—or getting little Greeks to do it for us. And that went on piling up for a couple of hundred years. The great days of the Republic. Yes, that's what was behind the great days, Balbus."

"Well, what of it?" Balbus said. "Even if what you say is true, it has nothing to do with us now. Or with what we intend."

"Hasn't it?" Scaevinus asked. "We were thinking about ways of government, and I have an idea that this money business has something to do with it."

"Naturally, the Empire has to be made to pay," Balbus said. "But we were discussing the individuals who were to run it under a new order of things. Ourselves, in fact. You don't accuse me of taking bribes, Scaevinus—or do you?"

Scaevinus shook his head, and Crispus interposed, worried. "My dear Balbus, nobody supposes for a moment that considerations of money could possibly affect the classes of person whom we have in mind as governing under a new regime!"

"I sometimes wonder, Crispus!" his cousin said, smiling at him. "Well, then, we pass on from Carthage to the great years of the Republic. The Empire going strong and men making money, and making it hard, and making it out of one another and against one another. Men beginning to hate one another because of money. Sooner or later bound to fight one another. For the civil wars were gang fights between one set of money-makers and another.

"No, don't feel you've got to protest in the name of all your pious ancestors, Balbus. That's how things were. It was in the great years of the Republic that we got our first millionaires, making money out of organized trade and usury, not out of anything they took or made in the old ways—men using money not as something to exchange with but as pure power. Now, was that or wasn't it social corruption?"

"No doubt," said Balbus. "But most of these were the new men, the speculators. Our own forefathers had standards of decency and honor unconnected with money."

"Had they?" Scaevinus said. "None of us were exactly born in poverty! The money was there, Balbus, however it managed to occur to those good forefathers of ours. But now let's take it a stage farther. Some of this suddenly increased amount of money had been used on these large-scale slave factories and slave farms. And at the same time had created an entire race of enemies inside civilization, hoping to wreck it if they ever got the chance. What with these enemies we import in chain gangs by the hundred, and the money enemies, each trying to serve his own interests and down his rivals, there was a pretty mess! Enough to pull the State apart, to crack it up completely. Gentlemen, that nearly happened. Several times. Between the end of the Punic Wars and the end of the Republic. In the great years."

"There might have been a better State built in its place," Crispus answered rather wistfully.

"Fairer? More equal? Simpler and kinder? All that? The Gracchi had something of the sort in mind—Tiberius, anyhow. Then came the revolts from the race of enemies. Spartacus, for instance. Why didn't Spartacus win when the whole trend of things was in his favor? Why didn't his revolt smash up the State completely when it was already cracking?

"How it looks to me, gentlemen, is that the State suddenly changed its nature, not in the way that Tiberius Gracchus would have changed it, when he wanted all the citizens to go back to small holdings and large families, but into a new form of the old money-making thing. Quite possibly what was the only way to save it. It was organized so that the money-makers shouldn't quarrel with one another and shouldn't use their money power to make civil war with. Now, the only way to do that was to subordinate them to the State. And that's where we are now. What do you think, gentlemen?"

"But must the State that's to keep order have a human head —a tyrant?" asked Balbus.

"I think so, men being what they are. We cannot escape from causality. And then the head gets drunk on power—thinks the power belongs to him, not to the State. And then— "

"Yes. That's where we are now. Pity you can't have a performing animal instead of Agrippina's son. A genuine wolf dressed in the purple!" Balbus laughed abruptly. "But you're making out, Scaevinus, that the only alternative to something of the kind is chaos—splitting the State."

"Exactly. So we have to keep the same kind of thing—modified. Not attempt any Utopias. I take it we've all been brought up on the fairy-tales—Plato and Iamulus and so on? They're usually included in any philosophical education!"

"Of course," answered Crispus, "but one didn't take them seriously." And suddenly he thought that perhaps Beric *did* take them seriously . . . because he was a barbarian . . . because he didn't have any money power . . .

But Scaevinus went on. "We *couldn't* take them seriously. Not now that we've come to depend on this excessively complex money system. When Tiberius Gracchus talked his kind of agrarian equality it wasn't, perhaps, quite impossible. Even a senator still depended in the main on land which he farmed himself, more or less. But now we don't know one end of a plow from the other!"

"No, indeed!"

"Funny about the Gracchi. You might have gone back to some kind of equality and simplicity then, but people didn't want it enough to make a revolution. But when things have got to the stage when enough people *do* want a revolution, equality and all that's out of the question. Which shows why we don't have revolutions, gentlemen."

"Yes. We don't want it, and the ones who do haven't got any power at all. Fortunate, that."

But Crispus was still thinking about Beric and what happened if one took philosophy seriously. If one let it influence one. As one might if one wasn't taking power seriously—not having it.

Flavius Scaevinus was definite about what was to be done. If the right precautions were taken, the danger was negligible. At any rate, as compared with the danger that all decent people ran now.

The other two both wondered whether he had heard about Flavia. It was an open enough scandal . . . but Candidus was the one who ought to act. And he would not do so and had asked his father not to.

However, it was agreed upon that Nero's friends could not be allowed to survive him. Gallio, on payment of a large fine, was to be released in a few days. That was relief at any rate. None of them discussed this evening's popular entertainment. They were out of sight and sound of it, and such things had better be left unmentioned.

The two guests rose to go, and Crispus clapped his hands to bring the slaves back. Mikkos was sent running to fetch Balbus's litter. Lamprion and Pistos brought the cloaks. The Spaniard and Phaon hung about helpfully. Argas and Sannio were the last to come in.

Crispus frowned at them and noticed that they both looked rather upset and untidy. Why? He hadn't yet replaced Manasses. In these times one avoided unnecessary expenditure.

After good-byes had been said and suitable gods invoked for a return visit, the slaves pulled the curtains aside and ushered out the guests to the entrance hall where their own torchbearers were waiting for them. But Argas and Sannio stayed and glanced at one another, then at their master.

"What are you hanging about here for?" he said. "Go and see to my guests!"

"Sir—" said Argas.

"And you have a spot of grease on your tunic, Argas—a large spot. You are disgustingly careless!"

But Argas went on his knees. "I've bad news for you, sir. Beric has been arrested."

Flavius Crispus's hand jerked up to heart level. He felt sick. "Is it—in connection with—this Christianity?" If it was, he thought, and steadied himself with resolve, he would kill Argas. And any of the others he suspected.

"No, sir," said Argas, "it was for trying to kill Tigellinus."

So that was it. The gallant boy. For Flavia. "But he didn't . . . manage it?"

"Sir, Persis is here. She's run with the news. Will you see her?"

He nodded.

Sannio dashed out and came back with Persis, white and panting a little still, her hair slipping down at one side. She too threw herself at his feet.

"Tell me as quickly as you can, child," he said.

"He came when my master was out and Tigellinus was with her," Persis said. "He asked for me, and after a little I let him in, God forgive me."

"Why did you let him in?"

"To kill Tigellinus," said Persis simply. "He made me think it was right to do it. And then my mistress saw him and screamed, and he and Tigellinus fought, and my mistress helped Tigellinus. Beric was winning and then—then my mistress tripped him—"

"Go on," said Crispus, very low.

"And then the slaves ran in, and they all got him down, and Tigellinus stamped on his face, and then Tigellinus said to my mistress, 'He was your lover, you little devil'—oh, I'm sorry, sir—"

"Go on," said Crispus again, stonily.

"So she said, 'No, he's a Christian. He killed one of your agents, he told me so—'"

"But *had* he?" Crispus asked.

"Yes, sir, that was true."

"How do you know?"

"He told me too, sir. He was wrong to do it. And, oh, I oughtn't ever to have let him in—it was my sin!"

"He was perfectly right in trying to kill Tigellinus," said Crispus fiercely. "Go on."

"Then, sir, they pulled him onto his feet, and he was bleeding—he had a tooth knocked loose, and he spat it out and said he wasn't a Christian. Oh, he swore it! But she said he was, and Tigellinus said it was another Christian conspiracy and he would arrest all Christians he could lay hands on, and she said, 'There are some in Father's household who were arrested before,' and he said, 'Yes, I'll get them all,' and she said, 'My maid was one of them'—I think she was frightened, sir; he did look awful!—and then I ran."

"Where were you, child?"

"I was hiding behind the bed curtains, sir, but I crawled out and got into the bathroom and jumped through the window."

"Why did you come to my house if there are going to be arrests here?"

"To warn the others, sir. The guards won't be here for an hour, sir."

"Are you a Christian, Persis?"

"Yes, sir."

"I see. And you, Argas?"

"Yes, sir."

"In spite of my orders. And you, Sannio?"

"No, sir, but they're not what we're told, sir. They're decent, sir—"

"Hold your tongue, Sannio. I can make my own deductions about them. Argas. I was aware that Beric had been—involved. Now it is exceedingly unlikely that I can save him." His voice shook and faded out.

Sannio quickly filled a wine cup and handed it to him.

"I know," said Argas. "I loved him."

"You—and others—will be arrested. I am afraid you have very little chance. I shall, of course, say you are not Christians."

"Don't do that, sir," Argas said. "I'm not going to deny it. And if Beric dies, I want to die."

Crispus reached his hand out waveringly. Argas took it in his. "Boy," he said, "Beric was like my son to me. I ought to have got him away from this."

"You couldn't have, sir. He wasn't to hold nor to bind when he thought he knew what was right." He hesitated. He was still holding Crispus's hand in his. "You aren't angry with me now—are you, sir?"

"No, Argas. Only—I'm your master. I've tried to do what was best for you and for everyone. I appear to have failed."

"It was stronger than you, sir. Stronger than anything you could do. Have we put you into danger through this, sir?"

"I don't think so. Beric may have. It doesn't matter. You will almost certainly be condemned."

"I know. I suppose there'll be a general house arrest, sir. All of us that they think may give evidence, and the Christians will be kept and killed."

"Yes," said Crispus. He looked at the three slaves. Sannio was kneeling too now. "My poor children!"

Argas said, "Sir, can you any way save Phaon? If you could—it's what Beric would want. Maybe it's the only thing you can do for him."

"Why, exactly, do you ask me to save Phaon? Tell me, Argas. Tell me the truth."

Argas let go the hand. He didn't know what to say to his master. It was Persis who answered. "He's the best of us, sir!"

"The best—Christian?"

"Yes, sir," said Persis. "He'd keep it alive. After we're dead."

"Is that true, Argas?"

"It's true."

"And you ask me to save *him*. To make your thing stronger. To help it against the State."

"I ask you for Beric," Argas said.

"Blast," said Crispus and wiped his eyes with the back of his hand. Then, "If I do this, I am involved. Myself. Do you see, Argas? No, why should you see . . . I thought Phaon at least would be cured of this, and now you say he's the one that will carry on! I can't deliberately encourage Christianity!"

"It wouldn't exactly be that, sir—" Argas said.

"Wouldn't it? Wouldn't it, Argas? What else would it be? No, I refuse to allow you to lie at this moment or myself to be side-tracked. Where is Phaon?"

Again Sannio ran out.

Persis had edged up close to Argas. He put his arm around her and kissed her cheek lightly and said, "It's our chance now, Persis!"

Sannio came back with Phaon. Again Sannio knelt with the others, partly frightened, confusedly hoping for protection from its only possible source, partly to be in with the gang that included Argas and the Briton—the one who'd said things to him that made him feel warm and good.

But Phaon stood with his head up. He was still wearing the long, deliberately archaic and Greek-looking singer's robe of fine white linen. It hung in folds to his ankles, and he had a wreath of green leaves on his hair. They had been Greek songs, in praise of virtue, friendship, and good wine.

"Are you a Christian, Phaon?" his master asked.

"Yes," said Phaon lightly, knowing the moment was come, looking down at Argas and Persis, who were half turned to watch him.

"You know what has happened?" Crispus said.

"I know we shall all be sent to prison, and in another day we shall be able to show people that we've got something to die for."

"If I save you for Beric's sake," Crispus said, "will you give up this Christianity?"

"No," said Phaon. He added, as a patient explanation, "It wouldn't do any good my living without this. Beric wouldn't thank you for my life alone. He has tried to judge God's will; he has tried an old way, which is proved wrong, instead of our new way. But now he will want that to go on. He will want to become somehow part of it himself."

"All this—" said Crispus and shook his head as though he were trying to wake up. "I don't understand."

Phaon said, "It's one way or the other for me. Either I die as a witness, or I live as a witness. The Kingdom shall go on through me."

"I can't waste time on all this!" Crispus said abruptly. "We— we can discuss this later, Phaon. I propose to send you over immediately to Balbus's house and then down to my mother in the country." He looked at them. "I see no reason why I should not do the same for Persis. My daughter has no right to own her after this. My tablets!"

They were on another table. Phaon went and picked them up and brought them. Holding them in his hand, he said, "I am and shall be a Christian. The same for Persis. We don't take our lives on any other terms."

"You are unreasonable, boy!" Crispus said and was suddenly caught by a shuddering sob. "Give me my tablets."

"I know I'm unreasonable, sir," Phaon answered gently, "but the whole thing's beyond reason." Then he passed over the tablets. "In Beric's name," he said.

Crispus wrote quickly.

While he was doing it, Phaon said to Argas, "Tell Manasses and Lalage, if you see them, that I will make their church again. I know I can and will. Nothing is lost."

Argas looked at Crispus and said, "Tell *him*."

"Yes," said Phaon. And then, "This is your doing, brother, when you were beaten for me."

Suddenly Persis said, "I shared the sin when I let Beric by to murder—I prayed he would be able to do it. I ought to die!"

But Phaon said, "You had a moment of wanting the old way again. You set that right not by dying but by living the new way. It will be hardest for us, Persis. We have our whole lives yet to live. There will not be many hours in them like this one."

"You have your whole lives," Argas said, "but I shan't be a slave much longer!"

Crispus finished writing and gave the tablets to Phaon. "Give these to Aelius Balbus yourself. You will be safe. Now, go on!"

"Come, Persis," said Phaon and pulled her to her feet.

Argas was standing now. He kissed them both and watched them go out.

"Argas," said Crispus, "if I don't see Beric . . . again . . . and you do, tell him I did this for him."

"I will," said Argas. "I promise."

"Good boy," said Crispus. "Now, who else is there? They'll know who was arrested before."

"There's Josias," Argas said, "and then there's Dapyx, but he's been frightened out of it. He isn't one of us any longer. He's going to say anything they want him to say if he's tortured, anything against Beric. He hates us all now because he thinks we made things worse for him."

"If he's been arrested before as a Christian, they're likely to kill him this time. But tell him, if you can, that if he denies he is a Christian and says nothing against Beric, I will—if he survives—send him to my country estate and see that he is well treated. The same applies to Josias. I take it that you yourself—"

Argas shook his head. "I'm going to die for it. But I'll say nothing they can get Beric on."

And then Mikkos came in quick past the curtains. "What's to happen to us, sir?" he gasped and knelt beside Sannio.

"I'm afraid you're all going to be arrested, boys," said Crispus, "and questioned for evidence against Beric—and the Christians."

"We'll stick it, sir, me and Sannio," Mikkos said, "but sir—"

"Yes, boy?"

"If—if they do anything to us . . . so we don't, maybe, look right for the dining room anymore, sir . . . you won't sell us . . . nor send us to the kitchen—"

"You needn't be afraid of that, Mikkos. I'd better see this other boy, Josias."

"You can't sir. He's gone and hanged himself, in the back kitchen, sir. When he heard, poor boy."

Argas crossed himself and stood stiffer.

"Such things happening in my house!" Crispus said.

"He was afraid of going back on us," Argas said, "afraid of the pain. Making him say things. Making him deny Jesus and the Kingdom. Don't think too badly of him, sir."

"How can I judge any of you?" Crispus said in a curious, strained voice. "I'm safe. At present. Argas, I wish there was anything I could do."

"You can't, sir. I thought this might happen. I'm ready, anyway. My death's my power. I've never had any power before."

"I wish I hadn't had you beaten," Crispus said.

"Let Phaon tell you about that," Argas said. "It's over. It's forgiven."

And then they all heard a loud and prolonged knocking on the outer door, and Sannio and Mikkos clutched one another, and Argas and his master stood facing one another, on a level.

20

State Methods

Blephano leaned over and trimmed the lamp. All night he had been copying out depositions from the slaves and others who were being tortured, and now it was nearly morning. He stretched and cut himself a new pen. Whenever the door was opened he could hear the noises or the equally unpleasant silences.

To take his mind off it, he thought about his little girl, a very pretty child, just four years old; danced like a proper little fairy and always ready with a kiss for her dad. The hot weather wasn't good for children, but, praise Juno, she'd escaped everything that summer. If they paid him a little extra for all this special work he'd been doing since the Christian trouble began—and they ought to in all conscience, but there, if you were only a freedman you had to take what you got—he'd buy her one of those pottery dolls that moved its head and arms. She was just the age for one. Regular picture she'd look, his little Philemation, with a big doll.

Toxilus came in, wiping his hands on his tunic.

Harpax lumbered after him, a middle-aged tough with a broken nose, stripped to the waist, trailing a nasty-looking barbed whip after him.

"There's no more to be got out of that lot," said Toxilus.

"You're on those household slaves of T. Flavius Crispus, aren't you?" Blephano turned back to another sheet. "Yes, here we are. Shut that blasted door, can't you, Harpax! Nice mixed lot of depositions you've gone and got. They'll have to be sorted out. Any of it true?"

Toxilus leaned over and looked. "This is all in agreement with our own list of questions. Got them pretty well all, sooner or later. Lamprion . . . Pistos . . . Chrysops . . . Dixippus . . . Syllis . . . yes, all that page. None of this lot are Christians, nor even suspects. We're taking the ones that *are*, separate. One of them's talking, a lousy little squirt of a barbarian. Thinks he's going to

336

save his skin. Dirty little coward. *He's* going to get what's coming to him anyway, or I don't know my job."

"What's this man who won't answer?"

"Hermeias—the old boy's secretary. A bit difficult. You can't do much to a valuable man. He wouldn't talk, not either way. I got the others properly rattled, but all he did was to go off on a boring set speech about death. Much he knows about it! He's in one of these blooming Mysteries."

"Better chase them all out first thing, Toxilus. They're all right, I take it?"

"We've not taken two pennies off the value of any of them. Tick 'em off." He picked up another sheet. "I'm keeping this lot. Sannio and Mikkos. Till they talk."

"What are they—suspects?"

"No. Just won't answer. Friends, as like as not, or may have been paid beforehand. There's another boy from that household we had on our list—yes, Phaon. Got to find *him*. And a girl. I've traced her to the other household, but she hasn't been brought in yet. Some of these girls are the devil's own job, worse than the men. I've a hunch I can get something about her out of this Sannio and Mikkos."

"What are they? Dining-room boys? Probably worth something. You can't do too much if they're not suspects, you know."

"Naw, I shan't do *too* much!" Toxilus hooted with amusement. "Not unless little old Harpax gets cross. Like he will if they keep him hanging about past breakfast time. I'm going to try just a touch of the irons now."

"Do it where it won't show, then, or there'll be a fuss. Who else have you got?"

"Casperius has got the Christians. He'll make them sing in a bit. The rest of mine are another lot—not in this case at all. Ready, Harpax?"

"No," growled Harpax and went out.

"Always affects the bowels," said Blephano thoughtfully, "even if you've been at it as long as he has." He yawned. "It'll be light in half an hour."

Then Cario came in, looking rather excited. He was wearing leather gloves and apron. There was blood on them. "Got to have a word with you!" he said to Toxilus and pulled him over into a corner.

"Here, your report!" said Blephano sharply. "Any results?"

"Oh—we've let that woman go again."

"Which woman?"

"The old poisoner. Euphemia. There's no more to be got out of *her.* She says this Briton *is* a Christian."

"That's the first definite admission apart from the house slaves."

"No, the man's spoken too. Says he was in their church."

"What, the metalworker? You've got to get some more names out of him. He didn't get properly questioned to start with."

"Yes, well, I've got to speak to Toxilus first, see?"

"Oh, don't mind me!" said Blephano. "You and *your* church, I take it! Wait till *they* burn Rome!" He got properly fed up with Toxilus and Cario talking their Mithraist stuff. He supposed they were going to arrange another of their feasts or fasts or some balls. He thought he'd go out for a minute and get a drink.

Cario was saying to Toxilus in an urgent whisper, "So I got him tied, see, and started in on it. Those cogs keep slipping too. I got to have them put right! Well then, his head fell back, the way they always do, and there on his forehead, under his hair, as plain as I see you now, he'd got the mark!"

"What, the mark of the Soldier?"

"Yes, that's what I'm telling you! Just as sure as I'm standing here, he's got it. Look, we've got to do something about it."

"He must have left us and gone off to these Christians."

"He'll come back to us. I tell you, Toxilus, I won't go on doing this to a man who's in that Degree. He may be higher for all we know! I tell you, me being the one that was told off to do him, that shows it was *meant!*"

"Well, what can we do?"

"Get him out and have it written off he died. When Blephano's gone home, we'll bring him through into the shed with the old stuff. There's sacks there we can get him under. Then he can be put into my room. I tell you what, Toxilus, when I first saw him I said to myself, he's different!"

"Bit of a risk," said Toxilus uneasily.

"By the Light of the Sun, I'm taking it!" Cario gave Toxilus a tug and pulled him out of the room. The lists on the table rustled a little in a puff of chilly wind that had come with the first signs of dawn.

Some of the assistants in this department of state were freedmen. But, of course, much of the hard work was done by tough and stupid slaves such as Harpax. They did not do any of the actual questioning, but it takes a good deal of physical strength to dislocate a man's joints, even if you have appropriate machinery, or to beat him till he faints and then go on beating him till he begins to feel again. Some of them were ex-gladiators who'd had luck. This was a permanent kind of job, and the conditions weren't at all bad, given you were the kind of man who didn't worry over certain aspects of it. Cario had been a gladiator. It was then he had picked up his Mithraism, which was the part of his life that really counted.

The man who was in charge of the examination of most of the Christians, Casperius, was something of a showman. He liked style in his tortures, and he was occasionally gratified by a visit from someone quite high up. In fact he had once or twice been called upon to give demonstrations at the palace. He was a Roman citizen and proud of himself as a servant of the State. He had a short, glossy beard on which he used a rather powerful scent. His prisoners would get to know that scent rather too well.

Lalage knew it now as an integral part of a complex horror, and so did Manasses. Argas was beginning to. He was slowly realizing what he had let himself in for. He had not seen Beric yet, though Beric might be quite near. In the next cell. But you didn't hear voices or groans or crying, only an extra loud or sharp scream. You couldn't always tell if it was a man or a woman, even. People's voices change when they scream. Once or twice there had been audible words, sometimes their Name. Was that Manasses?

When he was left to himself to think things over for a few minutes, he had time to wonder that. In those awful lonely spaces when you were bound to ask yourself if it was worthwhile holding on for another round.

So far he had said that Beric was not a Christian, since no Christian was allowed to kill. He had by now almost forgotten why it was important to say that, but he stuck to it. He also refused to agree to any other charges against Beric or the Christians, to give names, or to say where Phaon or Persis might be. From time to time he would become aware, with a sort of amazement, of what had been done to him already. Would he ever be able to keep his promise and tell Beric what Crispus had done? *Jesus, let me see him again. Only let me see him.*

Manasses and Lalage were in the same room. Casperius had made a mistake here. He had supposed from what he had seen that they were lovers and that he could use this to weaken their resistance. Actually they loved one another sufficiently to have made a pact, earlier on, by which each was to disregard the sufferings, present or to come, of the other. That was not too easy, but it was as well they had made it, for there was a good deal of threatening Manasses with what was to be done with Lalage, and the other way around too.

They were both nearly exhausted now and screamed easily and cried most of the time, yet when it came to speaking they kept their heads. Curious spirits of strength came to them from time to time, when they seemed on the point of swimming out of their bodies into an unassailable and painless state of pure being.

The deputy governor of the Mamertine was helping Casperius. He was in a rotten temper. He'd got that Briton where he wanted him at last, and he had got real pleasure out of the first few minutes.

But if only he *had* managed to kill Tigellinus! That was what Aelius Candidus kept on thinking, and sometimes he was so angry with Beric for not having pulled it off that he went for him in an unprofessionally violent way, which Casperius disapproved of. And the Briton went on saying he was no Christian, so perhaps he *had* tried to do it on other grounds.

Nor could you entirely disregard your father and father-in-law. He had made various assurances to Flavius Crispus in the middle of the night but, of course, had not let him see any of the prisoners. Nor did he propose to do so. But still you can't look a man in the eyes if you have lied to him completely, and, supposing things went so far that he could not stick his present career any longer, he might be glad to avail himself of his father-in-law's influence with other circles.

So Beric, though a good deal cut and bruised, especially about the eyes and mouth, had not been put through quite what the slaves were getting. But he, too, was exhausted after a night of it, and when in the early morning they suddenly went away, he spent the first half hour tensing himself against their return, but then fell asleep and, even on the stone floor and with his hands tied behind his back, went off into deep unconsciousness.

Lalage and Manasses were asleep too, though less deeply because they had been more hurt. Manasses had a couple of ribs broken. They caught his breathing, but fortunately he had been thrown onto a heap of straw and had fallen on the other side. Lalage was talking in her sleep about a dance that wouldn't come right, telling Sophrosyne she wasn't playing the right music. It was the burns that were hurting her the most.

Both of them had asked for water and hadn't been given any. Their mouths were dry and sour. But after the torturers were gone and before they slept, they had whispered to one another across the darkness and had made the great outward effort toward forgiveness.

Two cells away, Argas was half asleep in a huddle in the corner. Sannio and Mikkos were asleep.

Dapyx was dead. He had agreed to everything, denied he was a Christian, said that the Briton was a Christian, and ever since he had become one had been a murderer and seducer, forged letters, violated temples, talked treason, anything they liked! Yes, Flavius Crispus was a Christian and wicked too—oh yes, he was always talking against the gods and the emperor! What had he said? But here Dapyx broke down, and everyone began laughing, and Dapyx saw that they were going to go on torturing him. Nothing he said was of any real value as evidence, so he was left to Harpax and Sitas to finish off. At no particular point he stopped crying and died in their hands.

Blephano had gone home after putting his records tidily away. He knew he would be wanted again the next day. At home, he knelt down for a time by the edge of the bed, watching little

Philemation, rosily asleep. He renewed certain vows that he had made to Juno Educa and which had protected her, and suddenly he thought with hate and horror of these Christians who denied the divinity of the gods who were caring for his child, who would anger them and turn them away and leave his Philemation unprotected!

Euphemia, who had been turned out again into the prison yard, was awake and praying for Lalage. What they'd done to her this time wasn't much worse than they'd done before. They all thought she was an old fool who knew nothing. *I look my age now,* she said to herself. The men didn't get much kick out of doing things to her, but they did with Lalage. Euphemia had a kind of feeling that if only she stayed awake and prayed, it might somehow make things better for the others.

When Toxilus and Cario went back, they found that Rhodon had managed to wriggle half off the frame. Then he had got tangled in the ropes and had collapsed with most of his weight on the dislocated shoulder. He was pretty strong, but his old wounds were getting him, as well as what had been done. Indeed, Cario had noticed the scars. He always did, because he found in practice that there were often effective pain areas around these.

Rhodon became aware, though, when his torturers came in, and began floundering about again.

Cario caught hold of his head and pulled the hair back. There was the brand, clear enough. "Well?" he said.

Neither of them were in a high grade. Toxilus had only been initiated a few months, and Cario was in the Second Degree, a Nymphius. But he knew this mark. He hoped to have it himself some day, this brand that was utterly unconnected in function or feeling with the brands he had used so often.

The two of them heaved Rhodon, struggling, back onto the frame again and saw his muscles knot and swell, prepared to pull against them. But they only tied him lightly. His eyes were shut against them; his lips were pressed together. They eyed one another. The ex-gladiator Cario knelt by his head and whispered certain words. He had never been so excited in his life before. He shook as he waited for the answer.

As they lifted Rhodon, the pains in his shoulders and ankles increased and shot about. He was going to speak this time. He knew he was going to speak. If they wanted names and accusations they could have them. Even if it cut him off forever. If he could never face the others again. He had been in prison longer than the rest of them. He had stood it. He couldn't go on standing it. That was all quite clear. Only the pain was blurring everything. In a moment they would begin again. And he would speak. Out of darkness and pain, words came at him, an image, a savior and redeemer. As though once more a dog had been licking his hand. He answered the words as they should be answered.

"I told you so," said Cario triumphantly, and then, to Rhodon, with great tenderness, "We will save you, brother."

Rhodon opened his eyes and looked at the man who called him brother, the instrument of his savior. After a time he recognized the man as his torturer. "I am a Christian," he said, as he had said a hundred times already. It would begin again.

Toxilus nudged Cario and frowned, but Cario disregarded him. "No," he said gently, "that was all a mistake, brother. You are a Soldier, a Soldier of Mithras."

"A Soldier," said Rhodon. Yes, he was sure of that.

Again Cario whispered some words, and again Rhodon gave the answers. He had forgotten them for a long time, but now they came easily. It rested him to say them. It was like at the love feast when they were waiting for the Spirit to come.

"We'll get you out of here," Cario said. "It will all not have happened."

"No—more—questions?"

"No more." Cario was untying his ankles.

He did not move at all but lay stretched on the frame that stank of bodies that had struggled and contracted and loosed in the wrenching tides of pain. It would not any longer happen to him. He thought he said again, *"I am a Christian,"* but the words were only inside his head, never on his lips.

Still without moving, he watched Cario's face anchored in lantern light above him. That face had changed, had become good. He had known this to happen before, when a man was seized in some way by the Spirit. It was the sudden and definite moment when the metal becomes hot enough to work, to take the shape that it was intended for.

Toxilus was beside him now, holding a cup of wine and water for him to drink slowly. The torturers were expert at giving or denying drink to the terribly thirsty. But now the cup was given not in malice or for any end except that of human kindness. Toxilus was convinced and amazed at his fortune in having been part of the drama. It was all the kind of thing you hear about in stories! "There, brother," he said, eager to be recognized too.

They untied his arms and wrists. Then they did something to his shoulder that hurt terribly for a moment. That was so surprising that he yelled and clutched onto Cario, but almost at once he recognized that they had put his shoulder back into place. Now they were tying it around with a bundle of soft rags. He still held onto Cario, and Cario looked down at him and wiped the sweat off his face, touching the brand mark again. "The brothers will be all there in the Cave," he said, "to welcome you."

And all would be in order again. And he had not done anything wrong; he had not, after all, spoken. He had not denied anything. But yet he had been saved. He remembered the time before when his savior had not come. He tried to speak of it, to tell how this was different. "On the ship," he said, "the ship to Delos . . . and he never came . . . and now . . ."

But the others paid no attention. They put their arms around him and heaved him up. He could not stand alone, but he could hobble with their support at both sides. Toxilus picked up the lantern in his other hand. They went out through the room with Blephano's table and stool.

Light was coming in through the window now. They whispered that they would take him out to the shed and hide him there for a time. They would bring him food, and he would sleep long and deep there. He was in the hands of his brothers now; he trusted them to do whatever was best for him.

21

The Third Sacrament

Neither Paul nor Gallio had slept well that night. When the light began to filter through into their cells, both had despaired of getting any sound rest and had got up. Gallio looked at his Christian slave who was still calmly asleep. It seemed a shame to wake him, poor little devil, considering that any day . . .

But the boy had heard him and jumped up, apologizing and blinking and shoving his hand through his hair.

"All right, all right," said Gallio amiably. "Old bones up early! Get me some water, there's a good boy." Of course, the washing arrangements in the prison were none too good, but still you couldn't complain.

He dressed leisurely, leaving the boy to clip his beard and shave around the edges. He thought about some of the difficulties in the way of the removal of the emperor. It was never certain about the slaves and freedmen in the imperial household. You could bribe the underlings easily enough, but the chamberlains were a little different.

They were already so rich, some of them, that a bribe didn't mean much. What they liked was power, and the excitement of staking one's life on one's own individual capacities, and they would realize that the kind of regime the senators had in mind would remove all their power from them. They might even be genuinely devoted to their masters' interests; that was pardonable.

But Gallio thought with extreme distaste of Halotus, the cupbearer who had been so abominably insolent to him the last time he had attended an imperial function. And then of Helios and Polyclitos, who pretended to take all the dull routine work off the emperor's shoulders and who had wormed themselves into positions where they could sign edicts or do anything they pleased against senators, even! Intolerable that one's action for the well-being of Rome could be so easily thwarted by a pack of stateless, swordless, and often sexless Asiatics! Well, when it was over, they should be dealt with . . . appropriately. As benefited slaves who had become insolent.

While Gallio was considering this, he noticed a distinct shakiness in the hands of the boy who was combing and trimming his thick gray beard. "What's the matter?" he asked. "Hear something when you went for the water?"

The young slave swallowed and said, "It *is* today."

"Who for? You?"

"We don't know, sir. But a lot of our people are going to be taken. And the guards keep on telling us—what happened last night, sir."

"You mean, those burnings? Wasn't sure, myself, if they'd do that when it came to the point. A most deplorable business. Not, mind you, that I don't think *some* punishment necessary, but— know any of them, boy?"

"My father and mother were in the other prison, sir. Where they were taken from to be burned."

"Dear me!" For a moment Gallio found nothing to say. He was unused to consorting with criminals. Did slaves think about their parents, for instance, as one did oneself? He looked around at the boy who was half turned away, one arm across his face. Apparently slaves *did* feel the same.

"Come, boy," said Gallio, "don't cry! Be a man! Remember, it's over. Pain is of the body only, so it cannot endure. They are beyond it now."

"Yes, sir," said the slave and looked around again. "I keep on telling myself that. And they've been witnesses; they'll be part of the Kingdom now, won't they, sir?"

"Of course, of course," said Gallio awkwardly.

The slave took his hand and kissed it. "You're ever so kind, sir! I do thank you, I'm sure. Oh sir, I do wish I wasn't so frightened of the beasts! It's not—not being buried decent, nor even in one place, but to be in bits in the stomachs of a set of filthy animals!" He was crying again now.

What did one do about that? Scold him? Threaten to dismiss him or complain to the governor of the prison? No, didn't do. "Mustn't look at it like that, you know," Gallio said. "These lions

. . . just instruments of power. Injustice. You've got to show you can beat that. Whatever instruments it uses. Got to show *me* you can die well. No worse than being killed in war, really, and eaten by vultures like some of my own ancestors were. Just think of the worst the beasts can do to you. Think clearly. It's no worse than good men have suffered before you, and it will only last a little time."

"And I shall forgive the people who are making it happen," the slave said. His voice was steady now, almost glad. "I shall forgive the emperor!"

He began to trim up the other side of Gallio's beard, and his hands weren't shaking any longer. He had twisted the Stoic consolation his own way. Well, let him. But it made Gallio rather oddly uncomfortable. This slave was proposing to forgive the emperor whom Gallio and his friends were proposing to murder. There was something new about forgiveness. Something, perhaps, superior. The emperor could stop those who tried to assassinate him; apparently he could not stop his forgivers.

Paul, having combed his own beard, was already out in the yard. It seemed a little fresher in the early morning. He was trying to break through a curious entanglement of childish images, connected in some way with his parents, a complex of love and blood and punishment and inexplicable forgiveness. It was something to do with Jesus Christ and with the Kingdom, but he could not see just how.

Sometimes he thought it was a plain mirroring. He longed then to be a child again, in direct relationship with all this, a good and chastised and forgiven child, sitting quietly on a Sabbath evening with the candles lit, aware that all is well, that there will be kisses at bedtime, and that the great winged angels are keeping away all the bad dreams and the pains and the sickening giddiness that from time to time besets the child.

And sometimes he shook this off, knowing that he was a man and part of something greater than any family, because it did not merely hold him with love but must be made and shaped by his adult and unceasing efforts. Thinking this out, he paced up and down, shaking his head and muttering.

After a time Euphemia came out of the women's cells and went up to him. She was part of this pattern that must be made, even though she interrupted his thinking out of it. Any human being matters more to God than any ideas.

"Yes, Euphemia?" he said, then looking at her more attentively. "They've been questioning you again?"

She nodded.

Once more, as so often, Paul felt ashamed of his own citizenship and immunity to this. It made him rough and abrupt.

But she did not notice. She began to tell him what had happened last night in the punishment cells.

He asked a good many questions about Beric. He had heard of him from Manasses but hadn't thought much about him so far. "If they bring him out here," said Paul, "I shall see him. Come and tell me."

"Yes, Paul," said Euphemia. Then, "That other doctor put some stuff on Lalage's burns, but if Luke did happen to come—"

"I'll send him along," Paul said. "You know, Euphemia, it may be today—for all of you."

"I'm ready, Paul."

When Gallio came out, Paul went over to him and explained what had been happening.

Gallio's eyebrows twitched. "Pity the boy didn't get Tigellinus. As it is . . . Crispus may be held responsible."

"So may we. Not that one accusation more against the Christians will necessarily have any effect. I doubt if lies matter so much as one is inclined to suppose, in any case. He seemed a promising young man, this Beric. A pity, for his own sake, that he has made this deviation."

"Crispus will be very much upset. Perhaps I shall be able to see the boy."

"Perhaps. That depends on what they have done to him. They may prefer none of us to see. But if I see him, and if he is repentant, I intend that at least he shall not die unbaptized."

"Think it matters a lot, don't you? I wonder if Beric will." It was really very peculiar, Gallio thought, the company one found oneself in. The Christians talked to him openly enough now, and he was fairly certain that if they did normally do anything shameful or criminal, he would have found out about it.

By now there were more of them about. He nodded to a few, hoping that this might give them a shade more courage. Some of them were looking horribly frightened, and he was becoming extremely anxious that Nero should not have the satisfaction of seeing too many of these his fellow prisoners screaming or running when the lions were set onto them.

By and by Luke was let in. Paul spoke to him, and he went off toward the main block of the prison, where those who had been questioned were most likely to be.

He had been gone only a little time when Megallis was let in. She found Euphemia almost at once. "Whatever have they been doing to you now?" she asked.

"They wanted me to talk," Euphemia said, "but I wasn't talking. Funny, me always such a one to chatter!"

Megallis began to stroke Euphemia's face very lightly over the bruises and little edgy cuts. "There, and there, and there," she whispered, "and your hands. Oh, your poor nail! Euphemia, you didn't ever go forgiving *that,* did you?"

"It takes your mind off what's being done if you start in on forgiving it," Euphemia said, "and this is nothing to what some of us have had done—and forgiven."

"Euphemia," said Megallis, "there's something I got to say. It was my man, Tertius, that told on you. You could be safe at home but for him, Euphemia. But for us, that is, because if I hadn't gone and brought him to your house . . ." She began to cry.

Euphemia put one arm around her, a bit stiffly because the elbow felt no end funny after what they'd done. "If I'd been safe at home, I'd have been missing this, Megallis. And it's what my whole life's been for, in a manner of speaking. You see, dear, it's not much, is it, even having a little business and the right kind of customer? Not much, I mean, if you think of the sun and stars and that. But this is big enough to match all the big things. Don't you go doing anything silly about that man of yours, not on account of me, dear, will you?"

"You mean—you're forgiving him?"

"Why, of course I am. There, dear, don't take on so! Like a daughter, you've been." And there was something else that was so funny if you thought it out—the way Euphemia, who was going to be torn to pieces by wild beasts, was comforting and petting Megallis, who might be going to live to a comfortable old age and die in her bed like any nice woman wants to!

Beric was pushed out into the yard among the other prisoners. He recognized it as the same yard he had been in before, first when he and Hermeias had fetched out the house slaves and then when he had come with Crispus. A long time ago.

He sat down on a bench and tried to shift the chains on his ankles a little and began feeling in his mouth for the broken teeth. It was annoying to have one's teeth broken—and distinctly painful. He spit out another mouthful of blood. But why worry about teeth when you are going to die in a day or two? Probably after another night of it. Which you deserved for having failed. Yes, deserved it. You'd got more or less used to the idea of dying but not to being hit and hurt and being quite unable to hit back. Like a slave. Like Argas. And where *were* the others!

He knew they'd been there too. He'd been told that, all right, and what was being done to them, hour by hour. To make him admit they were his friends and the whole thing a Christian plot. Well, he hadn't done that. And it was because of his bungling that it had all happened. What would they be looking like now? Thinking of that, feeling sick, he knew he couldn't face them. Best just to die and end everything.

Somebody sat down beside him, said, "Are you one of us? Have you been beaten and chained for Jesus Christ's sake, brother?"

"No," he said and was left alone again.

Was this going to involve Crispus? Had he just messed up everyone he was fond of? It looked like that. They'd get them all, Argas, Phaon, Persis, Eunice, the whole of the little church. If they hadn't taken him, tried to make a brother out of him, been decent to him the way they were decent to one another, it mightn't have happened.

He was crying a bit now. One of the cuts on his cheekbone opened again and began to bleed, a sore tickle through everything he was thinking about.

He became aware that someone else was sitting beside him, had been for some little time. "Listen to me, son," said the other person in an energetic, educated voice.

Beric looked around. "I am not a Christian," he said. "I am a murderer."

"I know all about you, son," the man said. "I am Paul of Tarsus."

Beric shifted uneasily. He had heard plenty about Paul. He couldn't just chase him off. "Then you know I'm not one of you," he said. "I haven't been baptized."

"You'd like to be baptized, wouldn't you, son?" Paul said.

"How could I be! I'm here for trying to murder Tigellinus."

"I know. Why did you want to? Wasn't it because you thought you could help us that way? Yes? Well, then, you made a mistake. It can be washed out before you die."

"I knew it was wrong," Beric said. "They told me. And I did it in spite of them, and they were arrested and tortured . . . Oh, I don't begin to be fit for baptism!"

"It will change everything. You will begin again and afresh, bought out of your sin and fear by the love of Jesus."

"What I did will go on," Beric said, "for me and for others. I can't begin my actions again, and they're what count."

"No," said Paul, "your soul is what counts with God. Give it to Him, Beric. Make a sacrifice of it. That sacrifice will not be rejected."

"I don't see it your way," Beric said. It was all making him feel more miserable than ever. This wasn't his idea of baptism, nor what Manasses and Argas had made him think it was. It seemed to him now that it was being offered to him as something magic, a kind of private mystery. He didn't want that. He wasn't a child or a fool. He only wanted to be with the others again. And yet he couldn't bear that either—to see what he'd done to them!

Luke came out. His hands were bloodstained, and he went over to the prison well. One of the women drew up a bucket of water for him and poured it over his hands while he rubbed them with a palmful of oil from the little flask at his belt. Then he came over to the two on the bench and nodded gravely at Paul, then said to Beric, "You're the Briton. I've been hearing about you."

351

"Oh—who from?"

"Manasses and Lalage. And that new boy, Argas. You want to know what's happened to them, do you? Well, they're not too good. They've got some bones broken among them. I'm going to get them out here; they want to see you."

He came close and took Beric's head between his hands and tilted it toward the light. He lifted one eyelid, and Beric winced away. "That hurting?"

"I keep on seeing flashes that hurt a bit. I expect I was hit there a good deal."

"I might be able to patch you up," Luke said, "but—"

"It's not worth it, is it—honestly?"

"No," said Luke, "I'm afraid not." Then he saw Euphemia helping Lalage out and went over to them.

As he did so, Beric got up and shuffled away towards the far side of the yard, as fast as his chains would let him. He had got a glimpse of Lalage, not strong or light and steady on her feet as a dancer should be, but weak and hobbling, a bandage around her head and ears, her hair loose and draggled over it. And it was more than he could bear.

Then he saw Gallio. He hesitated. If he was seen talking to Gallio, it might make danger for Crispus. Nor would Gallio necessarily care to speak to him.

However Gallio beckoned to him. "Well, young man," he said, "most unfortunate you didn't do what you intended to do."

"Perhaps I was wrong," Beric said slowly. "Perhaps I was spoiling something."

"Wish you'd spoiled Tigellinus's beauty for him! Have they hurt you much, Beric?"

"They've hurt the others worse."

"What, the slaves? Yes, hard on them having no rights. When they happen to be human. That's not contemplated in most legal codes—so far. *Are* you a Christian, Beric?"

"I don't know. I meant to be. I can't think about it now."

"Afraid you'll have to," Gallio said. "Here's Paul."

"Oh," said Beric, "isn't it enough to be beaten up without Paul talking at me too!" He went over to the wall and leaned against it, pressing his hurt face and eyes against his hands.

Gallio intercepted Paul, tapping him on the shoulder. "Better leave the lad alone, hadn't you, Paul? He's had quite a beating."

"How can I leave him alone?" Paul said. "His soul is in danger."

"Paul, he is certain to be executed for this attempted assassination, poor boy. Will it make any difference whether or not you get him into your society or church or whatever it is?"

"Most certainly it will! Either he accepts his redemption or he does not. If he does, he has accepted an event for all eternity, an event not only in the eternity of the universe but also in his own individual eternity. Surely it's plain to you by now, Gallio, after all the times I have spoken to you about it!"

"Afraid I never quite manage to take it in, Paul! Somehow this business of the immortality of the soul never strikes me as very convincing."

"What you cannot realize—what you will not allow yourself to realize!—is that something new has happened, not before Adam or Troy, but quite lately. Something has at last emerged from the current of the world's being which can reverse that current, which is no longer part of it nor under its power. Men have died and their souls have died with them, but we who have become one with the new event will not die except in the world's way."

"As most of you here will do within the next few days. And you think that the laws of natural science will not take effect on them!"

"Your natural science is only of this world. I am speaking of another world, of the spiritual world."

"I could understand," said Gallio slowly, "if you insisted that this world is also a spiritual world, if you claimed for it a reality beyond phenomenal reality. But this split you make! No, that may seem easy for a scholar of your Eastern classics, but I fear my own Western scholarship cannot allow it.

"The curious thing is, Paul, that a good many of your people here are certainly not thinking of any other and separate world. They are thinking of your Kingdom, and all that it implies, in *this* world. Which is a sufficiently subversive idea, in all conscience, but at least a rational one."

353

"Some of our people have not understood—they are poor and ignorant. But because they have accepted the event, they will receive its consequences."

"Immortality? Taking back their poor little slaves' bodies to wear forever? Or other bodies in which their souls would be most uncomfortable? Senatorial bodies, no doubt! That's not what they're here for, Paul, nor why they're dying. Frankly, if I thought they'd been taking that kind of drug, I should cease to respect them. As it is, I do respect them. Indeed, I find them—singularly persuasive. Ah, Beric, you're back."

"Yes," said Beric, "I've got to face Paul sooner or later. I've got to say I can't be baptized."

"Paul says it's to save your immortal soul, Beric. No, Paul, let me speak! Don't you care about that?"

"No," said Beric. "I did care about the Kingdom. I did care about the new way of living for everyone. I wanted to help that. And I'm not even going to be able to die for it like the slaves now!"

Paul said very gently, "You will be able to die for it if you are one of us, Beric. Come, let Manasses and Lalage stand for you. It is the one thing you can do for them now. There will be no need of questions on doctrine, nor of prayer and fasting, for any of you. Come, Beric, and be part of the Will."

"I can't!" said Beric but more desperately and less certainly than he had said it before.

"You must face them," said Paul. "Beric, you must face the moment of your own birth."

"No!" said Beric again.

"Coward," Paul said quietly. "Come."

Then Beric tossed his head back, ignoring all kinds of pain. "Oh, very well!" said Caradoc's son and stalked off, his chains rattling and jarring down on his ankles, ahead of Paul, back to the others.

"Clever chap you are, Paul!" Gallio said. "But keep off the mystery stuff with that lad. It won't work."

The others were out in the yard now. Lalage was sitting up on a bench, stiff and pale, one foot propped awkwardly in front of her, the bandage around her head discolored at one side.

Manasses was half sitting, propped up on the ground beside her. Every now and then she stroked his forehead a little. Luke had just had to take a couple of fingers off his already hurt right hand, which had been crushed again, but he did not feel this very much at the moment. The hand was done up in rags and lay loosely on his knee.

Argas lay on the ground, sometimes twitching and rolling over onto his other side. He had been very sick, and now his face was drawn with shock and pain. The flies were on all of them, and they hardly had strength to try to knock them away. There was not much more any of the doctors could do for them; it was no worse than what had happened to a good many others. Several markedly unpleasant things had not been done to any of them yet. They could all stand up if they had to.

Beric came up to them and took it all in, smelling stale blood and vomit and the doctor's ointments and the peculiar smell of a hurt woman, very nasty, very disconcerting for any man to have in his nostrils. He knelt down beside Argas and took his hand. The terrible thing was that they were all smiling at him.

Argas held his hand pretty hard. Then he said, "We didn't say anything against you. None of us did. And we said you weren't a Christian if you'd tried to kill. And Manasses and me, we wouldn't say anything against Crispus."

"That was good of you," Beric said. "I said I wasn't a Christian. They wanted me to say it was a Christian plot. I didn't. Argas, I suppose I've killed you. All three of you."

"We were going to be killed anyhow," Manasses said. "But a sin has to take its consequences."

"It was my sin, and it's you who are taking the consequences."

"Surely I should be my brother's keeper," Manasses said. "Besides, you take the consequences too, just because we are really together, really part of the same thing. Beric, you denied you were one of us for the sake of the Kingdom. But you *are* one of us —aren't you?"

"I can't be," Beric said. "I don't deserve anything except to be killed myself. I've smashed our church. Argas, did they get Phaon too?"

"Crispus saved him," Argas said, sitting half up, Beric's arm behind him, "and Persis too. I promised to tell you. He got them safe away because it was the only thing he could do for you."

"Did he know they were Christians?"

"He knew. Beric, there was a minute when I was talking to him, oh, as if he were you! That wouldn't have happened but for this."

"And the others?"

"Josias killed himself," Argas said.

Beric looked quickly at Manasses, and Manasses said, curiously sad, "Me and Josias, we're separated now for the first time in our lives. You see, Beric, the masters hurt him so much early on when he was a boy, that they broke his spirit. And I wasn't there to help him past this time."

It was beyond anything Beric could say. He couldn't even look at Manasses. He stumbled on. "Dapyx?"

"Don't know," Argas said, his mouth contracting as one of the burns began to throb again.

But Euphemia had come up to them and had sat down by Lalage. "I'm afraid I do know," she said. "Dapyx is dead. And—well, he didn't die right, not as one of us. They just killed him the way you'd kill vermin."

"The way us slaves always have been killed," Argas said. "Oh, Beric, why couldn't you have talked to him? You might have got him back to us."

"Rhodon?" Beric asked in a low voice.

"They took him off to be questioned last night, with us, and none of us have seen him since," Lalage said.

It gave Beric new pain in his body and legs to hear her hurt whisper. "So that's what I've done," he said.

None of them answered. He had to face it. He said again, "I meant to help you. I thought I was only risking my own life. I've done just the opposite of what I intended."

Lalage sat forward a little, brushing the flies away from her eyes and the sticky edge of the bandage. "As if it mattered whether any one of us did or didn't do just what he intended!" she said. "Still thinking you're God, Beric? Still thinking you're so very important? Forget you've been a master, Beric. Be meek."

"Is that what's wrong, Lalage—my pride? That's gone now. You can be proud, all right, all of you. You saw what the right way was, and then you stuck to it, whole. You just did the day-to-day ordinary things that are so terribly difficult until one does take it whole. You managed to live in this way of yours that's really a threat to the world as it's always been. And when the world saw you were a threat, you still went on. And you're here. And other people will go on because of you. Others like you. But—I had too terribly much education, and I thought I knew better than all of you."

"It wasn't exactly that," Lalage said. "Education's lovely—to read all the poets in the world! And if what we've got is sense, then learning more sense ought to help us to be better Christians. But maybe it was just because of its being a rich man's education, sort of teaching you that you could learn anything by yourself out of books without caring about other people, and saying your judgment that you'd made up in a nice, clean, quiet room was fit to deal with living and acting. That's what was wrong. Wasn't it, Beric?"

"Yes," he said, "it was like that, Lalage. I'm only just beginning to learn anything real. And it's too late."

"It's not too late for you, Beric. You can be part of it yet. We wouldn't baptize you before. We will now—you're ready."

"Am I?" he said. "Do you think so, Lalage? Oh, I can't be. I'm not fit to be one of you!"

"That's for us to say. Isn't it, Manasses?"

But Manasses was suddenly looking neither at her nor yet at Beric, but beyond—at the deputy governor of the prison, who was coming toward them, who was standing over them, whose presence jerked them all, somehow, onto their feet, expecting whatever would have to be forgiven next.

Euphemia had one supporting arm around Lalage, and Beric one around Argas, but awkwardly, because they were both chained.

Then the deputy governor snatched Beric away by the chains between his wrists and ankles and ordered him to follow.

Beric went stumbling after him, dumb and darkened with hate and trying to deal with the nasty stabs of physical fear coming from all the bits of his face and body that had been hurt. They were new on him, and he didn't like them at all.

And then it occurred to him that there was a connection between this hate and this fear, which might perhaps be broken by the only action he could take.

As he followed Aelius Candidus across the yard he began to put himself into the other man's place, to try to know what he was feeling. It must be misery all right with Flavia; that was bound to make you act like a devil, even if you weren't one already. Aelius Candidus certainly had it in him to be a devil.

Would he have been if things had been different? If he hadn't been brought up as a Roman nobleman, to power, to having absolute rights over the bodies and minds of other men and women? There was no law or justice to hold him back in his dealings with them, or so little as to make no odds, and nothing had happened to make him question that or admit any principle of general justice, as opposed to Roman citizens' law.

So then he gets hurt by Flavia, thought Beric, *and on top of being a bully and really lawless, he's angry and frightened, and so he wants to hurt me. But if I'm angry and frightened too, I'm no better than he is. So I'm not going to be. I'm not going to want to hurt him. I* don't *want to hurt him. He is hurting himself very thoroughly by being part of the Thing, which also includes Flavia and Tigellinus and which he can't escape except by changing his whole self. But I can think of Flavia now without being hurt. That all finished when she said those things to Tigellinus after they got me.*

He followed Aelius Candidus into his office and stood for some time while the deputy governor, carefully ignoring him, gave orders to a sergeant about the transfer of a large batch of prisoners to the Circus Maximus. There were huge dungeons there under the seats and among the foundations, suitable for the temporary reception of criminals. No, there would be no need to feed them while they were there; it would be a mere waste of public money. He dismissed the underling, sat back, and made a note on his tablets.

Then he looked at Beric and found that his prisoner was regarding him quite calmly, as though from across a dinner table.

As though he had never been beaten up. As one gentleman to another. Which left one to make the decision whether to treat him as such, having regard for his patron, Flavius Crispus, or whether it was too intolerable altogether that any prisoner should look at one like that, in which case measures must be taken to stop it. Aelius Candidus tapped on his teeth with the end of his pen. At last he decided, leaned forward, and said, "You realize, of course, that your execution is only a matter of days?"

"I know that," said Beric. He was not sure what this comparatively civilized, man-to-man tone meant.

"Your patron has asked to see you, but I fear that would be inadvisable. However, there are certain concessions which might be made. It might, for instance, be possible to allow you a citizen's death, in which case your body would be returned for burial."

Beric said nothing.

"A death without previous—unpleasantness, such as you have already experienced. That would be preferable, I think? We reserve our other forms of death, of which there are a great variety, for treasonable and disgusting offenses . . . such as Christianity. You have, of course, committed a private crime—for private reasons. We realize that."

Beric looked at him carefully, wondering what all this was about. It would be rather a bore, really, to have to make decisions and choices at this stage. He knew he was going to be killed; couldn't it just happen to him? Couldn't he at least say good-bye to his will?

"Yes," he said, "it was a private quarrel." But as he said that, he thought how much it had nothing at all to do with a very worthless individual called Flavia! When Tigellinus got in that first kick after they'd roped him, he had said to Flavia that he wished he'd killed *her* anyway. Now he was sorry he had said that; he didn't either love her or hate her.

"Quite so," Candidus said. After all, the Briton was behaving decently. It might even be possible to allow Flavius Crispus to see him in a day or two, when it would be less obvious what had been done to him.

Candidus slightly regretted last night's procedure. Not much, of course. In any case, Tigellinus would have been content with nothing less. There had been a time, not so long ago, when he had admired the prefect of the Praetorians quite immensely, liked being with him, feeling he was sharing in that toughness and power. Well, he didn't want to do any sharing now. One must get power for oneself. Not be involved in the fall of Tigellinus, when that happened—as it was pretty well bound to. Stand alone and not necessarily give away such knowledge as one had—knowledge about people, giving one power over them.

"Your patron," he said again, "must have been very much disturbed at finding all those Christians in his household. We shall have to get hold of this other boy, Phaon. He appears to have run away. However, I think there will be no difficulty in tracing him. The fact that he has bolted is in itself a proof of his guilt. Unfortunately, suspicions exist in certain quarters about your patron himself. Naturally, I am anxious to dispel them. Are you sure there is nothing you could tell me, as man to man, which would prove a help over this? You will be aware, from what I have already said, that certain concessions might be allowed. Or even further ones."

He was not, certainly, going to promise the Briton his life, but if the Briton thought he was . . . "The greatest service you could do for your patron," Candidus went on, "would be to indicate what other members of the household might be infected with this Christianity. So that the whole thing could be stamped out and all suspicions removed."

"I told you last night that I was not a Christian," Beric said. He was tired of all this.

"You have obviously had some connection with them," Candidus said but still in quite a reasonable voice. "After all, you have been seen with them. With this notorious woman Lalage. Of course, I am not classing you with them. Especially if you can help me to clear your patron's name." He paused invitingly.

And Beric suddenly felt that it was quite impossible for him to be in any kind of fellowship with this man, in the world of noblemen outside of which slaves were tortured. "Candidus," he said, "I was quite certainly not a Christian last night. But just as certainly I have become one since. And I am a Christian now."

The deputy governor stood up, and he was all at once looking just like he had looked in the night. But Beric was not afraid of him now, not even in the body.

The deputy governor took a step forward. "Very well," he said. "If that is the case, then back to the Christians you go. There will be no concessions. You will die with them—publicly—in the arena. Your body, such as is left of it, will not receive burial. I shall arrange for you to die in some manner which will be thoroughly amusing for the cheap seats."

He picked up a metal-studded glove that was lying on the table and hit Beric across the face. Then he shouted for the guards and had Beric marched out of his office. As they came out into the yard, he gave Beric a hard, angry kick, and Beric, not unnaturally, stumbled, lost his balance, threw up his arms but had them jerked down by the chains and fell over onto his face. One of the guards kicked him up.

People were watching from all over the yard, and especially Lalage, Manasses, Euphemia, and Argas. When he went down, Lalage began to pray hard and quietly.

Then Beric came over to them. His face and arm were both grazed and bleeding again. But it was apparent that he was not paying any attention to that.

Beric was with them again. He had not been fit for baptism; he had been deeply ashamed before them; he had failed; he had been one of the oppressors. Now he was no longer ashamed. He had said he was a Christian. He knew he was. Clearly he was in the Kingdom with them. Since he had said what he was, things had been done to him that should have made him wild with fury and frustration. They had not done so. He had been hurt, yes, but only on top of an excitement that blanketed that pain from penetrating to anywhere it could harm him.

"What happened to you in there, brother?" Lalage asked, with a kind of respect in her voice that was new to him.

"He wanted me to talk," Beric said. "He tried a clever new trick on me. But I said I had not been one of you yesterday; and I said I was one of you now. And I am!"

361

The four looked at one another and up at him, standing chained and sore and happy in front of them.

Then Euphemia got up and went over to the well and let down the bucket to draw some water. Here in the prison it could not be running water. It could not even be clean water. It had to be prison water. But it would do for baptism.

Paul said to her, "I see he is back. What does he say now? Will he accept his redemption?"

"I am drawing the water for his baptism, Paul," Euphemia said.

"Has he repented, then? Of everything?"

"He is one of us, Paul." She hauled the bucket up and now rested it for a moment on the edge of the well. It had strained her hurt arm a bit.

"Good," said Paul. "I knew he would come. I knew he would listen. I will baptize him."

"I'm not sure," said Euphemia, "and, or course, it's not for the likes of me to say, but I do somehow think, Paul, that he'd sooner it was us." She picked up the bucket and took it over, hobbling rather, and letting it down to the ground once or twice. She had been in longer than the others, and the bad food was telling on her, as well as everything else.

As she said that, the sudden darkening in Paul's mind that his immediate anger made, warned him not to answer. He stood looking down into the well, accepting the lesson in the spirit of the fellowship they were in together. Yes, he had been proud, and he had been rebuked. He had in him this terrible capacity for work and pride; they went with one another. He could see through people, he could see their weaknesses. He must guard against using his own power.

Yet were we not all means toward the one overwhelming end? Yes, but each must be so in his or her own way—one way for the Greek and another for the Jew. Not only Paul's way. Ah, if one way only were possible, then how easy for the shepherd. Then indeed no need for any shepherds; all could be in the one flock.

God did not allow any such easiness, putting us above the animals. So Paul of Tarsus, God's shepherd, must never rest, never until death. Nor must he complain when men, not being sheep, went tortuously or must be lured around barriers of prejudice and old wrongs and ideas out of a past world.

But now the pride and darkness had cleared out of his mind. He crossed the yard, on the way stopping to speak to two prisoners who were quarreling bitterly over a few sour-smelling beans, letting their poor, half-starved bodies get the better of them, until they were stopped and reminded of the great thing that they carried in them, the Christ.

Would there become, Paul asked himself, a tradition of suffering for Christians, before the end and the judgment and the establishment of the Kingdom? It was easier for men to act by help of a tradition, above all in suffering. Being one of a race that had suffered much, he understood that; although here was something beyond what any of the prophets had known. And the future?

He came to the others.

Manasses was on his feet now, but, seeing Paul, he hesitated. "Do you want to question him, Paul?" he asked.

Paul said to Beric, "Are you surely repenting of what you were?"

"Yes," said Beric. "I was one of the oppressors. But I am forgiven for that by God and by my friends." He knelt in front of Manasses.

And Argas and Lalage, being witnesses for him and having known his temptations and tests, knelt one on each side.

"I've got to do it with my left hand," Manasses said, "but I don't think it matters."

Euphemia held the bucket for him.

For a minute they all stayed quiet, waiting and aware, in the grip of the validity of what they were doing. Others had gathered around, forgetting their pain and hunger and lice, and they, too, were very quiet or whispered the word *Jesus*, the one word that did not break their love for one another but was part of it.

Then Manasses took water in the palm of his hand and spilled it, three times, over Beric's head. "Beric," he said, "with this water I baptize you into the Name of Jesus."

"And into the fellowship of Jesus," Lalage said.

Then Beric bent and kissed the feet of the man who had baptized him, who had been a slave in the same house where he had been a master, and as he did so a few drops of blood and water ran down his cheek and rested on Manasses' instep. But none of them noticed that.

He stood up again. It had not been magic nor childish. He was not suddenly changed. It was only a sign that marked a change that had been happening and that was now complete.

Lalage slowly got to her feet beside him, holding onto his arm. But at the other side Argas still knelt, half doubled up, head against the side of his knee.

Beric's hand reached down to his hair and neck and bruised shoulders, alive still and warm, an object of affection and respect and brotherhood, so soon and stupidly to be destroyed. And Beric smiled across at Paul of Tarsus, the older man, rather outside their group. Paul had been preaching the Kingdom all these years, founding churches in one place after another, away overseas; and whatever he might have said, these churches had made their own image of the Kingdom and all its implications, not out of cobwebs but out of the way men and women were acting by one another. And so it would go on living. Queer to think that Paul had organized all this, seen all those separate people, lighted all those flames, keeping a purpose in front of him through all the long, tedious years of middle age, the years none of the rest of them were going to have.

Beric said to his friends, "The deputy governor says I am to die with you. And probably today. I shall be a witness too. I shall be some use."

"I wonder how long they'll go on killing us," Manasses said.

"Until they see they can't win," Lalage said. "But then they'll try and stop us some other way. They'll try and change us back into ordinary people, under their rule, obeying and worshiping them. When they find they can't do it by frightening us, they'll try something else. I hope we'll always be strong. As strong as we five are now." She crossed herself.

Manasses said, "Perhaps they'll try and tempt them that are in our place, so to speak, by offering them money or power. Trying to make the churches into part of their rule, perhaps. Do you think that would be possible, Lalage?"

"I hope not. It would be so terribly difficult to resist that. If they're offered all the kingdoms of the earth in return for giving up our Kingdom. Or changing it. Oh, Manasses, we're lucky to be now, when the temptations are so easy to see and resist, when we need only be brave and steadfast for a little time. And that's a thing that any slave can be, or any poor girl who can't read or write."

"Those'll be the ones that'll go on remembering us, Lalage," Euphemia said.

Argas said, "It'll be hard for all them that are coming after us. They'll need more strength than us really. They'll need to learn to be cunning, to see around everything. But maybe there'll be others in it then. Not just us slaves, but free men and women who've had a proper education so they can understand and not let themselves be tempted. Folks like you, Beric. Would you rather be then?"

"No," said Beric, "I'd rather be now. With all of you. But we *shall* need courage. We're sure of ourselves, brothers and sisters, aren't we?"

"I think so," Euphemia said. "You see, dear, if those gladiators could die well—I used to look on, you know, in old days, when my patron took me—then it stands to reason we can. And just think of all the people we'll be witness to! Hundreds and thousands, I dare say. It isn't like being beaten up all alone."

"Most of them are going to laugh and yell at us, Euphemia, and throw things too," Beric said, remembering what Candidus had been saying.

"There'll be some that won't," Euphemia said.

"What's more," Lalage said, "there'll be some of the ones that do who'll go home and later on, in the night it might be, they'll wake up and remember us. And they'll wish they hadn't laughed and made our deaths harder. They'll feel bad about that. They'll feel, well, maybe they ought to do something about it.

"You see, we'll have looked at them with love, Beric, because they're our brothers and sisters, though they're separate from us now because they haven't understood yet. They're going to understand, though. Through Jesus and us. But we won't know which they are, not yet. They won't look different; they won't know themselves that they've been chosen, not till later."

"There'll be plenty that we can't move," Argas said. "The ones who want all this to happen."

"Yes, there's some that no one could change, not even Jesus. Like He couldn't change all those men who were running things in Jerusalem in His time. They'd refuse the Kingdom even if they were shown it; they're turned the other way on purpose. They don't see the point of faith and love and freedom and justice.

"But there's more of the others, the ones who may see the Kingdom yet. And we'll be loving them. We'll look at them so they'll remember it always, won't we, Euphemia?—and it'll give a bit of a twist to their minds, so that the world won't ever be quite the same for them. They'll begin to look new ways and feel about for something they can't exactly lay a name to. And then, under God, they'll begin to get to know the Kingdom."

Argas said, "If Crispus is there, I'll try to look at him—that way."

"Yes," said Beric. "He'll be there. I hadn't thought of that." He rubbed his hand across his face. His eyes were suddenly stabbing him again.

Manasses was watching him. "Why do you mind, Beric?"

"We were there together so often. I was watching the races with him . . . yesterday, I suppose it was! We were enjoying them, in spite of everything. He kept on turning around, talking to me. And now he'll be watching, and I'll be down on the sand, and I won't even be able to tell him to look away. He'll be up there alone, with the ghost of me sitting beside him, in the best seats. And between me and my ghost there'll be just a few yards of sand and a wooden barrier that the lions can't jump over. But that'll be enough."

"Are you afraid of the lions, Beric?" Manasses asked.

"One likes to die at one's own moment, not at a beast's."

Manasses shook his head. "We've never had time of our own, we slaves, have we, Argas? It's been all a master's time. And might be a beast's that way, as like as not. You haven't been used to being wasted by someone else, nor to being hurt, the way poor folks and slaves are. It's something with us, pain is, day to day, so we need to get able to bear it. You haven't ever been used to being handed about at someone else's will and pleasure. It's hard for you, son."

"Not really," Beric said. "I'm glad I'm in this. It's the only thing that matters that's happening in the world. I'm glad I found it in time. I'm glad you took me. I'm glad God took me"

Euphemia looked up and asked suddenly, "Your father really was a king, wasn't he, dear?"

"He was a king all right, Euphemia," Beric said, "and made people fight for him and get themselves killed." And then he added, "And my brother was coming to Rome for the games! I'd forgotten. He may be there too."

"You will be bearing witness to many, brother," Lalage said. She was sitting on the bench again, her back to the wall. If only one could go to sleep in the sun and not wake up for a long time, stop being a hurt piece of flesh, gather one's strength. "Jesus," she whispered, "Jesus."

She fixed her mind on that woodworker who had taught the poor how to live and die, who had also taught such of the rich as would take His teachings. Beric. The pain stood away from her a little as she thought of how he had come to them at last and in time.

But he was saying, "I remember now Clinog telling me that most of our people, the British fighting men who'd been taken prisoner during that war of my father's, were made to fight one another in the arena. I hadn't thought of it from that day to this. I was only a boy; I didn't know what it meant. Clinog must have known, because he was so angry. I suppose our people were too tough to be slaves. It was a way of getting rid of them."

"I bet they fought well—your people, Beric," Argas said.

"But they were got rid of," Beric said, "so that even I, who was their king's son, had forgotten them. But we shan't be. No one's going to be able to get rid of the Kingdom."

Now it became apparent that something was happening in the yard. Here and there came a thud and a scream and raised voices. A rather fat woman, running stumbling in terror, her hands clutched over her breasts, cannoned into Euphemia. "They've come!" she cried. "To take us to the beasts! Oh, I can't!" And she bolted through into the darkness of the cells, to escape for another three or four days, perhaps.

Manasses saw a sergeant pointing to their group, and the guards coming with their hide whips ready. He stood up with his church around him. "It's time," he said. "Come, children. We are set to die now."

Beric helped Argas to his feet. They were in every way equals at this time, and all the way to the arena, in the streets—with the cabbage stalks and pieces of tile being thrown at them—Beric would have his arm around Argas, as far as the chains would allow, helping him to walk.

As they were being marched through the prison, Paul was standing there, blessing them all, his face tense. When he saw the worst need, he would walk by someone or some group, urging them to courage and faith and above all remembrance of their love for one another, pulling it up into their minds past the terror and pain. They had known all along in the love feasts and the crossing of the threshold that happened there, how this put them forever beyond death! And the hungry, frightened eyes were on him the whole time, and the hands clutching and slipping, and the souls slipping and rocking too, that had to be brought to the pitch of crucifixion. And he must, oh, by giving all the strength that was in him, he must succeed in getting across to these men and women, his brothers and sisters, what would keep their hearts and heads high for those last hours that faced them. And after that it was in God's hands. But when any passed him who looked as Manasses and Lalage and their church looked, then he got strength himself to help the weak. Then he knew that the Kingdom was present and actual.

Gallio walked by Beric for a minute, the guard respectfully not hurrying him. "Good-bye, Beric," he said. "I'll tell Crispus."

"Thank him from me," Beric said. "He'll know for what."

"Am I to tell him," Gallio asked, "boy, am I to tell him you chose to die this way?"

"Of my own free will," Beric said. "I might have had things otherwise. This was the best way. I and my friends—we die because we choose!"

At the gate Gallio dropped back, heard the yell of hate and derision in the road, and saw some of the prisoners duck their heads, saw the guards lifting their whips, then the crack and cry as the lash came down. He went back to his cell.

The young Christian slave was there; he hadn't been taken yet. They eyed one another. At last the slave said, "What did you think of it, sir?"

"Always a fine sight when men and women die well—for anything," Gallio said. He took down a book roll at random and opened it. The letters blurred in front of him, and he blinked and wiped his eyes. It would not be at all amusing to tell Crispus. "Almost makes one think there might be something in it, after all," he grunted at the slave, not looking at him, and began to read. After a time he noticed that he didn't even know what the book was.

22

The Seed of the Church

By afternoon the Circus Maximus was practically full. Most of the cheap seats had come in the morning, half of them bringing their lunch along with them, so as to miss nothing and above all not risk losing their places. You didn't see details so well, naturally, not if you were one of the ordinary common people in the upper blocks, but on the other hand you did see clear over the division down the center, the long, low, broad walls you knew so well, with the bronze dolphins spouting on it and the bronze basins always lipping over, and the great eggs they hoisted, one more up to seven for each lap of a chariot race till the screaming final, and the gilt bronze statues—only nobody cared who they were meant to be now—and the sixty-foot red stone obelisk jabbing up between the feathery spoutings of the dolphins, and the shrine of Castor and Pollux with the bunches of spiked boxing gloves hanging up in it, and the other shrine of Venus, who was Mother of Rome.

You'd have woke up that morning thinking it's the games again, and you might have been dreaming about them, hot, tangled kinds of dreams, mostly. And the dream would go on getting at you while you combed your hair and cut your lump of bread that was to have a bit of dried fish or ham for a relish, unless it was a free-lunch day with drinks on the emperor, and the dream would go on as you walked there through the early morning with a snap of September chill in it already. But it would warm up, and you'd hurry rather quietly, tasting the dream still.

You'd get near and begin to hear the noises, the crashing, the sudden shrill, the quickening noises of men and animals. And you'd elbow in, stamping on toes and swearing, to read the notices, red and black lettering of a whole new day of the games for you citizens: Out of the pairs of the first act of gladiators, fifty percent kills guaranteed, no fumbling or cheating; river scene with Leda and troupe of trained swans; female prisoners thrown in snakepit; blacks hunt ostriches, tigers hunt blacks; attack on castle, flame throwers in galloping chariots; whole Circus filled with dancers, nude dancers, armored dancers, feathered dancers, eighty nude dancers raffled among audience; display of jumping lucky piebald horses with flags; simultaneous net-and-trident or sword-and-club fights; genuine Alexandrian brothels, living Sphinx and crocodiles; the great cleanup, Christians eaten by bears, lions, hyenas, and wolves, the emperor lending animals from his private menagerie; Greek torch race; acrobats and elephants; illumined tightrope walk across the Circus; grand firework finale.

Well then, the next thing was getting to your seat, pushing your way through and a difficult job that was, and you'd need to look out for your money too! And sometimes you'd get barged into by one of the noblemen with his heavyweights all around him and his scented hanky up to his little nose, in case he caught a whiff of Genuine Old Rome, that being you. And sometimes there'd be a tart sidling along after you, with a clever soft touch and a "Meet me tonight when you've won your bet, big boy." Drink shops and fortune-tellers and quack doctors and massage establishments, and women and boys in all of them, because when you come out after a day of it, or in the middle for that matter, well, you know what you want.

But it takes you maybe an hour to get in, for there's thousands and thousands of you—two hundred thousand, they say the place holds—and that's more than any other place in the whole world or that's likely to be in the world again, either! But all the time you're edging along, there's shouting and singing, and, of course, there's plenty to laugh at, on the outside of the big crowd, acrobats and dancers and performing dogs and one-legged hoppers and fat women, or someone gets up a fight between a blind beggar and another with no hands, and you chuck the pennies into the ring. And you hear the beasts that have been kept hungry for today, roaring and howling and angry, all to give you a good show, and you know what they'll get for their dinners!

And in the end you come to your entrance and up the stairs and scramble for the seats, with your wife screeching and pushing after you—if you've brought her, that is—and then you can settle down nicely for a day of it. And in no time you hear the big trumpets and the drums and bells, and in comes the procession from under the arches at the east end of the Circus, like you've been waiting for, with horses and elephants and gladiators all set to fight to the death, and flower girls in flimsies, and blacks carrying trays full of monkeys, and a lot of little kiddies with no more on than cupids, firing off gilt arrows, and a lashing great tiger in a gold cage or what looks like gold, and dogs with frills on their necks, and more gladiators and girls on stilts and a painted dragon with ten men inside him spouting fire, and Indian snake charmers and young boys leading gazelles with silver collars, and the six-foot boxers showing off their great chests and arms.

And now they all line up, and there's the emperor and empress in their box, bless them, and everyone stands and yells, and today's games are going to begin!

Of course, the gods are called on first, as is only right. The gods and the emperor and us. And the procession goes snaking out again, all but the gladiators.

And then. The smell you'd been dreaming of, that's never gone quite out of your head, and the sudden bright splash on the sand, and all a man's got inside him emptied out all at once. And you gasp and tighten and feel it creeping and tingling in your stomach and loins. And already the day's getting hotter, and between turns the awnings are shifted about to let in the air and keep out the sun for you.

In the great top blocks are thousands who don't get the detail at all, though they do get the whole of a spectacle, better perhaps than the respectable in the middle tiers and the aristocracy, a bit less crowded, unless they choose to crowd themselves with cushions and slaves and mistresses. Most of them would have left home with enough slaves to push a way through the mob for them, but these would be dismissed to wait outside till the end of the show.

Balbus, for instance, had only one of his young secretaries, and Lucan was by himself except for another poet. He did not approve of bringing his wife to such places. Balbus was expecting his friend Crispus with some anxiety. If, as he could not help su-

372

specting, Crispus himself *was* in some way involved with these Christians, then it was important that Crispus should be seen at the games.

Much of it, of course, was tedious, yet it was a fine bracing sight to observe the contempt for death among the fighting pairs. Even though they were only common gladiators, they could teach you something, yes, by Jupiter, they could!

He had seen Crispus early that morning. Crispus had been very much upset about that poor lad, too much upset for a good Stoic. It was as though Beric had actually been his son. Well, well, it wouldn't be the first judicial murder, the first blood crying for blood again. Calpurnius Piso was no doubt at the games too. The Briton would probably be beheaded . . . unless he was mixed up with these Christians. Very awkward. And if on top of that Crispus didn't turn up . . . Above all it was necessary to avoid a scandal, for Candidus's sake. Why couldn't he manage that girl better!

Balbus had got those two slaves that Crispus had sent over safe out of sight, bolted into one of the cellars with the wine casks pushed back in front of the door. A pretty pair—wonder what they'd do in there in the dark!

Before the next act, while the Circus hands, dressed as Greek sailors and reapers, prepared the river scene, letting in the water from the tanks, Balbus went around to see some of his friends, and especially Flavius Scaevinus. To do that, he must pass behind the imperial box, in the space kept sufficiently clear for the police agents to notice anyone or anything.

Erasixenos was talking to one of them. He was absurdly over-dressed, with a collection of rings—oh, well, that was the kind of queer thing you found at the Roman games nowadays! He hadn't seen him since the supper party when the betrothal was announced . . . and then they had consulted the astrologers . . . why had the stars foretold nothing but good omens?

He nodded briefly to Erasixenos and went on. He hoped Crispus would have shown up by the time he got back to his seat. Not that either of them would want to see the Leda performance—couldn't be bothered with that kind of nonsense these days.

From the upper seats, on the other hand, the Leda scene was marvelous. Some of the swans were real birds, and some were dancers, but they all made the same rush. What a long, sharp quivery scream Leda did give—you heard it from one end to the other—just like a girl surprised naked would have.

Tertius Satellius squeezed his wife ever so hard while that was going on. She was all right now—didn't do to take notice of her moods. There'd be the snakes next. You didn't see that so well, but they'd do it while the river scene was being cleared and the hunt scene put on.

Clinog was sitting beside the friend with whom he had come, Sextus Papinius Calvinus. Owing to the fact that he had been kept at the Municipal Offices to finish putting through an important contract, Clinog had missed the first day of the games, and he had not even had time to call on Flavius Crispus. He wondered whether perhaps his brother was somewhere in the audience. It would be fine to see young Beric again.

He noticed that today's program would include some executions of Christians. Well, that would be a warning to his brother—though he could not think that there was anything in the story that Beric might have had something to do with the sect. Not if they were the criminals you heard they were, and indeed there was no doubting it on the evidence.

In the meantime, Clinog was exceedingly impressed by the whole thing. If you could give all this to two hundred thousand people, well, that meant, surely, that you could do what you liked with most of those thousands. They'd go on wanting more and more, and they wouldn't, so to speak, notice what was happening to the rest of their lives. You could take anything away from them except the games. The Romans were the first people in the world who had thought of that way of ruling. He would remember.

Candidus and Flavia had excellent seats quite close to the imperial box, and Flavia was, as usual, the center of an animated conversation. Just at the moment, she didn't care ever to stop talking or laughing or giving witty answers to compliments. If one stopped—but everyone said she was in splendid form. One of her best friends had whispered that the emperor had been asking who she was!

Candidus, also, was being particularly amiable and as complimentary as though she'd been someone else's wife. But that made her feel the tiniest bit uneasy. It wasn't the way for him to behave unless—well, unless he had some kind of nasty surprise for her. But anyway, even if he had, it wouldn't be till after the games! She was certainly going to enjoy herself till then. She adored these hunting scenes. There was so much movement and life, you couldn't be bored for a moment. There wasn't time for any of these thoughts you would rather not have sneaking into your mind. About last night. No!

One of the ostrich hunters, with his scarlet loincloth and anklets and little knife, had made his kill just below her seat. You could hear him panting after the run, a glorious, glossy black, muscles standing out like a racehorse's.

"Positively," said Flavia, "a man in good condition is the finest animal of all!" And she threw him down a rose. Several of her friends followed with pink and white flowers pattering onto the ostrich killer's ultramarine-shadowed shoulders.

He looked up, gesturing and grinning. The ladies all waved back, giggling. Caelia Pulchra in the front row actually tossed him over a bracelet, which set the man prancing with delight and shouting his gibberish at them.

Did he understand that the tigers were to be let in now? Apparently not, because when he turned and saw a great orange cat close on him, he screamed and ran, the flowers hopping off him. But the tiger in two utterly breathtaking bounds had got him down, you could see him wriggle and flap for a minute; and that was the end of the black ostrich hunter.

Caelia Pulchra threw herself back simply bathed in sweat. Her maid had to fan her for ten minutes. There was nothing like the games!

While the tigers were finishing their meals, rasping and purring and twitching their strong tails, the scenery of the castle was being rolled into position. The tigers were perfectly harmless now, so long as you didn't disturb them, and when they had finished they could easily be driven or lured back into their cages.

Even if one of them turned nasty there was a hundred-percent-efficient barrier with a smooth ivory rail at the top, beautifully pivoted so that it merely rolled over if a leaping animal so much as got a paw onto it—or a man trying to escape for that matter.

There used to be a ditch, but one of Nero's new architects had devised this method, at the same time extending the seating capacity of the Circus. It might have been designed by a Greek, but it was the kind of invention that Romans appreciated!

Tigellinus was reporting to the Master of the World. His police agents had been around during the last hour. It was all most satisfactory. The Divine Emperor was thought to have excelled himself. Last night's show in the Imperial Gardens had undoubtedly caught the imagination of the populace. The important thing now was to see that everything was carried out to its logical conclusion. There must be no protection of Christians. Not even in high places . . . supposing that by any chance evidence were found. It was probable that the Divine Emperor knew in what direction the prefect of the Praetorians was hinting, but he had leaned forward to give the signal and pretended not to hear. Through a blast of trumpets the attackers came galloping on, wheeling all around the castle. There was too much noise, from Circus and audience both, for Tigellinus to get the attention he needed. He had not really been certain how his imperial master had taken the news of the latest attempt on his life—the Christian murder plot. Nero had seemed amused and had merely asked for details about the lady.

The attack on the castle having successfully culminated in real flames, real burns, real pain, and real death, it was time for lunch. As soon as the debris had been cleared away, the dancers came on, in groups and lines and singly, or displayed on slowly moving platforms. Dancing was more conducive to digestion than sudden death. Perfume sprayers dashed about in all directions; the smoke from the castle had a way of lingering unpleasantly, tainted now also with the roast-meat smell. Sweet sellers were busy too.

During the lunch interval, the emperor would be approachable and affable to his people, would read petitions and remedy injustices. Amidst thunders of applause, an old blind woman, defrauded by her stepson, had her little home given back to her, as well as a dozen gold pieces from the imperial purse, charmingly presented by the empress in person. And the wicked stepson was chased across the Circus by the fine fellow with the cat o' nine tails, who set him dancing with a flick on the buttocks now and again.

But most of the better seats had retired for a peaceable luncheon at home. Very few of the dancers were quite up to standard from nearby—the makeup was crude and the nudity distinctly flyblown. They had no desire at all to take part in the raffle, when tickets were showered all over the upper blocks from catapultish mechanisms, and someone was quite sure to get hurt in the scramble.

Balbus was particularly anxious to find Crispus and bring him along to the Circus if possible. He decided to walk over to his house, across the Forum. A walk was just what he needed.

Felicio, following at a discreet secretarial distance, nodded, also discreetly, to a new acquaintance, one he had made at the wedding at Crispus's house, the Epicurean freedman Nausiphanes, who had been Beric's tutor.

Nausiphanes was standing outside the Circus, getting into conversation with people, not, however, in the way you would have imagined, as a pimp, but in order to spread certain doctrines directed against the State. Being middle-aged, Nausiphanes did this with care, knowing when to laugh and when to be very serious and decisive.

Felicio followed his master away from the noises of the Circus, the continuous varied rustle and jar and babble of human voices, and the echoing, long, chromatic roaring of the hungry beasts.

But Nausiphanes stayed. The lunch interval was always a fruitful time. Out of two hundred thousand, an uncertain percentage had been disgusted or bored or were in some way prepared to see through this particular activity of the State. Some, again, might be interested in popular science—the mechanics of the Circus enabled one to start a conversation of this kind. And science, interpreted, left very little of any of the gods, including the Divine Thing, which was, strictly speaking, being worshiped in there to the accompaniment of torture and death, at the September games, the Ludi Romani.

Nausiphanes saw the Christians who were to feature in the next part of the program being marched across to the cells under the tiers of seats. The man he had been engaging in conversation turned and ran over to look at them. So did most of the crowd. A good many picked up things to throw.

Nausiphanes followed, a little depressed. He suddenly wished he were back in Greece, where people were cruel on an impulse or by accident but not in this heavy, unanimous, Roman way. But perhaps Greece was just as bad now. He didn't know; it was a long time since he had been there.

He really knew very little about the Christian superstition. Obviously most of what he had heard was nonsense—all these orgies and murders. But probably they were hysterical and irrationally worshiped some kind of god, believing blindly without proof, as all worshipers do, and sooner or later the god would become a symbol of power and exploitation, as all gods do. Yet at the same time they were being persecuted because they were against the Roman State.

No Roman ever really bothered about a difference of gods. In religious matters they were profoundly tolerant because their own gods were not of the individual heart but only social inventions— or had become so. Yet politically they did and must persecute and equally must be attacked by all who had the courage.

He hoped these Christians had courage, in spite of the irrationality of their minds. Standing still and quiet among the yellers and throwers, Nausiphanes watched the faces for courage. And saw Manasses. And saw Beric.

Somebody threw a piece of jagged tile, and Beric jerked up his arm as far as the chains would let him to protect his companion, whom Nausiphanes, pushing through, recognized as another of the dining-room boys. The prisoners were halted outside the Circus while official notes were interchanged.

Beric was licking the new cut on his arm that the tile had made, just as he had done when he was a little boy out with his tutor and had tumbled over a stone. He was not looking beyond his group at the outside world.

Nausiphanes had to call his name twice. "Beric! Beric! Are you really one of them?"

Beric looked at Nausiphanes for a moment as though he did not recognize him, then nodded and spoke evenly, as though, in some way, he had expected to be asked. "Yes," he said, "and now I can prove it."

It sounded as though he had courage all right, the courage that you needed to stand against Rome, yet Nausiphanes had to make sure, had to twist and bruise his heart into asking and watching. For a moment he couldn't think how to ask. He had been fond of the boy and then, after his years of tutoring were over, had rather forgotten him, had been dealing with other, quicker brains. But none with more courage. He had taught him riding too. He asked in a whisper at last, "Ready for the fence, Beric? And all of you?"

"That's easy!" said Beric, and he tossed his head the old way, and Nausiphanes saw how bruised he was. "I should have made mistakes if I'd been living for it. I've only got to die for it now, and nothing's going to stop me doing that. Don't look so down about it, Nausiphanes. I'm not. You wouldn't be if you were one of us."

"To save you when you were a child, Beric, and now—to do this to you. Oh, that's Rome."

"But it's this that'll smash Rome in the end. You'll see. Nausiphanes, we're winning just because everyone wants the Kingdom really, at the bottom of their hearts. It's bound to come. Even the emperor's bound to want what we want. And we'll show him!"

Now the bars were pulled back, and the Christians were being shoved through into the dark. Beric and Argas were jerked forward, with only a look back at Nausiphanes. Some of them ahead were singing. A very few were crying.

Euphemia turned to the guard next her and said, "Good-bye, brother. I saw you stop them poking sticks at me. I do thank you ever so much, I'm sure."

"Get on there!" said the guard. A poor brother he was being to them! Oh, you'd *got* to do it. But this silly lot of women—what *were* the Christians, anyhow?

"Come in and watch us die," said Lalage, looking at him as though she knew what he was thinking. "We aren't crazy; we've got something to die for. And thank you, brother."

And all along the line, here and there, some man or woman would be saying that, and after the last Christians were in and the bars up and the guards standing easy while the sergeant was getting his note countersigned, Nausiphanes said to the one who had been next to Beric, "I knew that lad, guard. What did you think of them?"

The man looked around. "Peculiar. That's what they are. Going like that to the beasts. 'Tisn't natural!"

Another guard said heavily, "It made me feel quite bad. Getting thanked. I can't see what they done to deserve *that*."

The noise of the beasts, the yapping and roaring and howling, was very unpleasant from where they were.

"Hope the poor victims in there don't hear it," the guard said and suddenly turned in sharp anger on Nausiphanes. "Here, clear out, you! Nosing around—you one of them, hey?"

But Nausiphanes, expert by now at dodging and disappearing into a crowd, was gone. And this—this was being effective in shaking the primary roots of men's being. Once these are shaken, the reasonable mind, which is fed by such roots, can itself be approached. And this Kingdom of theirs seemed, Nausiphanes thought, the same as the Epicurean Garden, the place of love and equality and trust. So that was all right. But for Beric—his Beric . . . There were things you couldn't quite believe. Not at first. No doubt, since they were facts, you would come to believe them later.

The jumping horses, again, were a spectacle for the upper seats, pretty enough when you saw them all together but not so exciting.

However, most of the audience were back for the net-and-trident fights. These were highly skilled and had the necessary element of the exotic. The net-and-trident man had to fight a swordsman with armor and a far better weapon, who could only be overcome when netted. Then the comparatively useless, clumsy trident could be plunged into an unarmored throat. If the net cast short, its bearer must run, gathering it behind him, pursued by the swordsman, dodging among other couples, unlikely to escape.

The eyes of the spectators were constantly busy. Many of the combatants were old friends, known by nicknames to thousands, shouted at and encouraged, or booed if they were thought to flinch. An old favorite had more chance if downed. Several were spared this time for future amusement.

Balbus had persuaded Crispus to come. Indeed, it was necessary, in view of the position, but Crispus was in no mood for it. He had got no satisfaction from the prison, only promises. He did not know if there would really be a chance of his interceding for Beric. Perhaps if he went straight to the emperor . . .

It was just possible. If he did that, and if by any chance he had some kind of success, then he must be out of the Piso conspiracy. It would be worth it. If he could save Beric, he would never touch politics again.

So far he had not even got all his slaves back. Mikkos and Sannio were still held on some excuse. However, Hermeias was with him again. The poor man had been somewhat shaken but after a rest in the morning had insisted on accompanying his master in the afternoon. He and Balbus's Felicio sat on the floor behind their masters' seats, getting a look around from time to time and noting bets. Balbus was insisting on Crispus betting with him; it would take his mind off anything else.

The big brothel scene was arranged on a series of raised stages, so that there should be an uninterrupted view from all parts of the Circus. Tigellinus was chaffing the Alexandrian Erasixenos about the habits of his hometown.

The main scene with the most interesting special effects was set in front of the imperial box. Nero was amused. Constant fanning and scent spraying and sprinkling of lily garlands had kept the box and its immediate neighborhood in a highly civilized though somewhat unreal condition.

But as the hot air, laden with other than floral scents, lifted hourly toward the top blocks of close and sweating thousands, the dream that they had come with and which was the reality of the Circus had become more and more charged, breaking down all common barriers, so that men, and women as well, abruptly emitted spoken desires towards actions of an extreme and final kind on human bodies opened and wriggling and twitching, either in perhaps assumed pleasure or in certainly genuine terror and pain and death. Curious hootings of appreciation or impatience came down in waves from above. Nor did the more aristocratic seats always disdain to be carried away with the rest into the unanimity of the wolves that were the symbols of Rome.

It was into this blood dream that about sixty Christians were driven out of the dark cells to be torn to pieces and eaten by a considerably larger number of carnivorous animals. They were marched around in groups, and each group was preceded by a large written board saying: Christian Murderers; We Set Fire to Rome; Christian Baby-stealers; Christian Traitors; We Rape Priestesses; We Abuse the Home; Christian Poisoners; and so on. There had been some trouble about these notices. The original idea had been that they should be carried in by members of each group, but it was found quite impossible to coerce them into doing so. That was the worst of dealing with people who knew they were going to be killed anyhow.

As it was, they shouted out that the notices were all lies and called their own slogans instead. This did not matter very much, though, because everyone yelled and pelted them if they could, and what the Christians were saying could only be heard in the best seats, whose occupants, in any case, probably knew that these notices were not intended to be the exact truth.

Naturally the best seats had the best views again. Faces were quite distinct. There were those among the better-class spectators who had to say to themselves firmly that these people were a danger to the State, to all that must be held sacred, that it was an unfortunate necessity, and anyhow, most of them were only slaves and foreigners and one had better not think too much about it.

Flavia, close to the front, suddenly in the middle of a group had seen and been seen by. And as she looked away again, as she must, *must,* look away, lips tight against gums, fingers tight against breasts, all there was for discomfort was only Candidus revenging himself in a long stare. No mother, no father even and what would Father think? Must pick oneself up, laugh, however that was done, the little noise in her throat. Ha-ha, yes, they had passed, everyone else was laughing, and Flavia was so afraid because she was not being able to laugh properly with the others, and Candidus was leaning cruelly toward her, and the king's son was going to die, and she wouldn't be able to help seeing that, and in a moment Father would know.

Lucan recognized the noble savage, about whom he had once nearly written a poem, and was taken very much aback. He then recognized a little dancer whom he had seen several times. Yes, it must be the same, though she looked distinctly battered. This new infection of life appeared to be everywhere!

Flavius Scaevinus recognized Crispus's Briton and also, since he had dined at the house less than twenty-four hours before, one of the slaves who had been waiting on him. He half rose in his seat and then decided, no, all the more reason to maintain a Roman and Stoic calm—to be oneself utterly unsuspected of dangerous thoughts.

Crispus, having been to some extent distracted by the gladiators and having sat through the next act with some impatience, had decided to leave. He knew it was possible that he might see one of his own slaves among the condemned. Though very unlikely, of course. Besides—but Balbus had pressed him to stay. And even to his oldest friend, he could not exactly say why he had so very much rather be away. Intolerable to find oneself in a position where one must lie to this extent!

When the poor wretches were marched in, he decided not to look. And suddenly Balbus, who had been chaffing him in a friendly way, became exceedingly intent that he should continue not looking. Nor would he have, but for Hermeias behind him, who saw Manasses first of all and completely lost his head and pointed. "Oh, sir, there!" And then realized that he was also pointing at Beric.

"Cover your face!" whispered Balbus urgently, leaning across, one arm around Crispus, the other pulling at a loose fold of his toga. "Keep still. Felicio, *hold him!* No, no, my dear friend, I understand, but don't—remember where we are! Crispus, don't look, you can do nothing, none of us can, it will be over—gods, he's seen you!"

And what would Crispus do then? How could Balbus save his old friend from some completely disastrous action?

It was Beric who did that, waving and smiling. You couldn't hear what he said, only saw the head up and the smile.

"My," said Balbus, "the boy's brave!"

And Crispus, having seen that too, allowed the slaves to pull him down, allowed his friend to cover his eyes and ears. The louder sound of the beasts, as the gates of the cages were opened, came to him dulled as part of darkness and nightmare.

Yet it was very certain that he would ask afterwards how it had been. So Balbus, who would now also much rather not have watched, yet, being a friend and a Stoic, did watch for him.

Felicio, his hands on the old man's arms, watched too. *Oh, I would have liked to see him again. We might have had fun with one another. And now the fool goes and gets himself killed. That night. And it never went on. I'd hoped it would. Oh, I liked him. Oh, he is brave standing there. All of them. The women too. Supposing they've got hold of the right end of the stick after all? If none of them scream, that's what they've done. And that's a bet. Right. I'm taking that on. Now. When the wolves . . . They're saying things—to us. You can't hear over the din. Oh, I love him. If he doesn't scream. Now. He did not scream. He shouted. Not to me. None of them screamed. I have lost my bet—or very possibly won it. That remains to be seen.*

Clinog had been enjoying himself thoroughly. There hadn't been a dull moment. How they'd laughed and shouted, he and Calvinus. Did you good, that. And now they were going to see these famous beasts, including the lions from the emperor's menagerie. Well, it was a fine way of discouraging criminals. There would not be many Christians left in Rome after this, no!

Now the criminals were being marched in. There were a great many women among them. Well, it might be Calvinus was right, women could certainly be as dangerous as men, and indeed more so because of witchcraft, although these ones were not his idea of witches. Now they were being tied up in groups all around the Circus so that there should be a good view for everyone. It was a pity they were not actually to fight the beasts. There was always more sport in a fight.

"But most of these wretches wouldn't put up a show," Calvinus said. "They don't even come from the country. They're a bloodless, gutless lot out of the gutters of the big cities. Bred there like sewer rats. Just a product of overcrowding, this Christianity."

"All the same," said Clinog regretfully, "there are a few who look to my eye as if they could be made to fight."

"What, that fair one down on the left? Looks a bit like one of your countrymen, Clinog, what!"

"Indeed, he might be. Calvinus, he looks—"

"What on earth is it? What's taken you? Sit down, man! Here come the lions. You're getting in everyone's light."

But Clinog was shouting at the top of his voice, shouting—fortunately, no doubt—incomprehensible words in a foreign language. And down on the sand, the fair, tall one had shouted back. As the wolf leaped. And Calvinus and several others had got hold of Clinog and were pulling him down, and he was throwing them off, fighting, as the men on the sand were not fighting. Had to be tied, kicked, trampled on before he was quiet. And by that time the act was practically over.

One of the police agents came up and whispered to Papinius Calvinus, but the latter, being a provincial citizen, without the proper feelings of respect that a pure Roman would have had, bluntly told the agent to get out of there.

There had also been a disturbance in one of the upper blocks some way farther along. A young woman had recognized someone she knew down there. No, she hadn't screamed, but she had begun in a loud voice explaining just how good the woman had been to her and how these Christians were really kind and decent and truthful and honest and all the things you had been told they weren't. Her husband had managed to shut her up at last, but he seemed a bit uncomfortable himself, and what the girl had said sounded true somehow. And if all those Christians weren't the set of wicked murderers they were made out to be—well, then it was like you murdering *them.* Down there on the sand.

One way and another, in fact, there was considerable disturbance. Tigellinus did not like it. The thing was not working out quite as he had intended. It was not his fault or his stage manager's fault. It was the fault of these Christians not looking like the criminals they were. Looking too respectable, blast them! He'd change that next time. Sew up the next lot in beast skins and have them chased by wild dogs! That was an idea. But this lot—they'd hardly run at all. It was as if—as if they wanted to die. So that hundreds of these fools who were too stupid to see past what was exactly under their noses, would start disbelieving what had been told them, shifting the blame for everything they happened not to like off the Christians and onto the Master of the World and his friends. Defeating the ends of justice.

But all the same, thousands had taken it the right way and were now shouting for more. Thousands. Well, they should have it! The others . . . it didn't matter. He'd get it under. See it didn't spread. After all, if a few hundred boneheads did take it the wrong way, even so, they wouldn't dare to *do* anything . . . not after this.

There, now everything was being cleared up again, clean sand spread for the torch race. Tigellinus didn't believe much in torch races and all that himself, but Nero had insisted.

It didn't seem that this was going to be quite what the crowd wanted, either. He listened closely to the shouting, then whispered an order and set one of his men running. Put on another show of dancers first, just a taste of them. Went better with blood. There was a good old stink now! Even in the imperial box. It was one of the smells you weren't quite sure about. Went to the head. And to the stomach. Made you feel uneasy. If he could get hold of Flavia and . . . You wouldn't get rid of that smell now for the rest of the evening. Not for any of those thousands. It was loosed into the dream until tomorrow and past tomorrow.

During the torch race, Crispus uncovered his face and sat stonily. Balbus watched him but could find nothing to say. Before the acrobats came on, Crispus rose to go out. Balbus and the two slaves followed.

A little way from the exit, beyond the talking, glancing crowd, Flavius Scaevinus was waiting. "Come to my house, Crispus, old friend," he said.

But Crispus shook his head.

"If you are going home, we shall go with you," said Balbus. They walked on together, silently, their slaves behind them, and each of the slaves, also, had his own thoughts about these things that had happened. At their backs, the sounds of the Circus died out; they were in the decent Roman streets again.

At a corner Crispus paused. He had seen Nausiphanes, and Nausiphanes had looked back at him very blackly.

Crispus held out his hand. "Nausiphanes," he said, "come here." And then, "Beric. You know . . ." And his voice broke.

"Yes," said Nausiphanes levelly. "I know." But he was not yet saying to his old master that he had seen his pupil once again.

"If he had got himself into such a position," Crispus said, with a great effort controlling his voice and stiffening his hand, "into a position from which there was no way out, why did he have to do this—public thing? Could he not have killed himself? They would have allowed that in the prison—to a person of education. To someone in his relationship towards me. Why did he have to die like a slave? Was all our teaching without effect?"

"Killing himself would not have done what he wanted to do," Nausiphanes said. "He had got beyond the old ideas of decency. He had to be a witness for this brotherhood of his."

Crispus stared back at the Greek blindly. "Come with me," he said, with a jerk of his head, and Nausiphanes, as became a good freedman in the presence of his patron, followed a little behind. He and Felicio did not speak to one another. If either had spoken just then he might have said too much. A now indefinitely great need for caution held them.

Before he came to his house, Crispus stopped, then turned down a small street and stopped again by a door that had a loaf of bread painted upon it to show that it was a bakery.

Felicio also knew that door but said nothing.

Crispus said to his friends, "Go on to my house if you will. Hermeias will escort you and see that you have everything." Then, to his freedman, "Nausiphanes, stay."

"What are you going to do, Crispus?" Balbus asked, more than a little anxiously.

"The boy—he came here—when he was a child, to eat cakes. With Nausiphanes, who was his tutor. Yes, he came here." But Crispus did not say that Eunice had come to him that morning. He did not say that he wanted to tell her that all was still well with *her* son. He did not know what else he wanted to say to Eunice, nor did he know why he thought that in the little bakery and with the man and woman who had been his slaves, he would be able at last to weep.

387

23

The Doctrine of Efficiency

Flavia was waiting alone in a long, narrow, empty corridor sloping gradually up to a curve at the end around which she could neither see nor guess. Anything might come around that corner, and the light was none too good. A seat ran all along the side, heaped with soft cushions, but she did not feel easy or secure enough to lean back. Her maid had been told to wait in an outer room from which another corridor had opened, then this one.

She looked up. It was very high, arched at the top and painted with clusters of small winged objects, flying tables and beds and wine jars, and cupids carrying necklaces. You could hear nothing. She began to hum to herself, defiantly, then couldn't go on.

Someone was turning the corner, and she jumped to her feet, just in case—but then sat down again, fidgeting with the pendant on the end of her necklace and pinching up a curl that might have grown lax with warmth and waiting.

For it was only two women. She did not know who they were. They were speaking Greek. There was too much Greek spoken in the palace. Both of them glanced at her, then one, with a light inclination of head and neck, passed on, and the other came and sat down beside her.

Flavia stiffened. She still did not know who this woman was, and she was less sure of herself than she had hoped she would be.

The woman said, "I know you, and I am sorry for you."

Flavia moved sharply away and then hesitated. Was it, oh, was it possible that there was a trap somewhere, that the message had not really been from the emperor, that Tigellinus—oh, this woman must know something terrible! "Why do you say that?" she asked, trying to speak evenly, "and who are you?"

388

"I am Claudia Acte," said the woman, "and people tell me things. I was told how you betrayed your foster-brother, who was afterwards killed in the Circus. You must feel very badly about that now."

Flavia gasped and for a moment could say nothing. Anger, and the sudden misery that she had to choke, both made her dumb. "How dare you!" she whispered at last. "Oh—saying things like that! I only did what was right. He was a Christian. It was a Christian murder plot!"

"Do you really believe that?" Acte asked.

"You've no right to ask me, and of course I do!"

Acte said nothing, only sat there. Nobody else came.

Flavia knew quite well who Acte was and knew it would be very unwise to order her away or be rude to her. Why did the emperor like her so much? She wasn't really pretty, not striking anyhow, and she certainly wasn't young. Sitting close to her like this, you could see the lines around her eyes and mouth. Then what was it—magic? Yes, that must be it.

Oh, it would be exciting to learn what magic Claudia Acte used on the emperor! Cautiously Flavia said, "It *was* a murder plot, you know. The police found evidence. Ample evidence. Why are you looking at me like that, Claudia Acte? Don't you believe me?"

"I don't think I believe in evidence got under torture. Do you? When they tortured Beric, Caradoc's son—"

"Oh, *that* wasn't my fault! Besides, they wouldn't have if he hadn't been a Christian."

"So Christians ought to be tortured. Is that it, Flavia?"

"They ought to be punished. They're a danger to all of us. They don't believe in anything."

"How do you know?"

"Everyone knows that. Don't you?"

"I've heard it. But you see, I've known some Christians, and they were kind and honorable and only wanted a chance for everyone to be happy—blessed, they call it. In a state of goodness towards one another. Do you understand that, Flavia?"

"You don't mean—magic?" Perhaps that *was* it, thought Flavia.

"No. Just what's in all of us. Being fully ourselves toward one another. That is, letting what is of God become free of what men do to other men out of pride and greed."

Flavia regarded this woman, this Greek, and suddenly she remembered Beric's saying that he wanted her to be fond of her slave girls or some nonsense—this kind of nonsense, anyhow! And she said at a venture, "So you're a Christian, too!"

"Yes," said Claudia Acte.

"Does—does everyone know?"

"I expect Tigellinus knows," said Acte. "So you think I ought to be tortured for it, like Beric?"

"Beric was a murderer," said Flavia harshly. She was not going to let herself be needled over that!

"That was before he understood," Acte said. "By the end he must have forgiven even Tigellinus."

"That's what *you* say! All I know is, he tried to murder him, and if I hadn't happened to be there—"

"Happened?"

"You shan't insult me, you wretched little Christian!" said Flavia and slapped Acte's face. It might be rash or even dangerous, but Flavia was the daughter of a Roman senator, and she was not going to be spoken to like that by a Greek freedwoman! Not even in the palace. And her fingers had left a red mark on Acte's cheek, and Acte just did nothing. She took it like the slave she'd been, she even turned her face slowly, so that Flavia had a view of the unslapped cheek.

"Go on if you want to," Acte said.

"I wouldn't dream of touching you again!" said Flavia. "I don't care to dirty my hand. Some of you Christians are murderers, and some of you haven't even the courage to stop anyone hitting you!"

"Is that how it all looks to you?" Acte asked, with a funny sadness in her voice.

"Yes! Yes and yes!" Flavia stamped. "And I'll thank you to get out of my sight, because I'm not going to look at it or you one moment longer!"

Acte hesitated, then stood up. "I'm still sorry for you," she said. "Truly I am. And if ever—"

"Get out of my sight!" said Flavia.

So Acte went away down the corridor and out of her sight. *Something went wrong there,* Acte said to herself. *I didn't handle her right. God wasn't speaking through me. She's had the shock, surely, the thing that should have twisted her roots and made her able to see the world in a new way. But it has not worked out this time.*

Perhaps just because Beric did kill and try to kill. This might be the punishment for that, and even his death in the arena could not put it right. Or perhaps Flavia was so deeply one whose heart was evil that nothing could shake her. And the end for her must be the hardening, the loneliness, the slow death.

But Flavia was flaming and shaking with anger, digging her nails into the soft cushions. No, the past was past, and she would not be trapped into thinking of it! And some day she would find a way to get this woman down, this woman who had tried to shame her! And now she wasn't going to let herself be bothered by anything. She had all the future before her. And she would be admitted to the Presence. He would be alone. Waiting for her, with only the emerald-set fillet around his curls to show that he was emperor. But one would know, would sense it. And then, how would it be—would she kneel and cover her face, and he raise her, drawing the hands away—or how?

Along past the curve in the corridor, and across the courtyard with the new marble basin and the new walls, which the masons were busily facing with colored marbles in meanders and rounds, and past the guards, and through a smaller courtyard where a dozen charming little deer, in the charge of as many pretty boys, came trotting to be fed or stroked, and up a flight of porphyry steps, there was a double-arched balcony room especially favored by the emperor. He and the empress sat there, studying an astronomical chart. Poppaea was pregnant again. This time it was to be the Divine Son. What had the stars to say of him?

Tigellinus came in, and Poppaea yawned. She knew what he was going to say, and she had heard it all before. It was boring. But then, what Tigellinus wanted was a boring world. Where nothing unexpected could ever happen.

She picked the chart up to look at more carefully. How fascinating the Egyptian names were, written in red between the stars, strange, shivery names, half bestial . . . no wonder that God, Jahveh, the highest of all, could not bear them, must trample on them and hate them!

Tigellinus was talking about the Christians again. "It may have been a mistake, Majesty," he said, "to do it so publicly. There are always fools to be sorry for them."

"But they were a sacrifice," the emperor said, "to Rome, to the great Thing—"

"And to the Master of Rome," said Tigellinus, "but it wasn't everyone saw it that way."

"There are always some who fail to appreciate one. As they did with my Olympic Games. You didn't appreciate them yourself. No, don't start telling me lies. I know it! But these scenes in the games—I was almost satisfied myself. The beauty of a dozen lions leaping together!"

"There were some didn't see it that way," Tigellinus repeated solidly. "And these horrid Christians—they didn't look bad enough, somehow. Next time we'll execute them in private."

"You're wrong, you're wrong," said Nero. "If we do that, people will call us tyrants. Even though we do it for the common good! I will not be called a tyrant. I am above that!"

"They'll call us names, anyway. But then they'll forget. The way we've done it this time they don't forget. They keep on talking about the Christians. That's not how to get it under our control."

"Well," said Nero, "tell me how you think it should be done, you great bull!" He stroked a finger down Tigellinus's golden breastplate, in and out of the wriggles, fascinated by the thickness and toughness, mental and physical, of the man inside it.

"I could put down anything," said Tigellinus, "if I had all the means I'd need for it. You see, Majesty, it's just a matter of that. There's the Praetorians and the police; well and good. But I'd want to be sure there was no one being protected. Nor protecting others." He paused to see if Nero was taking that in, but the emperor was apparently looking at his own reflection in the breastplate. "And I'd get up a good hate against them. Well, I've got that already. But I'd see it wasn't interfered with by any of this sympathy and nonsense, and so I'd stop these public executions or, anyway, pick my public."

"Just you and me," said Nero dreamily.

"Oh, well, Majesty, we could do better than that! More, I mean; not better. There's plenty who feel themselves braced and purified, so to speak, by being present at an execution. And I'd see that the little children at school were taught to hate the Christians, and I'd frighten the women of them, properly. You can do anything and stop anything if you're efficient about it."

"And then?"

"Then, Majesty? Well, then they'd be stamped right out."

"And we would have all the trouble of finding other men equally hateful if we ever again needed . . . to deflect attention."

"Don't say that, Majesty! You know, just as well as I do, that these Christians couldn't be tolerated any longer in the community. They were a bad influence on everyone. Measures had to be taken. They won't dare to raise their heads again, even if a few are left here and there."

"I wonder what they really believe in!" said Poppaea abruptly, raising her long dark lashes, one finger still on the chart.

"They don't believe in anything," said Tigellinus. "That's what I keep on saying. That's what's wrong with them."

"Nonsense," said Poppaea. "They believe in something they call the Kingdom, which is a form of love. Possibly a low form, but the same Eros, the Binder-Together. Eros who was before Aphrodite and all the gods. Eros who is Jahveh."

"I can't follow you into all that!" said Tigellinus sulkily.

"I didn't think you could, dear Tigellinus," said Poppaea. "But the need for love is universal, in all hearts. To be loved by all. Not to be afraid. There is the meaning of the Golden Age. Did you ever think of that, Tigellinus? Ah, you should read the poets. Our own Virgil first of all."

Tigellinus stood, looking hot and cross. He *had* read Virgil, of course, when he first began to think of making a real first-class career for himself. But it was only poetry; it wasn't about anything. Curse these women, anyway!

But Nero had been listening. "Not to be afraid!" he said, half aloud, and for a moment his hand strayed to the amulet round his

393

neck, the little luck-girl with the thin, rolled strip of writing embedded in her, the magic luck-girl who kept away plots and conspiracies. "But the Divine must always be alone. Without love. Without beautiful love. The Leader must be alone. The artist must be alone."

Tigellinus fidgeted. Such remarks were neither here nor there. What he wanted was to finish the Christian cleanup. "From what my agents report, Majesty," he said, "we've got it under control in Rome. But, of course, we've still got to tackle the provinces."

"That will mean a vast number of tedious letters," said Nero unenthusiastically.

"Only signing them, Majesty. But we've got to get things the same all through the Empire, or else something of the kind will crop up again. Christianity or worse. People setting themselves up against the State."

"We must take care," said Nero, "to avoid religious persecution, or even sameness. The gods have many forms. All should be worshiped."

"Perhaps they are all the same god," Poppaea said, turning over on her elbow, so that the shoulder-gathered pleats of her dress slipped a little on the lovely cream-brown of her skin. Her husband looked at her with soft intensity.

"Of course," said Tigellinus. "But these Christians and Epicureans don't believe in the gods. Whatever her Majesty is pleased to say they *do* believe in. And what's more they don't believe in you. Or in her. So I'm going to protect you both from them. That's me, the old watchdog! And I'll do it with all means. Or all the means you'll let me have."

"I'm sure I let you have plenty of means," Nero said. "Why, if these wretched Christians only knew what they cost the Treasury, they'd all die of swollen heads! Sometimes I think you take them too seriously, Tigellinus. After all, they've served their turn. One would think you believed yourself that they'd set the Circus on fire."

"One can't take things like that too seriously," Tigellinus said, "not if one's going to be efficient about them."

"Oh yes, one can. And one might contrive such a tedious world that ridiculous things like this Christianity would have to be invented in order to relieve the boredom. So mind, Tigellinus, no religious persecution. The empress and I abhor persecution. It should only be carried out when the utmost political necessity demands it. However, if you really think there is a danger to ourselves in the provinces, you had better draft me some letters to the governors. Mind, I shall read them over before signing them."

"But, Majesty—"

"Come back when you've finished them, Tigellinus. In the meantime there is a little lady to whom I must give audience."

"A little lady, Majesty? Do I know her?"

"Now, now, Tigellinus, I never ask these awkward questions, and you should learn not to do so. One never can tell, can one, which butterfly has alighted on which flower. You'd make a marvelous butterfly, Tigellinus." He watched the prefect of the Praetorians backing out of the Presence, and turned to Poppaea. "When I go on my Greek tour, one of the most thrilling moments will be saying good-bye to Tigellinus. I shall feel like the vine deprived of its oak. But . . . oaks are sometimes so inflexible. He will be splendid to leave in charge of Rome. And in Athens they will understand me at last. I might even go on to Jerusalem. I feel they would understand me there too."

Poppaea smiled. "And your new little lady—is she an Athenian?"

"No," said Nero, "the purest Roman. Like my Poppaea Sabina, who must now go to her own rooms and rest." He kissed her hand and raised her to her feet gently. "Yes, I may say I owe the introduction to Tigellinus . . . indirectly. I feel I may be able to mold the little lady's tastes towards higher things. I shall tell you how it passes, my love. You will be amused."

24

Business Meeting

Eunice said to herself that the days were drawing in, and she lighted the lamp and trimmed it. Then she opened the oven door to see how her batch of bread and cakes was going. For a minute she stood close to the table, quite quiet, thinking about Euphemia and Lalage and the others.

It was still a deliberate effort to remember them joyfully, without pain, as they'd want to be remembered, not just to miss them, not just to hate their murderers. She had to say over to herself, slowly and carefully and paying attention to the meaning, certain words and phrases. These told her exactly how and why her friends had died, agreeing to it. Then she would be able to remember them steadily, and it did not hurt, or at least the pain did not make her angry or frightened or anything but set and steady.

She lifted her head again and lit the second lamp, and there was a knock at the door, their new knock.

It was her son Phaon, the deacon.

She kissed him. "Well?" she said. "What's the business tonight, son?"

"If the meeting agrees, I think we should baptize Felicio and Eprius. No, Mother, I won't have anything to eat. I'm fasting for them. That'll bring us to twelve in this church."

Eunice counted on her fingers and verified it. "We're not up to what we were. Not yet."

"We're going to be, Mother. Megallis says that her friend will be ready for us soon."

"That's Marulla, isn't it? I'll have a talk with her, shall I?"

"You ought to have gone on being a deacon, Mother, instead of me!"

"You know I didn't have that gift of the Spirit, my lamb, not really. I wasn't somehow able to get everyone together and tell them the next step, the way you have. I was so glad to hand it over to you when you got back. How's things in the house now, son?"

"Not too bad. The old man's going to free me at New Year. I asked him to."

"You never did! But I'm so glad. Well, I don't see how you come to talk to him like you do!"

"Don't you, Mother?" said Phaon, curling up on the rug beside the hot side of the oven and looking up at her, smiling.

"Well, there, I suppose I do. Ever since that day he came here and sat down on that very stool with his hands over his face—but you telling him you'd got to come back from the country to be in Rome again!"

"Persis and I. We had our work to do. We just told him. He knows we're all coming tonight. And—well, Mother, it's a funny thing, but I like the old man quite a bit, and, what's more, he likes me."

"Maybe you can help him, son."

"It would be an odd thing if I couldn't help anyone who wanted to be helped. Asked to be."

"*Does* he?"

Phaon nodded.

"And I used to be that frightened of what he could do to you. Does he ever talk about—her, now?"

"Not much. Of course, she comes to the house, and everyone pretends not to know a thing, and Persis keeps out of the way."

"How does she look, son? She used to be so pretty. But she can't be happy now."

"If she isn't, it doesn't show. Not yet, anyway. But, of course, what she's doing is dangerous. It might crack up at anytime. Nero Caesar doesn't care what his women's pasts were, but he's apt to be nasty about their futures."

"I don't like to hear you talk that way, Phaon. After all, she's your master's daughter. But there, I suppose you're right not to respect anyone."

"Only for what they do. I respect a man like Paul, that can do things by letters. He can do things by remembering just exactly what someone is like in a church the other side of the Empire, and what they're likely to get wrong. I couldn't do that. Here's the rest coming."

It was the others from the household: Sannio, Mikkos, and Persis. They gave the peace greeting and sat down on the bed. Sannio still limped a little. They had done something to one of his knees. Blephano had apologized for that to his master—they had not intended it to have such a permanent effect, but the man had been extremely obstinate and a State department must take its course.

After that, four came together: Phineas and Sapphira, with Noumi, and Abgar, whom Phineas had helping in his shop now. Hadassa had been fetched by some of her husband's relations and taken off to the other side of Rome. They had word of her sometimes. Occasionally one of Phineas's brothers came to the church, as a kind of gesture, but it was not much of a success. Noumi almost always came, though, and her father allowed it. He had been very much shaken by the delay in the Coming.

Noumi always liked, if she could, to sit by Eunice. They had shared in an experience that nobody else was able to know about. When it was shared, it became more possible to think about it calmly and reasonably.

Then someone knocked and came in alone out of the darkness. He was a man with a short beard, tough and upright, in ordinary working clothes. He gave the peace greeting rather hesitatingly.

Phaon got up off the floor and came to the newcomer. "It will be tonight, brother," he said, "if the rest say yes."

The man held onto his hand. "Tonight," he said, "and then— then—"

"You will be forgiven," said Phaon gravely.

"And it will be all right," said the man. "You're sure—in spite of everything—oh, you are going to have me, aren't you?"

"We will have you, Eprius, even if you'd been the prefect of the Praetorians," said Phaon. "Brother, you've done the things I told you?" He looked closely and deeply at the man, who was nearly twice his age, and the man shivered and gulped and nodded.

Then Megallis came in with a dark, thick-set woman, veiled as she was. "Peace!" said Megallis, rather out of breath. "Oh, I'm not late, am I? You see, Marulla couldn't get away earlier. They gave her an extra lot of weaving to do. She was almost too tired to come, weren't you, dear? But I told her it would be worth it."

"This is your third meeting, isn't it, sister?" Phaon asked. He put his hands on her shoulders and watched her.

Her eyeballs were moving a little and her eyelids twitching, but that would have come after a whole day's weaving, if she'd been made to hurry over it.

To penetrate this, he said rather loudly, "Have you understood? You have. Good. And have you kept quiet?"

"I saw them die," the woman said, slowly and with a certain effort. "I know about holding my tongue."

"Even if you are questioned—directly?"

"Yes," said the woman. "Let alone I'm not the kind that gets spoken to unless they're after me about my work. Besides, I know you can't talk about things to do with gods."

For today Phaon let that pass. People took different ways coming to the same place. This woman's way had begun when she was sitting just behind Megallis at the Circus, with her husband and father-in-law, who were weavers. She had heard what Megallis had said so very plainly about the woman down on the sand. The woman, so little and far off, kneeling it looked like, and then her face and shoulder abruptly streaked with red where the beast had clawed her.

And the loud voice of Megallis going on explaining what kind of person this Euphemia was. And suddenly Marulla had sort of woke up and thought, *What can be happening?* And she looked down again, and the woman on the sand was tumbled right over with a nasty brown lion right on top of her, tearing, and Megallis had been pulled back with a hand over her mouth.

But still Marulla seemed to go on hearing what she had been saying, and still she didn't know what could be happening, only she did know she was bound to see Megallis again and find out. Even if her husband hit her the same way Megallis was being hit by hers. And so, after getting acquainted and asking first one question and then another, and after certain promises and delays and inquiries, Marulla had been taken to the bakery and had there discovered that, as she had supposed, there *was* something happening here in Rome and that it applied to women like herself and Megallis in their common day-to-day life. There was something new now. So that you weren't utterly bound down by that life, even when it wasn't so good. There was this Christianity as well.

Then Niger and Felicio came in together. Again Phaon met them and whispered to Felicio before they sat down.

And then Eunice said, "This is all of us that's likely to come, friends, but have I your leave to ask someone else to the meeting? I'll be guardian for him, and Phineas knows him a little too."

"Who is it, Mother?" Phaon asked.

"It's my neighbor Carpus, son. He works for the big potter, but he's hoping to set up on his own soon. He must have had his suspicions, because he spoke to me a little time after—what happened. Of course, I put him off then, the way we'd agreed to, but later on he spoke to me again. And he told me a bit about himself, enough for me to take a chance, with God's help. So at last we had a talk, and now he's asking your leave to come to a meeting."

"You bring him in, Mother," said Mikkos, and after a bit of talking they all agreed to have him, and Eunice went out to fetch him along.

Felicio, sitting on the edge of the kneading trough, said nothing. He felt a continuous kind of surprise, the same that he had been aware of all these weeks since he had made his decision. Was he really doing this? In spite of everything Nausiphanes had said. And, indeed, in all their arguments, Nausiphanes had undoubtedly had the best of it. But yet he was going tonight to do something irrational, as Nausiphanes had said, and he was glad that he was going to do it.

He knew also that it was dangerous and likely to lead to torture, domestic or public, and perhaps death in the arena, such as he had seen with his own eyes. And he knew that he was afraid of physical pain, much more afraid than Niger, for instance. But still he was glad—so glad that it was all he could do not to throw his head back and laugh out loud.

How, then, measure up this irrational gladness against the Epicurean truth that also he recognized? *Perhaps because peo-*

ple's motives are, in the end, not rational, although they ought to be in the direction of reason. And that was the direction of the action that he intended taking tonight, although it had also elements of gross unreason, such as had made Nausiphanes say that he would never speak to him again if he became an initiate. But this unreason was only in it so as to make a hold on the unreason in the human soul, which, if one is honest, one knows to be there.

And so, in an increasing bewilderment, but also with a gladness that became more overwhelming hour by hour, Felicio had done the things that Phaon had told him to do. He had prayed and fasted and fixed his mind upon the Way of Life, and, having decided that this was the right end of the stick, he had given over for a time his rational and ironic and individual will into the keeping of their Jesus, who would soon be his own Jesus, and must be also, forever, Beric's Jesus.

Now, sitting there, regarding all this process soberly and calmly and somehow lightly, Felicio knew as well that the black litter slave, the beast of burden who could not really understand all that was involved and could not possibly do so, since he had not even the words, let alone the reasoning powers, necessary for this, was yet feeling with him in a manner that had not been analyzed by the philosophers nor even expressed by the poets. Niger, whose back was still scarred and ugly from last summer's floggings, sat on the floor, cross-legged. Felicio reached down and touched his shoulder, felt the big rough hand on his own, and knew that they had both escaped from their common slavery.

But by now the meeting had started. Eunice had come back with her neighbor Carpus, a youngish man, his hands and arms and the front of his tunic flecked here and there with gray clay smudges. The members of the church had gone up to him with peace greetings and handshakes, and now he sat on the floor beside Eunice, staring all around him.

Then there was silence for a moment, and then all said the Words together, and Phaon spoke to them, shortly and gravely, reminding them of their dangers and their obligations.

Now anyone who had some matter to bring up before the meeting could do so. Phineas and Eunice told how they had distributed the money from the fund and answered questions. Then

Sannio said, "What I want to know is, what's due to happen now? Did any of us hear anything from the other churches?"

Eunice said, "Well, I did see Claudia Acte just once, last week. But she doesn't know. Nobody does. We've just got to wait."

"To wait for a sign," Phineas said. "A true sign."

"What would that be, now?" Eprius asked, humbly and eagerly.

"It's watching the times, and then coming to our own conclusions," said Phaon. "If we think something looks like happening and then it does, that's a sign. See? Or with people, when we know what ought to happen, and it does, that's a sign too. Each time that comes off, we go a step forward. I tell you how it is, Eprius. We've asked a certain kind of question—we've asked the world—and we've got our answer." He turned to his mother and Carpus, who was listening and puzzling. "Does he know what's been going on? How things have shaped with us in this church?"

"Part I know," said Carpus, "but couldn't you tell me?"

"Sum it up, like," said Mikkos. "I've kept on trying to, only I don't right know how."

Here and there the others nodded or murmured yes. Phaon, looking around, had the sense of the meeting. He stayed quiet for a moment, praying for it to come in order into his mind and onto his tongue.

Felicio knew that was what he was asking, and prayed, too, that all should be made clear.

"Out of us fifteen," said Phaon, "of whom ten are baptized, six were in the church that met here last summer. And one—that is you, Noumi—was in another church. Five months ago there were another nine in our church. And after that, one more. They are dead. They have become a sign. What we know to be true was manifested on them. Most of us knew them, but you, Carpus, you did not know any of them, so I will name them to you. There were two of our deacons in the church, Manasses and Lalage."

Suddenly out of the shadow, Niger cried out, "Oh, Lalage, you were so lovely! The way you said things made me see them right."

"They were beaten and tortured, and they stayed unshaken," Phaon said, his breath coming quickly now but his voice still high and steady. "We lost them for ourselves, but they are not lost. We are all better for them. Because of them the Kingdom is nearer for all the world, and they are part of it forever. They could have bought their lives, Carpus, but they never even thought of that. They had been given knowledge and experience of the Kingdom with us, as you will all be given it, and that is so good that there's never really any choice for any of us once we've known it.

"Because we had known it, Persis and I were ready to die, but that sign was not made on us. And Argas and Euphemia were also tortured, and they also died in the sight of all Rome for the Kingdom, and Sophrosyne was beaten and died in prison. They were all led into temptation, because all of them might have denied and might have saved their lives. But they were delivered from that evil."

Phaon was trembling a little now, speaking to Carpus, who had known none of the witnesses. But when he had said Euphemia's name, he had heard Megallis start and draw in her breath quickly, and he could see that Sannio was crying, and Persis was crying, and Sapphira and Phineas were holding onto one another, and he heard a deep groan from Eprius like someone who was going to be sick. Yet all he had said was simply what had happened.

Yes, that was all, Felicio thought, *and I have faced this. I will not even move when it comes to Beric's name.*

"And Rhodon was tortured to death in prison, and he was a witness too," said Phaon, remembering the metalworker with his scarred hands and orderly mind, who must have been hard to kill. And now it was Abgar who cried out and beat on himself in barbarian fashion.

And then Megallis suddenly said, "Stop!" And she stood up from her place, her hands twitching at her veil, and then said, "I saw him in prison when I went to see Euphemia. I'd be bound to know anyone that I saw there, wouldn't I, friends? And not a word have I said until this day, but, oh, I'd swear it was him I saw a month ago, alive and well, only he'd grown a beard, like so it was—"

"Where?" asked Abgar, standing too and shaking from head to foot.

"It was near that temple in the new quarter," Megallis said, "the temple that's half dug into the hill. To some foreign god. To Mithras or someone. And he'd got such a big dog with him."

Phineas had been leaning forward to listen. Now he and Eunice glanced at one another, and then he backed out of the lamps' telltale circle. He did not want Eunice to remember what Rhodon had been. But Eunice did remember, very well.

Sannio said, "It couldn't have been him, Megallis. Just couldn't. You got it wrong. I know. Mikkos and me, we were in that prison, and we heard he was dead. Heard it read out of a book when they took us through to the office. You couldn't have a thing in the prison book if it wasn't true. You heard that too, Mikkos?"

"I did," said Mikkos. "Listen, Megallis, they'd just taken the chains off us, and there was our master come for us at last—not that he could have before—and he kept hold of us, me with one hand and Sannio with the other, and I know I kept holding onto the end of his toga, fair like a baby I was, and the chap at the desk was reading out the names. And Rhodon was one. Not that I knew anything about him then. Only, times like that, you keep any little thing you hear in your head afterward. You must have seen wrong, Megallis."

"I never told till now," said Megallis, half crying. "I didn't want to! I wouldn't have if I hadn't been near sure!"

"But if Rhodon lives," said Abgar slowly, "Rhodon couldn't not—be seeing me—after him doing that for me—and I would do—the same or anything—"

"Oh, let it go then!" Megallis cried out, and her tears got the better of her, and she choked and hiccuped, and Eunice brought her over a mug of water.

But if it is true, Eunice thought, *it is doing harm to the rest of us already. He has sinned against us as well as against God.* And then she thought, *If he is alive and has left us, either he hates us and wants to break us up, or else he still loves us in his heart and wants to help us—and he will do that best by keeping away from us. Most of all, away from poor Abgar. And maybe that's what he's done, and it shows he's partly with us still.* And she patted Megallis and kissed her forehead.

But Phaon was going on.

Felicio listened. No, it was not yet.

"There were three of our people who were tempted in ordinary ways," Phaon was saying now. "And they were not delivered from those temptations. You who are hearing about us now, you will be bound to be tempted, the world being the way it is. One of them was tempted by money, because he was poor, and he betrayed us and lost the Kingdom and cannot at all be part of the future. Money and that, it's the commonest temptation. It was the very first temptation Jesus Himself saw through and dealt with. Sotion, the man who was tempted that way, is dead, squashed out like a bug on the wall. Mankind is the worse for his having been born. It would be most terrible to have that said in truth about one.

And two others had the temptation of fear. They were afraid of pain. Josias and Dapyx let their bodies overcome their spirits. Dapyx denied us and died badly, and Josias killed himself. Their deaths were useless. And made their lives useless. It was as though they had never lived the new way."

"Josias never denied us, son," Eunice said.

"Except that he was afraid to be a witness. But we remember him still with love. And not one of us knows his own strength or his own weakness during life. It will only be known after we have made a good death. If we get that blessing." He stayed quiet a moment. He had been very near death himself, and he was still very young.

It was Persis who said, "We'll get strength for that if we ask for it. Oh, brothers and sisters, I know! I'm only a girl, and I don't know much about anything, but I thought I was to die as a witness myself, and I did feel the strength coming to me. Like something you could lay hold of."

And Eprius said painfully, "They had strength. Oh, Jesus, you gave them strength to die!"

Then Phaon said, "There was another. He was tempted too. In a different way. But in the end he was a witness too."

It's coming now, thought Felicio, *and I am prepared.*

"Carpus, he was one of the rich, but he saw the Kingdom, and he came to us. His name was Beric."

And Felicio, to his extreme surprise, cried out aloud and threw his hand out, groping, and Niger had hold of him, had brotherly care.

And again Phaon was going on. "When the powers of evil tempted Jesus, they said to Him, 'Set Yourself up as God, cast Yourself down from the top of the temple, do things which only God can do.' But Jesus said no. He said, 'I am a man, under God.' So He dealt with that temptation.

"But Beric set himself up as God, making judgments of right and wrong, saying that it was good to do evil at times which he himself might choose. Most likely he did that because he was a master and used to his own will being other people's law. Like a god's. Like the old gods whose wills were evil and unbounded. Until justice, which was always beyond them—which is another name for our God—laid hands on them in the end."

"But was this man a master," asked Carpus, "truly?"

"He was my master," Phaon said. "He used to make me do the things a slave has to do. Against my will." And he thought of parties where Beric had made him be this or that for the guests. And it all seemed a very long time ago. In the days when he had cried easily, when songs and drawings were always coming into his head. Before Argas had taken the beating for him.

"What happened?" Carpus asked again.

"He murdered a man," said Phaon slowly. "He took the life of that one who had betrayed us. Although the rest of us had forgiven him. He did that almost without thinking, in the way of a master. But afterwards he tried to kill again, and this time he had thought about it, and in spite of what the rest of us said and what he knew for himself, he made out that he would be right to do it. He sinned, and God punished him for it, so as to save him in the end. But others were punished as well, because that's how sins are, spreading like the rings on water when the chucked stone's already deep and quiet in the bottom mud. And it was worst for those who loved him most—that's how sins are too. It was worst for Argas."

"That's right," said Sannio, who had seen something he couldn't ever forget through the grating across a prison cell.

"Brothers and sisters," Phaon said, "you have said our Words often. You know them too, Carpus? Well, did you ever think what it means, us asking not to be led into temptation? These Words mean, maybe, everything. But one of the special things they mean is this: we ask not to be put where there's no good way out, but only bad ways. And that's where we're apt to be in Rome and Rome's world. We can't see how to alter the state of things that's keeping the Kingdom from us all except by murder and violence. You who're new to us, you know the lies that were told about us starting the fire.

"And we are all very sure that no true Christians would have done that. But sometimes I ask myself whether it mightn't have been started by someone who perhaps even called himself a Christian but had got so crazed by the state of things that he was trying to finish them even *that* way so as to get the Kingdom quicker. You can't hurry the Kingdom. We know that. But someone might have been tempted to think you could."

"Can't we be sure when the Kingdom will come?" the silent woman Marulla suddenly asked. "Can't we have a promise?"

"Sister, it will come when God wants it. But things as they are stop people from wanting it. They're offered the devil's kingdom instead—the kingdoms of the world—money power and power over people. Oh, it's difficult to say, friends, but to my mind, what's tempting us is to try and smash the kingdoms of the world and their power instead of smashing what's behind them. See, friends?"

"But we can't fight evil except in other men," Phineas said. "We see it in the rich. We see it in Nero and Tigellinus, and in them we have to destroy it!"

"We've got to keep ourselves from hating them—most of all from hating one or two men and saying to ourselves that they're evil itself. Oh, Phineas, if we do that, we're done! We'll go back. We've got to get at the will for evil that they have—find out, first of all, why they have it. That's half the battle."

"Surely we must fight the evil will in people first," said Phineas slowly, "but how?"

"The worst of it is," said Phaon, frowning, "that the evil will wield the power, yet I can't see but how the power also aids the evil will. It's a circle. But there's a weak place somewhere. There must be. That's where we've got to break it, friends.

"And meantime people are tempted like Beric was, to do evil that good may come. And they'll go on being tempted just so long as things are this way. So long as the rich are oppressing us, making us want to kill them. And that's why we ask every day in our prayers for the ending of things as they are. And remind ourselves that we've all got to help this to happen. Though not by doing evil. But always by some kind of doing. We can't just sit back and say it's none of our business. That's the death of the soul, that Jesus died to save us from. Oh, friends, it's difficult being a Christian! Especially when brother Paul says that slaves should obey their masters."

"We need to keep our thoughts on it, brother," Niger said soberly, "doing just what we see in front of us."

"But what happened to this master?" Carpus asked, "after he had sinned?"

"He took action," said Phaon slowly, "and he was forgiven. And he was one of those who were eaten by beasts in the Circus Maximus. You must have seen him among the prisoners, Eprius."

But Eprius groaned, his head down on the table, his hands beating and picking at the wood, so that the air grew dusty with unshaken flour.

"And others saw him too." Suddenly Phaon was staring at Felicio, drawing him to his feet.

And Felicio had to speak. "He bought me. Beric did that. With his love and his blood. Because one can't be bought with less than that or the certain promise of it." Across the lamplight, Felicio and Phaon seemed to be speaking directly at one another. And Phaon had been bought by Argas. And both of them were fasting and a little dizzy, seeing things more than usual from the outside, and each could see the tears shining on the face of the other.

Eunice said to Carpus, "So there was nothing lost. Not really. And there won't be if we die too. Because we've made ourselves part of something that never stays still but always keeps on growing and changing."

He tried to take it in.

One of the lamps was beginning to burn down. She went over to the corner for the big oil jar. It must be getting quite late. Eprius still had his head down on the table in a fierce agony.

Noumi had said nothing at all the whole time. Now she said in a half whisper, "But for those who do not see with their own eyes? How can they believe?"

Nobody answered at once.

Then Eunice said, "It's funny, now I come to remember it, but whenever we talked about it before, like, we didn't think how *big* the Circus was. So that there was thousands who never saw— not faces. Not so that you'd know it was real people. It was only the ones in the best seats that were sure to see. And some of them were the kind that can't be got at, not by blood nor yet by love. I don't see how you can alter people's minds if you can't, so to speak, get near them."

"And for the ones whose faces are seen—for *us*," Noumi asked again. "Can we show our forgiveness of those we do not see? Can we even love them?"

"I don't see that you can do anything except you get close to them," Eunice answered, bothered.

"That's something we'll have to find out," Phaon said, and his voice had hardened again.

But Felicio suddenly had the idea of books—if a poet could write a book that was about something here and now, not hundreds of years ago. But could you do that with a book?

"Didn't change old Hermeias, seeing it," said Mikkos thoughtfully. "He knows about us; bound to. But he keeps himself away from us. Sort of embarrassed."

"He had something else," Felicio said, "which did for him instead of the Kingdom. Some kind of Mystery." He realized, with a certain amusement, that he was considering this Mystery, which Hermeias was so serious about, as a mere bit of superstition—just in the same way that Nausiphanes considered the thing which he himself was about to do.

"And seeing may shake a man up, but not to go our way," said Sannio, "like with that brother of Beric's."

"What really happened about that?" Phaon asked. "I never knew, not being in the house myself then."

"I wasn't there either, not when he came," Sannio said. "We were still in the prison. All I know is, he came around that night, and he went for the old man—it was Lamprion told me—something savage. As if it had been *his* doing. Went for him good, shouting and yelling, oh my! Not even in Latin, it seems, but in that language of theirs.

"This Beric of ours and his brother, they were king's sons, see, Carpus? From some place up north. Right barbarians they were, to start with. And then, all of a sudden, he hit the old man, hit him real nasty, and then Lamprion and Pistos and the rest, who'd been sent out but were just behind the door, as I'd have been myself, well, they all ran in and caught hold of him and were all for sending him to the police.

"But the old man, he said no, and he told them to let Clinog loose, and then they went out together—past midnight it was, then—and neither Lamprion nor any of us so much as allowed to follow. Hermeias was asleep then. So he wasn't in on it, either way."

"But was that all?" Phaon asked.

"Seems so," said Sannio.

"Not like Beric, to let it go at that," Phaon said, puzzling. But he had never seen Clinog. It might be true.

But after a minute Eunice said, "I can tell you the rest. I don't see why I shouldn't—not among ourselves. You see, it was here that Flavius Crispus brought him. To my bakery. I was asleep, and it was all dark. I jumped up. Oh, I could tell it was bad news! About you, son.

"But it was those two. And when Crispus said it was Beric's brother, I fell to crying, silly it was, but I was all shook up. And then Crispus told me, very quiet, how this Clinog had struck him and said what should he do. So I said, 'He'd best hit you again, if that's how he feels, or me for that matter.' Who cares about being hit now? And then Crispus said, 'You tell him about it, Eunice, for I can't.' So I did tell him."

"Everything?" said Phaon.

"Yes. But it didn't take, son. He listened, yes, but then he began to laugh. Not right laughter, but strange. And he said, 'So that's what my brother died for,' and he struck me. And Crispus would have stopped him, but I said, 'No, let him.' And he said, 'This is what Rome has done to both of my brothers.' I never knew there'd been another brother, even. And at last he said, 'Get me a transfer to Britain. I'm going back before it's too late.' And Crispus said, 'I will try and do that for you, Clinog.' And I believe that's just what he's been doing."

"And that's that," Phaon said. Then, "Has anyone any other business?"

Megallis looked up. "Any news of Paul?"

"I've heard no more, not definite," Phaon said. "Has anyone else?"

Phineas said, "I saw one of the believers from Aquila's old church. She said he'd come up for trial next month. It's certain to be a capital sentence. Well, we know, and he knows. And we needn't fear any temptation for him. He'll die for us, just as he's lived for us all these years."

"I'd liked to have seen him," Sannio said. "It would be something to remember forever. Will it be a public execution, him being a citizen?"

But nobody knew that.

"I tell you who's seen him," Phaon said, "and that's Junius Gallio. Heard him say so at dinner one day. He went back to the prison to visit him—seems they had quite an argument. Got a nerve, Gallio has, going back to the Mamertine. I wish I knew what those old birds were after, though. They send us out after dinner and, what's more, they see no one's listening."

It occurred to Felicio that he half thought he did know, putting two and two together. But how did it fit in with Christianity? That was what he did not know yet, could not begin to consider until his mind was calm again. If it ever was.

And then from beside him Niger spoke. "Friends, I got someone. He works by me, sleeps by me. I tell him all the stories. I tell him the Name some time. Can I bring him here? My brother Felicio, he'll help us, maybe, over us getting out?"

Felicio thought quickly, *Who is it? Who sleeps in the shed by Niger?* "Is it the new Cappadocian?" he asked, and Niger nodded. *And I didn't know,* Felicio thought, *not a thing! Those two in that stinking shed, chained and sore half the time, whispering to one another, and old Niger helping this other poor soul—I ought to have been doing it. Well, anyway I'm glad I washed Niger's feet last time. I'm glad I wanted to when it came to him. It was a strange experience that was. I shall be doing it again. I shall be washing the feet of this newcomer, this Cappadocian—can't even think of his name—when he comes. There will be this joining us forever. As you showed us, Jesus.*

The others were discussing it now, questioning Niger. Phaon said he would go over to Aelius Balbus's house next time there was a chance and try to see this man. Better not to let him meet the whole church yet—in case . . .

They decided to hold the next meeting in Phineas's kitchen. It was better, these days, not to have it twice running in the same place. They had not held one in the old boiler room since the troubles. Phaon and the rest were all very careful in the house. None of them ever said a word to Lamprion and the others. But it was probable that any of the rest of the slaves who might have their suspicions would also know that anyone who informed the police of Phaon's or Persis's whereabouts would be liable to be dealt with himself by the master.

Carpus had some questions to ask. And he wanted to show that he knew the Words. He only had the first meaning so far, the meaning on the surface.

But which of us knows everything? Felicio thought. *Not I.*

Then Phaon looked all around from one member to another of his church. "Friends, there are two who want to join us. Do we take them?"

Eprius went dead still, listening.

After a moment Phineas said, "Let us hear them, friends."

"Who stands guardian for them?" Phaon asked formally.

"I stand for Felicio," Niger said.

"I stand for Eprius," said Eunice.

Phaon answered, "These are good assurances. We accept

them." Then he spoke again. "You who are with us but not of us yet. Abgar, Marulla, and Carpus, you must go now."

The two men said they would walk back with Marulla; it was safer. Phaon warned them not to say anything in the street that ought not to be overhead, even if they thought they were alone. You never knew, now.

Abgar said good night and peace on them, rather gloomily, and suddenly Sapphira said, "Oh, I'm sure it's going to be you soon, brother! God will give you understanding." When he had gone she excused herself. "He does want so much to be in! But he always gets things wrong, poor thing."

There was a short pause and a little shifting and whispering, while Eunice opened her oven and took out the loaves, Niger helping her. Persis changed over to sit by Noumi. All came rather closer together. Counting the two new ones, they were twelve now. This was a number that made them happy.

The delicious smell of the hot bread filled all the bakery, making Felicio so faint that he had to slip down from the edge of the kneading trough and sit on the floor with his head between his knees. Bread. The common, the necessary thing, so dull or so desirable. Common life and necessary actions might also be beautiful, given love.

The possibility of love. He hadn't wanted love before. He had been content to be alone and intelligent and ironic, taking lightly what pleasures were to be had. Then he had loved Beric, and that had been taken from him. And then? Was this feeling in his breast and head now love of humankind, or was it rather the urgent necessity for something obviously reasonable that was pressing on him? That was pressing them together, breaking down barriers, making them feel toward one another in an unreasonable and irrational way. You might call it love. He looked up and realized that Eprius was in the middle of his confession.

Eprius had lived an ordinary life. He came from the poorest-citizen class, and he thought it a bit of luck getting into the city guards. He was proud of his detachment. He'd had enough money for drink and women. Sometimes he'd gambled away half his pay, but he won almost as often as he lost. He'd taken part in official religious ceremonies with a certain feeling of awe and satisfaction. On private matters he had consulted an astrologer.

He had not heard of the Christians until the time of the fire. When it came out that they were to be publicly disposed of at the games in the Circus Maximus, he thought it was only right; that was where they'd started the fire. He'd been on sentry duty at one of the prisons and had been one of the squad detailed to take a batch of them across Rome to the Circus. So he was beside them, close to them for quite a while. And instead of being real criminals, the kind it was a pleasure to poke a spear into, they were a lot of decent-looking old women, and children even, and ordinary folk. That made several of the guards feel bad, as if they'd been cheated, though they didn't quite know what of.

And as for Eprius himself, the lid had been put properly on it when one of the women turned and thanked him. As if she'd meant it. And you couldn't get out of it by saying they were mad. She just wasn't mad. Or if she was, then everyone was!

"So later on that afternoon, it was their turn," Eprius said, his voice getting more and more choked, "and we knew because of the noise the beasts were making. And then the commotion stopped. And I couldn't speak. Dumb I went. Like I'd been hit on the head. And when the bugle went for fallout, I couldn't seem to want to go anywhere nor do anything. Some of my mates, they wanted a drink bad. But I wanted something more, and I says to myself, 'What?' But there wasn't a thing I could do then, not a thing.

"Oh, friends, you don't know what it was like those next days. You can't ever know. I kept on—dreaming. You see, friends, before, when I'd been on prison duty I'd not taken notice, and I'd knocked one or two about that happened to be in my way, and then in the street. But it wasn't only me. Friends, you're all one church here, and what happens to all happens to each of you in a manner of speaking. And it's all my regiment I keep on thinking about—what we did to them, among us. To the girls and all. Not giving it a thought. And now . . . now . . . it's burning me . . ."

"You shall be cooled in the water that washes away sin," Phaon said. "And if any of your mates get to feeling the same—later on, maybe—you'll know what to do about it."

Eprius, on his knees, caught the edge of young Phaon's tunic. "Oh, we did sin bad! And then they called us brothers. She did, that woman with the bandage around her head. I don't see how what we did gets forgiven."

"You don't know how," said Phaon, "but you do know why. Jesus forgives you. *She* forgave you. *We* forgive you. Don't we do that, brothers and sisters?"

"In Jesus' name, yes," said Phineas, and the others repeated it, some of them coming over to Eprius and touching him, and he, looking from face to face, began to believe it.

Then one after the other questioned him to see that he understood the Way of Life and the meaning of prayer and the intention of fasting and why the Christ had died for his sins.

Felicio listened and was suddenly aware that it was his own turn. He took a step or two, hesitating, into the middle of the group. What was there to be afraid of? He knew them all. But it wasn't that. It was something beyond any of them. Because of which you had to go down on your knees in a need to worship stronger than any other of the body's needs.

What was it? *Oh, let me catch it, let it be plain, why do I want the Will of the universe to be done more than my own will? It is not that I want a father or a mother—nothing as simple as that. Not merely that I am lonely—I was that before. Not merely that our world is obviously not just a chance scattering together of particles that may by chance equally be scattered apart—it is behind all that and yet nearer, yet in me, oh, I have early found it—*

"Brother," said Niger, "don't you be afraid now. Just you speak to us."

And he must speak. He must leave whatever it was uncaught, perhaps because it was uncatchable. Yes, he was on his knees, and they were all around. "Brothers and sisters," he said, "I thought I could live without this. Forgive me."

Eunice kept on thinking of others who'd come for their baptism, most of all young Argas. He was a sweet boy, the nicest of all, maybe. But now they'd decided it was safest not to baptize in the Tiber. You'd got to take some risks, agreed, but this wasn't one of the necessary ones. It would have meant half the night, getting far enough beyond the city to be certain you were out of sight.

415

That wasn't fair to the slaves who'd have to be back or they'd catch it.

Besides, you'd got to pass out of the gate, and that meant being seen by the guards, and you never quite knew . . . Well, there were some churches that managed with a rainwater cistern. They were full now after the October rains and plenty of them all over Rome, but there wasn't one near Eunice's, and you couldn't use the well.

But you could draw water from it, and so Eunice did, while the questioning went on. Herself, she didn't want to ask Felicio anything. She didn't doubt about his being all right. Noumi came and helped her. It took a good few bucketsful to make much impression on the big kneading trough. How her arms and back had ached over that trough, to be sure, working methodically and evenly through the dough, every two or three days, according to what orders she was getting. Good bread, Eunice's, as good as any in Rome.

The questioning was over now. The cold water, dark and swingy from the last pouring, three-quarters filled the kneading trough. The young women moved away into the farthest end of the room. The two who were standing guarantor and the others came to the trough.

Phaon stood, thinking about the confessions, and the sins that were to be wiped out. There was so much that he hadn't experienced at all himself. Could he know enough about it to forgive? He'd never even slept with a woman, though he and Persis had held one another very closely and kindly that time in the pitch-dark cellar, waiting and wondering and trying to be brave.

But sin? *I've got that to come,* he thought grimly, *unless I'm very lucky. Unless by the help of Jesus I can keep single-hearted. And I don't believe my life's likely to be that easy. You might keep single-hearted if you lived in the middle of the desert, but in Rome? I'm sure to be tempted soon, and sometimes one doesn't see it's a temptation till too late.*

We've all got the capacity for making the wrong choice, for sin. That's why it's so exciting to be a Christian and be aware of that capacity and of what it means to take so as to deal with it, and then it's possible to be different— or, if one fails, to receive forgiveness.

But they were waiting for him. He had now to become the channel between those two and this expression of their salvation. He signed to them to take their tunics off and noticed, casually, the hard, jutting body muscles of Eprius and how he shivered all over from moment to moment.

He took Eprius first. There was just room for him to kneel, crouching down in the cold water of the trough. He got into it as far as he could, and Phaon took a jug and poured the water three times over his head. The man's dark, rather curly hair straightened down into wet rats' tails, and he stayed very still, and his eyes seemed to look at nothing.

Felicio, watching him, thought, *In a minute I, too, am going to do this fantastic thing! I, too, am going to squat ludicrously in a trough of cold water like a boy's game of forfeits. I shall have these words said over me by young Phaon, and all of us will understand them differently.*

And now Eprius had been half lifted out by the others and stood on the floor smiling and dripping. Someone was drying him with an end of blanket that had been hanging by the oven, helping him into his tunic again, surrounding him with brotherly help and friendship.

And Phaon had signed for Felicio to step into the trough.

On the edge of the water Felicio noticed a little dusty patch of flour. The sudden cold, which he must not dissipate by any natural movement, stopped him from noticing what was happening for a moment. Then there was water on his head, cold again but not cold enough to get through to the racing thoughts in the brain underneath, tucked in there, sheltering itself behind the senses, only making human contact through them, never directly.

And the rite was over. He had deliberately accepted danger, yes, but he had already weighed that, had made up his mind, and now old Niger had him by the arm, was helping him out, looking no end happy, smiling with all those white teeth of his. Still wet, Felicio kissed him; it was the obvious thing to do.

Then he and Eprius and Phaon were given bread to end their fast, and milk and a little honey to show how sweet forgiveness and acceptance were. Everyone was talking a bit, feeling release and happiness.

Then Eunice asked two of the men to help her empty the trough. It didn't do to leave anything about—anything that might look suspicious. So, after lightening it by a few pailsful, they carried it out and poured the baptismal water away into the gutter and then tipped the trough up near the warmth of the oven to dry out, ready for the next batch of dough.

"Well, I'm off," Megallis said abruptly and stood up.

Eunice went over to her and took her hand. "What does your man think of you going out so late at night, dear? Does he—know at all?"

"He ought to know if he's not dense," Megallis said.

"But suppose he tried to stop you?"

"He wouldn't dare."

"Or—well, there's the police."

"He'd not do *that* again," Megallis answered, low and somberly. "He's never so much as asked me where I'm going. Keeps off it, sort of. Sometimes he'll try giving me a present, a comb, it might be, or some beads. Trying to get back to where we was. But it can't be done, not now. Not unless he comes right over—to us—and I don't see him doing that."

"Everything's possible," Eunice said earnestly. "You must believe that, dear. I've been praying for him to see—oh, ever since. I do hope you're praying too. And it might happen. Oh, how happy we'd all be if he did!"

Megallis rubbed her eyes with her hand. "Oh, well, I'll pray. Yes. I'd be happy all right. I'd be so happy I wouldn't know what to do. Well, good night, all, and peace be with you."

Niger stood up. "I'll walk your way, sister."

"All right," said Felicio, "and then back to the house? I'll be looking out for you by the door,"

"You are quite a size, Niger!" said Megallis, a bit more cheerfully. "I feel very safe with you!"

"Peace, brothers and sisters," said Niger, and the two of them went out together.

Then Phineas helped his wife and sister to wrap their veils thickly around themselves, and all three left.

Mikkos got up. "Coming, young Phaon?"

"In a minute," said the deacon. "You go on."

Sannio got up stiffly.

"You'd better let me rub that knee of yours, son," Eunice said. "Just you come on over tomorrow."

Mikkos, Sannio, and Persis all said good night and peace, and went out.

Phaon was still talking to Eprius, but at last the elderly man said he must be going back to his barracks. "Are you happy now, brother?" Phaon asked.

"I am," said Eprius. "I feel like an honest man again. I'll be back next week, that's sure. Give me a blessing now." He knelt for Phaon's blessing, then went out, steadily and joyfully.

Eunice blew out one of the lamps. You couldn't go wasting oil. Phaon picked up some bread crumbs and ate them. He was rather hungry still. He drew a fish with his finger in the flour dust on the table between the new loaves.

Felicio thought he must be going, but he didn't want to go. His hair was damp still. He rubbed his fingers through it. Anyone would have thought he'd been out in the rain, instead of—where he had been.

There was a knock on the door, not their own special knock. All looked up, surprised, because it was so late now, and, well, one didn't know, these days. Phaon brushed his hand across the fish, rubbing it out.

Eunice went to the door and saw who it was. "Why, come in!" she said and brought Nausiphanes over to the warm oven and the light of the one lamp.

Nausiphanes said, "I watched the lot of you coming out. Lucky I'm not a police spy, Eunice! Well, have you done it?" He motioned with his head toward Felicio.

"It is done," Felicio said. "I am a Christian now, for all my life."

Nausiphanes said nothing for a time, then, "I meant never to speak to you again. That's stupid perhaps. However great an intellectual disappointment may have been, there should still be the possibility of friendship. And so you have gone through this rite, Felicio. Do you feel different now?"

It was difficult to answer. Difficult to get back into this other world. Felicio made an attempt to regard himself scientifically but somehow could not get that focus.

Phaon said, "It's not always the one who is changed that sees the change clearest, Nausiphanes."

"All the same," said Nausiphanes, "I want to know what Felicio himself thinks."

Felicio could only be truthful. He said, "No, I don't feel changed. Eprius, the guard who was baptized with me, was, I think. But if anything sudden did happen to me, if it wasn't just slowly getting to think that the whole thing was too good to be out of, then the change came at the moment that Beric was killed."

None of them spoke for a little.

Nausiphanes sat down beside the oven, stretching out his cold feet in cheap sandals towards the warmth that remained in the bricks. At last he said, "And you others—do you accept that?"

"There's no holding nor binding the Spirit," Eunice said. "He's always coming unexpected, from behind the outside look of things, if you see what I mean, Nausiphanes."

"Phaon?"

"It's not magic, our baptism. We don't any of us suppose it to be that. It's just a sign. It's the accepting of a kind of question and answer, a new kind. It's difficult to find words, Nausiphanes, though I'll need to find them sooner or later."

"Perhaps it's too soon for any words," Felicio said. "We can't just explain the thing which we are in the middle of experiencing. Words come later."

"Whatever else there is going to be in the world," Phaon said, "this will have happened."

Again nobody spoke for a time.

Niger will be waiting, Felicio thought, *my new brother. And when he sees me he will feel suddenly happy. I have done that at least.*

"If I thought it was you Christians," Nausiphanes said, abruptly yet slowly, "who could break the power and rule of Rome, I might think differently of you. But it is an irrational power and rule. It is the Platonic State gone bad—as everything does

420

when it comes to Rome. How can it be attacked except by reason?"

"People don't listen to reason," Felicio said. "That has been tried. They aren't made that way—not yet. We don't understand our own minds. Only we know they do not work predictably, as machines work."

"If only they did!" Nausiphanes cried out, suddenly so tired of arguing all the year round in the streets of a great city, with fools.

"Then there'd be no need for us to pray," Eunice said.

"We've all got to go the best way we can," Phaon said, troubled. "But if we can get help, like Mother and Felicio and I have got it—"

"Yes?" asked Nausiphanes.

"We can bear the pain and death better," Felicio answered for Phaon.

"And somehow we don't get so tired," Eunice said. She'd had a long day of it, what with the kneading, and the baking, and the customers, and the housework, and then the meeting at the end of it.

And her son had fasted for two days, but he didn't show a thing! And there was Felicio, who could read and write and do regular accounts and all that, and he'd fasted too, but he didn't show it either. And there'd been the others who were dead now after having been witnesses. And she did somehow like Nausiphanes, for all he wasn't one of them.

She looked around at the three men, still sitting there, wanting to talk. If only you could be kind to everyone in the world like you could be to your neighbors. *I'll cut one of my cakes for them,* she thought. *I can't really afford to, I suppose, but there, what's the use of saving up these days. And maybe I can make them a hot drink too.*

Historical Note

The Piso conspiracy, in which several of the people in this book were involved, gathered supporters and strength for another few months. Then it was betrayed by a freedman of Flavius Scaevinus on the very night before the day fixed for Nero's assassination. Those who were first denounced, including Scaevinus himself and Lucan, were tortured into giving other names.

Nero and his advisers insisted on a thorough purge. Seneca was ordered to kill himself and did so. Others were exiled. It was the final breach between Nero and the old aristocracy. Tigellinus and his secret police were given a free hand. A year later Gallio, who had been under suspicion since the conspiracy, had to kill himself.

There is no official record of the trial or execution of Paul.